KEMPER ON KEMPER:

INTERVIEWS & ENCOUNTERS WITH A KILLER

EDITED BY

PETER SCOTT JR.

CONTENTS

Introduction   vii

Beginnings   1
"Boy, 15, 'Mad at World,' Accused In Fatal Shooting of Grandparents" Reno-Gazette-Journal (August 28, 1964)   10
"Judge Weighs Fate Of Young Slayer" The Fresno Bee (September 22, 1964)   12
"California Jails Youthful Killer" The Billings Gazette (September 23, 1964)   14
Imprisonment   16
Released Into the World   19
"Fresno State Coeds Missing" Santa Cruz Sentinel (May 19, 1972)   23
"Head Identified" The Times Standard (October 2, 1973)   25
"Law Authorities Seek Second Missing Coed" Santa Cruz Sentinel (October 8, 1972)   26
Aiko Koo   29
"Missing Girl Clues Sought" Oakland Tribune (September 23, 1972)   30
Cindy Schall   32
"Body Is Identified - SC Girl" Santa Cruz Sentinel (January 24, 1973)   33
Rosalind Thorpe and Allison Liu   35
"Two Coeds Missing" Santa Cruz Sentinel (February 8, 1973)   36
"2 Headless Torsos Are Bodies of Coeds" Santa Cruz Sentinel (February 22, 1973)   38
"Slain Torrance Girl Praised; Santa Cruz Probe Continues" Santa Cruz Independent (February 22, 1973)   40
Clarnell Strandberg and Sally Hallett (April 20, 1973)   45

"2 Women Slain In Aptos Home; Son Of One Held" Santa Cruz Sentinel (April 24, 1973) - Tom Honig ... 47

Confession #1 to Pueblo, Colorado Police Department (April 24, 1973) ... 49

Confession #2 to Pueblo, Colorado Police Department (April 25, 1973) ... 63

"Calls Police On Slayings, Is Seized" Press & Sun-Bulletin (April 25, 1973) ... 80

"Kemper Friends React In Shocked Disbelief" Santa Cruz Sentinel (April 25, 1973) - Tom Honig ... 82

"Suspect Names 9th Victim" The Independent (Long Beach, California) (April 26, 1973) ... 85

"Head Found In Aptos" Santa Cruz Sentinel (April 26, 1973) - Tom Honig ... 88

Confession #3 to Santa Cruz Sheriff's Department (April 28, 1973) ... 92

Confession #4 to Santa Cruz Sheriff's Department (April 29, 1973) ... 134

"Kemper Is Charged With Eight Counts Of Murder" Santa Cruz Sentinel (April 30, 1973) - Tom Hong ... 153

"Suspect Leads Deputies To Mountain Graves Of Victims" Tulare Advance-Register (April 30, 1973) ... 157

"Cal Slay Suspect: He Seemed Sane" Albany Democrat-Herald (May 2, 1973) ... 159

"Kemper's Young Fiance In Shock" Greeley Daily Tribune (May 5, 1973) ... 161

"Transcript Reveals Details In Kemper Case" Santa Cruz Sentinel (June 12, 1973) ... 162

"I'll Show You Where I Buried The Bodies" Front Page Detective (August 1973) - Hugh Stephens ... 165

"8-Death Suspect Slashes Wrist" Des Moines Tribune (October 29, 1973) ... 182

"Explosive Hatred Motivated Kemper" Santa Cruz Sentinel - Marj Von B ... 183

"Girl's Courtroom Gesture Brings Kemper Trial To a Halt" Register-Pajaronian (October 25, 1973) ... 187

"Gruesome Details On Tape At Trial" Santa Cruz Sentinel (October 25, 1973) - Tom Honig ... 189

"Jury Looks At Kemper's Car" Register-Pajaronian
(October 26, 1973) - Marj Von Beroldingen   194

"Allyn Kemper tapes relate grisly details", The San
Francisco Examiner (October 31, 1973) - Don West   196

"Kemper Explains Why He Murdered Coeds"
Register-Pajaronian (November 1, 1973)   198

"Kemper In Another Jail Battle In R.C." The Times
(November 5, 1973)   206

"Kemper Found Sane, Guilty Of Murdering Eight
Women" Argus-Leader (November 9, 1973)   208

"Kemper Gets Life Term" Santa Cruz Sentinel
(November 9, 1973) - Tom Hong   210

"Kemper Victims' Families Sue" Great Falls Tribune
(January 11, 1974)   212

Interview - Front Page Detective Magazine (March
1974) - Marj von Beroldingen   214

"Killer Pleads For Psychosurgery To Gain Parole"
Sacramento Bee (July 10, 1976) - Paul Avery   231

The Press Democrat (May 2, 1979) - James E. Reid   236

"Reluctant Edmund Kemper Denied Parole" Santa
Cruz Sentinel (May 2, 1979)   239

"No Parole For Homicidal Giant" - The Press
Democrat (May 1st, 1980) - James E. Reid   246

"A Day With Kemper" (May 1980) - a remembrance
by Joey Tranchina   250

From The Killing of America - Interview (1981)   257

"Mass Murderer Kemper Denied Parole Again"
Santa Cruz Sentinel (June 25, 1982) - Mark
Bergstrom   261

Interview from "Murder - No Apparent Motive
(1984)   265

"Killer Of Eight Women Waives Parole" The
Lompoc Record (June 4, 1985)   276

"Kemper Parole Denied   Psychiatrist Says Killer
Suitable For Release" Santa Cruz Sentinel (June 16,
1988) - Mark Bergstrom   278

FBI Academy Interview (1989)   283

From Forgiven (circa- 1990)   286

From Serial Killers (1991) - Stephane Bourgoin   292

Excerpt from "In At The Kill" GQ (Britain)
(February 1991) John A. Jenkins   343
Excerpt from Kemper Letter To An Unknown
Recipient (May 20, 1999)   346
"Mass Murderer Denied Parole For Third Time"
Santa Cruz Sentinel (June 13, 1997) - Robert
Gammon   348
"Kemper Waives Parole Hearing", Santa Cruz
Sentinel (June 28, 2002) - Jason Schultz   352
From The Believer - Werner Herzog /Erroll Morris
remembers Ed Kemper (March 2008)   354
Parole Hearing - 2017   358

Afterword   475
Acknowledgments   477

Why another book on Ed Kemper? What could such a collection of "interviews and encounters" add to our knowledge of him? He is, after all, a convicted murderer, multiple-times over. His crimes are well-documented. *Kemper On Kemper* includes never-before-published full confession transcripts of the interviews between Kemper and the police and district attorney and used for his Grand Jury indictment. Reading these and the other interview transcripts given to the media, it is clear that Kemper is nothing more or less than a solid source of what it's like to be a psychopathic serial killer.

In this collection, we follow Kemper's wayward path of destruction using newspaper sources, personal encounters and interviews. Out of the many books spawned from the true crime genre, this is the only book that attempts to collect contemporary reporting on the history of this tragic figure, and the harrowing West Coast journey he took through from 1964 to the early-1970s. There is still much left to be uncovered. He was, what the FBI classify him as an "organized nonsocial offender." Once he is apprehended, Kemper has proven to be more than amicable in sharing the sordid details of his crimes. He wasn't a thief or murdering for nefarious reasons other than to kill for the simple act of post-mortem possession. In his case, the means didn't justify the end, but that the end justified the means. Through the pages of this book, in snippets throughout the numerous articles, until Kemper talks, we can start piecing together some semblance of rationale for his behavior, even if that rationale is steeped in a psychopathic tea unfit for casual consumption.

Like many other serial killers, Kemper is a victim of his own compulsion. He is cognizant of this isolated deficit in his behavior which, to the rest of us, seems jarringly at odd with his giant intellect. Kemper doesn't write books, or express himself in a way that exhibits this casual intelligence. It is just there, in the mannerism of his speech and the scope of his storytelling abilities. If he wasn't Ed Kemper telling us his stories, he could just as well be Stephen King. We begin to like the guy against our better judgment. We almost feel sorry for him.

And what could be wrong with that? It's called radical empathy ... a theme explored by Fyodor Dostoevsky in novels like *Crime and Punishment* (which Kemper read) and *The Idiot*. Kemper, in his struggles to overcome his homicidal addiction does what he feels is best for humanity, he turns himself in knowing full well that if he does not, he will keep on killing until he is either captured or dead. This way, the way he chooses, he divines the course of his own fate and rises to accept it at the cost of his freedom and to save innocent lives. Kemper's intelligence would have kept him active for an even more devastating body count. It was his better judgment on display, a character attribute that he had when he wasn't driven by a compulsion to kill that made him turn his hand to pick up the phone and dial the police. In killing his mother, Kemper had both ascended his culminate goal and fallen from grace. For this, we as readers and as fellow human beings must be stirred, for he is one of our own kind. He is a killer, we are his judge and jury. But we are also better than that, we are also capable of radical empathy, to follow the path of the flaming comet that rises to only fall.

In the end, we are the sum total of our deeds, for bad or for good. We are tempered by our understanding of what is good in our world, and for what is evil. We know night and day, black and white. However, we are mystified by the gray areas between, that which keeps us intrigued. Curious. I took on this book because I was curious, too. I'm not totally attracted to the genre, but I feel in focusing my attention on this one person, in knowing him, I could learn from a life gone awry. I am compelled to listen more closely from the wisdom of one seeking to retrieve their burnt-cinder soul from a heap of cold ashes. It is easy to celebrate heroes and worship saints, but can one find it in a universally-scorned figure? Ah! That is my intrigue, and so I put together this book so as to have it in my hands, even if I was the books sole reader, and between its covers, find the shining diamond in a heap of human wreckage. If I could not, would there be then hope for any of us?

Are we not all flawed? Not cold-blooded killers, but flawed, in our way? That if we reveal our worst tendencies to our friends, co-workers, or family, that we risk their turning their faces away and being ostracized.

If so, this book is for you because we can all learn from a man like Ed Kemper.

EDMUND EMIL KEMPER, III, was born in Burbank, California on December 18, 1948. He was the middle child and the only son born to Clarnell Elizabeth Kemper and Edmund Emil Kemper II. Edmund II was a World War II veteran who, after the war, tested nuclear weapons in the Pacific Proving Grounds before returning to California, where he worked as an electrician. He was also in Special Forces. He was a formidable man, who had proven his courage and fortitude in the theater of war. Because he was in Special Forces, it was expected that he would be an unmarried man. However, that did not stop him from marrying Clarnell in secret. It was perhaps the first in along line of bad mistakes he had made in his life. He had set in motion a fatalistic spree of events that he would regret to his grave.

Clarnell was a chronic complainer and perhaps mentally ill. Among her roster of complaints was that her husband's chosen occupation as an electrician was menial. She was deeply unhappy and expressed her unhappiness to anyone within earshot. Edmund II later stated that "suicide missions in wartime and the atomic bomb testings were nothing compared to living with her." Clarnell's affect on him, and later their son, affected him "more than three hundred and ninety-six days and nights of fighting on the front [line] did."

Of Edmund III, Clarnell complained that he was a difficult baby. She did not take to motherhood, and suffered its duties at the behest of her entitlement of perhaps deserving a better life for herself. Their son was a fast grower. By the age of four, he was almost a head taller than the rest of his classmates.

Beneath the veneer of the odd-looking Kemper, there was a boy who also developed a fixation toward animal cruelty. By then, he had buried the pet cat alive. He waited a few days to make sure it was dead and then exhumed it so that he could decapitate its head and mount it on a spike. With the pet cat's disappearance, there came a bed of lies that Guy easily conjured. He enjoyed lying to family members. He found it was easier that way, though he would not make it a lifelong habit. After his murder streak, Kemper was all too zealous to tell the truth about them. He became a compulsive chronicler of his killings

Three years after the first cat, another disappeared. This cat seemed to favor his sister, Allyn, and so in a fit of jealousy Kemper deprived Allyn of her cat and the cat of its life. He had had cleaved its skull to expose the brains. He stabbed it to death to put it out of its misery and dismembered the animal and kept pieces of it as souvenirs, pushing them toward the back of his dark closet.

Afraid for her daughters, Guy was forced to sleep in the basement to which she locked the single entrance and exit to the subterranean depths of the house through a trapdoor located beneath the kitchen table.

Clarnell had an inkling that her son was deeply troubled. He was harboring morbid fantasies that were beginning to manifest both in his killings of the family pets, but also during playtime with his sisters.

Their toys suffered the same fate as the second cat. They were losing their hands and heads. He was fascinated by a mock guillotine he saw at a children's carnival. Try as he might, Kemper could not shake away his obsessions. One day, sister Susan was teasing him.

"How come you don't try to kiss your teacher?"

"If I kiss her, I'd have to kill her first."

Kemper was also a voyeur. He loved to watch his 2nd-grade teacher through her windows. In his hands was his father's bayonet kept from his military years.

Playtime consisted of playing "Electric Chair and "Gas Chamber." In the former, he asked Allyn to flip the switch after she tied him up with rope. To this, Ed would be mock-electrocuted, demonstrating his extreme torture by writhing on the floor in spastic contortions.

Kemper also flirted with death after his sister pushed him into the deep end of a pool. He almost drowned. Another time, she attempted to push him in front of an oncoming train.

And he continued to grow. To this, he was mercilessly teased by his peers for his height. His own mother mocked him, calling him a circus freak.

Then his father left home again, after several attempts to sever ties with Clarnell, and they eventually separated in 1957. She became in essence a single mother who had to both raise the three children and work a full-time job as a secretary at a bank.

She made Guy sell newspapers on a street-corner, charging him not to return home until every one of them were sold. Ed II, hearing about this, went out to look for him to bring him home against Clarnell's wishes.

Rudderless, Kemper was without a father figure. His father reminded him of his hero, John Wayne. In his absence, all he had left to show was his articles of war: bayonets, guns, and medals. These passed through Guy's hands again and again. He developed an early fascination with guns and soon became an excellent marksman.

Guy was emotionally emasculated by his overbearing mother. She drank to indulgence. Drunk and disgusted, Ed III reminded her of her failed marriage to Ed II. He was their poisoned progeny. He was the product of their failure. Though one tentative return by Ed II to the family disclosed to him that his son was being maltreated— he found out that Clarnell had made Guy sleep in the basement for almost an entire year—he did little to help, and so things continued to downward spiral.

By the age of 15, he was 6'-4". She suspected he was a monster, and shrunk from his affections. If she shown affection, she warned him that he would turn into a homosexual.

And the resentment grew.

And so then his fantasies.

He authored a "death list" comprised of the female friends of his mother. To this, he amended the list with exacting detail whenever they changed their names from marriage or if they moved to a different address.

Ed II and Clarnell formally divorced in September 1961. She took the three children and moved to Helena, Montana. She promptly re-married to provide a father figure for her son. Her first husband after Ed II, was 45-year-old Norman Turnquist. He was a plumber by trade, and it is hard to believe that she did not eventually consider his chosen occupation as menial as well. One laborer was as good as another. Turnquist tried to befriend Guy, He taught him to hunt. He took him fishing. Yet, Guy harbored a desire to bash his brains in with an iron bar, steal his car and drive to Southern California to be with his father. However, he could not do it, and lowered the weapon any time it came close to fruition.

Kemper's victim of choice had to be weaker than he was, and female.

And he was sexually-driven though he seems to have been devoid of any education on the matter. He looked at women differently, now, not as merely playthings, but of fleshly sensual beings that seemed to be out of his reach. He had few outlets to recover his skewed observations, to right his compass to true north. He was the only male in a house filled with women. His sisters were developing from girls to women. For a boy as confused as he was, brooding in nightmarish fantasies vacillating from sex to violence, he posed an ever-present danger.

Then Ed III was accused at 13 of shooting a neighborhood dog. To this end, because the dog was the pet of a neighboring boy, his male peers ostracized him. He was left an outcast, exiled from family and friends.

He retreated more and more to the inner phantasmagoria of his fantasies. At least he felt safe in a place where he could dominate his kingdom without fear of retribution, humiliation or judgment.

When Ed turned 14, it was the autumn of 1963. President Kennedy had just been assassinated and the country was in mourning. Black-and-white flickering images of the black-veiled First Lady and saluting John-John had endeared the country to the idea that they were experiencing a gradual plundering of American ideals. Non-plussed by the nation's attitude, Ed ran away from home by Thanksgiving time. Without asking, he took his mother's car and drove it as far as Butte. He abandoned it and boarded a bus westbound to Los Angeles. He was returning to his father, whether he wanted him there or not.

He needed his father who was then living in Van Nuys, California. During his absence, Clarnell found the remains of the cat in her son's closet. She found bloodstained clothing. She wrote him asking if he was responsible for it. He vehemently denied it.

Things had changed for Edmund II. He had found a new German immigrant wife, and a teenaged step-son shortly after his divorce. For that brief time, he felt bound to his son and agreed to let him live with them.

Ed II's new wife was Elfriede Weber. She had a son from a previous marriage (and two years older than Ed III) was Gilbert Otto Brechtefeld. It didn't take long for Ed III's presence to physically shake her, and a series of creepy incidents made her urge her new husband to dispatch his biological son to some other address. Ed III sensed that they were just as needy for his father as he was, and that she possessed the one thing that he could not provide for his father, an arresting sexual allure. Things felt wrong with Big Ed creeping around the house. He had a sexual curiosity bordering on obsession, and so, after catching his steps-mother naked, he harbored a simmering yet confusing attraction for her. Her son, Ed III's step-brother didn't like him either, and once chased him out of the house with a hammer after his mother asked him to leave.

By Christmas time, Ed II took his new wife and step-son and Ed III to visit his parents in North Fork, California. After the visit, Ed III was left to stay with them. His father told him hat he could not afford to keep him in their home. Kemper did not enjoy his stay with his grandparents, sensing inches grandmother the same domineering frustration that plagued his mother. He had no place to go. His mother did not want him for the time being (over the cat business), nor his father. She sought to replace her first husband as swiftly as possible as a continued means of support. Through Ed III's childhood, he experienced two more step-fathers, both of which had left shortly after marrying this shrill and emotionally-exhausting woman. They, too, didn't like Big Ed, and so she did not want him around. Ed III had no choice but to remain with his grandparents through the rest of the winter through August 1964.

Clarnell phoned her ex late at night after drinking, and she warned him that he was taking a huge chance on sending their son to live with his elderly parents. Ed III was unpredictable. He was, in her estimate, a "real weirdo" and she told Ed II that there was a real and lethal possibility that their son harbored homicidal impulses. She thought that maybe he may wake up one morning only to learn that his parents were dead at the hands of Ed III. He hung up the phone and returned to sleep

On August 27, 66-year-old Maude Matilda Kemper was sitting at the table writing a by-lined article for *Boy's Life* magazine. She thought of herself as a writer, and liked to author stories for teenagers. Her husband, 72-year-old Edmund Sr., had gone to buy some groceries. Ed III sat at the table with her and, before long, they began to argue. She had little in common with his grandson other than to try and make a man out of him. They thought maybe gifting him with a hunting rifle would give him something to do around their many acres of farmland. Edmund Sr. told Ed that he could shoot any small mammal that walked on four feet, but to leave the birds alone. Ed III found his grandfather somewhat dull, with his routine and errand-driven lifestyle. His wife was a domineering bitch that lived to make her husband miserable. To both grandparents, Ed III harbored a desire to desist and defy everything they told him to do, including shooting birds.

They enrolled him in Junior High, where he was a quiet and cooperative student. His grades were marginally-good. He was non-committal, giving only as much as he had to prove himself.

After school had ended, he returned home to his mother. After two weeks, she sent him back to Montana. His mood had darkened considerably.

And Maude continued to chide him, trying to make a better boy out of him using a tough love approach.

And then they were arguing in the kitchen one hot August day. He told is grandmother that he was going hunting. She reprimanded him, that he better not be shooting birds. Angrily, Ed III stalked away and retrieved his hunting rifle. He returned to the kitchen and leveled the barrels straight at her head. He pulled the trigger and swiftly dispatched her, eradicating from his world-view one of many matriarchal icons that tortured his mind. He shot her twice more in the back. A kitchen knife committed further outrage, as he stabbed at her stilled body almost amazed by how much blood a human body contained. Kemper wrapped her head in a towel and dragged her into the bedroom.

Panicked, he heard his grandfather coming up the drive. The sound of his car was immediately identifiable.

Ed went outside, clutching his rifle. His grandfather opened the passenger door to permit Ed III to grab the grocery sacks and bring them into the kitchen. The only resolution toward preventing his grandfather from seeing the bloodied corpse of his wife was to kill him, too. Ed III raised the rifle to the back of his grandfather's head and shot him. He dragged him into the garage and shut the door. Outside, fearful that neighbors would have heard the gunshots, Ed III sprayed the earth with a garden hose until the blood soaked into the dirt.

Now his back was at the wall, and he was afraid. The rage that prompted the shootings had now subsided. There was no clear way out, with the one exception that he could shoot his way out. If he wasn't isolated, he would have gone on a killing spree. However, thankfully, he was alone. In a panicked state he called the only person in the world who would talk to him, the one he hated the most ... his mother. He told her what he had done. He lied at first, telling her it was an accident. However, she knew better, because she had already predicted it would happen. Clarnell told her son to call the Madera County Sherrif's office and tell the truth.

Law enforcement pulled up and saw him sitting on the porch. They asked him why he did it.

"I don't want to live with either of my parents and I don't like living at North Fork." They pushed him for more information, and he gave it to them

"I just wanted to see what it would be like to kill my grandmother." He told them that he had been thinking about it for some time.

"Why you're Grandpa, then?"

I didn't want Grandpa to see his wife dead and have a heart attack and die."

Ed was also "mad at the world."

They clapped on the cuffs on strapping young Ed and brought him in the station.

"BOY, 15, 'MAD AT WORLD,' ACCUSED IN FATAL SHOOTING OF GRANDPARENTS" RENO-GAZETTE-JOURNAL (AUGUST 28, 1964)

MADERA (AP) — A six foot four inch 15-year-old boy who told authorities he was mad at the world was booked on suspicion of killing his grandparents.

Madera County authorities received a telephone call from Helena, Mont. Thursday afternoon from Mrs. Clarnell Stanburg who said her son, Edmund E. Kemper III, had called her and told her he had killed his grandparents.

The boy was staying with his grandparents, Mr. and Mrs. E.E. Kemper in North Fork, a Sierra foothills community northeast of Madera.

Deputies were dispatched. Before they reached the Kemper home, Guy called the sheriff's office and said, "there's been some trouble up here."

He met the officers in the front yard.

Chief deputy William Helm said the grandmother, Maude, 68, was found in a bedroom shot in the head and stabbed in the back. The grandfather, 72, was lying in the garage shot to death. The weapons used were a .22-caliber rifle and a butcher knife, Helm said.

Helm said Guy said he was mad at the world and did not want to return home to his father, Robert Kemper of Van Nuys.

Guy said he shot his grandmother and then stabbed her because he "did not want her to suffer."

Mrs. Kemper was killed in the living room and then dragged to the bedroom.

His grandfather was slain as he stood by a pickup truck after returning from shopping. The body was then dragged into the garage.

Helm said Guy has high intelligence, but apparently was upset emotionally.

Kemper was a retired State Division of Highway electrician. They had lived in North Fork bout a year after moving there from Southern California.

Edmund Emil Kemper III, age 15

MADERA, Madera Co. - - A closed hearing was being held in the juvenile court this morning for Edmund Emil (Guy) Kemper III, the admitted killer of his grandparents.

Judge Mason A. Bailey probably was to rule today on a probation office report charing Kemper, 15, with the double murder of his grandparents, Mr. and Mrs. E.E. Kemper, in their North Fork home on August 27th.

If the petition is upheld, the youth probably will be committed to the California Youth Authority.

Kemper admitted shooting his 68-year-old grandmother in the head and the back with a .22 caliber rifle and then killing his 72-year-old grandfather with the same weapon so that the grandfather would not see what he had done.

The openly reason the youth gave for the slayings was that he was "mad at the world." He told officers that he was tired of staying with his grandparents and did not want to live with his father, Edmund Emil Kemper Jr., in Van Nuys, Los Angeles County.

"CALIFORNIA JAILS YOUTHFUL KILLER" THE BILLINGS GAZETTE (SEPTEMBER 23, 1964)

California Jails Youthful Killer

MADERA, Calif. (UPI) —Edmund Emil Kemper III, 15, who admitted killing his grandparents last month because he was "mad at the world," was sentenced to the California Youth Authority Tuesday for an indefinite term.

Juvenile Court Judge Mason Bailey handed down the sentence but declined to give the results of psychiatric examinations which he ordered for the boy early this month.

Kemper admitted firing three shots into his grandmother, Mrs. Maude Kemper, 66, at a cabin near North Fork, Calif., Aug. 27. He said he shot his grandfather, Edmund Emil Kemper, 72, later to keep him from learning of Mrs. Kemper's death.

The only reason the youth gave at the time of the shootings was that he was "mad at the world" and did not want to continue living with his grandparents.

Mrs. Clarnell Strandberg of Helena, Mont., the boy's mother, and Edmund Emil Kemper Jr., of Van Nuys, his father, are divorced.

The boy will be sent to the CYA's Perkins Reception Center at Sacramento where it will be decided to which CYA facility he will be sent.

MADERA, Calif. (UPI) - Edmund Emil Kemper III, 15, who admitted killing his grandparents last month because he was "mad at the world," was sentenced to the California Youth Authority Tuesday for an indefinite term.

Juvenile Court Judge Mason Bailey handed down the sentence but declined to give the results of psychiatric examinations which he ordered for the boy early this month.

Kemper admitted firing three shots into his grandmother, Mrs. Maude Kemper, 66, at a cabin near North Fork, Calif., Aug. 27. He said he shot his grandfather, Edmund Emil Kemper, 72, later to keep him from learning of Mrs. Kemper's death.

The only reason the youth gave at the time of the shootings was that he was "mad at the world" and did not want to continue living with his grandparents.

Mrs. Clarnell Strandberg of Helena, Mont., the boy's mother, and Edmund Emil Kemper Jr., of Van Nuys, his father, are divorced.

The boy will be sent to the CYA's Perkins Reception Center at Sacramento where it will be decided to which CYA facility he will be sent.

At Atascadero, where he was entered on December 6, 1964, 15-year-old Kemper was given a battery of psychiatric tests. California Youth Authority psychiatrists and social workers disagreed with the court psychiatrists' diagnoses. They had diagnosed him as a paranoid schizophrenic at the Superior Court hearing.

He was insane, pure and simple.

Their reports stated that the boy showed "no flight of ideas, no interference with thought, no expression of delusions or hallucinations, and no evidence of bizarre thinking." They asked him if he was remorseful. Instead, he said he resented not undressing his grandmother but would not elaborate further. They thought him intelligent. Introspective. His initial testing measured his IQ at 136, over two standard deviations above average. After further testing, he was re-diagnosed with a less severe condition and classified a "personality trait disturbance, passive-aggressive type." Later at Atascadero, Kemper was given another IQ test, which gave a higher result of 145.

Kemper, they felt, was sporadically psychotic. He was "confused and unable to function." They suspected a major part of his psychosis was how he perceived women, with the main cause to be his mother's influence: "He is psychotic and a danger to himself and others. He may well be a very long-term problem."

Kemper was found to be unnaturally passive. He feared injury from other boys. He had severely impaired judgment. The only thing that prevented his own suicide was that he didn't want others to clean his mess up.

Kemper endeared himself to his psychiatrists by being a model prisoner. Because of his natural intelligence, he was trained to administer psychiatric tests to other inmates. One of his psychiatrists later said, "He was a very good worker, and this is not typical of a sociopath. He really took pride in his work." The pride in his work he would carry with him through adulthood.

Kemper also became a member of the Jaycees and said he developed "some new tests and some new scales on the Minnesota Multiphasic Personality Inventory," specifically an "Overt Hostility Scale," during his work with Atascadero psychiatrists. After his second arrest, Kemper said that being able to understand how these tests functioned allowed him to manipulate his psychiatrists and he later admitted that he learned a lot from the sex offenders to whom he administered tests; for example, they told him that to avoid leaving witnesses, it was best to kill a woman after raping her.

The incarceration of Edmund Kemper III was in fact, a sort of warm-up for his lifelong prison stint. He was not among his peers who were rising into the Age of Aquarius. He would not be drafted into Vietnam or wallow in the acid, mud and shit of Woodstock. He bypassed that era altogether and remained in the company of child molesters, rapists and other sexual deviates whom had no problem sharing the darkest depths of their depravity with the boy.

It was a nefarious coming-of-age.

ON DECEMBER 18, 1969, his 21st birthday, Kemper was released on parole from Atascadero. Against the recommendations of hospital psychiatrists, he was released into the care of his mother Clarnell—who had remarried, taken the surname Strandberg, and then divorced again—at 609 A Ord Street, Aptos, California, a short drive from where she worked as an administrative assistant at the University of California, Santa Cruz. Kemper later demonstrated further to his psychiatrists that he was rehabilitated; and on November 29, 1972, his juvenile records were permanently expunged. The last report from his probation psychiatrists read:

> If I were to see this patient without having any history available or getting any history from him, I would think that we're dealing with a very well adjusted young man who had initiative, intelligence and who was free of any psychiatric illnesses ... It is my opinion that he has made a very excellent response to the years of treatment and rehabilitation and I would see no psychiatric reason to consider him to be of any danger to himself or to any member of society ... [and] since it may allow him more freedom as an adult to

develop his potential, I would consider it reasonable to have a permanent expunction of his juvenile records.

While staying with his mother, Kemper attended community college in accordance with his parole requirements and had hoped he would become a police officer, though he was rejected because of his size—at the time of his release from Atascadero, Kemper stood 6-feet-9 inches tall—which led to his nickname, "Big Ed". Kemper maintained relationships with Santa Cruz police officers despite his rejection to join the force and became a self-described "friendly nuisance" at a bar called the Jury Room, a popular hangout for local law-enforcement officers.

Kemper worked a series of menial jobs before gaining employment with the State of California Division of Highways (now known as the California Department of Transportation). During this time, his relationship with Clarnell remained toxic and hostile, the two having frequent arguments that their neighbors often overheard. Kemper later described the arguments he had with his mother around this time, stating the following:

> My mother and I started right in on horrendous battles, just horrible battles, violent and vicious. I've never been in such a vicious verbal battle with anyone. It would go to fists with a man but this was my mother and I couldn't stand the thought of my mother and I doing these things. She insisted on it and just over stupid things. I remember one roof-raiser was over whether I should have my teeth cleaned.

When he had saved enough money, Kemper moved out to live with a friend in Alameda, California. There, he still complained of being unable to get away from his mother because she regularly phoned him and paid him surprise visits. He often had financial difficulties, which resulted in his frequently returning to his mother's apartment in Aptos. At a Santa Cruz beach, Kemper met a student from Turlock High School to whom he became engaged in March 1973. The engagement was broken off after Kemper's second arrest, and his fiancée's parents requested her name not be revealed to the public.

The same year that he began working for the Highway Division, Kemper was hit by a car while riding a motorcycle that he had recently purchased. His arm was badly injured in the crash, and he received a $15,000 settlement in the civil suit he filed against the car's driver. As he was driving around in the 1969 Ford Galaxie he bought with part of his settlement money, he noticed a large number of young women hitchhiking and began storing plastic bags, knives, blankets and handcuffs in his car. He then began picking up young women and peacefully letting them go. According to Kemper, he picked up around 150 such hitchhikers before he felt homicidal sexual urges, which he called his "little zapples," and began acting on them.

ON MAY 7, 1972, KEMPER WAS DRIVING IN BERKELEY, California, when he picked up two 18-year-old hitchhking students from Fresno State University, Mary Ann Pesce, and Anita Mary Luchessa, with the pretext of taking them to Stanford University. After driving for an hour, he managed to reach a secluded wooded area near Alameda, California, with which he was familiar from his work at the Highway Department, without alerting his passengers that he had changed directions from where they wanted to go. It was there that he handcuffed Pesce and locked Luchessa in the trunk, then stabbed and strangled Pesce to death, subsequently killing Luchessa in a similar manner. Kemper later confessed that while handcuffing Pesce, he "brushed the back of [his] hand against one of her breasts and it embarrassed [him]", adding that he said, "'Whoops,

I'm sorry' or something like that" after grazing her breast, despite murdering her minutes later.

Kemper put both of the women's bodies in the trunk of his Ford Galaxie and returned to his apartment. He was stopped on the way by a police officer for having a broken taillight, but the officer did not detect the corpses in the car. Kemper's roommate was not at home, so he took the bodies into his apartment, where he photographed and had sexual intercourse with the naked corpses before dismembering them. He then put the body parts into plastic bags, which he later abandoned near Loma Prieta Mountain. Before disposing of Pesce's and Luchessa's severed heads in a ravine, Kemper engaged in irrumatio with both of them. In August of that year, Pesce's skull was found on Loma Prieta Mountain. An extensive search failed to turn up the rest of Pesce's remains or a trace of Luchessa.

i

"FRESNO STATE COEDS MISSING" SANTA CRUZ SENTINEL (MAY 19, 1972)

Two MISSING Fresno State College coeds are believed to be in the Santa Cruz area after disappearing in the San Francisco Bay Area at the first of the month.

They are Anita M. Luchessa and Mary Ann Pesce.

Miss Luchessa is 5-1, with long brown hair and brown eyes. She was last seen wearing a red shirt under white bib-type overalls. She wears gold-rimmed glasses.

Miss Pesce is 5-1, with brown hair cut in a shag style. She was wearing a maroon colored sweater, faded blue jeans and hiking boots.

Anyone knowing the whereabouts of the girls is urged to ask them to call home. Miss Luchessa's mother is seriously ill. Or they are asked to telephone Bob Heitman, a Modesto private investigator, at 209-522-5006 collect.

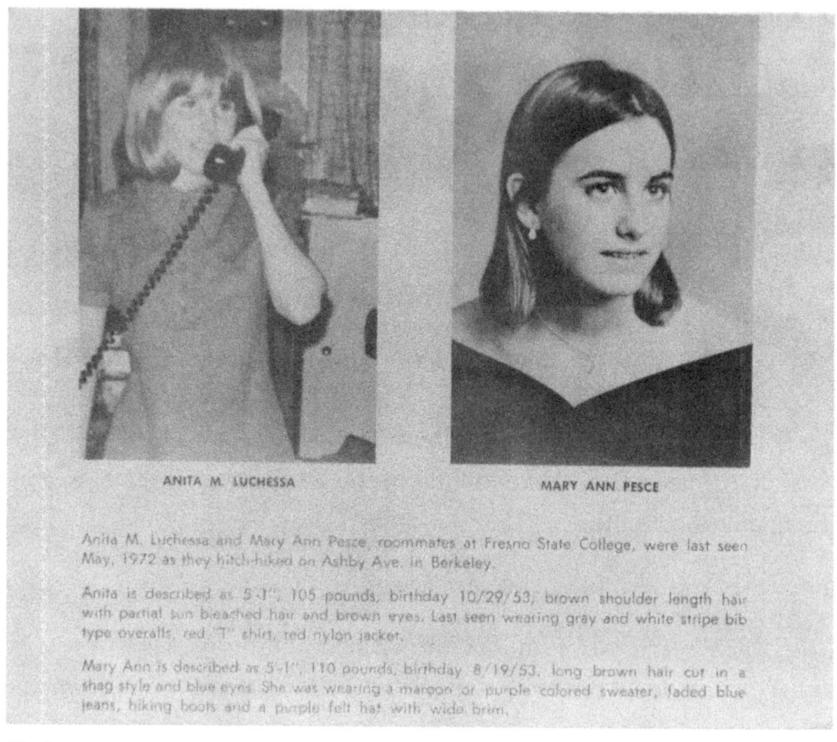

ID sheet used by Santa Cruz police to help identify and locate Anita M. Luchessa and Mary Ann Pesce.

SANTA CRUZ (UPI) — A human head found in the Santa Cruz Mountains last month has been identified as that of 19-year-old Mary Ann Pesce, one of two girls reported missing while hitchhiking between San Francisco and Meno Park almost five months ago.

Santa Cruz sheriff's deputies reported the identification was made after exhaustive pathological tests.

Miss Pesce of Camarillo was reported to have disappeared on May 11 while with Anita Luchessa, a girlfriend, who also has disappeared. Miss Luchessa's address was unknown.

Santa Barbara County sheriff's deputies said Miss Pesce's disappearance was reported by the girl's father, Gabriel, Pesce was on vacation at the time.

He told the sheriff's office that he had learned from friends the two girls disappeared while hitchhiking from San Francisco to Menlo Park.

THE SANTA CRUZ sheriff's department has released a picture of Mary Anne Pesce, the 19-year old girl whose severed head was discovered last August in the Santa Cruz Mountains at Loma Prieta.

Traveling with Miss Pesce was Anita M. Luchessa, 18, and who is believed by sheriff's deputies still to be alive.

According to a press release by the sheriff's department, the two girls left Fresno State College with a friend on May 6 at 9 a.m. They went to the University of California at Berkeley and spent the evening with friends.

On May 7, friends drove the girls to Ninth and Ashby Streets in Berkeley and were led to believe that the girls were going to San Francisco. Both girls had mentioned a desire to go to the Stanford and Menlo Park areas.

The girls were observed hitchhiking in Santa Cruz on May 13. They were seen getting into a blue Pontiac on Ocean Street at Highway 17, and then on Skyline Boulevard in the Santa Cruz Mountains, just inside San Mateo County.

Another positive sighting of the girls was reported in Berkeley on June 6. An unconfirmed sighting of Anita Luchessa was reported in Larkspur on July 1. Since then, there have been no reports of anyone seeing either girl.

Authorities are requesting that anyone knowing the location of Miss Luchessa, or the activities of either girl since their disappearance, contact the Sheriff's department ay (409) 425-2129. All responses will be kept confidential.

Anita Luchessa (courtesy of SCSD)

AIKO KOO

On the evening of September 14, 1972, Kemper picked up a 15-year-old dance student named Aiko Koo, who had decided to hitchhike to a dance class after missing her bus. He again drove to a remote area, where he pulled a gun on Koo before accidentally locking himself out of his car. However, Koo let him back inside, as he had previously gained the 15-year-old's trust while holding her at gunpoint. Back inside the car, he proceeded to choke her unconscious, rape her, and kill her.

Kemper subsequently packed Koo's body into the trunk of his car and went to a nearby bar to have a few drinks, then returned to his apartment. He later confessed that after exiting the bar, he opened the trunk of his car, "admiring [his] catch like a fisherman." Back at his apartment, he had sexual intercourse with the corpse, then dismembered and disposed of the remains in a similar manner as his previous two victims. Koo's mother called the police to report the disappearance of her daughter and put up hundreds of flyers asking for information, but she did not receive any responses regarding her daughter's location or status.

AIKO KOO
Last seen Sept. 14

BERKELEY - POLICE ARE STILL SEEKING clues to the disappearance of a 15-year-old high school student last seen Sept. 14 at a bus stop waiting for transportation to a San Francisco ballet class.

The girl, Aiko Koo, has been described as an "extremely attractive" Korean-American who has danced professionally in several Bay Area performances.

Miss Koo, who attends school in Oakland, lived with her mother at 1818 Hearst Ave. Mrs. Koo told police that she had a good relationship with her daughter and had not had any major conflicts. Aiko was to leave later this month for a dance performance in St. Louis. She is described as about 5 feet

4 inches tall, weighing 105 pounds, with long black hair and looking older than her age,

On January 7, 1973, Kemper, who had moved back in with his mother, was driving around the Cabrillo College campus when he picked up 18-year-old student Cynthia Ann "Cindy" Schall. He drove to a wooded area and fatally shot her with a .22 caliber pistol. He then placed her body in the trunk of his car and drove to his mother's house, where he kept her body hidden in a closet in his room overnight. When his mother left for work the next morning, he had sexual intercourse with and removed the bullet from Schall's corpse, then dismembered and decapitated her in his mother's bathtub.

Kemper kept Schall's severed head for several days, regularly engaging in irrumatio with it, then buried it in his mother's garden facing upward toward her bedroom. After his arrest, he stated that he did this because his mother "always wanted people to look up to her." He discarded the rest of Schall's remains by throwing them off a cliff. Over the course of the following few weeks, all except her head and right hand were discovered and "pieced together like a macabre jigsaw puzzle." A pathologist determined that Schall had been cut into pieces with a power saw.

Cynthia Ann Schall,

THE SLICED portions of a human body which have drifted into shore during the last week have been positively identified by the coroner's office.

The victim has been named as Cynthia Ann Schall, 19, 220 Cleveland Ave. She had been reported missing Jan. 9, one day after she reportedly hitchhiked to a class at Cabrillo College.

It has not been determined by authorities whether the severed arms and legs found in Monterey County belong to Miss Schall. A coroner's spokesman said that a meeting between local authorities and Monterey County officials will be held Thursday in an attempt to see if there is a connection.

According to the coroner's office, the victim was identified by two different methods. The first was a comparison of fingerprints of the severed hand which washed onto the beach Friday with fingerprints in Miss Schall's room. The second method was a comparison of chest x-rays of the torso discovered in the surf last week with x-rays which had been taken of the woman in October.

The coroner's office said that Miss Schall had been working as a live-in babysitter for the Arthur Windy family. Her mother has been identified as Susan McEvoy of San Rafael, her father as Forest Schall of Fresno.

The investigation of the crime is being handled by the Santa Cruz police department, which was originally notified of the missing girl.

On February 5, 1973, after a heated argument with his mother, Kemper left his house in search of possible victims. With heightened suspicion of a serial killer preying on hitchhikers in the Santa Cruz area, students were advised to only accept rides from cars with university stickers on them. Kemper had such a sticker because his mother worked at the University of California, Santa Cruz. He encountered 23-year-old Rosalind Heather Thorpe and 20-year-old Alice Helen "Allison" Liu on the UCSC campus. According to Kemper, Thorpe entered his car first, reassuring Liu to also enter. He then fatally shot Thorpe and Liu with his .22 caliber pistol and wrapped their bodies in blankets.

Kemper brought his victims back to his mother's apartment; he had beheaded the corpses in his car and carried the headless trunks into his mother's house to have sex with them. He then dismembered the bodies, removed the bullets to prevent identification, and discarded their remains on the next morning. Some remains were found at Eden Canyon a week later, and more were found near Highway 1 in March of that year.

Two UCSC COEDS described as "frequent hitchhikers" by Santa Cruz police are reported missing in two different cases.

The first is Alice Liu, 20, 431 Locust St. Her roommate, Julie Chang, reported the woman as missing since Monday. Miss Chang told police that the missing woman told her that she was about to hitchhike to campus Monday afternoon, and has not returned.

Miss Chang said that the coed has never stayed away from the residence all night before. Police have issued an all points bulletin for the coed. She is described as Chinese, wearing bell bottom blue jeans, a pullover sweater of an unknown color, a gray pea coat and brown desert boots. She is 5 feet 2 inches and weighs 111 pounds.

Police are also looking for Rosalind Thorpe, about 22, 220 Mott Ave. who was last seen Monday at 7 p.m. heading toward a lecture at UCSC. A friend of Miss Thorpe, Lynn Nakabayshi, told police that

Miss Thorpe missed the bus to the campus and has been known to hitchhike if she misses the bus.

Miss Thorpe is 5 feet 6 inches and has a heavy build, according to police. She is white, has long light brown hair and was wearing black pants, a pea coat and pink and purple boots. She also wears glasses, police said.

SANTA CRUZ – BECAUSE OF THE "SKILLFULNESS" of the decapitations of the two UCSC coeds found near Castro Valley last week, Police Lt. Charles Scherer said today that they were probably slain by the same person or persons who killed Cindy Schall a month ago.

"From all appearances and from listening to the pathologist, it appears that all three of the girls were killed by the same person," Scherer said.

The headless bodies found in Castro Valley last week were identified Tuesday afternoon as Alice Helen Liu, 20, and Rosalind Thorpe, 23. They were found in a canyon near Castro Valley, discarded over a cliff near a remote country road, authorities said.

Parts of the butchered body of Cindy Schall washed ashore in both Monterey and Santa Cruz counties in January.

Scherer said that there are no clues in the case, and there are no suspects.

No connection has been made at this time between the slayings of the coeds and the killing of Mary Guilfoyle, the Cabrillo College coed whose skeletal remains were found in the mountains near Bonny Doon Feb. 11. Sheriff's investigators reported that there is no evidence to indicate that Miss Guilfoyle's body had been dismembered. They said she was stabbed five times.

But autopsies of the three other slain coeds showed virtually identical cutting techniques and that extremely sharp instruments were used in all the cases, Scherer said.

In another development, Municipal Court Judge Donald O. May has revoked bail on Herbert Mullin, accused murderer of 10 people. Acting on the court's own motion, May "reconsidered the question of bail in view of events occurring subsequent to the arraignment." May had set bail at $300,000 at Mullin's arraignment which charged him with six murders. At that time, May indicated that "there should be no bail at all."

Since the arraignment, Mullin was charged with the murder of David Olicker, 18, Robert Michael Spector, 18, Brian Scott Card, 19, and Mark Johnson, about 19. Because of this development, May indicated that under state law, the court had the right to revoke bail.

Earlier this week, District Attorney Peter Chang said that he will ask for indictments charging Mullin with 10 murders.

Presently, Mullin is being held in custody at San Mateo County jail. Authorities said he is not being held at the Santa Cruz County jail because of the lack of facilities to keep him protected from the other inmates.

A Torrance girl who wanted to change the world lies dead while Santa Cruz law officials wonder whether her killer is a man already charged with 10 murders [Herbert Mullin] or is still at large and unknown.

Alice Helen Liu, 21, had been reported missing Feb. 5. A week ago, authorities advised her parents that one of two bodies found at Santa Cruz might be that of their daughter. The possibility became stark fact Tuesday when Mr. and Mrs. James C. Liu were formally notified that dental X-rays and other evidence had confirmed the identification.

A car parked in the driveway of the Liu home at 22714 Fonthill St. still bears the UCI decal of Alice's freshman year at the University of California at Irvine. Two years ago she had transferred to the University of California at Santa Cruz, where she was a junior.

"Originally she wanted to be a teacher but more recently she became interested in Oriental studies," her father said Wednesday in a voice that fought to control his emotions.

James Liu never mentioned his daughter by name during the five-minute interview. The name would have caught in his throat.

Other names were avoided for another reason: to protect friends and relatives from prying reporters.

The records at Torrance High School, from which she graduated in 1969, show she was an active girl with wide-ranging interests. She was a member of the Future Teachers Club, served as treasurer of the California Scholarship Federation, was an officer in the Creative Writing Club, French Club and Interclub Council, and a member of the Tartar Ladies service organization.

Principal Harold Klonecky recalled her as a vibrant girl, who had appeared in the senior play and in modern dance recitals on behalf of the Youth for Nixon organization during the 1968 Presidential campaign.

"Alice was probably a sophomore when she was involved in the Indian project," Klonecky said. "We brought a number of Papago Indian students here to Torrance High and she escorted them around. After they left she was active in collecting clothing and other items to send to them."

In Alice's high school file is this paragraph she wrote as part of a standard form for scholarship counselling:

"I want to change the world through government. I want to be involved with the core of people, and I can do both by being a political science teacher."

Torrance City Councilman James Armstrong, a political science teacher at Torrance High, remembers her for those very reasons.

Armstrong said that the Torrance High political science teachers assign upper-classmen to become involved in the campaign of their choice as a class project during election years. He had these observations of her work in the 1968 campaign:

"She was interested in people, cared about all kinds of people. She understood about coming from a good home like hers and going to a good school and the difference it makes for those who don't have the same advantages."

"A death in these circumstances would be tragic enough with anyone," he finished, "but with Alice you feel a real sense of loss and of waste."

As a thousand University of California students listened in silence at UC's open air amphitheater in Santa Cruz, Robert Edgar, provost of one of the colleges eulogized Miss Liu: "She was bright and lively. Like a bird, she was full of song. Struck down. I'm full of sorrow."

Classes were canceled at Santa Cruz for the memorial convocation for Miss Liu and another coed found slain [Rosalind Thorpe].

Alice was last seen alive Feb. 5 in the college library. A week later her decapitated body and that of Rosalind Thorpe, 23, of Carmel were found near Castro Valley, a semirural area southeast of Oakland.

Santa Cruz authorities, continuing their marathon probe of the area's 15 murders, are studying possible relationships between their deaths and those of two other coeds, Mary Anne Pesce, 19, and Cynthia Ann Schall, 19, and the disappearance of another girl, Anita Luchessa, 18. Pesce's head was found on Loma Preita Mountain near Santa Cruz last August but her body has not been recovered. Parts of Miss Schall's body were carried ashore by the tide near Santa Cruz and Monterey in January.

Miss Luchessa, a friend of the Pesce girl, has disappeared and is feared dead, but no traces of her have been found.

Meanwhile 10 murder indictments are being sought by Santa Cruz County District Attorney Peter Chang against Herbert W. Mullin, 25, of Felton. Mullin had already been arraigned on six counts and was in custody when four more bodies slain with the same two guns were discovered Saturday.

His fingerprints also were found in the confessional booth of a Catholic priest who was stabbed to death in Los Gatos, but no charges have been brought against him in that case.

Investigators have reported no links between Mullin and the four dead coeds, but are still examining that possibility.

Burial site of one of Kemper's victims. (Photo provided by SCSD)

On April 20, 1973, after coming home from a party, 52-year-old Clarnell Elizabeth Strandberg awakened her son with her arrival. While sitting in her bed reading a book, she noticed Kemper enter her room and said to him, "I suppose you're going to want to sit up all night and talk now." Kemper replied "No, good night." He then waited for her to fall asleep, returned to bludgeon her with a claw hammer, and slit her throat with a knife. He subsequently decapitated her and engaged in *irrumatio* with her severed head, then used it as a dart board. Kemper stated that he "put [her head] on a shelf and screamed at it for an hour ... threw darts at it," and, ultimately, "smashed her face in." He also cut out her tongue and larynx and put them in the garbage disposal. However, the garbage disposal could not break down the tough vocal cords and ejected the tissue back into the sink. "That seemed appropriate," Kemper later said: "as much as she'd bitched and screamed and yelled at me over so many years."

Kemper then hid his mother's corpse in a closet and went to drink at a nearby bar. Upon his return, he invited his mother's best friend, 59-year-old Sara Taylor "Sally" Hallett, over to the house to have dinner and watch a movie. When Hallett arrived, Kemper strangled her to death to create a cover story that his mother and Hallett had gone away together on vacation. He subsequently put Hallett's corpse in a closet, obscured any outward signs of a disturbance, and left a note to the police. It read:

> Appx. 5:15 A.M. Saturday. No need for her to suffer any more at the hands of this horrible "murderous Butcher". It was quick— asleep—the way I wanted it. Not sloppy and incomplete, gents. Just a "lack of time". I got things to do!!!

Afterward, Kemper fled the scene. He drove non-stop to Pueblo, Colorado, taking caffeine pills to stay awake for the over 1,000-mile journey. He had three guns and hundreds of rounds of ammunition in his car, and he believed he was the target of an active manhunt. After not hearing any news on the radio about the murders of his mother and Hallett when he arrived in Pueblo, he found a phone booth and called the police. He confessed to the murders of his mother and Hallett, but the police did not take his call seriously and told him to call back at a later time. Several hours later, Kemper called again, asking to speak to an officer he personally knew. He confessed to that officer of killing his mother and Hallett, then waited for the police to arrive and take him into custody, where he also confessed to the murders of the six students.

When asked in a later interview why he turned himself in, Kemper said:

> "The original purpose was gone ... It wasn't serving any physical or real or emotional purpose. It was just a pure waste of time ... Emotionally, I couldn't handle it much longer. Toward the end there, I started feeling the folly of the whole damn thing, and at the point of near exhaustion, near collapse, I just said to hell with it and called it all off.

THE UNCLOTHED BODIES of an Aptos woman and her woman friend were found stuffed in closets at the woman's home early today, the sheriff's department reported.

Authorities in Pueblo, Colo. have arrested the slain woman's son, Edmund Emil Kemper, 24, in connection with the deaths.

He was arrested while making a telephone call to Santa Cruz police to confess to the double slaying. While on the line with Santa Cruz police, Colorado authorities were notified and were able to arrest him before he hung up, the Associated Press reported.

The sheriff's department at presstime wasn't able to positively identify the victims, although Sheriff Doug James reported that one of the victims was Kemper's mother.

One source identified the suspect's mother as Clarnell Strandberg, 52, 609A Ord St. Aptos. The other victim has not yet been identified, but authorities are checking to see if she is Sally Hallett, 59, who was a co-worker at UCSC with Mrs. Strandberg.

A missing person's report was filed with Santa Cruz police last weekend by Mrs. Hallett's son, who arrived at his mother's house Saturday following a trip. Christopher Hallett told police he came to the house to pick up his mother's car, which he was going to use to drive to Berkeley to fetch his daughter and bring her back to Santa Cruz.

Hallett told police he arrived home Saturday afternoon, and his mother was gone. He found no note, the back door was unlocked and the car was gone.

Hallett then called Mrs. Strandberg, who he said was his mother's best friend. She too was missing, police said.

Following Kemper's telephone call to Santa Cruz police, authorities rushed to the Order Street duplex, where they found the bodies about 5:30 a.m.

By mid-morning, investigators had sealed off the apartment which is on the bottom floor of a two-story duplex.

At a press conference late this morning, James told newsmen he refused to speculate on Kemper who may have been involved with other slayings. He admitted the suspect had been doing a lot of talking to Pueblo police, but added he would "hate to speculate on anything because I have no idea what he is saying."

James did reveal that one fo the women had been beheaded, although he did not specify which one. He said cause of death of both women would be determined by a pathologist's investigation.

Pueblo Police Chief Robert Maber told reporters today that Kemper also had confessed to "six coed murders."

"I believe him," Maber added.

CONFESSION #1 TO PUEBLO,
COLORADO POLICE DEPARTMENT
(APRIL 24, 1973)

Reported by Inv. M. Aluffi
Address: Santa Cruz Sheriff's Department
Date: 4-24-73
Crime: Homicide
Classification: TAPED INTERVIEW
Victim's Name: Strandberg, Hallett, et. al.

THE FOLLOWING IS *u lupe recorded statement by suspect Edmund Kemper taken to Pueblo, Colorado shortly after his arrest on the above charge.*

⌊Interviewer will always be in *italics.*⌋

Scherer: *All right, now we get through Thorpe. Now let's get into Liu again. When you fired the shot into Thorpe ...*

Kemper: Yes, and she slumped over, Miss Liu panicked and she went unconscious, but she was making a very strange sound. I almost threw up as we were going down the hill. It was a sigh, a constant over and over sigh.

This was after the shooting?

Yea

Would you describe the shooting again?

With her, I fired the first time and it went through her hand. She was moving around quite rapidly, trying to get away from the gun because I had to fire right handed because of the cast, or in both cases, I would have fired left handed. It was awkward in both cases. I had to turn it around like this, so I was at a bad angle with her and I missed, they were bad shots the first two times. But the third shot, I moved it almost out of my hand and around at a direct angle. The first shot through her hand, missed her head completely and the second one grazed her head and also went through her hand and embedded itself in the car, and ricocheted back out the front. Then the third shot, I was positive that she was unconscious, but I really don't think I needed to do that. She was very slumped over in the seat and she was scrunched way down in the seat and was only maybe two thirds the height up off the seat. So her head was not visible above the cushion like it normally would be. So I just put the coat over her and grabbed the blanket and unfolded it enough ... and I tried to push Miss Thorpe over down into the floorboard area, and she wouldn't budge. She was just sitting there, slumped over completely, and so finally, I just pulled her over sideways on the seat, and put the blue velveteen sort of blanket over her and made sure it stayed below the level of the windows there and that it wasn't an obvious shape or anything. I kept it double thickness, and just opened it enough so it looked like a flat blue surface and started and continued right down the hill and never hit the brakes. Actually, maybe only once or twice when I reached back. Right after I put the blanket over Miss Thorpe, a car came down, so I smoothly accelerated so there wouldn't be a blast of gas and a jerk or anything. So I'm sure to them it appeared as if I was just cruising along. They came down behind us, and I came right down in front of the guard station at the bottom where the cars were parked and everything and there were two guards standing right by the road out there having a little conversation. They were maybe 20 feet from the car, on their side of the car.

Liu was moaning or gasping?

Yea, it was a sigh, a very strange sigh. It would start out very sharp, almost like a snuffle and then it would taper off and a little bit more like a masculine sigh than a fine girl, petite type of girl like she was. It wasn't low or anything, but it was very disconcerting and it was constant. After we stopped and went on down Bay, obviously, there was quite a bit of blood because of the wounds and there was blood from that last hole in the forehead.

Just a second, you made a stop where?

Right by the guards, I made a stop right next to the guards, and they glanced over and were talking. I stopped right there at the stop sign and continued right down Bay.

What were your movements from there?

I went straight down to Mission, turned right and headed out on [HWY] 1, making sure I broke absolutely no rules and was doing my damndest to look cool while I was freaking out about Alice Liu in the back seat there, which I'm sure she was unconscious. At first I didn't think so and I made a couple of loud statements and just continued right on through, so I knew she was unconscious. But the blood started running and started gurgling and the sighing was still there. So as soon as I got out to the edge of town, I stepped on the gas and got the hell away from there and a little farther down the road, where no cars were coming, I slowed down very slow, turned her head around to the side, and fired point blank at the side of her head. The reason she didn't go instantly like the Thorpe girl, was that the automatic had a kind of quirky ramp and it would not, you couldn't load all the points into the clip, or I would have always used those. I could only put one in the barrel and nine regular solid head long rifles in the clip and everything I fired at Miss Liu was solids. So that one solid slug she got in there and she was doing the moaning .... I got out of town and turned her head to the side and fired point blank and the flash was so great that I could see some of the tissue coming out. She stopped immediately, silence, then I turned back around about two seconds later and it started up again and it was really getting to me, so there's a place down the road, you know, that popular beach area where the sign is like it says "Davenport" and all that ... Bonny Doon, etc. A lot of people park there. Well, the next one back from there is the loop. Some people get on that and think they're going to Bonny Doon and it loops right back out.

Laguna

Yea, I circled back down through that and went up on that little cul-de-sac up in there and parked. I had the parking lights on, jumped out and put both of them in the trunk. Unfortunately, Miss Thorpe was very hard to handle. She didn't look as heavy as she was at all. As I was moving her and trying to get her up over into the trunk. She slipped and came down and landed on her left side. I picked her back up and pushed her on in. I just dragged Miss Liu and put her in and her back up and pushed her on in. I just dragged Miss Liu and put her in and lost a shoe doing so, and went back and got it. I was very careful about things like that because I knew that those were the details that get people every time. Also, I heard a plastic bag underneath the car blow out of the car as I pulled around and it had blood on it. It was a blue laundry bag, so I reached under the car and fished that out and put it back in. But it rained later that night, so anything that had been there would probably have been destroyed as far as evidence. But I put them both in the trunk, drove home, went in the house. I had told her I'd gone to the movie. So I came home and by this time ...

After you loaded them into the trunk, did you go straight home?

Straight home.

Did you talk to your mother as soon as you got home?

Yup. I went home and what I did was, I walked straight in and I noticed as I got into the light, there …oh, wait a minute. I stopped at Freddy's Fast Gas on the left there coming back into town. There was a Chinese girl pumping gas. I went into the rest room and cleaned off as much off the cast as I could, 'cause it was a new cast, and a little bit off my pants. To myself I called them my murder clothes because it was these dark pants. They were a dark blue denim western-type pants with very very light, not quite white markings, but they were very dark. That was in case I got them splattered. I used them on the first two girls. I think I used them when Aiko Koo and Cynthia Schall were killed. I'm not sure, but in the vast majority of the cases, I used those pants and shirt. The shirt is still at home and I know it has some stains in it, but they look more like rust stains than blood.

What happened when you got home?

Well, I stayed there quite a while at that station talking to the girl and acting nonchalant. Then I went home and talked to my mother a little, and crabbed about how I had fallen asleep in the movie. I said, "How do you like that, you go and pay all that money and then fall asleep?" Then I said I'd go back and see it tomorrow night and that gives me an alibi. So I went on in and acted nonchalant. Pretty soon I needed some cigarettes, so I told her and the way the house is laid out, there's a big picture window that's enclosed with curtains and the TV is right over here against the wall, and my mother sits right where that picture window is. All she'd have to do is get up and take a couple steps and open the curtain in order to see if I'm still out there and she hasn't heard the car leave. But what I didn't realize was that she wouldn't hear that over the TV. So I just went out there, pulled the car around and opened up the trunk, and this is the way the entire series happened. I took out the big knife and I cut both of their heads off right out there on the street. It was maybe ten o'clock at night, or possibly eleven, but that's where I did that because of the blood problem because they both had bled very badly in the trunk during the time of riding around and sitting at that gas station. It was getting all over everything. Then I went down and got my cigarettes at this little bar down by Seacliff, walked back out, got in the car, drove home, went back in the house, watched TV and went to bed. The next day, my mother was at work and it was drizzling. About ten or eleven in the morning, I started the process.

You left them in the trunk all night?

Yea. Their clothing was drenched with blood, and there was a tremendous amount of it. Anyway, that next day I took Miss Liu out of the trunk and into the house. I just carried her in, right through the back store, 'cause I knew the old bitty in the back there was never out in the rain. So, I just wandered on in there and committed this act which actually was rather difficult. Actually I think that was the last time I did anything like that. It was rather distasteful. I guess maybe the first time I did something like that there was a little bit of a charge, you know?

OK, both girls were in the car all night long with their heads removed, right?

Yes.

Did you say you took both girls in the house?

No, the other girl never left the trunk. Thorpe never left the trunk except for her head and I took that in the house the next day and removed the bullet. I cleaned the blood off of both of them in the bathroom for disposal later, so I wouldn't get all bloody.

Now you took Liu in the house and then what?

At that time, I took the clothes back out and put them in the back seat of the car.

Did you immediately attempt to have sexual relations with her?

Yes.

Did you wash her up or anything beforehand?

A little bit with a little rag or something or a dishtowel or a wash cloth or something. But there wasn't too much there. She was on top and to the back.

Whereabouts in the house did you have this act?

In the bedroom. I was very careful though about any blood stains or anything like that.

Whereabouts in the bedroom?

It was on the floor. There aren't any blood or blood related stains on the bed at all. I bleed from little zits and things on me and there's a stain on the white pad, that I think is a baby stain.

All right, these sexual acts took place on the floor?

Yea.

All right, she still has her hands at this time, is that correct?

Yea. That was one of the last things I did after she was back in the car. It was an afterthought.

Now she was stripped nude and you took her clothes out to the car, was this before or after the sexual act

After.

Now you said you washed her to where it would not look like there was any sexual activity. How did you do this?

With I think it was with a paper towel napkin-type thing and some Kleenex-type napkins, and there was quite a bit of material there. She was built ... her vaginal area was built a little differently than most girls I've seen. It seemed a little bit lower and the bone–I don't know what that bone is, above the bottom of the pelvis–is very very formidable there. It was very definite and like I said it was a rather difficult position. Anyway, I more or less poured it out with wet cloths. Then I disposed of them, but I was very careful doing so.

Now these two acts that you had with these girls, did you strip down yourself?

I think I did. I changed my clothes while I was at it, too, because I had the clothes from the night before and they were formidably stained on the pants from the night before because Miss Liu was quite bloody in the back seat there. When I removed her from the car I got stains all over the side.

Now, we've got Liu in your room, what happened after the sexual acts?

Well, like I said, I cleaned her up. I carried her back out and there was a party going on upstairs. This was about 2:00 in the afternoon.

Did you have her wrapped in anything?

I think very casually in a blanket or something very small, 'cause her legs were hanging out. I was carrying her like a mannequin sort of. She was very lightweight. I just wandered right out there with her and put her in the trunk right under the window. That's one thing that amazes me about society, that is, that you can do damn near anything and nobody's gonna' say anything or notice.

All right, then you got her back in the car, then what happened?

That's when I removed the hands. I noticed them especially then. I had a red tub, sort of like a dishwashing plastic dishpan, and I placed the heads and hands in there in the corner in the trunk away from everything else. At this point, Miss Thorpe was mostly clothed. In moving around and stuff, certain things got half-pulled off, but mostly, she was clothed but in a state of disarray. But like I remember her bra, she was well-built in the chest and that was still on, but a lot of it was exposed because the shirt was torn open and the coat was almost pulled off around sideways from trying to move her around in the car there. I removed the boots then, I remember. She didn't have any socks on. This was just before I left. I took the coat off and I pulled down her panties and I noticed that she had a tampon placed, and I removed that and I just tossed that off up in the corner of the trunk and again, because that could possibly lead toward her identification which at this point I wasn't too concerned about because I had decided I was just going to, rather than hassle with dismemberment which would have been a super hassle at that point, I was just not caring if somebody finds those portions of their bodies, but hoping that it would be at least a few days in case somebody happened to drive by while I was doing it. But then again, in fact, it wasn't even a pretense. I went up and visited that friend, a good friend of mine up there that lived in the same neighborhood as I did when I worked with the state, and I dropped by and I was fairly agitated that night and she noticed it. I was kidding around a lot and was very nervous. My stomach was killing me. I think I'm developing ulcers because of all this. Not so much now, but I was in a great tension whenever something like that was happening, especially people in the trunk and having to dispose. I'd get very close to the point of panic until it was done. Then I would just completely relax. But this tension would build and build and build to the point of removal, and I'll tell you on that road, Eden Road there, uh …

What did you do when you left your house and had both girls in the trunk?

Well, it was afternoon and it was raining. I went up [HWY] 17. I was gonna' go up to visit my friend and I had definitely decided to dispose of them up in the Bay Area.

All parts of the girls were there?

Yes, and I decided to get rid of them up in the Bay Area because you could tell they'd been from Cabrillo and I figured these girls were from the university and as far as the authorities knew, the first two could possibly have been killed in Santa Cruz too, and I wanted to distract the heat away from Santa Cruz. So I figured that I know both areas and the authorities wouldn't necessarily know that I knew the Bay Area well, because the job that I do entails extensive travel through those areas, especially like with the disposal of Miss Koo's heads and hands. I knew that particular area really well and knew that people at 2:00 in the morning would not be traveling that road at all, so they would think it would be at least somebody within five or ten miles of that area and that's what I wanted people to think.

All right, you drop up 17 to Alameda.

Yup, and I stopped by and saw my friend for a while, went out to dinner and then went out to a movie and I couldn't eat the dinner. I got in the car, and just to kill time, filled up with gas at the other Union station, the one to the right of Park Street as you turn off the First Street bridge, by the police station. It was the one I went to with the first two girls for gas. I went to the other one with the trunk loaded and very low and very obvious, filled it half way up with gas, went out, parked right in front of the theater, went in, watched two movies. I wanted to be sure it was good and late. I arrived on the scene up at Eden Canyon Road about 2:00 AM. In fact, I think it was very close to 2:00 AM when I actually got rid of them. It was probably 1:30 when I got up there and it was a good half-hour or forty minutes before I had the nerve to get rid of them. I went up and down the road looking for places. I had a big flashlight, and was looking all over vetoing different spots for different reasons. Then I decided upon this one because of the steep grade down from the road and the fact that there were discarded items down there already and probably nobody would go by looking down there as a habit. It turned out that that panned out. I dragged both bodies over to the edge and laid them horizontally and pushed and rolled them down. Unfortunately, Miss Liu, both of them were in rather contorted positions because of their positions in the trunk.

Did anything happen while you were disposing of the bodies at that location?

No. Wait a minute ... yes. When I was pulling Miss Thorpe out of the car, she fell on the back side and left a rather large deposit of excrement and I'm sure some of it stayed because it was a rather good size of discharge there, then I just pulled her straight over to the edge. That's the only unusual thing I can think of. There were no cars at all the whole time I was down that road. If even one car had come by while I was down checking things out, I would have vetoed the whole place.

Did you deposit all parts of the bodies there?

No. Like I said, I had the heads and hands in the red container and at that time, I moved them to the front floorboard on the passenger side and put a blanket over it so I'd have quick access. I was trying to make up my mind what to do with that and I decided what I'd do is go up to the Devil's Slide area. My first choice was to go up to Devil's Slide and actually just drive by because it's very dangerous to stop there. I decided with these high banks there at Devil's Slide, I'd drive by to find a likely spot and heave them over as hard as I could hoping they would go in the water. But I vetoed that idea because of all the different chances involved and also, because just before I got there, I can't remember the damn name of the town, it's the little town at the base of the hill, the last little hamlet that you're gonna' hit before you hit Highway 1 and Devil Slide on down. Pacifica, that's it. As I passed through Pacifica and went on up, I noticed to my left there was a great wide parking area there and even better yet, there was a mound all the way around, kind of a ridge around the edge of it and so that made people have to get out of the car, go to the top of that ridge to see down. I got to the top with my flashlight and looked down and it was almost deserted in that valley and quite far away and no cars off on the little streets in the background. I noticed as I went through Pacifica all the patrol cruisers were having coffee in the coffee shop there, so I had it made there. I made sure no cars were coming either way when I stopped, checked it out and took off again, came back around, made sure no cars were coming, pulled up, leaped out, and one head at a time, went up to the very top and heaved them as far as I could and they both landed in the vicinity of that barbed wire fence, and I guess later on, the hair detached itself and the heads rolled on down father.

Where did you learn that from?

I went back later about two weeks ago, in fact, two weeks to the day, at night worrying, worrying, worrying, thinking that was a dumb thing to do. Why didn't I skip those heads and bury them somewhere, and I vetoed that originally, 'cause I was just too worked up and I didn't want to put out any more hassle and take a chance of getting caught. So, I went back two weeks later. I had another appointment with my doctor on the cast. So, I went up there about four in the morning and parked and went all over that hillside with that damn flashlight and all I found was the one clump of hair. It belonged to Miss Thorpe, definitely. It was not scattered. It was sort of in a bundle and was by a bush or in a bush. That's apparently where it had landed and it had rained a few times. But I guess something like the next day or the day after, those boys up there messing around found one of the skulls.

Let me ask you one thing, Ed, before we wrap it up for today. There are three cars involved here evidently. #1 is your car. #2 is your mother's car and #3 is Mrs. Hallett's car. Can you give us the location of these three cars?

Generally. Specifically, on my mother's car. Do you know the Union Station off Seacliff? Turn up that side street and there's two cul-de-sac type things on the right. It's in the second one. You can see it once you approach it. It's a little green Mustang with the A sticker on it. My car is on the other side of Seacliff out on one of those little sketchier streets. In fact, it's in front of a house construction site. I don't know the name of the street, but it's fairly close to the area. There's a little drive along the beach or cliff there. It's maybe a few blocks away from that. It's on a fairly flat road where there are not a lot of obstructions and it'd be easy to see. Mrs. Hallett's car is at a Texaco Station in Reno. The Main Street in Reno is Virginia and as it goes through town past all the big casinos, you hit the base of the hill and as you go up the hill you run into the University of Nevada and right at the base of that hill I believe this is where the Texaco station is.

Is that near where you rented the car?

Well, what I did was I parked the car a couple of blocks away from there, walked down to a hotel, to a pay phone and called a taxi and called the airport. The taxi took me out to the airport and I rented the car and drove back up to where her car was parked, right up on the University property, just inside it, and that's when I transferred the weapons and the ammunition into the trunk and car and stuff like that.

This is the conclusion of the interview at this time, the time being 2345 hours Colorado time, the date being 4-24-73. Interview to be continued on 4-25-73 AM.

RECORD CROSS REFERENCE COPY OF DRIVER LICENSE
OR IDENTIFICATION CARD APPLICATION ON FILE WITH
CALIFORNIA DEPARTMENT OF MOTOR VEHICLES
FOR DMV OR LAW ENFORCEMENT USE ONLY

RIGHT THUMB PRINT

Int.
I.P. MAR 3 1 1972
Ext.
T.L.
(DATE)
other
name

Fingerprint card of Edmund Kemper III - this was provided by the Santa Cruz
Sheriff's Department. The date stamp of March 31, 1972 is from the Department
of Motor Vehicles and used to cross-reference latent crime scene(s) fingerprint
evidence.

SYNOPSIS: *The following is a taped interview held in Pueblo, Colorado with suspect Edmund Kemper and investigating officers, D.A. Peter Chang, Lieut. Scherer of SCPD and Inv. M. Aluffi of this Department, regarding this case.*

REPORT:

Scherer: *Where did you make the removal on this girl, Schall?*

Uh, it was similar to, in fact, identical to the Koo girl, with the exception of the splitting of the torso across the middle, the midsection, and I used an old Division of Highways axe, a large plastic chipping axe that I had. It was rather sharp.

Where is it at?

It's up at the dump, but I think you can get it. I threw that away after you [referring to Inv. Aluffi] came up. He caused me quite a bit of consternation and he was very cool about it, too. The axe is out at the Santa Cruz City Dump, as you come down into that thing off towards the left in the back, there's a little shack back there along with piles of pilings of wood and things and it tapers off down into like a little valley thing. There's piles of rocks and stuff. I can show you, but it tapers down and goes off into some bushes where I threw it.

You washed this axe?

Oh, yea. It still had some ... she was rather fatty and there was ... I had a bad problem there where I didn't with the others with the body fat, a grease-type coating and there's some of that still on that axe I'm sure.

Ok, now you have the body in your apartment all night long, right?

Yea.

When did you start dissecting the body?

I think it was around eleven o'clock the next morning. It took a hell of a long time.

Where was it down at?

In the bathtub, there's two bathrooms. The one I used was the one closest to the living room. I removed the sliding glass-type plastic doors in the shower and there was an aluminum rail above and I just removed that whole assembly, so it would be like a regular bathtub, and I was very careful and meticulous in cleaning it up. I poured lots of Drano down the thing and made sure it fizzed real good and removed any hair or tissue that got caught in the drain, and things like that, made sure there was no spots of blood laying around. I used that special foam bowl cleaner stuff in any suspicious areas where I thought something like that might be there. Then there's immeasurable baths and showers since then. Anyway, the reason they found that bag, or suspected that bag out there on the cliff was because the upper part of the torso was the heaviest and I double-lined the bag. I was kinda' panicky watching for cars and everything and ran over the edge, thinking it was straight down, 'cause I had only looked hastily with my flashlight and dumped it out and I forgot about the inside bag and they must have separated down the cliff somewhere. I saw it tumbling. I didn't know if there was water down there or a beach or what. I saw a little sliver of beach off to the right, and for all I knew, it landed right smack dab in the middle of somebody's beach party, so I was very quick about the whole thing and ran. In fact, when I dumped the bags with the parts of the arms and legs, one arm I think propped up a little bit out of it, I think it was very noticeable and even back from the guardrail, I could see it. I skidded down the side of the hill there, slipping in the mud. I was afraid somebody got footprints off of that, it must have drizzled up there. But this was like two o'clock in the morning, and then three o'clock that afternoon, that highway patrolman discovered the parts, so I was pretty well blown out about that. I was sure there must be tire prints or one possible tire print or a possible large foot print. All I was worried about was a large foot print, because I wear a size-15 shoe and that would tell you a hell of a lot.

When you thought you might have left a tire print, did you do anything?

No. I thought seriously about getting my tires recapped.

Were all parts of the Schall girl deposited at that one spot?

Everything but the head.

Where is the head?

That's what I didn't want to say. It's in the backyard at my mother's place. There's a stone stepping thing in the backyard. [A sketch of the backyard is made by Kemper as he explains where the head is buried.] What I did was like I only cut the hole with a trowel that big around. It was about 11-inches deep. That was on January the 8th, so maybe that was the 9th that I did that. The reason was I was gonna' let it stay there a few months and was gonna' dig it back up and take the bullet out of the skull and then dispose of the skull, rather than hack and chop. Because my thing was no evidence at all if I could possibly help it. If I stand there with that certain type of axe, chopping into the skull and dispose of the skull, you're gonna' have a pretty good idea what type of axe it was.

Okay, we've got Cynthia Schall's shirt, and her head over at your house, but all the other parts of her body were deposited over the cliff?

Yea. That was at Sand Creek. I couldn't find the specific spot again, because I'm not familiar with that area. I chose the first steep appearing cliff and apparently it wasn't steep enough. Also, since then I've disposed of property of Rosalind Thorpe and Alice Liu out in that area.

What about the clothing of Schall?

I took that up to Alameda, this on the pretense of telling my mother I was going to visit friends, and very late at night, when nobody was at this all-night laundromat that I used to use. I went in there, and I put the coat in the dryer and put it on about four dimes worth and put it on full hot, figuring it would ruin the coat, because it was inexpensive and had a little tear here and there, I figured it would melt certain spots of the plastic and the owner would come in, he's a little ole' black guy, and he'd get pissed and throw it in the garbage. I threw the pants in with it and I think I threw her bra and something else in the trash. The shoes I think, I'm not sure, but I think I tossed them in the Goodwill thing, down there. Maybe not, I might have thrown them somewhere. I can't remember, but I know at that time I was very touchy about continuing any patterns, like disposal of clothes for instance. By that point, investigators might be looking for anything like that that might show up. Oh, wait a minute, on the way up on Highway 17, past San Jose, I just heaved it off the side of the road, one of the shoes, and on the next off-ramp, I came back this way and heaved the other one, so that the highway crews wouldn't find them at the same time and they'd just figure it fell off a trailer or something.

All right, we've got the stuff in the laundromat.

Yeah, that was disposed of. I came by the next morning. I didn't even visit my friend. I just parked out in the front of his apartment and slept all night. He was already asleep. I just got up about five or six in the morning, started the car, drove back to the laundromat and he had already taken the trash out, the coat and everything was gone, so there was no sweat.

There was no struggle out of Schall?

Absolutely nothing, there was no hanky panky, no assault or anything like that.

Was there anything out of the ordinary you haven't told us about this particular girl?

Yea, she had a joint of pot in her pocket that I got rid of very quickly. All I needed to do was to get busted for dope. I don't like that stuff anyway. But she had that in her coat pocket. What do you mean as far as "unusual"?

What I'm making reference to is the time that she was shot or after she was shot, had she been tied or gagged?

No, not at all. I imagine you have some very deep marks on her wrists appearing to be a handcuffs and that's how I moved her around, you know, with a broken arm, not being able to pick her up. Then I reached from the back between the body and the arms and dragged her that way. That was after she was dead. I didn't put anything on, she was very, very touchy about that. It was hard enough just getting her to get in the trunk, and as soon as she got in, that's when I shot her.

And you put the handcuffs on after that?

Yea, after she was shot, two times. Once in the morning in the house and once in the bedroom and the bathroom.

When you took her into the house, some time after 8:45, the time you fixed the shooting, did you leave with her?

I think it was about ten o'clock when I took her in. I just left her outside 'cause I thought possibly my mother would come home, so I just left her in the car for a while.

Did you leave her in the closet all night long? What did you do with her all night?

She stayed right in there till about maybe thirty or forty minutes after. I got her in the house. It was very hard getting her in the closet because I couldn't pick her up and place her anywhere. It seemed to me almost immediately after that, but I knew if I tried any messing around or anything which I believe would have been very difficult anyway, she was a rather large girl, but I did disrobe her before I put her in the closet. I took her clothes off and hid them under my bed. Then, I put them in my car the next day, and got rid of them.

You put her in the closet in the nude, then? You didn't put her on your bed?

Yea. I don't know if you'd know what the layout of my bedroom is, I've got a narrow angle bed that a. ...

Did you try and have sexual relations with her?

I did.

You did have sexual relations with her?

Yea, on the 4th, the next morning. This sounds terrible, but that night, she was still quite limp and very hard to move around as it was and I just . . . no way that, uh ... but I'd never had sex with a large girl like that before and I decided to see what it was like. Actually, you can't really check that point off, I understand, because of the state of the body, but I will say that the next morning I did. Also, that pretty much finishes that one because that brings up something about the next two. I did have relations with Alice Liu after her death. Also, I imagine the heavy rains up in the area after I disposed of their bodies helped.

What type of knife did you use to dissect her?

I used the same knife in all of them. It's a buck knife. It's called the "General" and it's the largest. It's something like a Bowie knife but it has more of a straight blade, rather than real fancy or curved.

Where is it at now?

It's at home. It has a black case. I think it's . . . there's two pink chest drawers, one right beside the door and there's one over by the closet, and it's the one right inside the door. That's where I kept my guns and pistols, ammunition, and the knife.

Is this knife sharp or did you sharpen it?

It still had the factory sharpened . . . it's an extremely hard-tempered steel. In fact, I had a hard and a soft sharpening stone for it and they wouldn't even touch it. I had to get a carbide steel rod to sharpen it with and then use the others to finish it off. So, actually, it was a semi-sharp knife but it had an extremely fine edge to it, but I had to use quite a bit of effort. Like where I had just bought the knife, and I used it on Aiko Koo, it was no problem at all. It was extremely sharp and brand new. I had bought it maybe that day or the day before, something like that.

Is this a different knife than you used on the first two girls?

Yeah, I used the pocket knife on them because all I removed was heads and it was extremely sharp, too.

Okay, let's go over to . . .

The last two, that was the 5th of February, and I'm not really sharp on the time. I think it was around 8:30 and I figured there'd be a lot of cars going up through there, as they had a seminar up there that night,. I noticed, I always paid attention, I went in at night when the guards were at the kiosk, since I did have an "A" sticker, an "A" parking sticker on my Ford which allowed me open access without suspicion. I had a badly crushed left rear fender with a Mickey Mouse-type tail-light wired on it which is extremely noticeable, and very easy to remember, but I watched him very closely as I passed by and he didn't even look. He saw the front of the car, the number and saw that "A" thing flash and just looked right on to the next car and started waving him up to stop at the kiosk, and he just waved me on by. So, I knew he wouldn't ever be able to say what kind of car it was and I imagine they'd start looking for unmarked cars that went up there that didn't have tags. When I did get that tag from my mother, I did get it for the purpose of doing things like that. I told her I wanted to be able to go up there and park and go into the library and drive through, and things like that and park where I wanted to.

You say this was about 8:30 when you picked up the girls?

I picked up Miss Thorpe first and I guess it was up around Merrill College, up towards the top and I had passed her actually. I think the time was around eight or eight thirty, I didn't watch the time too closely but, apparently, this seminar was about in the middle and she had either decided she didn't like it or she had a class, I can't remember, but I had just passed her and as I was passing her, I said, "Well, she's not bad looking," so I stopped and she hesitated, she was probably about 20 yards behind the car and looked to the rear and she saw the wrecked-up car there and hesitated for a moment. Then, I'm sure she saw the "A" tag and ran right along and hopped in. I told her, she asked me where I was going, and that had always been a problem with me, 'cause when they ask me where I'm going and I say the wrong thing, they won't get in. If I say I'm going down to Mission, and they say they're going up the other end of Mission, or something like this, sometimes it's an excuse to not get in. Sometimes they're actually going the other way and I'll blow an awful good opportunity, 'cause I didn't think quick enough.

Could you describe her to us?

Yea, she was 5' 6" I think and probably close to the weight of the Schall girl, about 150 pounds, something like that. She was very hard to handle because I still had problems with my arm. It was still in a cast.

What about her hair?

It was light brown with blondish tints in it, but she wore it short that night so it looked like a dull brown. It was kind of a bun-type ting,. She had pictures and her college ID card and they showed long hair and it looked dark completely, That night, after I cut their heads off, the hair got disheveled, and you know, you could see there were highlighted streaks of blond through it as you got farther down.

What about her clothing?

She had ... this is one way I identified myself to the man on the phone this morning in Santa Cruz, the Police Department. I said, "Hey, on those two girls, I remember in the paper you didn't say anything about physical evidence, or what type of physical evidence that helped identify them besides x-rays," and I knew what they meant because she had pink and purple zip-up boots that were halfway to the knee with a medium-sized heel. She had black felt bell bottom, front button-up sailor pants which were also torn because I grabbed her when she was sitting in the front seat when I went up to this place where I was gonna' put her in the trunk, I grabbed her by the leg and by the back and as I pulled, it just tore. I grabbed her by the other leg, or else by the same one in another spot, and it tore again, and I said, "the hell with it," and I tugged her out by the arms. But at any rate, she had on a blue crew work-type shirt thing and a black pea coat that was rather tight fitting.

Was she carrying anything?

Yeah, she was carrying a purse. It was a brown purse with a kind of a lock-clasp thing. It was like a metal spring thing that would keep the top of the purse closed. It was built into the top lining, where instead of having a flap over it, the top of the purse was open, but it stayed shut. I'll repeat this, but basically that's what I was talking about, about getting rid of some of the property, the two bags. I had to keep those for a long time, because things blew ups really quick,.when they disappeared and I didn't dare go out because they were both very noticeable things, especially that purple book bag. Actually, aside from statements, I had thought about it, and there's some physical evidence in the car, like the last two, there's two bullet holes and there's also some blood. But I understand you know in court proceedings, just used by itself, that would be circumstantial evidence or supporting evidence ... well, it wouldn't be supporting, because there's nothing to support it. So, I figured, like Miss Schall, there was absolutely no evidence against me. I even had the sash thing on my robe replaced. I had my mother make me another one. It was a homemade robe. I very nonchalantly asked her to make me another one after I disposed of the first one, telling her it was torn.

You picked up, you think, Thorpe some time around 8:30 up at Merrill College?

Yeah, out on the road. That was Sunday, out on the other side of the road.

All right, let's go into Thorpe here. You had her in the car what was your next move?

I started talking with her. Basically, she carried the conversation. She was very outgoing and I was just trying to be amicable and I was trying to think of what I was gonna' do. I had decided after we had rode a little ways that that was it. I was gonna' get her, definitely. I had my little zapple through my body there and that always confirmed it. I never had one of those where it didn't actually happen. It's just where everything would click just right, circumstances were perfect. Nobody else was around. The guard didn't notice me coming in, nothing that looked unusual going out and she was not the least bit suspecting. Also, it was somebody that I didn't know in any way, shape or form, or knew anybody that I knew about. So, those were certain things I held as absolute. One I had held as an absolute for a long time was don't ever do anything like that around the Santa Cruz area, because that's too close to home, and having the past I had, I would naturally come under suspicion. But then I started getting sicker and sicker later on and a little more and more careless in my approach in taking care of hings and afterwards, which I'm sure got obvious, because more and more evidence started popping up, in different forms.

Well, let's go on to the sequence of what happened.

Okay, what happened next is we were talking and she's more or less popping little questions here and there, talking along. I noticed Miss Liu standing on the side. She saw us coming, threw out a great big beautiful smile and stuck her thumb out very hopefully and you know, not a cheesecake-type thing, but you know, throwing her best foot forward there. I figured later on, what happened was, that she looked to me for just different little details, that she was probably a careful hitchhiker, and very good looking, built nicely and everything and intelligent and moderate in her dress and everything, nothing outlandish. From some of her ID, college friends, stable background and all that, I imagined she was a cautious hitchhiker and she always made sure of her ride before she got in, and we appeared to be a couple, and with that "A" tag on there, and a man and a woman, you know. So, she didn't hesitate at all about getting in.

Did the girls appear to know one another?

No, not at all. That's one thing I noticed before I stopped was, she just glanced at her and just kept looking forward, and then I stopped. We went on down. I stopped in front of Liu's college ... Kreske ... somewhere out there, but it was farther down from where we picked up the other girl. We went over there to the front kiosk and I was very careful in eyeballing the guards as I went by and he glanced and I'm sure he didn't see Mis Liu in the back seat because of the lighting and the fact that her clothes were dark, except for the top, light-colored tweed peacoat.

Describe Miss Liu.

Well, I think she was 5'2", very nice build for her height. It surprised me, her being an Oriental, that she was built like she was. Nothing fantastic, I mean, but you know, very nice build. Anyway, she had long black hair, rather coarse, and very square sort of a face. Very wide, high cheekbones.

What about her clothing?

Her clothing, she had, I think, desert-type boot things, and shoe goodies. Suede-colored. The pants were Levis bell-bottoms. She had a brown wide belt on, and the pants and belt were very stylish, laying nicely right around the hips, not trying to be funny or anything, but that's something that appealed to me immediately. She had a very short coat on and this was noticeable as she carried her bag up in front of her. It was slightly pulled up and she had on a bra–a supporting bra–to accentuate her figure. She had on a light blue turtleneck sweater that had a zipper in the back, up to the top of the neck and she had on this old grey-colored pea coat and she had bright red socks on.

Was she carrying anything?

Yes, a purple book bag with white Chinese lettering on the front and a strap over the shoulder and several papers inside. She had a wallet, a lot of IDs and pictures and things like that. What struck me about Miss Thorpe was that she didn't have any money at all, not even change in her purse. She had just gotten a letter from home with a check in it.

Where's the check?

At the bottom of the ocean . . . I left everything in both bags, kept them for quite a while, sweating the whole time, wondering if somebody was gonna' come out there and investigate me, or if my mother's gonna' go through my closet and stumble across it and immediately know what it was without even opening it. So, I went out past that rocky creek point, farther out to Big Sur, well not Big Sur, but out where the road curves around and starts to go down the coast to one of the cliffs out there and threw both bags out as far as I could.

About how much time spanned between the time you did it with these girls and threw out the bags?

Well, that was the 5th of February, and I did the thing with the bags in late-April. Getting rid of the bags was at least a month or maybe five weeks after.

How do you place the 5th of February? Do you recall what day of the month this was?

It was a Monday night. I remember that. Well, see, that was the thing. I kind of made a point of the dates in my mind originally and I might have gotten it wrong, but I'm pretty sure it was the 5th of February. There was May 7th, September 14th, January 8th, and February 5th.

What happened when you had both girls in the car now?

I passed the guard and made sure he didn't take special notice of us. I was sure he only noticed the girl in the front. Both of us were in a stabilized mood sort of, chatting as we went out. Miss Liu was quiet in the back, sitting in the back right behind Miss Thorpe. We started down around the first curve there. We went down a ways to where it straightens out and you can see the city and the lights, and I slowed down and remarked about the beautiful view and asked if she minded if I slowed down and she said, "Not at all." She was watching, and I looked back at Miss Liu and asked her the same question and she said no. But I got the impression from her she was just saying no because she was getting a ride, and didn't mind slowing down a little bit and was disgusted for maybe five or six seconds which were long because I knew there were no cars coming at that moment and I didn't see any coming up and I hesitated for several seconds because I was very scared, really. I had never done something like that before, where I just come out and shoot somebody, just right out in the blue.

But I was mad that night, My mother and I had a real tiff. I was pissed. I told her I was going to a movie and I jumped up and went straight to the campus 'cause it was still early. I said the first girl that's halfway decent that I pick up, I'm gonna' blow her brains out. As it was, I improvised. It was two in a perfect situation. That's the only reason there were two that night, just because they happened to be there. Miss Thorpe almost didn't get picked up you know, 'cause I almost passed her on by and if I hadn't picked her up, Miss Liu wouldn't have got in with a single guy. A young guy. I don't think she would have gotten in.

Anyway, we slowed down there, almost to a stop, we were just barely moving, and I had been moving my pistol from down below my leg in my lap, a solid black pistol, and the interior of my car was black, so she couldn't see it and I picked it up and had it on my lap talking with her and I moved it up to the side like this and I just picked it up and pulled the trigger, 'cause I knew the minute I picked it up like that the girl in the back was gonna' see it and I didn't want any problems. So, as soon as I picked it up, I hesitated maybe for a second at the very most, and then pulled the trigger.

This was on the straight stretch, coming down from the campus, overlooking the city?

Right, that would be on the eastern side of the farthest eastern part of the campus. It's the only major straightaway there. It was halfway between the bottom of the hill and the kiosk, so I was confident there wouldn't be any noise heard. I had a blanket in the back, folded up, right in the back seat and I had a large coat sitting there, too. A green coat. There's some evidence for you. There's a small blood stain on that green coat for you, inside the lining.

Was your car still moving when you shot her?

Very slowly, yeah, just barely moving, just like maybe 1/4 mile an hour, almost to a stop. Like I didn't want the brake lights on in case somebody was around the corner, 'cause that would be something to stick in their memory.

What did Liu do at that particular time?

Well, as I lifted the gun up, I heard a slight gasp in the back and I think possibly Miss Thorpe heard it because she started to turn her head as I pulled the trigger. She instantly just fell over against the window.

Do you recall what portion of the head or body that the bullet went into?

Right square in the middle of the left side of her head. It was just above the ear, maybe an inch. But basically, I was sizing up, looking at her head, She had a rather large forehead and I was imagining what her brain looked like inside, and I just wanted to put it right in the middle of that. So it was above and a little behind the ear, or not actually above and behind the ear I was centering on the temple, not aiming at it but so it would be a little bit back and above the temple, so it'd be towards the front portion of the top of the ear, just above the hairline.

Did that bullet remain in the skull?

No. It did not exit because she was right by the window. It was one of the first things I checked. What happed was, I fired and Miss Liu panicked and started covering her face up and that's why I cut her hands off, 'cause she had four bullet holes in her hands. Two in each hand. I had to fire through the hands. She was moving very quickly around and was down into the corner and I missed twice. One just went through her hand, I guess. It went right into the padding of the car. The next shot I fired, went into one of her hands, the back of her hand, and hit her just right around the temple area on the right side of her head and it had a glancing blow, 'cause it took a long tearing cut in and went right along the bone. I'm sure it broke the top of the jawbone, 'cause there were broken bones up in that area. It creased along there, came out and exited through the ear. There was a hole in the ear and hit the same padded area as the first bullet. It hit at a glancing angle and it was flattened out ... the bullet was. It hit in and ricocheted off of the inside, came back out, right in front of the cushion, hit the cushion, it bounced out into the front floor mat and I found it there. That, I think, stunned her. She was making quite a bit of noise. No loud shrieks or screams, but quite a bit of fuss there, and then as I fired a second time, it quieted down but she was still making noise, and her hands were starting to come down and she was moving over a little bit, and I thought she was still going so I aimed carefully and fired. That was the bullet that would be in this area on the right front forehead, just about the middle of the forehead, and that was the last shot I fired at them. But there was one more fired later.

THE INTERVIEW WAS CONCLUDED AT THIS POINT UNTIL A LATER time.

Edmund Kemper III assists the Santa Cruz Sheriff's Department in locating
bodies (courtesy of SCSD)

*"CALLS POLICE ON SLAYINGS,
IS SEIZED" PRESS & SUN-
BULLETIN (APRIL 25, 1973)*

Santa Cruz, Calif. (AP) — Edmund Emil Kemper III walked into a telephone booth in Pueblo, Colo., dialed authorities in Santa Cruz and told them he had killed his mother and a woman visitor. He later said he "just got worrying about the murders" and had to tell someone.

Police converged on the telephone booth Tuesday and apprehended the 6-foot-9, 280-pound Kemper while he was still talking to Santa Cruz sheriff's deputies who had traced the call.

Pueblo authorities later said Kemper, 24, told them he had killed six other women in the Santa Cruz area.

The former mental patient was being held today by Pueblo police pending extradition to California.

Santa Cruz deputies, acting on Kemper's tip, hurried to his mother's home in the nearby coastal community of Aptos and there found the nude bodies of Kemper's mother, Clara Nel Strandberg, 52, and Sara Taylor Hallett, 59, hidden in closets.

Sheriff Douglas B. James, at a news conference late Tuesday declined to comment on the reports from Pueblo that Kemper was quoted by Police Capt. Robert Simon as saying he had killed six other young women in this area. Santa Cruz police say they know of four unsolved coed slayings.

"KEMPER FRIENDS REACT IN SHOCKED DISBELIEF" SANTA CRUZ SENTINEL (APRIL 25, 1973) – TOM HONIG

Law Mum On Link To Slaying Of Coeds

By TOM HONIG
Sentinel Staff Writer

FRIENDS OF CONFESSED slayer Edmund Kemper, 24, streamed into the sheriff's department Tuesday to tell detectives of their disbelief that their 6-foot-9, 280-pound friend could be involved with the two latest Santa Cruz area murders.

Many of the nearly 20 friends who talked to detectives were aware that nine years ago Kemper confessed to killings grandparents in North Folk, Calif.

Records indicate that in 1965,[1] Kemper admitted shooting his grandmother as she was sitting at her typewriter and also stabbing her with a kitchen knife.

When his grandfather came upon the scene, Kemper said he shot him in the back of the head. He then reported the crimes to the local sheriff.

One friend interviewed by authorities Tuesday said Kemper "wasn't proud" of the killings, but he wanted to let people know what was in his past.

Following the murder confession, the 15-year-old Kemper was sent to Atascadero State Mental Hospital, where he remained through 1970, authorities said. After his release from there, he reportedly spent a couple of months at the California Youth Authority.

In March of 1970, records show he went to work as a laborer at the Green Giant Corporation in Watsonville. He lasted there a couple of months, and then jumped around to other labor jobs. Most recently, he worked for the state division of highways in Alameda. Detectives said he was one. A leave of absence because of an injury on the job.

The portrait of Kemper described to investigators Tuesday showed the man as friendly and slow fused. "He never focused on violence," a good friend noted.

What Kemper did focus on was his long-time hobby, motorcycle riding. In connection with this interest, he expressed a desire to get into law enforcement, especially the highway patrol. But at 6-foot-9, he was over the maximum height requirement.

His motorcycle riding did cause him some problems. In February of 1971, he filed suit in Santa Cruz Superior Court asking for damages which resulted from a motorcycle collision.

In the suit, he asked for $45,000 in damages from Irene Moulton Withrow, for injuries sustained in a collision involving her car and his cycle in November of 1970.

Among other injuries, Kemper claimed he sustained a skull fracture and a concussion which resulted in swelling and flushing of the face. He also complained of "giddiness at times."

The suit was settled out of court Dec. 9, 1971.

Another friend told Sheriff's deputies he had spent much of last Saturday with Kemper. He said he met him about 11 a.m., and they spent the next few hours just "riding around."

They stopped briefly at Kemper's apartment at 609A Ord St. Kemper told his friend his mother was out shopping with a friend. Then, Saturday night, the two men met with other friends at the Jury Room bar on Ocean Street, where they stayed until after midnight.

"He seemed a little quieter than usual Saturday night," one man told investigators. But he added that he didn't seem extremely upset about anything.

Sheriff Doug James reported Tuesday that the two slain women were killed prior to Sunday.

Kemper's friends reacted with further disbelief to reports coming out of Colorado that he claims he killed six women in the Santa Cruz area.

"To his friends knowledge," said an investigator, "not only wasn't he violent, he never picked up hitchhikers."

Friends also reported to detectives that Kemper has a fiancée living in Turlock, but her identity has not been established.

---

1. Correction: 1964.

"SUSPECT NAMES 9TH VICTIM" THE INDEPENDENT (LONG BEACH, CALIFORNIA) (APRIL 26, 1973)

SANTA CRUZ (AP) — *Mass-slaying suspect Edmund Kemper has claimed yet another victim, authorities announced late Wednesday. Berkely police said they were informed by Santa Cruz authorities that Kemper claimed responsibility for the death of Aiko Keo, 15, of Berkeley. The girl disappeared Sept. 14*

A SEEMINGLY UNCONCERNED YOUNG GIANT HEADED BACK TO California Wednesday in his getaway car top race charges of killing his mother and a family friend – two of eight women he confessed slaying in the Santa Cruz area in the past year.

Edmund Kemper, 24, a 6-foot-9, 290-pound laborer who killed his grandparents nine years ago, agreed to return to Santa Cruz during a court hearing in Pueblo, Colo.

The mass murder suspect voluntarily signed extradition papers after turning down a judge's offer of a court appointed attorney.

Three Santa Cruz homicide detectives leftPueblo with him in a car that Kemper had rented in Reno, Nev. They planned to drop the rented auto there and pick up the care of one of his alleged victims, which was abandoned in Reno during the weekend.

Dist. Atty. Peter Chang requested extradition of Kemper on charges of beating his mother, Mrs. Clarenell Strandberg, 52, and her friend, Sara Taylor Hallett, 59, to death with a hammer last weekend in the town of Aptos.

Santa Cruz Police Lt. Charles Sherer said Kemper "definitely" ties in with the other six murders he confessed by long distance telephone—the mutilation killings of six hitchhiking college coeds.

Kemper was arrested Tuesday in a phone booth in Pueblo, a southern Colorado city of 120,000 while talking to detectives.

Kemper, wearing a gray shirt and baggy blue jeans, refused District Judge Jack F. Feaby's offer to appoint an attorney.

"I don't think it's necessary, your honor," Kemper said, then signed six copies of extradition papers.

He laughed aloud on his way back to his jail cell when police lost the keys to his handcuffs. Kemper had asked them to remove the cuffs while he smoked.

"He was very very cooperative," Chang said after he and homicide detectives questioned Kemper for several hours about the killings.

Kemper—described by Pueblo Police Chief Robert Mayber as "big enough to beat a mountain lion with a switch"—was released on parole to his mother four years ago after his release from a California mental hospital. He had been institutionalized in 1964 after shooting his grandparents to death in North Fork, Calif., and then stabbing his grandmother to make sure she was dead.

Neighbors said the young man, who had collecting workmen's compensation since an injury last year on a highway construction job, went to his mother's Aptos apartment last Saturday carrying an Easter lily.

The lily was still blooming on a table when sheriff's deputies entered the apartment Tuesday and found the nude bodies of the two women stuffed into a closet. Mrs. Strandberg had been decapitated and one hand chopped off.

Neighbors said Kemper quarreled frequently with his mother about whether she loved him. "You're embarrassing me in front of my friends," they quoted him as saying after she upbraided him for "laying around and drinking beer."

Kemper also admitted slaying six college coeds who disappeared in the Santa Cruz area in the past year. Portions of the bodies of five of the girls have been found.

Chang labelled Santa Cruz county "the murder capital of the world" because 18 slayings have occurred this year in the beach and mountain resort area about 80 miles south of San Francisco. Another young man, Herbert W. Mullin, 25, Felton, Calif. has been charged with 10 of the killings.

A SEVERED HUMAN head was uncovered late this morning from the backyard of Edmund Emil Kemper's residence at 609A Odd St., Aptos.

Authorities refused to comment on the find, other than saying they had received information which led them to the Kemper yard.

Representatives from the Santa Cruz sheriff's office, city police and the district attorney's office looked on as detectives dug a 16 inch deep hole and found the decaying head. Because authorities pinpointed the head's location, it is speculated they were acting on information from Pueblo, Colo., where Kemper was arrested and has reportedly been giving detailed information on not only the slaying of his mother Clara Nel Strandberg, 52, and her friend Sara Taylor Hallett, 59, but also the slaying of six young women.

At prestige, no identification had been made on the head. Two possible identities are Cynthia Ann Schall, 18, and Anita M. Luchessa, 18.

Parts of Miss Schall's butchered body floated ashore in both Santa Cruz and Monterey Counties in January. Her head was never found.

Miss Luchessa, a Fresno State College coed who was last seen hitchhiking in Santa Cruz County, has never been found following her disappearance last May. Sheriff's deputies found the severed head of her roommate and traveling companion, Mary Ann Peace, in the Santa Cruz mountains last August.

The head found today had been buried about four feet from the rear of Kemper's house. For the last several months, Kemper and his mother lived in the duplex apartment.

While the skull was being removed from the hole, the upstairs neighbors glanced down at the yard through a window.

People living next door to the duplex were visibly shaken as they occasionally looked over to where detectives located the head.

"To think we've been living here so peacefully with that laying in the ground," said one woman, pointing to Kemper's backyard. A young woman next to her, wearing a Cabrillo College T-shirt, nodded silently.

Meanwhile, Kemper is heading back to California from Pueblo, accompanied by investigators from the sheriff's department, city police and the district attorney's office.

Dist. Atty. Peter Chang returned Wednesday night from Pueblo, but made no statements to the press. Local authorities have refused to comment on reports from Pueblo that Kemper has described fully and confessed to the slaying of six young women.

Slain in recent months in Santa Cruz have been Miss Schall, Miss Pesce, Alice Helen Liu, 20, Rosalind Thorpe, 23, and Mary Guilfoyle, 24. Miss Luchessa is still listed as missing.

Berkeley police said Wednesday they had been told by Santa Cruz authorities that Kemper had claimed responsibility for the death of Aiko Koo, a 15-year-old Berkeley girl missing since Sept. 14, the Associated Press reported.

Just before noon today, Sheriff Doug James issued a press release saying he has formally asked the district attorney to file first-degree murder complaints against Kemper in connection with the slayings of Mrs. Strandberg and Mrs. Hallett.

James also said Kemper will be arraigned Monday in Municipal Court. Kemper is due back sometime Friday or Saturday.

The sheriff again refused to speculate on Kemper's involvement in the coed slayings, except to say that intensive investigation is continuing.

At an extradition hearing in Pueblo Wednesday, Kemper was led into the courtroom by Pueblo and Santa Cruz police. The AP reported while Kemper was led into court with his handcuffs in front of him, he nodded a greeting of "Hi, Mr. Chang" to the Santa Cruz district attorney.

When asked if he wanted an attorney, Kemper replied, "No, I don't think that will be necessary," according to AP.

Backyard of Kemper residence at 609 Odd Street in Aptos, California, where he
buried the head of one of his victims, Aiko Koo.

CONFESSION #3 TO SANTA CRUZ
SHERIFF'S DEPARTMENT (APRIL
28, 1973)

SYNOPSIS: *The following is a tape recorded interview between Edmund Emil Kemper, III and Inv. Michael Aluffi of the SCSD. The interview taking place at the SCS Jail on 4-28-73 at approximately 2045 hours.*

REPORT:

Aluffi: *Ed, for the purpose of this tape, would you please state your full name and date of birth?*

Edmund Emil Kemper, III, D.O.B. 12-18-48.

Ok Ed, you were arrested in Pueblo, Colorado?

Yes.

At that time you were advised of your rights a few times, is that correct?

Several.

Upon the arrival of Lt. Scherer and myself, we also advised you of your rights, is that true?

Yes sir.

Do you still have those right in mind?

Yes.

Having those rights in mind, do you still want to talk to me?

Yes.

You're aware that you have the right to remain silent and all that other stuff?

Right, and I have the right to an attorney if I can't afford one. I don't see the reason for an attorney during these interviews.

All right, if you remember in the last interview Ed, we covered the six homicides involving Mary Ann Pesce, Anita Luchessa, Aiko Koo, Rosalind Thorpe and Alice Liu. Is that correct?

Didn't you leave out Cynthia Schall?

I'm sorry, I left out Cynthia Schall. That's six. Is that correct?

Yes.

This interview will be based around the incidents that occurred at your home last Saturday. Is there anything that you want to tell me that led up to this incident?

Not really.

Well, let's start with the reason for it.

That's rather involved. The reason for it is these murders were coming to a head, I felt that I was going to be caught pretty soon for the killing of these girls, or I was going to blow up and do something very open and get myself caught, and so I did not want my mother …

A long time ago I had thought about what I was going to do in the event of being caught for the crimes and the only choices I seen open is that I could just accept it and go to jail and let my mother carry the load, and let the whole thing fall in her hands like what happened last time with my grand-parents or, I could take her life. Well, I guess that leaves me two choices: I could either do it in the open with her knowing what was happening or I could do it when she didn't know what was happening. Last Friday night, whatever date that was, I had decided it was the night before the killing, or the day before the killing really, I had been thinking about it for quite a while and I just started working myself up towards the act of killing her. I guess that answers the reason.

All right, you want to get into the actual crime?

Ok. I got home Friday night, or I got back to her home from Alameda, where I'd been working early Friday in the afternoon and I sat around the house and took care of a few business problem, you know, calling and making a couple phone calls that were unrelated to the problem, and I called my mother at work and let her know I was in town and she told me that she was going out to a dinner, some faculty dinner or something, and she'd be home late. So I sat around and drank some beer, watched television, stayed up as late as I could and I had wished to talk to her really, before anything had happened. It was my hopes that she would go on good terms and that was impossible because, well I guess it would be good terms because we hadn't really argued or anything when we talked on the phone. I went to bed about midnight I guess and I woke up a couple of hours later. Well, let me see, that doesn't work out right. I think I went to bed around two and she still wasn't home and I went to bed and went to sleep. I woke up a couple of hours later, around four, and she had already come home, done whatever she does when she gets home late at night and had retired for the evening. This was after I had gone to bed around 2:00 AM, Saturday morning.

She was in bed, reading a book and I woke up about four o'clock in the morning, two hours after I went to sleep roughly. The lights were pretty much out in the house. I didn't see any lights on. I hadn't heard anything and I thought, 'gee, it's four o'clock and she's still not home.' So I got up and I walked out of my bedroom, noticed her small light was on and walked into her bedroom, just as she had taken off her glasses and turned the light off. Without her turning it back on, she commented that uh … I said "Oh, you're home." She says, "You're up, what are you doing up?" I said, "Well, I just wanted to see if you were home. I hadn't heard anything." She said, "Oh, I suppose you want to talk?" This has happened several times before, when she'd come in late and I wanted to talk and we'd talk and then she'd go to sleep. She didn't say it in an abusive manner, it was more or less just jive, and I said no. She said, "Well, we'll talk in the morning." I said, "Fine, good night." She left the light out and I walked out of the room and back to my bedroom, laid down and decided at that point, I was going to wait another hour or so, until she was asleep before it happened. I looked at my watch. It was about a quarter after four, something like that, and I laid there in the bed thinking about it and it's something hard to just up and do. It was the most insane of reasons for going and killing your mother. But I was pretty fixed on that issue because there were a lot of things involved. Someone just standing off on the side, watching something like that isn't really going to see any kind of sense or rhyme or reason to anything. I had done some things and I felt that I had to carry the full weight of everything that happened. I certainly wanted for my mother a nice quiet, easy death like I guess everyone wants. The only way I saw this possible was for it to be in bed, while she was asleep. The next thing was to decide how to do it. The only possible answer to that I saw was to take a hammer and hit her with it in her sleep, and then to cut her throat.

So I waited till about 5:15 AM. I went into the kitchen and got a hammer. We have a regular claw hammer at home, picked up my pocket knife, the same one I'd used to kill Mary Ann Pesce with, opened it up, and I carried that in my right hand and the hammer in my left, walked into her bedroom very quietly. She had been sound asleep. She moved around a little bit and I thought maybe she was waking up. I just waited and waited and she was just laying there. So, I approached her right side, to my right on the right side of the bed, on her side. I stood there for a couple of minutes and spent most of that day, and most of that week I suppose and most of that night, trying to get myself, I guess you'd say, "hopped up" to do something like that, thinking nothing but reasons to do it and the need to do it, trying to keep everything else out of my mind. I stood by her side for a couple of minutes, I suppose, and about 5:15, I struck and I hit her just about the temple on her right side of the head, the side of her head, the side that was up from the pillow. It was above and behind her temple on the right side of her head. I struck with a very hard blow and I believe I dropped the hammer, or I laid it down or something. Immediately blood started running down her face from the wound, and she was still breathing, I could hear the breathing and I heard blood running into her, I guess it was her windpipe. It was obvious I had done severe damage to her, because in other cases where I had shot people in the head, I heard the same, or it had the same effect, blood running into the breathing passages, and this all happened in a few moments. After I struck, I moved wherever in the bed on her back and with my right hand holding her chin up, I slashed her throat. She bled profusely all over and I guess it was an after thought. I hadn't really thought of it, but her being my mother, and me doing those other things, and I knew right now I had torn everything out in the open, and my plan which I didn't mention earlier, had been to just ... well, everything's getting to an end and I could either kill her and turn myself in, or I could kill her and head out with everything I had. My arsenal. This was my choice at the time. So I decided at that time, it's a hell of a cliche to use, but I guess what was good for my victims was good for my mother. So, after I slashed her throat, I went ahead and slashed the rest of the way around her neck and took off her head, and I guess half as much of that was to make absolutely sure in my own mind that she was dead instantly and right then, so the whole attack took maybe, less than half a minute, possibly even as little as 20 seconds. Then after this, I moved her out of the bed and her nightgown was very bloody and I didn't want to make a big mess in the house because if I did and someone in our family, or a friend came by, it would be obviously noticeable and it would give away what I was doing before I wanted it to be. I pulled off her nightgown, tore it off and then pulled her body and put handcuffs on her wrists because it was very hard to move her, and pulled her into her closet, into the very far back, and put her sideways in the closet in the back, took all the bloody bedding off of her bed, put that in on top of her and flipped the mattress over because it was very bloody, changed the bedding on it and arranged the clothes in the closet to cover her up and I cleaned off the blood where it hit the wall. It hadn't gone very high on the wall, at the most, maybe 10" above the bed level. There was quite a bit of blood running down the wall and into the carpet.

I cleaned off the blood down below the top of the bed level and by this time, well, several little things happened in-between. A lot of running around the house that seems inconsequential at this point. But anyway, it was well after dawn, in fact, dawn was breaking while this happened. It was barely visible in the light, but this was well into the morning by now when all this was accomplished. The house looked back to normal and some time early in the morning, I got in my car and went out and drove. I had become quite ill immediately after it happened and hadn't eaten anything the night before, but I had the dry heaves a few minutes after it happened. I was unable to do anything then, when I did these things I mentioned. Finally, I went out. I couldn't stand being around the house any more, so I put a couple of guns in my car, well, I think I put them all in my car, but this was real early. I started driving around town. I was looking for a hardware store and a saw. Possibly a hacksaw blade. Not having any sidearms, I'd hoped to take the carbine that I had and cut the stock down to the pistol grip and possibly cut down the barrel to the forestock, making it a semi-pistol automatic weapon. There were a few other things I'd wanted to buy. I can't really remember now what they were. I think they were minor essential uses to that project or had no importance to it. It was early in the morning, 8:30 or 9:00. I ran into a friend, an associate.

What's his name?

Robert McFadzen, and he had owed me $10.00 for several weeks, and a mutual friend of ours had informed me that that was a stupid mistake. Loaning him that money. I had before and he hadn't paid it back, but I was drunk when I did, and he said that he had been avoiding me. We both had citizen band radios and talked frequently on the radios, and for the last week that I had been trying to get in touch with him, I had been gone all week working. But on the previous weekend and that weekend, I had been trying to get in touch with him and this mutual friend had said that he (McFadzen had heard him before and that he had heard me before) and had deliberately avoided communication contact because he knew that I would want my money back. I didn't press by calling him at home and trying to get it from his mother or anything like that. At any rate, I was driving down 41st Avenue from the ocean end, and just before reaching Capitola Road, I spotted him in front of me. He pulled up behind and gave me my up-and-down beams. He didn't immediately recognize my car until I hit the light beams, because I didn't have my whip antenna on the car anyway, saw it from the front. But I removed it and left it up in the Bay Area when I had come down that weekend. So, he recognized me when I gave him the high beams and we pulled into the Sears parking lot, and decided that we ought to go have some breakfast, meaning let's go get drunk. So we left my car there with the weapons in it, him not knowing what was going on. We drove out to several places, several bars. They were all closed that early. I think it was till 9 or 9:30. In fact, it wasn't even that. It was 8:30, I remember.

We approached the Caravan down by the Greyhound Bus Station and it was closed. It was 9:00, then. We went to a liquor store, Lloyd's Liquors right on Soquel and he cashed a check. We went over … I think it was the Fireside Lounge on Water, and there, he offered me the $10.00, which to tell you the truth, saved his life. Because with his little excuses, I needed to kill somebody at that point, and I think he deserved it more than anybody. He offered me the $10.00 without my having to mention it, so I just took five of it and figured we'd drink on the other five. It was also my intent during that day to cash some checks which were not covered by my account, because I did need money. I had planned on leaving the state that day or the next. So, anyway, we drank and we drank and I told him I had to leave around eleven or 11:30. I left, went back home for a couple of hours. Let's see, wait a minute, I forgot something. We went over to Gray's Gun Shop. It was his suggestion that possibly I could get … we had talked about going out to the DeLaveaga range and shooting that day. I thought this an opportunity to get a pistol from him or a friend, and not being able to … him not knowing that my .44 magnum had been seized, I told him it was loaned. So, he suggested that rather than go out with his .357 magnum to the range, I tried to get one and we went over to Gray's Gun Shop for the purpose of either borrowing one of the owner's personal sidearms or possibly, renting one. So under the guise of having gotten an opportunity to go to work for a security company and having to have a pistol before I could start, and telling this person that I had told the company that I did have a sidearm when I didn't, it was a common ruse, I suppose. Anyway, I was turned down flat by the owner of the store, Joe Desmond, and he explained to me that he, being the owner of a Class I federal firearms license, he could not loan or rent any of his firearms, personal or sales merchandise. So I left with McFadzen and decided to try and borrow another friend of his' .38 Special, which had originally belonged to Robert McFadzen, and was now in legal possession of and ownership of Roy Libel, who had recently quit the same security job McFadzen had and we both knew he had no use for the gun, so I tried to get in touch with him and he apparently wasn't home. His phone didn't answer. So at that point, McFadzen and I split up. I told him I had several things to do that day and would be busy the rest of the weekend, and that I'd see him next weekend, which would be this last weekend, or would it? No, it would be starting today, with the full belief and knowledge that I would not be here next weekend. So we split up.

I went home and sat around the house for a couple of hours trying to think up some sort of a plan. I realized that my mother not being there Easter weekend would be highly suspicious by the family and friends, and a cause for alarm, and I realized that her not appearing at work Monday would be alarm enough, without having people pre-alarmed on Easter weekend. So, I decided that someone else had to die, too. A friend of hers, as a cover-up. An excuse. Something that would be believable by other people involved and other friends, and possible family that might get in touch and call. So, I started thinking about who would be a victim, who would be most available, who would be the easiest to kill and who would be likely to be gone with my mother for the weekend. So I fell upon a friend of hers, Sara Hallett, or Sally Hallett, who had frequently gone places with my mother and done things on weekends. There was another friend, Mrs. Victoria Sims, who would have been just as easy if not for the fact that she was married and was with her husband for the weekend, and possibly with her daughter and her daughter's boyfriend. So, that completely ruled that person out because it was too involved. So I tried to call Miss Hallett's personal home phone, which was unlisted. I had the number from my mother's phone book and I got no answer. I called several times in the afternoon, but she was not there. I went out for a while again that day and I forgot all about buying a sale for that carbine, and was quite worried about this Sally Hallett possibly being gone for the weekend, probably with her son. The reason I thought this, was because the upstairs neighbors to her apartment had been gone all weekend from late Friday until sometime before I had gotten there. They were completely gone and the oldest daughter of the woman upstairs was there out front, which indicated to me that she, her mother and the youngest daughter were gone. By Saturday, when the car was still there and the house lights were still out and it was quiet up there, I realized that they were not going to be there that weekend, most likely. So, I drank some beer I think that afternoon, Saturday, and was sitting around the house. I had some time during Saturday also, took the keys to my mother's car and drove it out to an area not far from our home, but a street that I knew our family and friends wouldn't be driving up. I parked my mother's car there, locked it up, took the keys home and I think I left them there. I'm not sure. I may have taken them along. At any rate, that left my car out front. I drank some beer that afternoon and Mrs. Hallett called on the phone around 5:30 and wanted to speak to my mother and before telling her she wasn't home, I asked her what she was doing that night. She said, "Why?" I told her I had just gone back to work and had gotten a raise while I was home recuperating for 4 1/2 months with my broken arm. This previous week had been my first week back at work on a regular job in Oakland and I told her that I was celebrating and that I'd like her to come along with my mother and I to dinner and a movie. The reason I did this was I knew she'd accept. I don't know if I should say for selfish purposes she would accept, but I had surmised from past acquaintances with her and past sessions let's say at home and out, that she would leap at something like that, so that's what I thought to say. Of course, she jumped at the idea. I told her that my mother was not home, that she would be home a little later and I said said, "Why don't you come over about 7:30 and we'll supervise her and go out to dinner and a movie?" She said, "fine."

She told me she had been doing her laundry and had things to straighten out. This was around 5:30. So then I … well it must have been around 6:00 when all this went on. I prepared for her coming. I closed all the windows and the doors in the house, making sure all the sliding windows were shut and all the doors to the various rooms to the house were shut, leaving the living room very quiet, which was where I planned on killing her. Next, I had to decide how to do it. I felt upon the idea of strangulation and so I had a cord that I had taken from the first two girls that I had killed, Miss Pesce and Miss Luchessa. It was a strong nylon rope-type cord and it was probably three-feet in length, maybe a little longer. I took that into the living room. I took in a large bludgeon-type broken piece of equipment that I had had from the state. It was a top end of a drill shank, which is approximately 1 5/8ths-inch diameter and was close to a foot long, I'd say about 10 or 11 inches long. I was backing myself up in case of possible difficulties in my attack. I also placed my carbine in the next room against a wall, just in case again. I figured one shot was better than a lot of screaming in case something went wrong where she was lucky and possibly incapacitated me partially. The neighbors were quiet, very quiet in the neighborhood. Some were not home and others didn't have lights on and were entertaining or some such. So, at any rate, by 7:30 she hadn't arrived. I waited and waited and just before, maybe six minutes to eight, she did arrive, went into the house.

I met her at the door. We spoke and she came inside. I removed her wrap, which was a sweater. We talked about where my mother was, and I said I was sure she was coming soon, that she had just called from a friend's house, which was something that was very common around there, so she accepted it fully. We moved across the living room towards the couch. It was an oblong living room, rectangular-shaped and some of the preparations I had also ... I hate to break off at this point, but some of the preparations I had made, I had used some 3" wide medical tape that I had used in the Aiko Koo killing. I just pulled off a long piece of that and stuck it partially into the wall in the kitchen, right around the corner from the living room and also, I had brought two clear plastic bags that I had bought from a laundry for use in these killings, the coed killings, and for my car. I placed them in a readily-available area and also my handcuffs that I had used in some of the killings, I put into my pocket. So then anyway, she came and we talked and we were crossing the living room towards the couch. I was balking at what I had to do, or what I felt I had to do and that was the last thing I wanted to do. I didn't want to seem obvious at anything being wrong. I was stalling around as we moved across the room.

My first intention was to strike her in the mid-section and around the solar plexus and knock the wind from her, so that she couldn't cry out and then strangle her. It was this first move that I was kind of dreading. I guess what really worked me into it really was that she saw that as a cue and I struck her in the stomach and she fell back or jumped back mostly, I guess. I was quite surprised at her reaction. I hit her hard in the mid-section and she jumped back and said, "Guy, stop that!" I struck her again immediately after the first blow and her last words were "Oh!" and sort of stumbled back. I pulled her around toward me, facing away from me, threw my left arm around her neck, it was hurting at that point, but I didn't realize it then because I was so wrapped up in what I was doing. It's almost like blacking out, you know what you're doing but you don't notice anything else around, but in striking her, I had held my thumbs wrong when I made a fist and I had jammed my thumb and hurt my wrist. It's weak anyway, being in a cast for so long. I grabbed her around the neck with the left wrist at her throat, put her into a choke-hold and pulled her up off the floor in fact, where she was dangling across my chest and there were absolutely no sounds coming from her at the time. She was holding my arm with both of her hands trying to pull away, apparently. There was no real tugging, just holding onto my arm. Her legs weren't really kicking at all. She was moving around a little bit, but very little, but no sound at all came from her and at that time, I thought that she was so embarrassed or so shocked at what had just happened, that she really couldn't say anything and that she was waiting for me to make a move. I didn't really think that I had cut her wind off so completely that not even a little squeak or any gasp or anything had come out and so I pulled her back farther and looked down into her face and her eyes were bulging badly. Her face was turning black at that point, and this was just moments after I had grabbed her. Her face was turning from a bright red to a black and I realized that I was actually cutting her wind off completely, and later on, I realized I crushed her larynx or at least, dislocated it to where she couldn't breathe and I guess I had completely cut the wind off. When she went limp completely, I dropped her to the floor and tied the bags around head with a cord, after I had put the tape over her mouth, which really didn't work, so I just pulled that off. When she completely quit struggling, there were some automatic reflexes in the lung area. Her chest was heaving once in a while. When that all stopped, I put her on my bed in my bedroom, threw all of her belongings, other than her purse, in my clothes hamper, covered her up with a blanket, went into the other room with her belongings, and removed the money from her wallet. I don't really remember how much was in there, it was a slight amount of money.

Can you remember approximately how much?

I had been keeping track of things like that with the other victims, but in this case, I was blowing wide open. I just took any money that anybody had. It might have been $10.00 or $15.00. I don't know. Her credit cards, I had already taken some from my mother. I had several gas credit cards and took a couple I didn't have from my mother's pocket book which I had placed under the bed out of the way.

I thought I removed a couple of credit cards from Mrs. Hallett's purse, but I think I must have changed my mind and put them back, deciding that I had a reason to have my mother's cards, that they could be explained, but I couldn't explain having her cards. I also took my mother's Master charge card in case I might possibly be able to use it, cause it had not been signed on the back of the card. At that time, I put her purse in a drawer in my mother's desk and left.

I left the house. I got in her car, went down to the Jury Room in Santa Cruz, a bar, and drank for an hour or so, went back to the house, maybe it was a couple of hours, I don't know. But from that time I attacked her until I came back to the house, it was I think three hours. When I came back, she apparently had been set upon by rigor mortis already and that's why I stretched her out on the bed. I removed her from my bed and noticed that when I picked her up, that her neck was broken also, because everything else was stiff, and having dealt with dead bodies before, everything gets stiff, and the neck and facial area went first, along with the extremities. When I moved her head, I noticed that the neck was completely broke, completely dislocated from the spinal column. I moved her from the bed into the closet, or … wait a minute, now. That was the next morning. I left her on that bed and I slept in my mother's bed. The next morning, I didn't get very much sleep that night, maybe six hours. I got up early the next morning. That's when I moved Mrs. Hallett's body up to the closet and to the stand-up wooden closet in my mother's room and closed the door and put the desk back in front of that door so nobody would open it and it would be just like it had been before. If someone opened the other door of the closet, it was so packed with things that one would not see anything on the other side. Thus, with a body in each closet, I prepared to leave.

I got my things together and at about 9:45 AM I left Santa Cruz in Miss Hallett's car. I had transferred the guns from my trunk to her trunk and I believe that was that. Also, during the crime, I had kept pulling this cord very tightly around her neck before she was actually dead, leaving a very deep gouge around her neck from that cord where I had placed my foot on her neck and pulled very tightly as a noose-type fashion around that cord trying to get it tight around those bags and it wasn't working. Maybe the bag was torn, I don't know, but some air was still coming in and out of the bag. So I went to the bedroom and took a knitted muffler, white wool muffler that I had taken from one of the coed victims, Miss Aiko Koo, and wrapped this tightly around her neck in a single knot and just pulled it tight and this seemed to do the trick and that's when I moved her into the bedroom, and later on, removed the cord from her neck.

Did you remove the bag as well?

Yeah, yeah, the whole thing, and threw the bags in the garbage.

What about the cord that you used, what did you do with that?

It's hard to remember. I think I might have left it. I moved it several times. I left it on the desk in my mother's bedroom, then I moved it to my bedroom on the dresser top and then I might have put it in a drawer to get it out of sight. I don't really remember for sure where I left it because I had been thinking about more important things at the time, when I was doing this. It was more of an absent-minded gesture.

Did you ever handcuff Mrs. Hallett?

Yes, yes I did, come to think of it. Yeah. When she was unconscious and on the floor from being in that stranglehold from the rear, I put her down on the floor, pulled the handcuffs out of my pocket and put them on her with her hands behind her back and that's when I proceeded to cover her mouth with tape and placed the bags over her head.

So you say you left about Sunday morning around 10:00?

Yeah, about quarter to ten.

Did you ever go anywhere Saturday night, about midnight?

I don't really remember. I remember that I left the Jury Room, I had cashed a check there that afternoon for $20.00 and then one that night for $10.00 with another bartender, which wasn't uncommon for me. I don't remember what time I came back from the Jury Room. I know I stayed down there a while and came home,. I don't remember leaving again. I might have.

Okay, you say you left at 10:00 in the morning, you left in Mrs' Hallett's car?

Yes.

At what point did you get rid of the car?

Sunday morning before I left town, I drove my car over across Seacliff Drive, the approach to the black park, and it was on a small side street towards the ocean that I parked it and locked it up, and might have left my mother's keys in that car. I'm not sure whether I did, but I locked my car up and walked back to the house prepared to leave and left.

That was about 10:00?

Yeah, quarter to ten or ten.

From there, where did you go?

From there, I proceeded directly out of town, going to ... I had filled her car up the night before with gas at I believe it was the Union Station at 41st Avenue and Highway 1.

Did you use a credit card?

Yeah. I used my own Union credit card for the purchase. But anyway, Sunday morning when I left, I went straight to Highway 152 in Watsonville ... no, wait a minute. No, I didn't. I took 129 out of Watsonville over Highway 101 and drove up to 152 and went out 152 east to Highway 5, went up 5 to Sacramento, bought another tank of gas, I didn't know whether it was a Union or Chevron Station. I think it was a Union station. I paid for the gas with my own credit card. I drove from Sacramento right through to Reno. When I was in Reno, I parked Mrs. Hallett's car up on or inside the University of Nevada, up on Virginia Avenue and changed my shirt. I was wearing dress boots, blue denim bell bottoms that had been involved in most all of the murders, except my mother's. I put on a white shirt and my brown leather buckskin jacket, that had also been used in the first two murders and had blood stains on the inside of it. I walked from there down into the main part of town, the main boulevard and then to a hotel where I made a phone call to the Hertz Rental Agency out at the airport and reserved a large car. I believe it was a Monte Carlo or something like that. I took a Yellow Cab out to the airport, found that the car I had reserved was too small and so I changed my rental to a '73 yellow Chevrolet Impala and took that car back to the place where I had parked Mrs. Hallett's and removed the guns from her trunk to the trunk of the rental car, under a blanket and all the ammunition I had, an extra pair of shoes and another shirt. I removed some of the things I had inside the car, like a carbine clip and a map and some keys, I believe. No, I think I left the extra keys in her car, which were the keys I believe, to my car. I locked her car up. No, I didn't. I loaded everything into the new car, took her down to the Texaco Station, a couple of blocks away, and told the apparent owner that I was having electrical problems, having worked in gas stations before, I knew that I had to come up with a problem that he wouldn't be able to find right away. It would take a day to two. I told him I was having electrical problems somewhere in the car, and that sometimes it would cut out on the highway and not run. Sometimes, it would not start or have difficulty in turning over. I told him I'd be back to pick the car up in a couple of days. I indicated that my mother was with me without saying "mother." I talked about "we" and this was my mother's car, which was not true. I had removed at that time, the registration and some gas receipts that Mrs. Hallett had in the car, in case he started looking through the glove box. I left the keys to that car with him and told him I'd be back in a few days, that we were gonna' be in town and that we have friends with a car and at that point, I went back up to where the parked car was, took it down to the casino and gambled a little bit, went up to dinner in a restaurant, left town and drove for a day and a half, I guess, including that day of driving. I drove I'm not sure of the highway, it might have been 80 east until I got on 50, at which time I jumped onto Highway 50 east, I'm not sure at all.

Things were not too clear from that point because I was taking NoDoze quite heavily and doing very much driving and very little stopping. I'd only stopped for gas and once in a while, something to eat. I would drive until the tank was empty. I sometimes drove for five-and-six hours. I continued this until somewhere in Utah, I believe. Maybe it was Utah or maybe the far side of Nevada. I was in Utah, I was in Utah, the eastern side of Utah very late at night. I stopped and pulled off into a rest area and slept for three hours, until quarter to three AM, started driving again, taking NoDoze and stopping to buy those and sometimes pop and sometimes something to eat, but very little eating. I continued to drive right on through until I think it was 9:00 PM that night, so that meant, what 15 or 18 hours? I found myself on the eastern side of Colorado, and some time during the Colorado trip, I was stopped by a highway patrolman and another radar unit and the officer informed me …. at that time, I had the carbine in the back seat. I had not altered it from its original form, it was under a blanket. Anyway, I was stopped by this officer and he told me that I had the option of either … I can't really remember what he said … I got the impression that he said either go with him if I got a citation and have to appear in court on the citation, and not having to appear in court on the citation and paying cash in his presence to the state, whatever division of the state that you pay traffic fines to, and he and I went to the nearest mailbox and deposited $25.00 of badly-needed money.

At this point I left and I was very careful not to exceed the speed limits, obviously because I did not want, at this point I thought, this was well into Monday afternoon, and I had been afraid that if someone did give me a ticket, within the next 12 to 18 hours they got an APB for me or the car, it would be for the car and they'd be looking for my name, and I'm sure he would remember it. It was an odd name and my description was odd, and so I did not want to get any tickets at all. This would tell the authorities in California or possibly the pursuing FBI at this point, where I was, and which direction I was headed in, so at this point, I had the choice of either stopping and just going ahead and having a ball, blowing it, or with the weapons, or to continue on at a breakneck speed . . . I had wanted to break off driving for some time, but I didn't care in Colorado now. So I drove, ate more and more NoDoze and taking as many as three every half-hour or 45 minutes, drove far into the night. I was not that far ... I got as far as the far eastern side of Colorado by late Monday night, still not having heard anything about the crimes committed in California considering I had cut my mother's head off ... I had also cut off her hand. I didn't mention that ... her left hand which was symbolic, I suppose. I believe between the two the authorities would immediately surmise that I was the person they were looking for in the other slayings.

Was this the purpose the hand and head were cut off?

Partly the head, I told you that was also to make sure for myself that she was dead, even though I knew with the cut throat that she was, but I did it so quick, I wanted to make absolutely sure there wasn't any suffering. But the hand I think, it's like that left hand of God thing, I had always considered my mother very formidable, very fierce and very foreboding. She had always been a very big influence on my life and whether I hated her or loved her, it was very dynamic, and the night she died or the morning, it was amazing to me how much like every other victim of mine had died, how vulnerable and how human she was. It shocked me for quite some time. I'm not sure that it still doesn't shock me. I felt quite relieved after her death, a lot of it was guilt that I had been building up, and fear that she would find out about what had happened and what it would do to her. I was glad that it had been quick. Anyway, I was afraid by this time over in Colorado, that the authorities were looking for me, and not for two murders, but for several. I continued on into almost to Kansas, I was eight miles away from Kansas. I'd passed through a little town named Holly, Colorado, nearing the Kansas border.

It was very late at night, I was exhausted and I was past exhaustion. I was just running on pure adrenalin. My body was quivering at times and my mind was slowly just beginning to unravel. I felt I was losing control and I was afraid that anything could cause me to go off the deep end and I didn't know what would happen then. I had never been out of control in my life. I had lost control of my body. I experienced this in the killing of my grandparents when I was 15 over there, I just completely lost control of myself, but as far as my mind went, I had realized what was going on and I just couldn't stop it. In this case, my body was just exhausted and my mind was starting to go. I was hallucinating, not so much seeing things that weren't there, but I was imagining things happening that weren't happening and normally, when I'm driving too long, I experience visual hallucinations and in this case, it was emotional and mental hallucinations. Physically, I guess my body was overly alert. I was completely wound up.

About eight miles from the Kansas border, still headed east, I finally had a thought. I was trying to think, 'Wow! I've got to stop this because it's getting so far out of hand, I'm not going to be responsible for what happens any further, it's just going to happen.' I didn't know what it was and I didn't like that idea. I came upon the idea of calling up Lt. Charles Scherer at the Santa Cruz Police Department long distance, knowing I couldn't wait till morning. I just had to talk to someone and I didn't want to talk to some desk duty officer that wouldn't know what was going on or couldn't really do anything. I wasn't going to identify myself. I was gonna' tell him I'm the one he's looking for and already feeling that he knew who I was, I just wanted to say where I was and see what I could arrange as far as a surrender, and if it was not satisfactory, then I would continue on. So I returned to a small town that I can't remember the name of at this point, but it was east of Pueblo, 50-to-60 miles. I remember it was only 19 or 20 miles west of Holly. I returned to this town late at night, maybe 11:00 to 11:30, got some change from the bar, went to an outside pay phone, called Santa Cruz Police Department and I got Officer Andy Crane on the phone whom I knew from previous times in Santa Cruz. I told him that I wanted to talk to Lt. Scherer, and he said he's not in and I said I know that. I said, "I'm the one he's looking for," and he says, "What do you mean?" I said, "Well, you want to know what I'm saying?" I said, "Do you want to know about those coeds." He said, "What's your name?" I said, "Don't worry about a name, I just want to talk to Lt. Scherer and get him down there as quick as you can. I'll call back." He said, "Well, I have to have a name." I said, "Okay, Andy," and I could feel him stiffen over the phone, and I said "This is Ed Kemper" and I don't know at that point whether he thought I was drunk and kidding around or dead serious. I told him it was very serious and that something was gonna' happen soon if I didn't get him on the phone.

He told me he'd try to get in touch with him. I hung up and called back 45 minutes later, as I said I would. Mr. Crane had gone home, it was change of shift, and the new man on was vaguely aware of what was going on. I didn't have the change at that time call back, so I called collect. He refused the call and indicated that Lt. Scherer wouldn't be in until 9:00 AM, when he was available. This threw me so far back and realizing at that time, that they were not at all aware of what had happened with my mother and her friend, and with the state I was in, this was a hell of a shock to me and that's when I started going off the deep end. I began driving back west from that town, trying to get somewhere near Pueblo, intending to call again, the next morning from a different town in case they had tried to trace the call.

I only got so far and figured I just had to get some sleep. I still wasn't tired. Oh, I was very sleepy, that's right, so I pulled over to the side, after I don't know how long I drove. As it turned out, it was only 19 miles from Pueblo, so I must have driven 50 or 60 miles. I pulled up to the side of the road and slept, tried to sleep. I jumped in the back seat and just had a fit. I tossed, turned, beat my head on the walls of the car, yelled at myself, I really felt I was going fast at this point, I was breathing very fast, very shallow and rapid and this was bothering me. I didn't know what was happening, it was scary. So after what I thought was a couple of hours of trying to get to sleep and being very unsuccessful at it, I looked at my watch and it was four hours later. By this time, it was 5:00 AM or something like that. I jumped into the driver's seat, took off in the car, headed west again and went back towards Pueblo, wanting to surrender in a larger town possibly. I figured at that point, I had to and I just had to screw all those people in Santa Cruz and get the nearest cop I could find. I drove 90 MPH+ back to a sign that I saw that said 19 miles to Pueblo, or something like that. I raced on into Pueblo, I think it was West Pueblo, got very confused, driving down the wrong way on streets and off-ramps and everything else and turning around and finally found a phone booth and called up Santa Cruz again, being told that Lt. Scherer was not there and would not be in until . . . this was maybe 5:30, telling the officer that I had a lot of guns in the car, a lot of bullets, that I had killed a lot of people and that if I didn't get somebody over there quick, it was gonna' happen again, I wouldn't have any control over it this time. So this officer got my name, I told him where I was, at what intersection, he wanted some identifying information about some of the coeds and I gave that to him and told him which coeds were involved, or how many and where my mother and her friend was, whereabouts, in the house, where the house was, asked them to call the SCSD and get Investigator Aluffi on the case because he had been out there at one point to seize a .44 magnum revolver of mine, which I thought was beginning to close the thing down on me, really. That was just a circumstance that apparently, I put too much . . . that isn't what really made me blow. It was just that things were really getting tight in my head anyway about the whole thing and I had to make a decision soon and that kind of helped me get going, and I realized that there wouldn't be much more time before they'd find out about my other weapons and take them, then I'd be up a creek. So anyway, he had been out to the house and it was hard to locate, so I asked to get him on the case, that he knew me and that then they'd believe that I was serious. About this time, a car pulled up and an officer jumped out and arrested me, took me into custody. Two more officers came and they took me back to the Pueblo Police Department, and I guess from there is a matter of record.

Ok, I have a series of questions that I'd like to ask you, pertaining to some of the details, also pertaining to how you might have felt or some other things that you might have done that you don't recollect. Let's start with this most recent incident involving your mother and Mrs. Hallett. Did you at either time sexually assault either one of them?

Uh, I believe there was an attempt. but there wasn't any ejaculation with Mrs. Hallett. I believe I probably penetrated her.

At what point was this?

I don't remember. It would have to have been the night before I left, some time after I killed her.

This was after she was dead?

Yeah.

How about your mother?

No. My mother was stripped. I suppose that would have been a possibility that would come into somebody's mind, but well, my mother was moved around quite a bit, and I did strip her clothes off.

Also, if you will remember on our trip back from Pueblo, you mentioned the fact that you had written a note and left it in the apartment.

Yeah. I was feeling kinda' salty at that point and I had been rather efficient in covering up evidence in other cases. There was quite a bit of blood under the bed against the wall and that really–not seeing any need to cover anything other than superficial doctoring of the evidence–I wrote a note to the people involved. I'm not sure, but I think it was for the time that Mrs. Hallett died and apologizing for the mess and saying that I'm not really that sloppy, but there wasn't any time to be any neater, or something along that line.

Okay, what was the note written on?

I'm not sure. I think it was an envelope.

Did you use a ball-point pen or a pencil?

A ball-point pen. It was in my handwriting anyway.

Do you remember when you left the note? Or rather, where you left the note?

Yeah, behind the bed after I pushed it to the wall, right next to the blood stains on the rug.

Do you feel that you've got urges to kill people or is it just something kinda' spontaneous?

Well, it's kind of hard to go around killing somebody just for the hell of it. It's not a kicks thing or I would have ceased doing it a long time ago. It was an urge. I wouldn't say it was on the full of the moon or anything, but I noticed that no matter how horrendous the crime had been or how vicious the treatment of the bodies after death or say, on the previous killing ... let's use an example, the Schall girl which was a particularly distasteful method of disposing of the body. It was very distasteful in the dissection of her body and it was very painful to me physically with a broken arm in doing this thing, and it was rather hard on my body physiologically going through that stress; still, at that point, in my crimes, the urge to do it again was coming as often as a week to two weeks afterwards, a strong urge, and the longer I let it go, the stronger it got, to where I was taking risks to go out and kill people, risks that normally, according to my little rules of operation., I wouldn't take because they could lead to arrest.

Did you ever make any plans or have any ideas of killing somebody that you know?

Oh, I did fantasies about that, but one of my rules of operation was that I not do something like that unless it was at that last moment and everything was up in the air and there was no chance of keeping it quiet, as in the case of my mother and Mrs. Hallett. After that, the door was wide open with the exception of not killing someone that would bring the attention to me any sooner than I wanted and I had wanted a couple of days head start.

You mentioned to me at one time that you had a fantasy of killing everybody on your block in Aptos.

Yeah, that was one of my things when I'd feel inadequate there, feel like everybody's catchin' up with me and I'm not doing anything, I thought ... and without I don't think too much hallucination considering the abilities I did have in creating a calm about me where people weren't excited or suspicious or nervous, and had the trust of most of the people around. I believed and I still believe that had I wanted to, just as a demonstration, and I thought of making this as a demonstration to the authorities in Santa Cruz, how serious this was and how bad a foe they had come up against or how difficult a one, or how crafty or whatever... I had thought of annihilating the entire block that I lived on, or had lived on in Aptos, which would include several homes, not only the block that I lived on, but the houses opposing it, which could have included as many as ten or twelve families or members of those families that would be there when I'd make my attack, and it would be a very subtle, very slow, quiet attack, where no one would be aware of what was going on in the surrounding area, and this would have happened very quickly. Of course, I wouldn't have been involved as I was in the other killings. I would have done it and left, I think, very unnoticeably by the other people that would still be there.

All right, and you mentioned your rules of operation, could you tell me basically what those are?

Yes, these were observance that I had made before I'd actually gone into operation let's say on the crimes, against the coeds. For a long time, I just drove around, originally with the purpose of just getting to know more people and seeing where people's heads were at, not trying to make a pun, that were my own age or younger, because I had quite a gap of existence there and quite a gap of awareness in my having been to Atascadero and going through quite a few different programs where my awareness of myself and my surroundings, I do believe I was a little bit more acute than the people I had to live with and deal with out on the streets. This is a problem we approached in the hospital and solved theoretically, but it was very difficult on the streets to gain an honest rapport with other people who weren't aware of the special problems of an ex-mental patient who didn't want to be known as an ex-mental patient. I drove around, picking up several people and noticing the different situations, like that girls were hitchhiking alone and in pairs and quite naively and quite innocently and people around weren't paying any attention, and I could pick up as many people as I wanted, as often as I wanted without authorities really becoming aware of it. They were about their own duties.

Some of them, I suppose, including watching certain characters that had been picking people up where there had been complaints. So rather than think of a rape type thing where threatening the people not to turn you in, I'd been through all that at Atascadero and watched hundreds and hundreds of rapists go through and always being caught eventually, so I decided to kind of nix the two and have a situation of rape and a murder and no witness and no prosecution. My first rule for operation was to be observant of everything around me, far before the approach. If I knew I was going to commit a crime on a certain day, I watched very carefully the situation, the flow of traffic, how heavy the police traffic was, how observant they were being of me in particular and the people around me, the mood of the hitchhikers, which pretty much was according to what day it was. On weekends, everybody was hitchhiking and nobody was paying any attention. Sometimes there were police, and sometimes there weren't. So rule number one was watch the traffic and try not to pick anybody up when it's too light or when there are too many people out on foot around the area. These weren't fantastically specific rules, it was more general things. That was one, don't do it if there are police around, don't pick anybody up when police are around, or if you do, make sure it's very obvious that you're letting them out, not getting in when police are around. From then on, I did not pick people up for sport any more, it was for possible execution. I didn't pick up males any more. It was all coeds and it would only be if they were a possible candidate for death, which would mean that they were young, reasonably, good looking, not necessarily well to do, but say of a better class of people than the scroungy, messy, dirty, smelly hippie-type girls I wasn't at all interested in. I suppose they would have been more convenient, but that wasn't my purpose. My little social statement was I was trying to hurt society where it hurt the worst and that was by taking its valuable members, or future members of the working society, that was the upper-class or the upper-middle class, what I considered to be snobby or a snotty-brat or person that was actually ... than ended up later being better equipped to handle a living situation that I was, and have more happily adjusted, I consider it a very phony society, a very phony world where people were so busy coping out to so many things to exist and fit into a group that they had lost sight of their individual aims and goals. I had become completely lost and very bitter about what I considered these phony values and phony existences, and I decided I was going to not necessarily weed things out because I would have ended up killing most of the world if I weeded it out, but I was striking out at what was hurting me the worst, which was the area. I guess down deep I wanted to fit in the most, and I had never fit in, and that was the group, the in-group. Like I said about these rules, one was besides the ones I've mentioned, I would not circle back if I saw a good prospect. I would not circle back to pick her up unless I was really out on a limb and I hadn't run into anybody all week. There were a couple of exceptions to that rule, like the first killings. I had turned around a couple of blocks up, but I realized then I was really sticking my neck out and being obvious to several people. I was quite lucky nobody noticed or had it stick in their mind, but I did turn around and go back and pick up those girls. Besides, they could notice me doing it and if they did refuse the ride, there would be a possible witness to a future crime for the police to work on. Realizing they couldn't come grab me, they could start watching me and I wouldn't necessarily know it.

So, to be inconspicuous as possible was the order of the day, I had no wild things on my car. No wild clothes. No flashy driving. It was all strictly down the line. Very casual. Very relaxed. Smiling only when I had approached the girls, because to sit around smiling a lot in the car would draw notice every now and then. I wanted to be absolutely nondescript. Being 6'9"? It's difficult. But sitting in the car with lots of leg room, I was able to scrunch down enough to where not even the passengers in the car would realize how tall I was. Other rules were that I would take no chances that I didn't absolutely have to take which meant mostly, condescending or ascending to the wishes of the victims before their deaths, which would always be to their benefit. their requests and their pleas would be to their benefit and not to my own, no matter how good it sounded. I had predetermined what exactly I was going to do, or not exactly, but down to a fairly fine point to where I could leave a little bit of leeway open to a random glance, meaning that I would pretty well have a plan or route of travel set up after the pick up and I would pick at certain points, unless just by a random chance, someone was in the middle of the block or in a wrong area.

I'd always work out in my mind a quick route and excuse to go to a certain place, and I would not threaten them or say anything to them committing myself until I was sure there was no one around in the immediate area, just in case they did panic, scream, yell or try to jump out. I also locked the door from the inside by placing the broken window turning knob from my side of the car into the opening mechanism on the passenger side which was not civil from the inside of the car. I would open the door from the inside for these people to show them that it would work from the inside, to let them in, and then place the window knob in the lock right after opening it and they'd never try it after they get in, they would just get in and that would be that. Oh, I would not produce the weapon. Usually, it was always a gun. I would never produce a weapon until I was sure that from then on in I had it pretty well licked, the whole situation. From that point on, I would take absolutely no chances if I didn't have to, which unfortunately was kind of ego damaging because I would love to have been the big bad effective rapist or the effective male ego-type where I could be in control of the situation without a weapon. I usually put the weapon away but let them know it was right there. But I would have to leave the area quickly. I would have to put them in the trunk or tie them up in some way that they couldn't, when I'm not looking, harm my plan. At that time, they wouldn't know what it is, they would never know they were gonna' die until they were under attack physically. I always promised this and that, release. Only in the case of the first two girls did I actually say that they were going to be raped and that was way out in the boonies with nobody around and no driving to distract me and even then, I didn't get to fulfill my promise. I would have loved to, but I realized at the time, that I really couldn't. It was two people and I realized I lived in a crowded apartment house and it would be impossible to get them in and out without someone noticing. There were too many risks, so they were killed on the spot. After that point, I realized that without someone else involved I really couldn't be considering a rape situation because it's just too dangerous. I couldn't watch out for myself and I couldn't do something like that out in the open because it's just way too chancy. So, the moment no one was around, the moment that was best to my advantage, the way I saw it, the victim would die, and being frustrated about the sexual end of the thing, sometimes sex was committed either during the death or after, but there were no sexual attacks or sexual assaults before unconsciousness was achieved in any of the cases.

Okay, during any of these killings, had you been taking drugs?

No, this was asked in the other cases by the police department if I had been under the influence of alcohol, drugs, or anything else. I told them no, I was not under any outside things, chemical or physical. I was legally sober every time. I got drunk quite often afterwards. Sometimes I was drunk before, but when I would go out looking for some victim to kill them, I was always sober, or legally sober, I wouldn't feel the influence. I never took any drugs at all.

How do you feel about your mental abilities at the time of these killings?

How do you mean that? Do you mean mental clarity?

Yeah. Well, your reactions, your mental stability, do you feel that . . .

Yes, I'm sure it's happened before, but the only time I actually noticed an ejaculation was as I was killing Mrs. Hallett on Saturday night, as she was dying, it was a great physical effort on my part, very restraining, very difficult, much less difficult that I made it. I went into a full complete physical spasm let's say, I just completely put myself out on it and as she died, I think with the Koo girl, in the case of a suffocation, the same thing happened. But I didn't really notice it, because I did have sex with her right after causing her to be unconscious.

All right, if you'll remember Ed, when we were in Colorado, you told us your account of the killing of Cynthia Schall, and you gave us a location of where her head could be found, and that location was in your backyard, underneath the stone in the dirt area. Why was the head placed there?

Well, because the rest of her body, or most of it, let's say, half of it, had been found less than 24 hours after I placed it where I had. I was afraid there was possible evidence up there, someone could possibly come by asking me questions. At that time, her head was in my closet, in a box. I had planned on getting rid of it the next night. I hadn't wanted to get rid of the hands and the head, along with the rest of the body, as in the Koo girl. It quite noticeably shocked me when I heard on the radio the very next day after depositing her body over the cliff that it had been discovered.

Which cliff was this now?

This was somewhere out in the Sand Creek area of Monterey

You dumped the body in Monterey?

Yes. Well, instead of that night, which was a work day and my mother was gone, taking it out and depositing it which I'm sure the police would have been looking for, and possibly even be watching me at that time, I didn't know, so I went straight into the backyard and buried her under the stone in the dirt area in the backyard.

Did you do anything to the head before you buried it?

Yeah, I sure did. I wanted it to decompose quickly because there was a bullet in the head and I didn't want it to be still attached to the skull area. I wanted the skull area to decompose quickly, anything left on it or in it. But hair and scalp I did not to put in there, just the facial areas of the head.

What did you do with the hair and the scalp?

I cut the hair off of the scalp, deposited it in the garbage of a service station in a sack, and I cut the scalp up in strips and flushed it down the toilet, figuring that it would not be discovered.

Let's get on to something a little more general now, why do you choose the campus area of the university for your picking up these girls?

Well, I didn't actually. At first that was one of my rules, don't ever hit around town. But then some time after that, I don't remember whether it was after the first two or the third one, Miss Koo, that Mary Guilfoyle was abducted and disappeared apparently from what I read in the paper.

End of tape

THE FOLLOWING IS A TAPED INTERVIEW BETWEEN SUSPECT Edmund Emil Kemper, III and Investigator Michael Aluffi, held at the SCSD Jail on 4-28-73.

WELL, LIKE I SAID, ONE OF MY RULES WAS DON'T HIT AROUND town. This Mary Guilfoyle, from what I had read in the paper and gathered, was an abduction and possible murder, because it stated she had no reason to disappear and she was going down to the … I think the welfare office or something, to get an unemployment check, and I couldn't see, someone of … like the paper said her apparent background, disappearing like that when they're going to college. So I assumed that someone else was doing the same thing I was doing and they had hit in town and that kind of made me mad because that could throw everything in my lap if an investigation started around Santa Cruz because up till that point, I had assumed that the authorities were looking for someone in the Bay Area that was depositing the heads in the Santa Cruz area. I remember this did happen with Miss Guilfoyle, I believe when I was disabled and staying with my mother, when I first started to live with her. When I sat around and realized that no investigation was coming my way at all, I realized that I was being a little too careful, and there was a much better opportunity around the Santa Cruz area to attack these coeds. I had been hitting primarily the Berkeley area and prior to this, the University of California and I saw no reason to leave my, uh ... completely leave out Santa Cruz, as long as I was careful. So this is why I started out with the Cabrillo school, quite by accident. I had been looking for university coeds when I picked up Miss Schall. I kind of picked her up as an afterthought. I was pretty pissed. These two girls I'd picked up on the university campus, had taken down the back route of the campus road, and at the last moment, had avoided turning down Western Drive which would have taken me immediately out of town, and that would have been my statement to them that they were abducted. I would have already made my move. I was afraid to do this. I guess I just emotionally wasn't quite prepared to jump anybody and they were quite beautiful girls and the opportunity was so great and everything, it just caught me off-guard. Before I knew it, I was dropping them off and apparently, they lived on Locust Street, where Miss Liu, a later victim, also lived. At that time, I circled back around and came back down through the campus again. No one else was really available and as I drove back down Mission towards the center of town, I saw Miss Schall and picked her up and that was my first attack inside town, let's say, with a citizen of the Santa Cruz area, and that worked out well enough that I went after the regular coeds

Could you possibly relate the reasoning behind the dissecting of the bodies and the decapitations?

Yeah. Originally the decapitations, I think part of it was kind of a weird thing I had in my head; it was a fantasy I'd had in childhood. I don't know where it came from, but it was always something I'd wanted to do, and it did facilitate part of my plan later, that is if someone was found, they would be harder to identify. I figured that the more odds that were in my favor, the better. There would be just as many odds that they'd find parts of the body as they would find the head, which would be the easiest to identify. But there was satisfaction gained in the removal of the head. In fact, the first head I ever removed was that of Miss Luchessa in the trunk of the car with the knife that killed Miss Pesce, and I remember it was very exciting, removing Miss Luchessa's head, there was actually a sexual thrill and in fact, there was almost a climax to it. It was kind of an exalted, triumphant-type thing, like taking the head of a deer or an elk or something would be to a hunter. I was the hunter and they were my victims.

Another thing that comes to my mind, is the fact of a time span between several of the victims, sometimes as much as what, three months? What would be the reason for that?

Uh-huh. Part of it was fear, some of it was regret, other parts of it were the opportunities. I didn't just rush out and look for the opportunities. If you'll notice, there was a greater time span between the 1st and 2nd and the 2nd and 3rd, then there was anywhere else. But I had started to really get into gear towards the end there, I was getting what I think is sicker and it was much more of a need for more of the blood and the . . . the blood got in my way, it wasn't something I desired to see. Blood was an actual pain in the ass. What I wanted to see was the death and I wanted to see the triumph, the emulation over the death. It was like eating, or a narcotic, something that drove me more and more and more. When I had the .22, it facilitated the killing, it stepped everything up, made it much simpler, much quicker, much easier, less of a threat to me personally. I was less afraid to attack. I don't like attacking people, I would have been in bar fights and street fights, and would have been physically and verbally assaulted. These I wasn't, it was a matter of ... I didn't care how I got there, I just wanted the exultation over the other party. In other words, winning over death, they were dead and I was alive, that was the victory in my case. I suppose I could have been doing this with men, but that always posed more of a threat. They weren't nearly as vulnerable and that would have been quite odd and probably noticeable, picking up other men and having them killed, plus, like in this case where sex is involved, or the thrill of having a woman around, alive and dead, wasn't there with a man.

So, like I said before, there was a threat of the possible retaliation or the possible defense that could throw me off and after I'd broken my arm, this was absolutely unthinkable. So it wasn't just deaths I wanted, it was, like I said, somewhat of a social statement in there too, and I was jumping upon, I could have gotten children I suppose, children are vulnerable. But there are two things against that, one is the most important, that is that children are innocent, children are unknowing and I've always been very protective of children for that reason. I was very sensitive as a child about the treatment I got and the treatment other children got and these girls weren't much more than children, I suppose, but I felt, excepting the Aiko Koo case, I felt that they were old enough to know better than to do the things they were doing and what they were doing when they were out there hitchhiking, when they had no reason or need to, was that they were flaunting in my face, the fact that they could do any damn thing they wanted, and that society is as screwed up as it is. So, that wasn't a prime reason for them being dead, it was just something that would get me a little uptight, the thought of that. Then feeling so safe in a society where I didn't even feel safe.

Let me ask you one question, Ed, on the theory you have of eliminating evidence. Have you ever done anything to a person's body or head to totally ...?

Yeah, now you're talking about the Aiko Koo case. That occurred somewhat after the discovery of Miss Pesce's head. Even though it was quite some time before the authorities discovered exactly who it was, I realized from the paper accounts, that it was quite difficult, because of the time it had been out in the hills. This gave me the idea of disfiguring the head enough to where it would be even more difficult to discover the identity, thus, giving me a longer time for any possible mistakes to correct themselves, due to time, or whether, or whatever. In her case, Miss Koo's, after she was dead, there was some time between the disposal of her body portions and the head and hands. The hands by that time were, let's say, the tips of the fingers were distorted enough by normal deterioration, that I wasn't worried about fingerprints by the time they could be found. So the head, I removed the hair from ... very noticeable long dark hair, and cut it short with a knife, but not so short that it would seem to be that of a man's or a boy's. I also removed the teeth from the head because this was one of the prime methods of identification on a head, that is, dental chart comparisons.

How did you remove the teeth from the head?

I used a chisel-type tool, a screwdriver and a hammer and not striking hard. I just struck them over against the face of the tooth .... the enamel portion and this would pull the tooth and the root out of the head, out of the gums.

About how long after decapitation did this occur?

It happened, let's see, she was killed Thursday night. Friday she was decapitated, and cut up and Sunday night, after I'd returned from Fresno and my sanity hearings, I removed the teeth from the head and the hair and deposited the head and the hands in Eden Canyon Road area.

What was the purpose of keeping the head and the hands with you for this period of time?

Well, like I said, I wanted to be more careful and take more time getting rid of those, because if the other parts were found, it would be very likely or very possible that there would be a very difficult time in identifying the remains , and time was almost always the most important thing. Because like I said, the time in my figuring, was the more time in picking someone up and the more time between me depositing someone and them being found or discovered is more time for any possible identifications to be forgotten or for clues to be muddled up enough to where they wouldn't be of value to the police.

Ed, you've admitted to the deaths of six coeds, your mother and Mrs. Hallett, are there any other homicides that you've committed other than your grandmother and your grandfather?

No.

None whatsoever?

None whatsoever.

What about in Santa Rosa?

No. There almost was a victim there, but I guess pretty much for the same reason I didn't kill so many others, was it was a surprise pickup and quite a lovely young lady, and I was just psychologically not prepared for it. But when I was psychologically in the mood for it and everything worked out right, the person didn't have a chance, when I knew ahead of time.

But you did pick up a hitchhiker in Santa Rosa?

Yeah, then deposited her safely. She was probably 16 or 17 years old.

What about Los Angeles?

No. I picked up people up down there for the same reason, only on one occasion, two girls, and I released them at their destination and picked up one girl in Santa Barbara that was headed for Santa Cruz. But at that time, all I had was my knife and I didn't really see an opportunity to use it.

Did you ever pick up any hitchhikers in Las Vegas?

No.

Have you ever been to Las Vegas?

Yes, long, long ago and only by bus.

So, in essence, the killings that you have admitted, those are the only ones that you've ever completed.

I'd love to take credit for more, not because I'm looking for a big score, but that I wouldn't take credit for any that I didn't do because, well, there's partially the guilt factor involved and there also is the, uh … well, I didn't do it, so I didn't get any pleasure out of it or any guilt out of it and why take somebody else off the hook who did it? Obviously, whoever did these other crimes that haven't been solved doesn't have too many clues against him. I'm not trying to pat anybody on the back or help anybody else get away with everything, but I figure I can't even cop out to these crimes because they're gonna' find out that I didn't do them and I wouldn't be able to give you any details, not even under a lie detector test.

Would you be willing to submit to a lie detector test?

Sure, as long as it only pertained to any cases that I didn't involve myself in. You know, there's always questions people don't like to sit there and have a lie detector test on concerning other parts in their lives.

But you would be willing to submit to a lie detector in reference to …

Any unsolved murders that you might think I had something to do with, or to verify certain statements I have made concerning the crimes I did commit.

You would submit to the subject of these coed deaths?

Certainly.

Do you think you could remember anything else that might be of any consequence in these investigations?

Not at this time I don't.

Would you be willing to talk to me at a later time if you did remember something like that?

Yes.

All right, for the purpose of this interview, I'd like to ask you a few questions. #1 - have you been making these statements freely and voluntarily of your own accord?

Yes.

Have you been promised, coerced or threatened in any manner?

No. It should be kinda' hard to promise anything at this point. I think right now, maybe it should not be on the record, I don't know, but I'm of the view that–and I don't think it would be out of accord with anybody else's thinking–is this whole situation, this whole process is merely a matter to decide by which method I won't see society again. But I certainly wouldn't trust me in society again, so not having any promises or threats facing me, I mean, who could threaten me? I could be threatened with death, decapitation, someone could threaten to even eat me.

Also, I'd like to put this on tape that this morning at approximately 1000 hours, we picked you up at Santa Rita Prison in Alameda County, at which time you showed us locations of where bodies and parts were placed both in Alameda County and Santa Crux County. Did you do this freely and voluntarily of your own accord?

Yes.

Were you promised, threatened, or coerced?

Well, actually, not of my own accord. I was asked.

You were asked, but you did it freely and voluntarily?

Yes.

Were you promised, threatened or coerced in any manner?

No, no way.

All right, Ed. Unless you can think of anything further, I guess we'll conclude this interview.

Oh, I can think of other things further, but I suppose I'll bring them up at a later date, when I figure it's appropriate. It's nothing that would affect the course of the investigation or the outcome, really. It's so much more detail I guess. It's obvious from the content and the extent of the interviews that all interviews together, there is quite a bit of detail to be gone into that isn't necessarily important to the outcome. The important things basically, what happened before and after the crimes, whether anybody suffered and how much, who can say? Basically, when I'm thinking back in the crimes, the first three did suffer to an extent, not deliberately, not intentionally, but the last three did not suffer, very definitely and if I had continued on with these crimes, if I had not disposed of that .22 pistol, that would have been the method of death and it would have gotten down to a certain level of efficiency I would have maintained that as my method of death and I'm actually quite glad I did get rid of that pistol because I would have been terribly tempted to use it in my travels in the last days of my freedom. Any other method with the other weapons would have been quite difficult and very hazardous. But I did intend when I took those weapons with me, not to hide in the corner and defend myself, but I hadn't planned to … make a last great outburst, but towards the end there, I started seeing the folly of the whole damn thing and at the point of near exhaustion, near collapse, I just said the hell with it and called it all off. I couldn't so much worry about myself getting killed or hurt, I just didn't want to see anybody else get hurt or killed trying to stop me from what I had been doing.

Let me ask you one final question, Ed. What is your ultimate purpose for surrendering yourself in a fashion and telling your complete story?

Well, there again, it's only mostly a complete story. Like I said, there are some things I'm sure are of interest to certain people. But my main purpose is getting it off my chest, because whatever's on my chest must stay, I'm sure, but let's say I had some accounts payable and I had closed my accounts receivable, and so I had balanced the accounts. I guess I could be facetious about it and say, "Well, I gave you guys a year to catch up with me, and I mean, shit, I coulda' kept goin' on forever," which is facetious. I really couldn't have. Emotionally, I couldn't handle it much longer, so considering, I don't know who would consider me lucky that I didn't get caught, there are times I wish I had been caught. But considering that I wasn't, there was a certain consideration that the police weren't gonna' do something. I had to do something. I'm sure they were trying, but, with the tools the police have to work with, and with the basic concept that society isn't as cold-blooded and ruthless and backstabbing as I am, they didn't really have, and you know, I was being rather cunning about the whole thing and it's obvious that I premeditated every crime, just by the fact that I didn't get caught on any of them. There's no way or odds or luck or anything else could have had anything to do with getting away with them, I think, forever, but I knew I wouldn't stop and I knew I didn't want to go out and kill all the young coeds in the world. As soon as this area would have dried up, I would have gone to another area to do it and I may have ended up driving a thousand miles to kill two or three people. But by that time, how many would have been dead? It was starting to weigh kind of heavy, so originally, my thought was that it wouldn't and that I could continue on forever. But let's say I started returning to some lucid moments where I started to burn out the hate and the fear and the disappointments on coeds that were already dead and the need that I had for continuing death was needless and ridiculous, it wasn't serving any physical real or emotional purpose, it was just a pure waste of life.

This is the conclusion of the interview. The time is approximately 2255 hours.

Car belonging to Clarnell Strandberg and parked at this location on the night of her murder.

CONFESSION #4 TO SANTA CRUZ
SHERIFF'S DEPARTMENT (APRIL
29, 1973)

SYNOPSIS: *The following is a tape recorded interview between District Attorney Peter Chang and Edmund Emil Kemper III: the interview taking place at SCSD, Investigation Bureau on 4-29-73 at approximately 2015 hours. Also present at the interview is Investigator Michael Aluffi.*

REPORT:

Ed, I want you to go through a few things we talked about this afternoon, primarily, would you go by as much as you know about the Aiko Koo case?

Yea, well right from scratch, I guess, happening on 9/14, I picked her up approximately at 7:00 PM, maybe a little before. Apparently from later missing reports in the papers, she had been waiting for a bus that she later told me was a regular bus that she took into San Francisco to the Mission District to attend a scheduled ballet lesson and she was not at this bus stop, she was at least one block farther down towards the freeway and she was attempting to solicit a ride. She was attempting quite actively, in fact, stepping out off the curb and looking very hopeful with S.F. written in large red letters on it and this was the type of hitchhiker I actually preferred picking up, that is, someone advertising where they want to go. That way, I didn't have to answer the question where am I going and possibly blow the ride. I had actually gone past her before I spotted her, I circled back around the block, picked her up and there was absolutely no problem. Apparently, she was not an accomplished hitchhiker. I didn't come across any of the normal problems I had with girls, with their curiosity as to where I'm going, what I'm doing and this set of questions along that line. I continued on down University Avenue in Berkeley, got up on the freeway towards, it should be in Highway 80, and headed towards San Francisco. But I didn't follow the normal approach to the freeway that you would take from University. I went down to the Marina on Frontage Road first and took what would amount to be Ashby Avenue on-ramp to Highway 80 West. At any rate, we crossed the bridge with no incident,. I had not told her what my intentions were at that timer. I was just listening to her talk, and asking questions and answering hers., It was a basically nondescript conversation.

After we crossed over the bridge, she apparently wanted to take an off-ramp. You know there are several off-ramps and arteries from that off-ramp that move out to different parts of the city and apparently she had a pattern set of which off-ramp the bus would take, and I appeared to blow it by accident, but it was deliberate. I kept on heading, I was heading towards 280 South, towards San Jose, which would cut me off at Highway 1, along the coast. Because I was trying to get as close to that as I could before having to inform her that she was being abducted. After blowing her off-ramp and making it sound like an accident, I said, "oops," and she said, "oops." I think it was slightly cutting. I continued on towards the 280 South cutoff, got up on this, no wait a minute… I didn't get up on it right away, both of us were talking back and forth about which one to take, and I took the next off-ramp thinking that was the one she wanted, and at that point,

I suppose I could have avoided the whole thing and possibly had been planning it. But when I realized, once we were down on the street, I realized she didn't know where we were and she thought I wanted to take that off-ramp, so I spent the next five or ten minutes trying to get back up on the freeway and found myself headed in the right direction again, which would be Highway 280 South. I got up in this highway and later, moved over towards the exchange that goes over to Highway 1, al along seeing Mission Street off-ramps and each one, she thinking to be the last one to take and I kept assuring her there were more, actually not knowing there were, but that's the way the luck ran. At any rate, she didn't realize that there was a serious, serious problem until after we passed the town of Half Moon Bay and at that point, she kept looking at her watch and saying, "Well, I've only got 15 minutes to get there." 10 minutes and five minutes and at two minutes after eight exactly, she said, "Well, I'm late. I'm gonna' be late for my class," and at this point, I had been balking at saying anything, but at this point I told her that's he wouldn't be making her class tonight, and with a worried tone, she said, "What do you mean?" I said, "I'm not taking you to San Francisco, I'm taking you to of San Francisco," and at that point, she didn't shriek but she like ... covering her head and moving away from ,e. She was in her seat belt and I was in mine. She was shaking her head and holding her arms up and saying, "No, no," and almost shrieking, "Don't kill me please," and I started shaking her and told her to knock it off, and I wasn't going to hurt her. She kept doing it, so I reached under the seat and picked up the gun I had under the seat which was a Colt Trooper, 6" .375 magnum that I had borrowed from a friend, him not knowing what I was using it for, and I poked this into her ribs and then asked her, "Do you know what this is?" I poked this into her ribs and then held it up in front of her. After two or three times doing this, she finally stopped this pleading not to kill her and don't hurt her. I told her to calm down and talk with me and she did. Right away, she stopped being nervous and upset and we talked down the coast for the next few hours, or I'd say about an hour-and-a-half down the coast, and as we approached Santa Cruz after passing through Davenport, we turned up Bonny Doon Road, the plan being that to avoid her possibly getting hurt and someone else trying to rescue a possible abduction. I told her I wanted to talk to her and I was desperate. I needed someone to talk to to keep me from killing myself, which of course was a ruse. I said that it would be suspicious if she was sitting in the car with me and the neighbors would be alarmed– which of course was not true–if she were in the car with me. So I wanted her to be in the back trunk to foil my plan. So, she agreed with this, but didn't want to get in the trunk. She asked if she could be tied up in the back seat instead and I agreed, and we went to Bonny Doon Road, from Highway 1 South, outside of Santa Cruz to a point that I thought was desolate enough, I turned up Smith Grade Road.

Now was she tied up at this point?

No. She was sitting in the seat with me and she said, in fact, she still had her seat belt on. As we went upon Smith Grade Road, I noticed a little road that dropped down from the right and this was pointing back towards Santa Cruz, I believe. Smith Grade Road was, the way I was driving up it from Bonny Doon Road. So in other words, I was basically headed southeast on Smith Grade I think, and headed down this little road to the right that lost sight of the road, stopped, turned off the lights, turned on the inside lights and asked her to get the tape out of the glove box, her already knowing what was gonna' happen to a certain point. She got the tape out. I pulled a piece of it off and placed it over vermouth and told her to get in the back seat where I would tie her up and cover her over with a blanket.

Did she help you in any way to put the tape on?

Yeah, she got it out of the glove box for me and when I pulled the tape open and tore off a piece, I placed it over her mouth and rubbed it on nice and tight and got it on straight and everything and asked her to blow against it and mover her mouth around to see if it would come off and she assured me it wouldn't following my instructions to the letter.

Do you still have this tape?

I had it for some time in the trunk, just laying there and I eventually threw it away. It is the same roll of tape that's still at the house.

How did you tear it?

With my fingers. I asked her to jump over the back seat and she did, and as an afterthought, she took off the chop she had been wearing, and at that time, her hair, she had very very long hair that fell down past her shoulders, then she went back over to the back seat and laid down on her back. At any rate, I got out of the car on my side, leaving the gun under the front seat on the driver's side, got out of my car, walked around to her side and realized that the keys being in my pocket, she had locked her side of the door when she got in and it was still locked. At this point, I started fumbling in my pants trying to get the key out quickly before she realized the advantage she had and when she saw that I was fumbling for the keys, she climbed back over the seat and flipped up the inside lock on her side, letting me in. At this time, I moved the front seat forward and flipped the twin cushion front seat, flipped her cushion forward, climbed in the back seat. She was laying on her back with her hands across on her stomach to be tied, and I asked her to turn over on her stomach, and she did and put her hands behind her back. At this time, I tied her hands and I took a lot of time doing it because I was realizing that as soon as I was done tying her hands, that I had to kill her or else take a chance on driving around town where someone could see her moving around under a blanket, or someone could stop me for a routine stop because my left rear taillight had been smashed out in an accident and I did not want to be stopped for any reason with her in the back seat in her condition.

So I fumbled around at tying her hands when I finally realized I was wasting my time and needed to get the thing done if I was going to do it. I turned her over back gently on her back, as if I were going to place the blanket over her and started to place my body over hers, on top of hers actually, placed my right hand firmly over her mouth from the right side. She looked slightly curious at that point, wondering what I was doing, not at all worried or panicked. I then took my left hand, the thumb and index finger, reached around over her head and plugged both nostrils, pressed both nostrils closed and for a moment there was actually no change in expression, then she realized what was happening and she went berserk. She completely panicked and struggled violently for what I can only imagine to be a half of a minute, maybe 45 seconds until she lost consciousness, possibly longer, but I don't think so because when I got up on her body, I heard quite an amount of wind being pushed out of her lungs by my weight and I did not notice her sucking in a lot of air after that.

How did she struggle in this 45 seconds?

Very violently, her hands not being tied closely together. I tied her wrists separately by knots and there was approximately six-to-eight inches of string or cord between the two knots, the two wrists; this gave her enough room to reach around her side, and flip partially over on her side, she reached and grabbed at my testicles and penis in an effort to get me off and make me release her nostrils.

Was she successful?

She was at first and I guess she didn't realize that she got me where she did. She kept grabbing and probing and I think two or three times she grabbed me by the testicles or by the penis and I broke away with that portion of my body and scooted it farther down towards her legs, which means that less of my weight was positioned over her body and her violent struggle got even more violent and she moved around all over the back seat, kicking at the cushion on the far side, under the rear window and kicking at the window right over her head even. I was trying to stay out of the way while this was going on with a major portion of my body, but I never let go of the grip on her nostrils or the tape over her mouth and when the struggle stopped and she collapsed back into the seat, I waited a few moments and then released her, leaving the tape on.

You mean you released her nose?

I released her nostrils and she apparently was still breathing, but unconscious. At that time, I opened her right eyelid I imagine with my left hand, to see how unconscious she was, how much eye movement there was and there was I guess a nominal amount of eye movement. It wasn't rapid, so apparently she was what I thought deep asleep or unconscious and after a few moments of watching this, the eye movement, the eye zeroed in on me and then her other eye thrust open and she started her movement again. For a moment she just looked at me and I guess she became conscious enough to where she remembered what was happening and went right back into the extreme panic she had been in and the whole process started over again for just about the same amount of time, identical to the other 45 seconds. Every move I mean, still grabbing at my testicles and still grabbing at my body.

What did you do, were you still pinching her nose?

Yes, this time I held her nose until all of the voluntary breathing was done, she was into great deep gasps with her lungs, her back was arching, unconscious, but the breaths became fewer and far between and she was still in a spasm type breathing.

Did you still have your fingers over her nose?

Yes, and at that point, I stopped because I knew she wouldn't wake up soon. I picked her up from the back seat, took her out of the car, around the back behind the trunk, thrust her body down on her back on the ground and pulled her pants down violently, not removing them but pulling them down below the crotch area, and spread her legs apart and forced sexual intercourse on her and I achieved orgasm in I guess it was in 15 or 20 seconds. It was very quick. At that time, I noticed her hair falling over her face and nose, she was still breathing and starting to breathe again. I took the muffler that she had around her neck still and just wrapped it very tight and tied a knot in it and her hands were still tied behind her back and the tape was still over her mouth. At that time, I even choked her around the throat for a moment, but by that time, I was convinced that she was dead, picked her up by the shoulders and she wasn't a heavy girl. I think she told me she weighed 104 1/2 pounds.

She told you that?

Yes. She had told me her height was 5'4" and she weighed 104 1/2 pounds. I picked her up by the shoulders and I think I laid her across the open trunk, across half into the trunk while I did something else. I think I took the muffler off her neck, checked around to make sure nobody was coming and made sure there was nothing laying around out on the ground and then moved her all the way into the trunk and wrapped the blanket around her that had been in the trunk. It was a blue velveteen blanket.

Now where had you gotten this cord that you tied her hands with?

I had gotten this cord from the first two coed killings, that of Mary Ann Pesce and Anita Luchessa. I believe the cords belonged to Mary Ann Pesce, but I'm not sure. It was a finely braided nylon cord that was probably I'd say between a sixteenth of an inch and an eighth of an inch thick and round, and it was burnt on the ends to keep it from unraveling.

Did you retain the cord after Aiko Koo?

Well I had three cords originally from the first two murders. This was the third murder and I used one of the cords that night and destroyed it. The one I had had her hands tied behind her back with, I later cut with a knife, rather than untie it and this was after I put her in the trunk, closed the lid, drove down the road. I stopped to make sure she was dead, got out, went around and checked for a heartbeat. I couldn't really feel her hands, her extremities to see if they were cold without moving her body, so I turned her over, cut the cords, threw the cords off the side of the road in some bushes and pulled her hands out and around and put them across her chest and the fingertips were cold and the hands had already changed from her normal body temperature of the rest of her body.

Was this before or after you stopped for a beer up there?

That was before. Then I next stopped at a little bar up on Bonny Doon Road for a couple of beers. Also, to check to see how apparent my whatever was ... grief, excitement, exultation, anxiety, whatever was showing. I wanted to test on these people in the bar and correct it before I went any farther. Besides, I was hot, tired and thirsty. I went inside the bar. Actually, I stopped, opened the trunk to check to make sure she was dead, not moving, not breathing, closed the lid, went into the bar. I had I think three beers, maybe only two, washed my hands in the washroom and left, again checking in the trunk, satisfied that she was dead. I suppose as I was standing there looking, I was doing one of those triumphant things too, admiring my work and admiring her beauty and I might say, admiring my catch like a fisherman, closed the lid, got back in the car, drove to Santa Cruz out to Aptos, where I stopped at my mother's home at 609A Ord Street, went inside the house, talked to my mother for approximately half an hour about non-essential things, just passing the time, telling her why I was down from the Bay Area which was a lie, a fabrication, testing on her whether or not anything would show on my face or my mannerisms or speech as to what I was doing and why, and it didn't. She absolutely took no alarm or asked any undo questions. I left her home and by then, it was probably 9:30 at night, before I got in the car, I looked in the trunk again admiring my catch knowing already she was dead, feeling her body to see which parts were still warm, partially out of curiosity, wrapped her body up very firmly in the blanket because there was a big hole in the back that would suck dust and road dirt and things in. The trunk was a very dirty area and started driving again, this time towards Oakland, up Highway 17 going to Alameda. I arrived there I think it was 10:30 or 11:00, probably 11, took her bag, her book bag and also the little hat and hat tie that she had had there into the house, up into my apartment, checked it over to see, make sure . . .

Let me ask you something. You kept this woolen or knit muffler that she had, is that right?

Yes sir.

Did it have a design on it?

No. It was solid white and it was crocheted, looked like someone possibly, either her or a member of the family had made it and from the things she had with her, she had a little pen pouch sort of that was very crudely made by crocheting, and she had crochet materials and tools in her bag, I gathered it was an article she had made herself.

Did she have some pencils with her?

Pencils and pens and a large typewriter erasure with a little brush on it.

Did one of these pencils have her initials or something on it?

Yeah, it was a blue pencil, fairly new, apparently that she didn't use much, but just kept it because it had her name on it. She had scraped the enamel away, down to the bare wood for about 1/2 or 3/4 of an inch and had written her name in blue ink with a ballpoint pen and had etched it actually into the wood, her full name, Aiko Koo. In fact, she had a little flower pattern in it, it was a little stem with four little dots around it.

Did she also have a book in there?

Yes, it was a second year Latin book. I don't remember who put it out.

Do you still have it?

Yes, I do. It's at my mother's house.

When you were conversing with her, did she give you any kind of idea what kind of family life she had or what kind of family she came from?

This was something I usually tried to talk to the girls about and gently probe about different things to find out their lifestyle, their living conditions, whatever. She was very free and prolific in her speech and I believed from her speech that she came from a home or meager means that her parents had either divorced or her father and left her at an early age and she and her mother apparently were living alone and possibly someone else, that wasn't quite cleared up, and there was no family car. The only transportation she had was a bus to and from where she would go. I got no indication at all that she was from a family of any means. Her clothing was rather plain and she apparently had taken pains to dress herself, well I don't know how to say it exactly, well, as clean cut as possible, rather than just wear her hair long, she apparently had gone to some efforts to look a little better dressed than she actually was.

Did she say how frequently she rode in automobiles?

She said she very infrequently rode in automobiles and she hadn't been in one in a long time, except to go on some ballet tours or some such, or dancing tours.

Now, when you first looked at her, did she look patently Asian or Oriental?

Yes.

Did she look like at first glance at least, like she may have had some Caucasian blood in her?

No.

What color hair did you notice she had?

At first, I only saw tiny bits of her hair from under the hat and it appeared to be black. But when she pulled her cap off and her hair fell out and also on the back seat when I was choking her, I noticed that it was a dark brown and almost had some auburn highlights to it, but it was not black. It was definitely brown and not black and that surprised me. She did look completely Oriental in her features.

Now what did you notice about the bag which she had and the books and pencils?

Well, she had several articles in there. She had a little leather coin purse with a little thong the draw string on it and I think little blue beads on it, with a few coins in it and also a housekeep. It was a nice new shiny house key that looked like it got very little use. This I later threw away. She had a great roll of yarn for crocheting and she had a crocheting needle and a couple of knitting needles or I should say a crocheting hook. She also had several papers, corrected math papers from some school, with her name on them and the dates.

Is that how you discovered her name?

Yes. She had told me her first name and I told her my first name and I thought it was Iko and she told me no, it was Aiko. I still was led to believe by her name that she was Japanese. I didn't realize until Monday, when I read in the paper about her being missing that she was a Korean girl which surprised me because she seemed awfully tall for a Korean girl, being 5;4".

She didn't tell you what extraction she was?

No, there was never a reference to it.

What did you do with her personal belongings?

I disposed of them, mostly through the trash.

Now you've told us before that this was the first body that you dismembered.

Yes, it was. At this time, I had broken my arm June 28th in a motorcycle accident–quite severely, my forearm–and I had a steel plate, four inches long with six one-inch screws through the bone holding it in place, but it was still broken and it was quite painful to use it to any extent, and it was quite an effort to carry her up to my apartment from the trunk and I knew, not so much from the pain of carrying her, but I knew it would be very difficult to carry her back down out of the apartment. I was quite fortunate to get up there without anybody seeing me. It was late at night, at least midnight. So I decided the only safe way to take her out of the apartment was to dismember her body and take her out in some form of container. The only container I could see that would be blood proof, waterproof, and would not give away what was in it would be a large green, heavy plastic garbage bags. I bought, I think, two big packages, boxes of these bags.

Was this before you or after you ...

This happened on a Thursday night and Friday. I called in sick and then went down to a store and purchased these bags.

Where was her body in the meantime?

You mean Friday?

Friday.

I had it on my bed in my apartment. It was a Murphy bed. I was in a studio apartment. I had the body well, in several places. I had it on the couch laying down and on the bed and possibly at one time, in the closet in case someone would come up there when I was gone.

Had the body in any way been dismembered at this point?

No.

Did it have any clothes on?

No.

Where was this that you had the body? What was the address?

916 Union Street in Alameda, apartment #207.

What time did you get back there Thursday night?

I think it was about 11:00.

How did you bring your body from your car up to the apartment?

Well, the garage is a drive-in underneath the apartment, it is ground-level and the apartments actually start one-floor up and I was up on the second floor of three and I had a choice of going up through the elevator, which is an old-fashioned elevator with a closing door and a sliding cage, or going up the stairs and I chose the stairs. I waited until I was sure there was no one up or about. In fact, there was a man that saw me at this time. I doubt if he'd remember it, but he . . . because it happened on other occasions when I wasn't concealing bodies or trying to move bodies. He was an IBM computer technician and he worked odd hours and I knew he'd be leaving some time around midnight. So I didn't go down to take her body up to the apartment until after I heard him leave his apartment and head down stairs. Then I went downstairs and as he was leaving, I waved to him and said goodbye. He went out with his Karmann Ghia and I went into ... I first went out and checked both doors to the garage, went out and check the front because I had had a problem on a previous occasion of someone almost discovering a body in the open. I closed the big doors and went outside and checked to make sure nobody was coming and made sure the front door was locked, opened the side door propped it open. There was a cord around the knob and tied to the wall to hold it open for people and I used this prop as a sort of noose, I guess, around the knob or loop, I guess. I went back to the car, opened the trunk, removed her body in a horizontal carrying position and carried her indoors and up the stairs rather quickly, to my apartment.

Was she covered in anything?

No. If anyone had spotted me, I had hoped to get out of the area quick enough to where they would think I was just carrying a girl up to my apartment and I held her in such a way that it appeared that she was awake and alive. I got into my apartment, I had already had the door open and unlocked and moved inside the apartment, laid her on the couch and shut the door.

How did you carry her in such a way that she looked like she was alive?

Well, the upper-half of her torso up was propped more in a vertical position with her arm around my shoulder and it would look like she was asleep from a distance.

Ed, did you keep that woolen muffler?

I'd used it in the killing of Miss Aiko Koo and it had been very effective. In fact, I had attempted to tie a cord around her neck, that same cord. You see, I had two cords with me that night, one around her hands and the other one was in the trunk. I grabbed that one out and tied it around her neck but it didn't stay tied around her neck. It slipped. So I used the muffler that was already around her neck and just pulled it tight and tied it into a knot and it stayed and it was very effective. In fact,. It had sort of a spring tension to it, so when I tied it tight and let go, it would pull tighter.

We're gonna' skip around here a little bit. Did you keep any other textbooks from any of your victims?

Yes. I kept the only book that Rosalind Thorpe, the fifth victim had in her possession. It was apparently a borrowed textbook, extra reading you know, and inside the leaf of the book was a girl's name and just "Merrill" after that, and I knew this to mean Merrill College, which was Miss Thorpe's college.

Do you still have that book?

Yes I do, but I removed that leaf inside the cover and destroyed it, possibly. No, I think I put that leaf and several other articles of paper with names on it of Miss Alice Liu and Rosalind Thorpe inside of a red book bag Miss Liu had and threw that ultimately over a cliff in Monterey.

And that's the cliff that we went to this afternoon?

Yes. It might be destroyed. It isn't destroyed unless I tore it up and flushed it down the toilet. There were a few pieces of paper that I did this too.

Now, the check that was with the letter in Miss Thorpe's …

I can even tell you what was in the letter come to think of it.

What was in the letter?

It was a letter of Miss Thorpe's mother to Miss Thorpe and it started out, "Dear Roz," and it indicated that she was quite happy to have heard from Miss Thorpe the previous evening, apparently by telephone, and at this time, it was apparent by the note she got from her mother, that Miss Thorpe had asked for $25.00. It stated in there, that here's the $25.00 that you asked for. She commented also that another female friend of the mother's and apparently the family, known to Miss Thorpe had borrowed a chair and had returned it and there had been something wrong with it. Apparently, one of the casters or something on it was messed up. She also stated that she had to end the letter and that apparently, her (Miss Thorpe's) younger sister and this woman's daughter, I'm not sure I got the name right, but it might be Wendy, had to be taken to a ride to a pick up point for the ballet class and . . .

That was why she ended the letter?

Right, and I believe it ended, "Love, Mom."

Now, there was a check with the letter, what about that?

The check was drawn on a Carmel bank, I think Bank of America, and was for $25.00 even and made out to Miss Thorpe.

This is the conclusion of the interview, the time being 2100 hours.

Kemper on location of crime scene (courtesy of SCSD)

Kemper on location of crime scene (courtesy of SCSD)

EDMUND EMIL KEMPER III appeared for arraignment on eight charges of murder this afternoon before Municipal Judge Donald O. May.

Kemper waived the reading of the eight specific counts and officially accepted the services of attorney Roland Hall for his defense.

SUSPECT IN SLAYINGS—Respectacled Edmond Emil Kemper III, a 6-foot-9, 280-pounder, is led to court in Pueblo, Colo., after he was taken into custody in a phone booth where he had called police, saying he had committed nine murders in Santa Cruz area. He waived extradition and is on the way to California.

In accepting the attorney, Kemper uttered his only words in court, responding "yes" to Judge May's inquiry.

Kemper was guarded by seven deputies and two bailiffs and was handcuffed as he entered court. The handcuffs were removed only when he approached the bench.

District Attorney Peter Chang asked the court for a three-week continuance so that he might take his case to the Grand Jury. The request was granted and May 21 was set as the date for entry of a plea by Kemper.

Hall asked the court for a gag rule on the proceedings and May in turn asked Hall to draw up such a rule "similar to the one n the (Herbert) Mullin case."

The gag rule forbids officials in the case from discussing it with newsmen.

One of the victims was killed two days before psychiatrists diagnosed him as no longer being a danger to society, Chang told a group of reporters crowded into the board of supervisors' chambers at the county building.

Aiko Koo was picked up by Kemper on the evening of Sept. 14 in Berkeley, Can said, and taken to the Bonny Door area, where she was murdered and later dismembered.

Two days later, the psychiatrists said Kemper's motorcycle "was more of a threat to his life and health than any threat he is presently to anyone else."

Kemper is officially charged with the murder of Mary Ann Pesce and Anita Luchessa, both Fresno State College coeds who were reported missing last May. Chang said they were last seen hitchhiking from Berkeley to Stanford. They were allegedly murdered May 7 near Hayward, and then decapitated and deposited off Loma Prieta Road above Soquel.

Chang is also charging Kemper with the butchering murder of Cynthia Ann Schall, 18, a Cabrillo College coed who was last seen Jan. 8 hitchhiking to a class at the school. She was taken to the Watsonville area, according to Chang, where she was shot to death. Her body was later dismembered and thrown off a cliff on Highway 1, south of Carmel. Her head was dug up by investigators last week in the backyard of Kemper's residence.

Chang also accused Kemper of murdering two UCSC coeds, Rosalind Thorpe and Alice Liu. Both girls were picked up by Kemper on the UCSC campus around 8:30 p.m. Feb. 5. Miss Thorpe was already in the car when Kemper picked up Miss Liu, Chang said. They were reportedly shot to death minutes after they got isn the car, beheaded and taken to Eden Canyon in Alameda County, where their bodies were dumped. Their heads were then taken by Kemper to the Devils Slide area north of Pacifica and dumped.

Last week, Kemper allegedly killed his mother, Clarnell Strandberg, by hitting her over the head with a hammer. After the killing, Kemper reportedly invited Sara Taylor Hallet to his apartment in Aptos on the pretext of taking the two women out to dinner. After she arrived, she was choked to death, Chang, said.

Then Kemper hid Mrs. Hallett's body in a closet, as he had done with his mother, and fled to Reno in Mrs. Hallett's car. He then rented a Hertz car and went to Pueblo, Colorado., where he phoned Santa Cruz police to turn himself in.

As for motives, Chang only commented that Kemper felt he would be caught shortly for other murders, and he did not want his mother to know what he had done, so he killed her.

Chang said Kemper had fantasized about the dismemberment-type slayings "for quite some time." Kemper told lawmen he never would have gone ahead except for the availability of "naive girls who were hitchhiking," Chang noted.

Although refusing to comment on his own personal feelings about the fact Kemper had been judged "safe" by two psychiatrists, the DA told newsmen, "If I didn't have thoughts on it I wouldn't have included it in the press release I gave you."

The psychiatrists examined Kemper because the accused murderer had asked to have his juvenile record sealed and expunged by the court. He confessed nine years ago to killing his grandparents in North Fork, Calif.

The final diagnosis by one of the doctors said the 6-foot-9 Kemper is in "excellent psychiatric health and is certainly competent mentally in all ways. He has made an excellent response to the years of treatment. I see no psychiatric reason to consider him to be of any danger to himself or any other member of society."

Chang also told the press Kemper himself has said it is not safe for women to hitchhike, "even when a car has a UCSC administration parking sticker on it." Chang noted Kemper was driving his mother's car, which had such a sticker, when he picked up Miss Liu and Miss Thorpe. Kemper's mother was an administrative assistant at College Five at UCSC.

Chang also commented Kemper has denied any responsibility for any other murders than the eight with which he is charged. In particular, he disclaims any knowledge of the slaying of Cabrillo College coed Mary Guilfoyle, missing since October, and the killing of Rosalinda Zuniga, a Watsonville High School student, last July.

"SUSPECT LEADS DEPUTIES TO MOUNTAIN GRAVES OF VICTIMS"
TULARE ADVANCE-REGISTER
(APRIL 30, 1973)

Grave inspection

Santa Cruz (UPI) —Edmund Emil Kemper III faced arraignment in Municipal Court today on charges he killed and dismembered nine women, including his mother and several hitchhiking coeds.

The 6-foot-9, 280-pound Kemper, 24, was held in Santa Cruz County jail Sunday after allegedly confessing the slayings to police.

During the weekend, Kemper–under heavy guard–led sheriff's deputies to several crude graves in nearby mountains where he said he left parts of the victims' bodies.

Kemper spent five years at the Atascadero state hospital for the criminally insane after he confessed slaying his grandparents when he was 15. He was examined by two psychiatrists and adjudged "normal."

Deputies found the headless remains of Mary Ann Pesce, 19, a Fresno, Calif., student who disappeared last May. Her skull was discovered in the same wooded area last August.

Kemper, 24, also led investigators to a ravine where he said he left the remains of Anita Luchessa, 18, also of Fresno, who was hitchhiking with Miss Pesce when they disappeared. A pelvic bone was found.

Kemper then directed officers to a wooded site where he said he left parts of the body of Aiko Koo, 15, a Berkeley girl who disappeared Sept. 15 on the way to a ballet lesson. A handless arm, pelvic bones and a rib cage were found.

The hulking young man—who spent five years in a mental hospital for the 1964 killing of his grandparents—allegedly told police by telephone that he killed seven girls, his mother and her middle-aged friend.

He was arrested Tuesday in a telephone booth in Pueblo, Colo., while he was talking with Santa Cruz police.

The nude, headless body of Kemper's mother, Mrs. Clarenell Strandberg, 52, and the body of her friend, Sara Taylor Hallett, 59, were found in the Aptos apartment Kemper has shared with his mother.

Other victims Kemper is accused of slaying were hitchhiking college coeds who disappeared since last summer. Parts of their bodies were found in isolated locations in three counties. Segments of one body washed up along the shore of the Pacific Ocean.

"CAL SLAY SUSPECT: HE SEEMED SANE" ALBANY DEMOCRAT-HERALD (MAY 2, 1973)

FRESNO (AP) — The former Santa Cruz mental patient accused of murdering eight women including his mother, could have deceived psychiatric examiners into believing him sane, says one of two psychiatrists here who examined him.

The doctor, who concurred with a colleague that Edmund Emil Kemper III was no longer a threat to society, examined him two days after he allegedly killed a 15-year-old girl and dismembered her body.

EDMUND EMIL KEMPER III
Charged with eight murders

"If someone wanted to deceive the examiners, regardless of the length of examination, he could present a picture of mental health which might not be there,: the psychiatrist said Tuesday in an interview. He asked not to be identified.

Kemper, 24, is charged with eight murders in Santa Cruz County, including the slaying of Aiko Koo, 15, on last Sept. 14. Two days after that alleged slaying, two Fresno psychiatrists examined Kemper and found him "no longer a danger to society," Santa Cruz County District Attorney Peter Chang said.

Kemper spent five years in a state mental hospital.

Santa Cruz, Calif. (AP) — Police say Edmund Kemper III, accused of killing his mother, her best friend and six coeds, became engaged to a Turlock High School senior last March.

The girl, 17, has gone into seclusion to recover from the shock of learning that her fiancé led officers to the bodies of the murder victims. Her family pleaded that her identity not be disclosed.

Kemper, 24, and his blonde girlfriend became engaged last March after meeting at a Santa Cruz beach. Police found a news clipping reporting the engagement in Kemper's Aptos apartment after his arrest.

The engagement date was three weeks before Kemper's Aptos apartment after his arrest.

The engagement date was three weeks before Kemper's mother and her friend were slain.

The girl's parents have sent her away from Turlock. School officials have consented to excuse her from classes and allow her to graduate with her class.

"TRANSCRIPT REVEALS DETAILS IN KEMPER CASE" SANTA CRUZ SENTINEL (JUNE 12, 1973)

GRUESOME DETAILS about the murder of eight females have been made public following the release of the transcript of Grand Jury testimony against. Accused mass-slayer Edmund Emil Kemper.

Much of the 94-page document detailed how each of the women were killed. Except for specifics, most of the information about the slayings had been outlined by Santa Cruz Dist. Atty. Peter Change four days after Kemper's arrest.

The transcript included testimony from Santa Cruz policeman Jim Connors, who talked to Kemper by telephone when the suspect was in Pueblo, Colo. According to Conners' testimony, Kemper said he had been driving for several days and was very tired. He said he wanted to talk to Police Lt. Charles Scherer about the killings, and expressed concern that he might go on another killing spree.

Also testifying before the Grand Jury was sheriff's detective Michael Aluffi. It was Aluffi who confiscated a revolver from Kemper some weeks before the suspect's arrest.

According to Aluffi, Kemper became convinced he was about to be "caught" because he had the gun taken away from him. Kemper told Aluffi he then killed his mother "to avoid her suffering any embarrassment" about her son killing several coeds, according to the transcript.

Alkuffi said Kemper killed his mother while she was asleep by hitting her in the head with a hammer. After cutting off her head, he then cut off one of her hands because, among other reasons, he wanted to link the homicide to the coed slayings, Aluffi testified.

Aluffi also told the Grand Jury about Kemper's "rules of operation." According to these rules. He wanted the victims of the killings to be of an "aristocracy" — members of upper class or upper middle class families.

Aluffi testified that the murder suspect took a trip to Camarillo, the home of murder victim Mary Anne Pesce, to see whether she fit into his rules of operation. This trip reportedly took place after Kemper killed Miss Pesce and her roommate, Anita Luchessa, according to the transcript.

Also testifying was Scherer, who along with Aluffi and Dick Verbrugge of the DA's office, rode in a car with Kemper from Pueblo back to Santa Cruz County.

Scherer said that Kemper seemed to be an intelligent person and "rather likable, believe it or not."

On the subject of the slayings, Scherer noted that Kemper "prided himself on his meticulous detail. Remembering names, ages, description of clothing, bodies and locations; almost like he had a fixation to recall specifics."

Monday, Superior Court Judge Harry Brauer declared that there is no "Gag order" restrictions on the release of information about the Kemper case.

A gag order was imposed when Kemper was arraigned in Municipal Court, but when the matter moved into Superior Court, the gag order automatically expired.

The issue about the gag order came up because of the release of the Grand Jury proceedings. Brauer said nobody had ever asked him to issue a gag order and therefore he had not done so.

YOUNG WOMEN DISAPPEAR EVERY DAY. They leave their husbands, their parents, their children and simply drop from sight. Police take the missing person reports, issue the required all-points bulletins and try to ease the fears of those left behind.

"She'll come home or write you a letter or turn up somewhere. Most of them do," is the standard response in cases where there is no indication of foul play.

A missing person case filed with the Berkley police department in the early morning hours of September 15, 1972, was typical.

Mrs. Skaidrite Rubene Koo, an employee at the University of California Library, called to report the disappearance of her daughter, 15-year-old Aiko Koo, from her home.

"She's been kidnapped," Mrs. Koo told the officer who drove out to her house to take the report. "I've had a premonition all summer that something was going to happen to change our lives. She has started hitchhiking ... you know we have no car."

Aiko was a student at the exclusive Anna Head School for Girls over in Oakland, she told the officer. She was a good student, a good daughter. She would never just leave. There was love in their family.

And Aiko was talented. She had great plans for a future in Korean ballet. Already, she was receiving invitations to perform. The last weekend of the month, Aiko and two other girls were scheduled to travel to St. Louis to perform at the World Trade Fair there. Just before Aiko left for her ballet class the previous night, they had been putting the finishing touches on the girl's costume for that anticipated performance.

"It's been such a busy time," Mrs. Koo told the officer. "Normally, I would have gone with her. I always go with her to her dance classes. But I had so much to do.'

"You know, I didn't want her to go. It wasn't that important for her to go to that class, but when my daughter wants things she wants them very bad.

"I'm no psychic, but I was afraid for her. She was so beautiful last night. I finally told her she could go if she took the bus, if she didn't hitch a ride.

"I know she's been hitchhiking. You know how impatient young people are these days. I know because she got a ticket for hitchhiking. When she told me about the ticket, she joked about it. She called it her parking ticket.

"I told her I was very much against her hitchhiking. But once people hitchhike and it goes well, they can't believe anything can go wrong. Now I think something terrible has happened. That's why Aiko didn't come home last night."

Aiko Koo never performed in St. Louis. She did not come home.

Police told her mother not to give up hope; the nicest young people were running away from home these days and they rarely gave their parents notice. Chances were at least 50-50 that Aiko had joined these wandering young runaways. The best thing she could do they said, is have some flyers printed with Aiko's picture and description

Mrs Koo was certain her daughter had met foul play, but she complied. She sent circulars to police departments and communes throughout the western states, asking any information about a beautiful young Eurasian girl, graceful in dance. She received hundreds of letters of sympathy but not one word of her missing daughter,

Last Christmas, three months after Aiko's disappearance, Mrs. Koo stopped sending the circulars. Ever since Aiko left, she had kept her daughter's Korean dancing drums and the dancing dress she was to have worn to St. Louis displayed on the living room wall. She took down the dress and packed it away.

"I never believed she ran away," she told an acquaintance. "Not even that night when she didn't come home."

The police, too, might have had hidden suspicions about the fate of Miss Koo. She wasn't the first hitchhiker to disappear in Berkeley that year.

Four months earlier, two 18-year-old Fresno State College girls—Mary Ann Peso and Anita Luchessa—bade goodbye to some friends in Berkley, saying they were going to hitchhike to Stanford University in Palo Alto, south of San Francisco. Their friends at Stanford told police later that they never arrived.

The parents of the girls filed a missing persons report and sent photographs of their daughters to local newspapers, asking for help in locating them. The police report was filed and forgotten until a month before Miss Koo's disappearance.

In August, someone found Mary Ann Peso's skull up on rugged Loma Prieta Mountain in Santa Cruz County. An extensive search failed to turn up the rest of her remains or a trace of her companion.

The discovery of the skull on Loma Prieta Mountain was recalled by Santa Cruz County lawmen five months later when a 19-year-old coed named Cynthia Ann Schall disappeared while hitchhiking from her home in Santa Cruz to class at Cabrillo College in Aptos.

On January 10, the day after Miss Schall disappeared, a California highway patrolman made a ghastly discovery while driving on Highway 1, 19 miles south of Monterey, near Big Sur. Just a few feet off the roadway, he found two severed human arms and hands.

Seven days later, a badly mutilated human torso was found floating in a lagoon near Santa Cruz. Two days after that, a surfer at Capitola— just south of Santa Cruz—found a left hand. And, three days beyond that, someone else found a young woman's pelvis along the shore near Santa Cruz.

Pieced together like a macabre jigsaw puzzle, this was the body of Cynthia Ann Schall. Every part but her head and right hand was there. Fingerprints from the left hand matched prints taken from Miss Schall's rented room. Chest X-rays she had taken in October matched X-rays of the torso found in the lagoon. Police and a pathologist decided she had been hacked to death, then sawed into pieces with a power saw.

Coeds at Cabrillo College and the University of Santa Cruz campus just to the north started thinking twice about hitching for rides. Lawmen warned them not to. There seemed to be a homicidal butcher in the area, preying on defenseless young girls traveling by thumb.

At the University of Santa Cruz, a warning was posted:

"When possible, girls especially, stay in dorms after midnight with doors locked. If you must be out at night, walk in pairs. If you see a campus police patrol car and wave, they will give you a ride. Use the bus even if somewhat inconvenient. Your safety is of first importance. If you are leaving campus, advise someone where you are going, where you can be reached and the approximate time of your return. DON'T HITCH A RIDE, PLEASE!!!"

At age 22, Rosalind Thorpe was a sensible, careful girl. She took the bus from her apartment in downtown Santa Cruz out to the university last February 5. And she was there all day. She left when the Science Library closed at 9 P.M. and headed for the bus stop.

Her arms laden with books, Rosalind stood there in an umbrella of light provided by a street light and hoped the last bus of the night had not left already for town. As she waited, a battered yellow 1969 Ford with a long, police type whip antenna pulled to the curb. There was a university staff parking sticker on the bumper. A big, friendly young man with a mustache leaned across the seat and rolled down the passenger window and called out:

"The bus is gone. I know. I've missed it before, too. Can I give you a lift? It's pretty late."

Rosalind got in the car and they drove off.

Two blocks away, 22-year-old Alice Liu, 21, was standing beside the road, wondering how she was going to get back to town. She had stayed too late in the main campus library. A car came toward her down the road. A street lamp behind it illuminated a couple in the front seat. As the car drew nearer, she saw a university parking sticker on the bumper. What could be safer, Alice probably thought as she stuck out her thumb and smiled.

Friends reported the two young women missing the next day. Santa Cruz police, recalling the fate of Cynthia Schall, issued an urgent "all-points."

Students at the university had no doubt about the fate of their two classmates. They formed search teams and began crisscrossing the wooded 2000-acre campus looking for their remains. They found nothing,

Ten days later, an Alameda County road crew was out checking for storm damage in the Eden Canyon area of the county north of Santa Cruz. Alongside a lonely road, up in a steep ravine, they made a horrifying find.

At first, at a distance, they thought that what they had come upon were discarded mannequins. Up close, they were two mutilated corpses.

Both women appeared to have been young, though the men were not certain. The bodies were headless. One seemed to be Oriental and also had had her hands hacked off. She was nude. The white woman was clad in bra and panties.

It was a week before authorities were certain that the mutilated corpses were the remains of Alice Liu and Rosalind Thorpe. The confirmation came through use of X-rays and physical descriptions provided by the Liu and Thorpe families.

Murder was the Number 1 topic of conversation in Santa Cruz those days. District Attorney Peter Chang even commented that the once peaceful tourist community might be "the murder capital of the world right now."

He wasn't just talking about the horrible attacks on young women hitchhikers. There already had been 16 murders in the area since the start of the year. His office just had charged a young religious zealot and LSD user from Santa Cruz--25-year-old Herbert Mullin--with ten of those murders [Chalk Up Another for Mr. Kill-Crazy, *INSIDE DETECTIVE*, June 1973].

When brought to trial, Mullin would be the second man Chang had prosecuted for mass murder in two years. He was the district attorney who sent John Linley Frazier, a drug-crazed ecology freak, to prison for the October 1970 murders of prominent eye doctor Victor Ohta, his wife, two small sons and a private secretary. Frazier killed them and dumped them in the swimming pool of Ohta's expensive and remote hilltop house because he felt their luxurious existence damaged the natural wonders of the area.

What concerned Chang most––with Mullin in jail––was that this time he seemed to have not one, but two mass killers on his hands. There was no way Mullin could be connected with the murders of the hitchhiking coeds. There still was a psychotic killer on the loose and any young woman with her thumb out, standing at the side of the road, was a potential victim.

The horror was underscored two weeks later when a hiker near Devil's Slide in Pacifica, up the coast in San Mateo County, found the skulls of two young women. Tests showed they had been chopped from the necks of Rosalind Thorpe and Alice Liu.

Everywhere in Santa Cruz, people looked a little more closely at their neighbors. The person responsible for this butchery must be living a very bizarre double life, they thought. Where could someone so thoroughly mutilate and dismember those young women without being seen? How could one be so sick as to even contemplate such crimes without giving some hint of dangerous instability to family, friends or neighbors?

One center for conversation about the murders was the gun shop in Santa Cruz where dealer Harry Ellis was selling handguns as fast as he did in the days when they were looking for the person who killed the Ohtas.

"I've never owned a gun before, but I'm frightened," a pretty office worker told Ellis as she slipped the snub-nosed .38 into her purse. "From now on, I'm keeping this handy at all times."

A tall husky man with a mustache stood near the counter and joined in the conversation. Ellis recognized him as "Big Ed," a gun freak who was in his shop quite often, sometimes to look, sometimes to buy, sometimes just looking for someone to talk to—about guns, mostly. They'd talked of the killings before.

"The guy who's doing this to those girls must be sick. He needs help," said Ellis.

"Sure does," said "Big Ed."

Another locale for intense speculation about the killer was the Jury Room, a bar frequented by off-duty Santa Cruz police officers and others from City Hall across the street.

"Big Ed" Kemper often joined in those conversations and he was welcome. He was a friend of many of the officers in the tavern. He idolized them, wanted to be a policeman himself. He would be, he told everyone, if he wasn't too big. He stood 6 feet, 9 inches tall and weighed 280 pounds. He was a security guard, instead, he said, and he had the gun and handcuffs to prove it.

Everyone thought of Big Ed as a pretty good guy. He got a little rowdy sometimes. Generally, though, the straight shots of tequila he downed seemed to have little effect on him. He played the role of a friendly giant—picking up smaller friends and setting them down on bar stools.

After the arrest of Mullin, there were no more murders. Memories faded. On the Santa Cruz campus, it once seemed as if no one could complete a sentence without mentioning the killings. Everybody joined the anti-hitchhiking campaign. Campus police passed out handbills reading "Everybody Needs a Body (Save Yours)." By mid-

April of this year, though, hardly anyone was talking about the killings. Hitchhiking was starting to pick up again. Those who did recall the attacks on the coeds wondered if it hadn't been that guy Mullin after all.

Then, at 4 A.M. on Tuesday, April 24, the telephone rang at the dispatch desk of the Santa Cruz police department: A man's deep excited voice came over the wire:

> "I killed my mother and her friend. And I killed those college girls.
> I killed six of them and I can show you where I hid the pieces of
> their bodies."

An excited dispatch officer waved at a superior to pick up an extension telephone. As the man continued to talk, the graveyard shift officers punched buttons on the telephone, frantically trying to set up a trace. Then the line went dead. Someone had pushed the wrong button and cut off the caller.

The startled officers in the police station began a tense wait, praying the disturbed young man would re-dial their number. While they waited, they arranged with the telephone company to place a tracer on the call immediately, if it came. Each time the telephone rang, the men started in anticipation. At 6 A.M., he called again.

A two-man patrol car originally had been dispatched to the phone booth when Pueblo police headquarters had been alerted about the agitated caller to Santa Cruz. The California officers had warned their Colorado counterparts of the man's size and said that he probably was dangerous and armed. Patrolman Martinez, who had been just a few blocks away from the booth, took the assignment because of his location and he was warned about the suspect, too.

When they said on the police radio that he was 6'-9" and 280 pounds, I couldn't see anyone that big," Martinez was quoted. "I moved into the area and spotted him in the phone booth with his back to me.

"Then I put on my red lights, pulled my revolver and eased from the cruiser," Martinez continued. "I wasn't taking any chances."

The 30-year-old officer, who is the father of three children, said that he had walked cautiously up to the phone booth, then tapped on the glass. "First I came up, he hadn't noticed me yet and I checked his hands to see if he was armed.

"He was still talking to Santa Cruz when I came up. When I told him to move outside, he asked 'What do I do with the phone?' I told him just to drop it."

His prisoner just walked out of the phone booth, Martinez went on, then leaned against it while the officer searched him.

"It took about four minutes for the backup car to arrive," Martinez recalled, "but to me it seemed like four hours.'" According to the arresting officer, a quick look in Kemper's car, parked near the booth, showed him there was enough ammunition in it "to hold off an army for about a week."

"It's not likely that I'll ever make as big an arrest again," Martinez told newsmen.

Kemper, who Pueblo Chief of Police Robert Mayber sized up as "big enough to beat a mountain lion with a switch," had surrendered without a struggle. He reportedly stepped from the booth with his arms together out front, indicating his willingness to be handcuffed. Asked where his weapons were, he indicated the trunk of a nearby rental car, obtained in Nevada. Inside, officers found a shotgun, a rifle, a carbine and 100 rounds of ammunition.

Kemper seemed almost driven to confess the Northern California murders, telling where and how he killed his victims, how he dismembered their bodies (usually with an ornamental saber) and where he hid the pieces. Chief Mayber, at that point, knew little of the string of killings to which Kemper was referring but he thought the man sounded authentic. Turning to another officer, he said:

"With that kind of detail, I believe he knows what he's talking about."

Kemper told them he had killed ten people in all and he was afraid he was about to kill some more.

It all started, he said, nine years ago —when he was just 15 years old and a mere 6-foot-4, 160 pounds. He was staying with his grandparents—Mr. and Mrs. Edmund Emil Kemper—at their farm house in North Fork, a Sierra-Nevada foothill community in central California.

He didn't like being there and he had heard some talk that he was going to be sent to live with his father in Van Nuys in Southern California. He didn't like that either. He was just "mad at the world" when he saw his grandmother sitting at her typewriter, putting the finishing touches to one of those boys' adventure stories she wrote. He took a gun and shot her twice in the back of the head. Then, taking up a ten-inch kitchen knife, he stabbed her twice because "I didn't think she was dead and I didn't want her to suffer."

When Kemper's grandfather drove up to the house later, he stepped from the car and greeted his grandson with a wave and a smile. When he turned back to take out some packages, Kemper shot him in the back of the head, "because I didn't want him to see what I had done."

He hid his grandfather's body in the closet, then experienced overwhelming feelings of sorrow for what he had done. He called his mother at her home, which then was in Helena, Mont., and sobbed his confession. She called the sheriff. As deputies were en-route to the farmhouse, Kemper himself called the sheriff to report his crimes.

Kemper was tried in Juvenile Court and found insane. He was sent to Atascadero (Cal.) State Hospital, where, five years later, he was pronounced cured. The hospital turned him over to the California Youth Authority, which released him after two years imprisonment.

The hulking young man went to work for the State Division of Highways as a laborer, but fantasized about going into police work of some kind. First, he had to get his juvenile court record sealed. To do that, he had to convince two psychiatrists that he was normal, no longer a danger to others.

But Kemper knew he was not normal. He had bizarre sexual fantasies about the young women he found in the free world around him. And they were so available. All he would have to do would be to pick up one of the pretty young hitchhikers.

On May 7, 1972, the tormented young giant gave in to his desires. He picked up Mary Ann Peso and Anita Luchessa on a Berkeley street corner. On the pretext of driving them to Stanford, he headed his auto south. Near Hayward, he turned off onto a lonely road and easily overpowered the young women, fatally stabbing each.

Stuffing the bodies into the trunk of his 1969 Ford, he drove back to his apartment in Alameda. After nightfall, he dragged their bodies to his room, then ceremonially dismembered them, experiencing great sexual release.

Later, he placed the butchered bodies in plastic bags and stored them in his bedroom closet overnight, he said, then carried them to his car in boxes the next morning and headed south. In Santa Cruz County, he dumped the remains on Loma Prieta Mountain. He remembered the exact place, he said, and would lead the police to it.

The urge overcame him again the night of September 14, he said, when he saw pretty little Aiko Koo hitchhiking near the bus stop in Berkeley. Once she was in his car, he forced her to ride with him to the Bonnie Doon area of Santa Cruz. He smothered her there, covering her mouth and nose with his oversized hand until she was dead. Using his ornamental saber, he dismembered her body with mounting excitement. He deposited her remains in scattered parts of the county the next day. He remembered most of the places, he said.

Actually, not all of Aiko Koo's remains were left in Santa Cruz County that day. He kept her head in the trunk of his car. In fact, he recalled with a smile, her head was in his car trunk on September 16, when he went to Fresno and was examined by two court-appointed psychiatrists in his effort to have his records sealed.

Kemper was given a clean bill of health by the two medical men.

"He has made an excellent response to the years of treatment. I see no psychiatric reason to consider him to be of danger to himself or any other member of society," one of them wrote.

The other suggested Kemper's motorcycle and his driving habits were "more of a threat to his life and health than any threat he is presently to anyone else."

The records were sealed a month later, despite the objection of District Attorney Hanhart that they should have been kept open for at least ten more years.

On January 8, 1973, Kemper said, he picked up Cynthia Schall in Santa Cruz and drove her to Watsonville where he shot her with his .22-caliber rifle. Since it was daytime and his mother was at work at the university, he brought the body back to his mother's apartment. Using his bedroom there, he thoroughly dismembered the young girl's body, placing most of the remains inside plastic bags in boxes in his closet. Her head, he said, he took into the apartment courtyard and buried near a stepping stone with the face turned toward his bedroom window.

The next day, he scattered the other remains over a two-county radius, driving up and down Highway 1, stopping at cliff sides to make his grisly deposits.

When he picked up Alice Liu and Rosalind Thorpe on the Santa Cruz campus on February 5, he drove them only a short distance before the girls realized he wasn't taking them back to town, he said. He pulled to the side of the road and hurriedly shot them both with his rifle. He beheaded them that night and dumped their bodies in Alameda County and heads in San Mateo County the next day,

He started brooding, Kemper said, after the sheriff's deputy came to his mother's apartment in April and took away the .44 Magnum revolver he had purchased. He felt lawmen must be "onto me" and had come to the apartment mainly "to size me up." He wanted to spare his mother the heartbreak of knowing he was once again a killer.

Early on the morning of April 21, he crept to his mother's bedroom and struck her a massive blow to the back of the head with a claw hammer. He then stripped her nude, cut off her head and right hand, then placed her in the closet.

Later that day, he inexplicably called his mother's close friend, Mrs. Hallet, and asked her to come over to the apartment. He was going to take them out for dinner, he said. When she arrived, he strangled her with his hands and placed her body in the other closet.

He loaded his guns into Mrs. Hallett's car, he said, and drove down to the Jury Room for a couple of drinks. Then he headed out of state. In Reno, he abandoned that car and rented one.

That, he said, was about it.

Santa Cruz County authorities, by that time, had confirmed the truth of Kemper's claim to have killed his mother and her friend. They found them in the closets in the bedroom. The bed, which Kemper apparently had used as an operating table, was soaked through with blood to the springs. A claw hammer and curved, three-foot saber with scabbard were found nearby.

As officers carried the bloodstained bed from the house, Claire Scali, an upstairs neighbor, told her sisters she had heard the officers say Ed Kemper had killed his mother and another woman and all the coeds.

The girls wondered if some of the young women had been cut up in the apartment below them. They remembered seeing Kemper carry cardboard boxes "in and out of the apartment all the time."

They also recalled talking with Kemper about the killings of the college girls.

"It must be some crazy person doing all this," he had told them, they recalled.

Two days later, the police reappeared at the Kemper apartment and went into the backyard. As the girls upstairs watched, they went to a stepping stone in the courtyard and started digging. Two feet into the. earth they stopped. One of the men, in plain clothes and plastic gloves reached down and carefully extracted a human skull from the hole.

"When we first heard he was confessing all this stuff, we thought it might be for the publicity," said Claire. "But we changed our minds when the officers dug up that head."

A team of three officers from the Santa Cruz police department and sheriff's office flew back to Pueblo to question Kemper further. When the big man waived extradition—telling the judge who offered to appoint an attorney for him, "I don't think that's necessary"—and said he wanted to come back and face trial, the officers set out with him for California in the rented car, but not before he had a laugh when the local police couldn't find the key to his handcuffs, which he had asked to have removed to smoke.

In Reno, they decided, they would leave that car and proceed to Santa Cruz in Mrs. Hallett's auto.

As they motored across country, Kemper rode in the back seat, shackled and handcuffed and scrunched down to avoid attracting attention. At night, Kemper stayed in local jails. During the days, they stopped for lunch at drive-in restaurants. At one point, they were stopped for lunch when two attractive young women walked by the car.

Kemper vomited violently, then apologized, saying that was a common reaction for him when he saw an attractive woman, police reported. While Kemper was en-route home, lawmen with a search warrant impounded his yellow Ford with the whiplash antenna found parked near the Aptos apartment. From the passenger compartment, they extracted strands of human hair—some blonde, some dark—a blood-streaked back seat, a whole clip of .30-caliber ammunition and a spent bullet lodged in an interior panel of the car.

From the trunk, they meticulously collected more hair snarled in the trunk latch, a short-handled shovel, a tan cotton raincoat, a plastic water bottle and an enamel dish pan.

When Kemper and his escorts arrived in the Bay Area, they stopped first in Alameda County, where he led lawmen through his apartment and to sites where he encountered his victims and where he deposited the bodies of two of them. They stopped briefly in San Mateo County where he had dropped off the skulls of the two Santa Cruz coeds.

After four days, they arrived at the Santa Cruz County line where 20 sheriff's deputies, anticipating further explorations of burial sites, were waiting. When Kemper saw the small army of lawmen, he was upset.

"This is no circus to me, man. Get me out of here," he bellowed.

When he calmed down, he led the sheriff's deputies on a six-hour tour of the county. The tour yielded:

—A decomposed, headless body believed to belong to Mary Ann Pesce in a shallow grave near Old Santa Cruz Highway, off Summit Road.

—A bone, possibly a human pelvis, and some clothing in a rugged canyon near Loma Prieta Mountain.

—An arm in a plastic bag at the bottom of a steep canyon off Rodeo Gulch Road.

—What may be the skeleton of Aiko Koo from a makeshift grave off Two-Bar Road near Boulder Creek.

—Personal items of some of the young women, on a ledge below a cliff where Kemper said he threw parts of Cynthia Schall.

All burial and deposit sites were within a 20-mile radius of Kemper's mother's apartment.

On April 30, Kemper was charged in Santa Cruz Municipal Court with eight counts of murder. He was arraigned and Chang said he would take the case to the county grand jury. The district attorney also had harsh words for the psychiatric profession for its apparent inability to identify persons who are dangerous to others.

On May 28, Kemper reportedly twice tried to commit suicide while being held in a Santa Cruz jail cell. He slashed his arm with a pen clip, obtained from an unknown source, and received hospital treatment, then tried again when back in jail.

EDITOR'S NOTE: THE NAMES HARRY ELLIS AND CLAIRE Scali are not the actual names of the persons who were in fact participants in the incidents described in this article.

REDWOOD CITY, CALIF. (AP) –– Edmund Emil Kemper III, accused of killing eight women including his mother, has attempted suicide for the third time since he was arrested, authorities reported.

Guards at the San Mateo County Jail in Redwood City found Kemper had slashed his wrist Sunday morning with a sharpened ballpoint pen, Sgt. Robert Cancilla said.

Kemper's trial in Santa Cruz County Superior Court was to continue Monday, but Dist. Atty. Peter Chang said the session might be shortened if Kemper is too weak as a result of the incident.

The defendant is charged with killing his mother, her best friend and six hitchhiking coeds.

EDMUND KEMPER's rampage of murder arose from two basic causes, an "overwhelming sexual curiosity and obsession with sex and rage, hatred, anger and aggressiveness."

"The murders were an explosive expression of hatred," Dr. Joel Fort of San Francisco, an internationally-known psychiatrist, testified today in Kemper's murder trial.

Fort was appointed by Judge Harry F. Brauer to examine Kemper to determine whether the young giant was legally sane when he committed each of the eight murders with which he is charged.

The doctor said under questioning by district attorney Peter Chang he had first been contacted in the case by Kemper's lawyer, public defender Jim Jackson, as a possible expert for the defense.

However, Fort, who made no secret of the fact on the stand this morning that he has little regard for "traditional" psychiatrists, said he had decided not to accept Jackson's offer.

"I decided if Jackson didn't like my findings then I wouldn't be free to testify in court."

Chang asked, "You wanted to be free to call the shots as you saw them?"

"Yes," Fort said with emphasis.

The doctor, whose qualifications took almost a half hour to recite, said he is "not actually a psychiatrist, if that label means I restrict my work to middle-class neurotic women," and went on to comment that in his opinion "traditional psychiatry is mainly irrelevant to the problems of society."

The "neurotic women" reference prompted the only question put to the doctor by Jackson concerning his qualifications as an expert witness.

"Don't middle-class neurotic women need love too," asked Jackson.

"Definitely," Fort instantly replied, "but they don't need it from a psychiatrist."

The doctor said he had spent five hours with Kemper discussing things with him and approximately 50 hours reviewing all available records relating to the immediate case and Kemper's past history, including all of his reports from Atascadero where he was held for five years after he ordered his paternal grandparents.

Fort disagreed completely with an original diagnosis by two court-appointed Madera County doctors who followed Kemper through Atascadero. The doctors had said Kemper was a paranoid schizophrenic.

Fort said he found "no basis whatsoever" for the diagnosis.

He described Kemper in layman's terms, a " sex maniac ... to a greater degree than anyone I have seen in 20 years."

In killing the coeds, sexually molesting them and dismembering the bodies, Fort said Kemper's motive was, "to have as wide a range of sexual satisfaction and sexual pleasure as he could possibly have."

The doctor said Kemper felt "inadequate sexually" and this was the reason in all but one of the coed murders Kemper participated in sexual acts with the victim after he had killed her.

He had only one sexual intercourse with a live woman and when he sought a second experience with her, he was rejected by her. The doctor said. (This woman was not one of the victims.)

"The sex killings also gave Kemper a feeling of power and control over his victims and dismembering their bodies expressed his hate and violence," Fort said.

The doctor also said that Kemper had admitted "taking pieces of flesh from some of his victims, cooking it and eating it."

This admission came from Kemper during a 2-1/2 half hour interview in which he voluntarily underwent sodium ambotal injections. The drug puts a patient into a relaxed state but allows him to maintain consciousness.

"Kemper's expression-of-violence pattern began in his childhood," Fort said. "He first expressed it by beheading and mutilating dolls belonging to his sister and continued similar things with cats and dogs."

The sexual problems of Kemper stemmed from a "total lack of sex education in his home, negative information from his mother, and misinformation from his peers," the doctor asserted.

"The misinformation Kemper received regarded sexuality continued when he went to Atascadero," the doctor said.

Fort also noted that Kemper was a very intelligent young man, well-versed in many subjects including police work, ballistics and psychology.

He said Kemper had administered psychiatric tests to "thousands" at Atascadero, and that he had memorized 28 psychological tests and knew what answers to give in order to appear normal.

"He is clever and manipulative," Fort said.

An odd sidelight was Kemper's apparent desire to be punished for the murders. Fort said Kemper had told him he wanted to "get the gas chamber," and in fact voted for the death penalty last November.

Kemper appeared to be in good shape in court this morning. Yesterday he seemed haggard and worn from his suicide attempt Sunday morning. Today he had a fresh haircut and was again wearing his own clothing ad looked neat and trim.

A THREATENING GESTURE by a young woman spectator seated in the rear row of the court brought the Edmund Emil Kemper murder trial to a halt for almost half an hour this morning.

The incident occurred during the playing of a tape interview of Kemper by investigators in which Kemper had described the killing of his mother, Mrs. Clarnell Strandberg on Easter weekend.

Kemper, who had said yesterday he would rather not be present in the courtroom during the playing of the confession tapes, was not allowed to remain out of the courtroom. This morning, when he came to court, his attorney said Kemper had been taking tranquilizers.

Despite this, Kemper was showing obvious strain listening to his own voice on the tape, and a number of times he turned from the counsel table and scanned the spectator section. After one such look at the spectators, Kemper turned back quickly and motioned to his sheriff's guard sitting nearby.

A whisper consultation took place and Kemper's lawyer, Jim Jackson, got up and immediately went to the bench and whispered something to Judge Harry F. Brauer, who promptly called for a recess.

Later, Judge Brauer told reporters Kemper had said a young woman in the back row had looked at him and drawn her forefinger across her throat in a throat-cutting type gesture.

Brauer gave Kemper time to calm down and then resumed the court session, continuing with the playing of the confession tapes.

Bailiffs searched for the offending girl but she apparently left the courthouse immediately following the incident.

"WHEN I WALKED into the courtroom I could just feel the tension."

So remarked Asst. Dist. Atty. John Bohrer after Wednesday afternoon's session of the Edmund Kemper murder trial. Bohrer, who attended the court session as an observer, was one of dozens of spectators who sat silently and listened to a tape recorded conversation between Kemper and lawmen in which the defendant outlined six coed murders in gruesome, explicit detail.

As Kemper's tape recorded voice droned on, telling investigators exactly how he killed six young women since May of 1972, not a whisper emerged from the spectator section of the courtroom. Some sat with mouths agape:.Others remained rigid, one or both arms supporting their heads. One young woman was unable to keep an occasional tear from running down her cheek.

Kemper's description began with the Anita Luchessa and Mary Ann Pesce slayings on May 7, 1972. "I asked them a few questions and determined to my satisfaction that they were not familiar with the area," he began.

"I didn't really make much of an effort to deceive them because they were terribly naive."

From that point, Kemper detailed the kidnapping and finally the stabbing of the two victims.

(At this point, the reader should be cautioned that several gruesome details follow.)

He remembered every detail of the crimes, as well as accurate physical descriptions of the young women. Referring to Miss Pesce, he said, "I was really quite struck with her personality and looks and there was almost a reverence there."

"I heard one news comment that she was a Camarillo girl, so I went down to L.A. after the slayings and checked out Camarillo and only found one Pesce in the phone book and that was a Gabriel Pesce, so I went up by that neighborhood, in fact right by the house."

Miss Pesce and her companion were beheaded and discarded in the Loma Preta area, according to the tape.

The next victim was 15-year-old Aiko Koo of Berkeley: "That was the first time I ever dissected a body and that was then, after I had broken my arm and that was why I dd it, because I couldn't carry her all the way."

Part of her body was disposed of in Alameda County, and part above Boulder Creek, Kemper indicated. He said he killed her by taping her mouth closed and then pinching her nostrils. "She was sexually assaulted after death," he added.

This murder occurred on Sept. 14, 1972. Kemper said. "Two days later, I had two psychiatrist examinations to get my juvenile record sealed." Listed on his juvenile record was the fact that he had killed his grandparents when he was 15.

"Cynthia Schall was the next one," Kemper went on. "That happened the night I bought a .22 Ruger automatic pistol with a six-inch barrel. And that night I killed her. Not so much to celebrate, but I had been eagerly awaiting that gun."

He said he bought the gun at Valley sport shop in Watsonville.

He picked up Miss Schall on Mission Street. "In that vicinity, I had been up cruising around the campus and I'd picked up three different girls, two of them together, that were possibilities, but I cancelled those out because there were too many people standing around that possibly knew them when they got in. But all the other conditions were perfect. It had been drizzling. It had been raining real hard and people were getting any ride they could get and windows were fogging up... But I had given up on those other two and I was kind of uptight about it and driving down the street I spotted her standing out there with her thumb out."

The young woman with her thumb out was Cynthia Schall. After driving her to the Watsonville area, he forced her to get in the trunk. Later, near Corralitos, he shot her.

He took her to his mother's house in Aptos and dumped her in the closet. He dismembered her in the bathtub the next morning, after having sexual intercourse with her.

He discarded her clothing in an Alameda laundromat, putting them into a dryer and putting in "about four dimes worth and (putting) it on full hot, figuring it would ruin the coat."

The next killings involved two UCSC coeds, Rosalind Thorpe and Alice Liu. "That was the fifth of February and I'm not really sharp on the time," said Kemper.

He said it was around 8:30 p.m. when he picked up Rosalind Thorpe, who was hitchhiking around Merrill College. A short time later, with Miss Thorpe in the car, Kemper picked up Miss Liu.

"I noticed Miss Liu standing on the side. She saw us coming, threw out a big beautiful smile and stuck her thumb out very hopefully ...I imagine she was a cautious hitchhiker and she always made sure of her ride before she got in, and we appeared to be a couple (Kemper and Miss Thorpe) and with that "A" tag on there, and a man and a woman, she didn't hesitate at all about getting in." The "A" tag refers to a UCSC parking sticker which Kemper's mother, an employee at the university, gave to her son.

"I was mad that night," he said. "My mother and I had had a real tiff ... I told her I was going to a movie and I jumped up and went straight up to the campus 'cause it was still early. I said the first girl that's halfway decent that I pick, I'm gonna blow her brains out. As it was, I improvised, it was two in a perfect situation."

While on the straight section of road overlooking the city of Santa Cruz, still on UCSC property, Kemper shot the young women. He dismembered their bodies, dumping their torsos in Alameda County, their heads in Pacifica.

After she was shot, Miss Liu was sexually molested, said Kemper.

Today, the tape recording continued, with Kemper's voice relating how and why he killed his mother and her best friend. "The murders were coming to a head, I felt; that I was going to be caught pretty soon for the killing of these girls or I was going to blow up and do something very open and get myself caught. I did not want my mother to know."

He said he hit her in the head with a hammer and slit her throat. Authorities found her a few days later, beheaded and her hand severed.

As for his mother's friend, Mrs. Sara Hallett, Kemper said he had to kill a friend of his mother's "as an excuse." In other words, Kemper said he had to provide a reasonable story for friends of his mother's to explain her absence. If she were away with a friend, Kemper reasoned, nobody would be concerned about her absence.

Kemper for the most part remained impassive throughout the playing of the tape. Late this morning, his attorney, Jim Jackson, hurriedly asked Judge Harry Brauer for a recess when Kemper became agitated. Reportedly, a woman in the spectator section, in an apparent attempt to upset the defendant, moved her finger across her throat in a slashing motion.

Before the tape was played Wednesday, Kemper requested that he be removed from court, a request that was denied by Brauer.

On the tape, which was prepared less than a week following his arrest, Kemper showed concern about the ultimate playing of the tapes in open court. "It's an awfully touchy subject, you know, what happened and what didn't happen … Still it's going to be awfully terrible for the family to have to listen to, just because they are in court, you know. 'Cause I've heard of things like where certain tapes are played just in front of the judge or just in front of the jury as evidence rather than just play it in front of the whole court … that starts to look like a whole arena, you know, and everybody is in there to hear all the gory details. That would get me very upset and I'd probably ask to leave the court. The judge would say, 'No, you're going to sit there and listen." Then I'd start throwing chairs and having a fit, scream on the floor and all that stuff."

EDMUND KEMPER'S CAR, in which six hitchhiking coeds were picked up and either stabbed, strangled or shot to death, was, in effect, "entered into evidence" today at his murder trial in Santa Cruz.

Just before the noon recess, Judge Harry F. Brauer, at the request of District Attorney Peter Chang, allowed Kemper jurors to leave the courtroom and examine the car, which was driven up and parked along the river levee walkway at the rear of the courthouse.

Kemper did not immediately join the group of persons from the trial, because he did not want to let his guard, sheriff deputy Bruce Colomy put handcuffs on him and a waist restraining chain before leaving the courthouse. Kemper has been allowed to appear in the courtroom, at Judge Brauer's instruction, wearing only manacles around his ankles, with his hands left free. However, Colomy, as a security measure, insisted upon the additional restraint outside the courtroom, and Kemper finally relented.

As the jury was examining the car, Kemper, flanked by two guards, filed through the crowd of spectators.

Crowds of curious onlookers gathered on the courthouse steps in the morning sunshine as the young giant, dressed in his jail-provided orange jumpsuit, towered above the car in which he has admitted taking six human lives.

Earlier, expert witnesses for the prosecution had testified about the physical evidence found in the car, including a dried pool of human blood found in the back seat where one girl, Alice Liu, a UCSC coed, was shot to death and another, Mary Anne Pesce, a Fresno State coed was stabbed to death. Traces of blood were also found in the trunk where other coeds had been shot to death.

TESTIFYING as the first defense witness in Ed Kemper's trial, Allyn Kemper, 22, revealed under cross examination that both she and her mother thought Kemper might have been involved in the death of Cynthia Schall.

Allyn Kemper testified that she asked her brother directly whether he had anything to do with the killing – one of eight of which he is accused.

"No," she quoted him in response, "but I was afraid you might be suspicious because of that cat thing. My mother has already asked me about it, and I'd appreciate it if you didn't bring it up again because it will just stir things up."

The "cat thing" Miss Kemper explained, involved an incident when the family lived in Montana and her brother decapitated the family cat with a bayonet.

Under questioning by District Attorney Peter Chang, she also related that she herself was almost killed by Kemper.

That, too, happened in Montana. Kemper, she explained, had always had an interest in guns, and one day as she walked through the living room she heard a click.

As she turned, she said, a bullet from Kemper's .22 rifle whizzed by her ear and buried itself in a bookcase.

"Oops!" she quoted her brother. "I thought it was empty."

THE TESTIMONY by Ed Kemper yesterday was no exception from the preceding grim testimony. With questioning from his lawyer Jim Jackson, he recalled his childhood fantasies which started out innocently and wistfully, later to become daydreams of murder and sex.

He said his first fantasy was that his "mother and father would be loving together and caring for their children."

According to Kemper, it was a fantasy that never came true. Instead, there was "much violence, hatred, yelling and screaming" between his father and mother who separated and were divorced when he was around seven years old.

Kemper said he felt rejected and unloved by his mother and his father as well, though he indicated he yearned for a good relationship with his father.

He spoke of his mother as "alcoholic," and said she once had beaten him with a heavy belt and buckle when he was a small child and told him not to scream, "because the neighbors will think I'm beating you."

This was at the age of nine, and Kemper said after that he was afraid of her and began to have a recurring fantasy about sneaking up on her and hitting her in the head with a hammer.

Later, in Atascadero [where he was incarcerated for five years after the murder of his grandparents], Kemper's fantasies turned to sex as well as murder. He said his final fantasy was, "I killed someone, cut them up and ate them... and I kept the head on a shelf and talked to it... I said the same things I would have said had she been alive, in love with me, had she been caring of me."

Asked by Jackson if he ever told anyone at Atascadero about the fantasies, Kemper replied, "No, I would never got out if I had told psychiatrists. I was having fantasies of sex with dead bodies and in some cases eating them. I would never have gotten out ever."

He paused, and then said, "Wow! That's like condemning yourself to life imprisonment, and I don't know many people who do that."

The young defendant, who worked for psychologists testing other inmates at Atascadero, said, "I hid it from them. They can't see the things going on in my mind. All I had to do to conceal it from them was not talk about it."

Six coeds murdered by Edmund Kemper died because, "I wanted the girls for myself, like possessions, they were going to be mine," he testified at his murder trial this morning.

Under examination by his defense lawyer Jim Jackson, continued from yesterday's session, Kemper revealed his "private world" dealing with the killings.

He related the killing of the coeds to a fantasy he had had in childhood when he admittedly killed his pet cat because its affections had been transferred to his two sisters and "I wanted to make it mine."

Kemper said he buried the cat alive in the back yard and later dug it up, fondled it and talked to it after it was dead.

This morning he described his frustrations in attempting to establish a relationship with girls his own age after his release from Atascadero State Hospital where he had been confined for five years for the murder of his grandparents when he was 15.

He said he couldn't communicate with people his own age.

"When I got out on the street it was like being on a strange planet. People my own age were not talking the same language."

He said he began picking up hitchhikers of both sexes just to "trying to communicate with them... just trying to make friends."

Then, later, he started relying on his fantasies "more than reality." It was apparently at this point that the killings began.

He was asked by Jackson to tell the jurors what he had in mind when each of six coeds died.

"What were you thinking? Death?" Jackson asked. "No," Kemper replied, "Death never entered as a factor."

Kemper said, "Alive, they were distant, not sharing with me. I was trying, to establish a relationship and there was no relationship there..."

"When they were being killed there wasn't anything going on in my mind except that they were going to be mine ... That was the only way they could be mine."

"Like the cat?" asked Jackson.

"Like the cat," Kemper replied.

Jackson asked him what the "real reason" was that Kemper disposed of the girls' bodies in the manner he did cutting them up and keeping parts of the bodies for a time.

Kemper hesitantly replied, "Because they were rotting and I was losing them."

He explained, "When the girls died I kept them a certain length of time, but couldn't keep them any longer,"

However, he declared, "I still have their spirits."

Kemper said he also visited the grave of one of the coeds, Mary Ann Pesce, because he wanted to be near her and talk to her.

"I loved her and I wanted her," he said.

In the death of another girl, Cynthia Schall, he said he buried her head in the backyard of his mother's apartment house facing the window of the bedroom where he was staying and "talked to it (the head) many times, saying affectionate things."

He said of the killings "I didn't want to hurt anybody... the deaths didn't exist to me. It wasn't as in dying. It was a transition to me."

"I wanted the girls to be mine."

Kemper denied that he had planned his operation carefully so he wouldn't be caught by the police. He said he "just didn't want to be stopped by anybody who'd take my girls away from me."

However, he admitted that while he was fleeing across the country after killing his mother and her best friend, he' felt "so horrified about what had happened," that he "wanted to be punished in the worst possible way."

Kemper said that by fleeing, he was "basically running from the whole world. My fantasies were gone and I had no place to hide."

He said that after his arrest he felt "convinced I should be shackled and hung upside down from the bars and beaten," and that he should be "tortured for what I did."

Shortly before the noon recess, District Attorney Peter Chang began his cross-examination.

Yesterday's afternoon's session in the Edmund Kemper murder trial started in a near riot as loud voiced and shoving teenage girls and middle-aged women, struggled to secure seats in the courtroom, and it ended abruptly when the defendant broke into tears on the stand.

Kemper testified for two and a half hours yesterday, probing into the events of his childhood which may have led him to the murders of his grandparents, the horrors of confinement in Atascadero state hospital for the criminally insane and his ultimate murders of eight other persons.

Kemper broke down shortly before 4 p.m. as he was being questioned by his attorney Jim Jackson about his suicide attempt Sunday morning in his San Mateo County jail cell.

Kemper's cell is under constant surveillance by jailers by the means of a television camera.

But Kemper told how he avoid signaling his suicidal actions by simply turning his back to the camera and slashing his wrist with the flattened and sharpened casing of a ballpoint pen.

He said he had cut an artery, which was spurting blood, and a vein, which also was bleeding.

Jackson interrupted him to ask why had he not, if he wanted to die, stuck himself in the throat.

Kemper looked up blandly at the question and replied quietly, "I would have died too fast that way."

He explained that he could have cut an artery in his throat but that he wanted to think about things as he bled.

"What were you thinking about, Ed?" asked Jackson.

Kemper looked down at his hands and began to reply slowly, "I was thinking about the girls who died…their fathers…" At this point, his voice broke and tears came to his eyes, which he brushed away. (Two fathers of his coed victims testified in court during the first week of the trial and Kemper had been unable or unwilling to look at them while they were on the stand.)

Momentarily, Kemper recovered his composure, and said, "Sorry," and then continued "…their mothers, and I thought about what I did…" At this point the young giant buried his face in his hands, apparently unable to continue.

Judge Harry F. Brauer immediately adjourned the court for the day, and Kemper jumped up from the witness chair and hastily tussled for the back door of the courtroom, catching sheriff's deputies across the room momentarily off guard.

Bailiff Don Chapman was the first to reach Kemper, and he patted him consolingly on the back as he led him into the jury room adjacent to the courtroom, where Kemper remained until Jackson went in to see him before he was taken back to San Mateo County Jail.

Earlier, following the mob scene at the courtroom door, Judge Brauer, coldly angry, admonished the spectators.

"There will be strict decorum, not only in the courtroom but outside," the judge said. "Anybody who pushes or yells will be excluded. This is not a circus," he snapped.

The courtroom has been crowded each day of the trial, with a number of persons turned away for lack of seating. Present daily have been students from local high schools who, with their teachers, have sat through the grim recitations of murder, violence and sex.

The testimony by Kemper yesterday was no exception from the preceding grim testimony. With questioning from Jackson, he recalled his childhood fantasies which started out innocently and wistfully, later to become daydreams of murder and sex.

He said his first fantasy was that his "mother and father would be loving together and caring for their children."

According to Kemper, it was a fantasy that never came true, he said. Instead, there was "much violence, hatred, yelling and screaming" between his father and mother who separated and were divorced when he was around seven years old.

Kemper said he felt rejected and unloved by his mother and his father as well, though he indicated he yearned for a good relationship with his father.

He spoke of his mother as "alcoholic," and said she once had beaten him with a heavy belt and buckle when he was a small child and told him not to scream, "because the neighbors will think I'm beating you."

This was at the age of nine, and Kemper said after that he was afraid of her and began to have a recurring fantasy about sneaking up on her and hitting her in the head with a hammer.

Later, in Atascadero, his fantasies turned to sex as well as murder. He said his final fantasy was, "I killed someone, cut them up and ate them... and I kept the head on a shelf and talked to it...I said the same things I would have said had she been alive, in love with me, had she been caring of me."

Asked by Jackson if he ever told anyone at Atascadero about the fantasies, Kemper replied, "No, I would never got out if I had told psychiatrists I was having fantasies of sex with dead bodies and in some cases eating them I would never have gotten out ever."

He paused and then said, "Wow! That's like condemning yourself to life imprisonment, and I don't know many people who do 'that"

The young defendant, who worked for psychologists testing other inmates at Atascadero, said, "I hid it from them. They can't see the things going on in my mind. All I had to do to conceal it from them was not talk about it."

MASS MURDER SUSPECT Edmund Emil Kemper III, who tried to commit suicide last week by slashing his right wrist, today ripped out the stitches, sparking another battle with San Mateo County sheriff's deputies.

It took three deputies, a sergeant and a physician, with the aid of chemical spray, to subdue the 6-foot-9, 240 pound Kemper.

The defendant was shackled and handcuffed and taken to Kaiser Hospital in Redwood City, three blocks from the jail, where a doctor determined it was unnecessary to sew Kemper's wrist back up.

But the doctor did inject a depressant to allow Kemper to fall asleep, authorities said.

A jury in Santa Cruz County was scheduled to begin deliberations later today on the charges that Kemper killed his mother, her best friend and six co-eds.

Asst. Sheriff Eugene E. Stewart, said jailers constantly monitor Kemper's isolation cell. A deputy spotted blood on Kemper's T-shirt at 2 a.m. today, the result of him tearing out the stitches. The 24-year-old defendant last Sunday used the sharpened end of a ballpoint pen to inflict his wound.

Kemper has been kept in San Mateo County because of better security.

Stewart said that Kemper had jammed the lock to his cell by putting a wooden tongue depressor in the lock. It took deputies several minutes to clear the wood and enter the cell.

"KEMPER FOUND SANE, GUILTY OF MURDERING EIGHT WOMEN" ARGUS-LEADER (NOVEMBER 9, 1973)

SANTA CRUZ, Calif. (AP) - - Edmund Emil Kemper III, who said he acted out homicidal, cannibalistic and sexual fantasies in the killing of eight women, has been found sane and guilty of first-degree murder.

The 6-foot-9 Kemper, plaid in an orange jail jumpsuit and with his wrists manacled, heard the verdict Thursday without showing emotion. The jury of six men and six women deliberated five hours over two days following a three-week trial.

Kemper, 25, had pleaded innocent and innocent by reason of insanity in the eight killings.

Judge Harry Brauer told jurors, "I agree entirely to your verdict." He ordered Kemper to appear in Santa Cruz Superior Court today for

Kemper Found Sane, Guilty Of Murdering Eight Women

SANTA CRUZ, Calif. (AP) — Edmund Emil Kemper III, who said he acted out homicidal, cannibalistic and sexual fantasies in the killing of eight women, has been found sane and guilty of first-degree murder.

The 6-foot-9 Kemper, clad in an orange jail jumpsuit and with his wrists manacled, heard the verdict Thursday without showing emotion. The jury of six men and six women deliberated five hours over two days following a three-week trial.

Kemper, 25, had pleaded innocent and innocent by reason of insanity in the eight killings.

Judge Harry Brauer told jurors, "I agree entirely with your verdict." He ordered Kemper to appear in Santa Cruz Superior Court today for sentencing. The penalty could be a life term for Kemper on each of eight first-degree murder counts.

Public defender James Jackson said Kemper expected the verdict and the attorney called it "reasonable enough."

Kemper, who tried four times to kill himself in jail and said he thought he should be "tortured" as punishment, cannot be sent to the gas chamber because the

Muskie Introduces Pollution Waiver

WASHINGTON (AP) — Legislation giving the Nixon administration emergency authority to waive environmental controls because of the energy shortage was introduced today by Sen. Edmund S. Muskie.

The Maine Democrat, in a speech prepared for the Senate, urged quick action on the bill so the Environmental Protection Agency can move "expeditiously to assure that environmental controls do not exacerbate the energy crisis."

Muskie said the measure must be looked upon as a temporary one. If not, he said, "our

Edmund Kemper

sentencing. The penalty could be a life term for Kemper on each of eight first-degree murder counts.

Public defender James Jackson said Kemper expected the verdict and the attorney called it "reasonable enough."

Kemper who tried four times to kill himself in jail and said he thought he should be "tortured" as punishment, cannot be sent to the gas chamber because the slayings occurred between May 1972, and last April, before California reinstated the death penalty.

Seven of the eight victims, including Kemper's mother, Clarnell Strandberg, 53, were beheaded. Six of the victims were young women student hitchhikers.

Three days after the killing of his mother Kemper was arrested in a Pueblo, Colo., telephone booth while he was giving details of the slayings to Santa Cruz authorities who had the call traced.

The defendant said on the witness stand he killed the women because "that was the only way they could be mine. I had their spirits. I still have them."

In his testimony, Kemper told of living in a world of fantasies from early childhood. He said his daydreams became increasingly violent during the five years he was confined to mental hospitals for the murders of his paternal grandparents nearly ten years ago.

EXPRESSING the sentiment "May God have mercy on your soul, Mr. Kemper," Santa Cruz Superior Court Judge Harry Brauer today sentenced convicted mass-murderer Edmund Emil Kemper III to life imprisonment.

Brauer told the defendant, "You are being sentenced to prison for the term of your natural life."

The judge added he was suggesting as vehemently as possible to the Adult Authority that he never be considered for probation.

In preparing the statement to the prison authority, Brauer asked Dist. Atty. Peter Chang to "buttress that request with certain exhibits." Those exhibits include taped statements made by Kemper stating that if he were freed again in society, he feels he would kill again.

Kemper was led into court by his two guards, Bruce Colomy and Ron Atkinson. The tension in the courtroom came to a climax following Kemper's sentencing when the judge commented, "May God have mercy on your soul, Mr. Kemper, but you understand I have to protect the rest of the people from people like you."

Following the hearing, Kemper, restrained by foot shackles, made his way over to the prosecution counsel table and shook hands with Chang. "Mr. Chang. I want to thank you for your restraint during this trial," said Kemper.

Colomy said Kemper would be taken immediately to Vacaville State Medical Facility where he has been imprisoned following a series of attempted suicides.

Kemper also expressed his gratitude to the judge for allowing hi to remain in court unshackled during the entire trial.

The private investigator who worked for Kemper's defense, Harold Cartwright, had additional praise for Kemper's two guards, Colomy and Atkinson. Cartwright commented that both men were responsible for "being as much counselors as guards," while transporting Kemper from court to prison each day. He said without the two guards, Kemper may not have been able to keep his composure in court.

The eight life-prison terms by statute, cannot be imposed consecutively. Instead, Kemper's sentence will be served concurrently.

After court, Kemper appeared relieved that the whole thing was over, and while walking from the courthouse, he nodded greetings to several officials he became acquainted with during his imprisonment and trial.

*"KEMPER VICTIMS' FAMILIES
SUE" GREAT FALLS TRIBUNE
(JANUARY 11, 1974)*

SANTA CRUZ, Calif. (AP) — A $1.25 million suit accusing state agencies and two psychiatrists of negligence in the treatment and diagnosis of convicted mass murderer Edmund Emil Kemper III has been filed in Superior Court.

Families of five coeds slain by Kemper named the State of California Youth Authority, the State Department of Mental Hygiene and two court-appointed psychiatrists as defendants.

Kemper's mother once lived in Montana.

It claims they "carelessly and negligently" treated Kemper, 25, "approximately causing the deaths of the five young women."

Last November, he was convicted of the mutilation slayings of six coed hitchhikers, his mother and her best friend. He was sentenced to life imprisonment.

At the age of 15, Kemper was sent to the state mental hospital at Atascadero for slaying his paternal grandparents. He was released five years later.

"The parents believe that professional negligence in the examination and treatment of Kemper was such that it resulted in the deaths of their daughters," said Bob Crawford, attorney for the parents.

The parents of the slain women contend the state agencies had wrongfully released Kemper five years ago and then the psychiatrists in 1972 "let him slip through their fingers again."

The plaintiffs include Mrs. Suzanne McEvoy and William Schall of San Rafael, parents of Cabrillo College coed Cynthia Schall, 19, Roland and Marjorie Thorpe of Carmel, parents of Rosalind Thorpe, 23, of UC Santa Cruz coed; Gabriel and Lois Pesce, parents of Mary Ann Pesce, 19, a Fresno State coed; and James and Phyllis Liu of Torrance, parents of Alice Liu, 21, a UC Santa Cruz coed.

Crawford said the family of Berkeley student Koo, 15, did not join the suit because they "felt they had been through enough."

JUST A FEW HOURS after California's mass murderer Edmund Kemper, 24, was convicted on eight counts of first-degree murder, he kept a promise and granted me an exclusive interview. It was not my first person-to-person talk with the young killer.

As a reporter assigned to cover the grisly murder investigation ["*I'll Show You Where I Buried the Pieces of Their Bodies,*" INSIDE, August 1973] and the trial, I had, by chance, chatted with him a few weeks before his trial, as he was waiting at the Santa Cruz County courthouse for a conference with his lawyer.

I wrote a story about our meeting and my impressions of him and he liked it, thus came his promise of an interview once the trial was ended. Kemper had warned me the court hearings on the gory sex-killings of six coeds and the subsequent murders of his mother and her best friend probably would turn my stomach. They did.

As a sex-starved young man in what should have been a peak of his virility, he was sexually and socially so uncertain of himself that he began to prey on hitchhiking coeds, not as a rapist, but as a murderer and necrophiliac.

"At first I picked up girls just to talk to them, just to try to get acquainted with people my own age and try to strike up a friendship," he had told investigators. Then he began to have sex fantasies about the girls he picked up hitchhiking, but feared being caught and convicted as a rapist So, he said: "I decided to mix the two and have a situation of rape and murder and no witnesses and no prosecution."

Kemper's first two victims were 18-year-old Fresno State college coeds, Mary Ann Pesce and Anita Luchessa whom he stabbed to death May 7, 1972, after he picked them up in Berkeley.

"I had full intentions of killing them. I would loved to have raped them, but not having any experience at all..." he trailed off.

He disclosed that, despite the fact he killed Miss Pesce, she had awakened a feeling of tenderness in him that none of his other victims did.

"I was really quite struck by her personality and her looks and there was just almost a reverence there," he said.

Kemper decapitated the girls' corpses, burying Miss Pesce's body in a redwood grove along a mountain highway and casting that of Miss Luchessa out in the brush on a hillside. He kept their heads for a time and then hurled them down a steep slope of a ravine.

The girls were listed as "missing persons" for months until Miss Pesce's head was found by hikers and, subsequently, identified through dental charts. Kemper later led investigators to the grave where he had buried her.

"Sometimes, afterward, I visited there ... to be near her ... because I loved her and wanted her," he said on the witness stand.

Miss Luchessa's head and body never were found.

A month after Miss Pesce's head was discovered, Kemper chose another victim. Beautiful Aiko Koo, 15, a talented Oriental dancer, was hitchhiking from her home in Berkeley to a dance class in San Francisco. She never arrived. Kemper literally snuffed out her life in the darkness of an isolated spot in the mountains above the city of Santa Cruz.

Her mouth was taped shut and he pinched her nostrils together until she suffocated. Then he raped her inert body and put it in the trunk of his car. A few miles away, he stopped at a country bar "for a few beers."

Before going into the bar, he opened the trunk to make sure she was dead. He told investigators:

"I suppose as I was standing there looking, I was doing one of those triumphant things, too, admiring my work and admiring her beauty, and I might say admiring my catch like a fisherman."

Kemper also spoke of a sense of exultation in his killings:

"I just wanted the exaltation over the party. In other words, winning over death. They were dead and I was alive. That was the victory in my case."

He said of the act of decapitation, "I remember it was very exciting ... there was actually a sexual thrill ... It was kind of an exalted triumphant type thing, like taking the head of a deer or an elk or something would be to a hunter.

"I was the hunter and they were the victims."

On the witness stand, though, Kemper testified that "death never entered as a factor" in the coed killings. He said:

"Alive, they were distant, not sharing with me. I was trying to establish a relationship and there was no relationship there...

"When they were being killed, there wasn't anything going on in my mind except that they were going to be mine ... That was the only way they could be mine." (Kemper testified that as a child of eight he had killed his pet cat, which had transferred its affections to his two sisters, "to make it mine.")

His desire to possess the coeds led Kemper even further than murder, he revealed in court. In his fantasies he literally made two of the girls "a part of me" by eating "parts of them."

Of all his coed victims, he said: "They were like spirit wives... I still had their spirits. I still have them," he declared in the courtroom.

Kemper did not kill again until after he bought a .22-caliber pistol in January of this year.

"I went bananas after I got that .22," he told me.

The day he bought it, he fatally shot coed Cynthia Schall, a 19-year-old Santa Cruz girl, in the trunk of his car. He carried her body into his mother's apartment near Santa Cruz, kept it in his bedroom closet overnight and dissected it in the bathtub the next day while his mother was at work.

He buried the girl's head in the back yard "with her face turned toward my bedroom window and, sometimes at night, I talked to her, saying love things, the way you do to a girlfriend or wife."

Less than a month later, Kemper picked up two girls, Rosalind Thorpe, 23, and Alice Liu, 21, on the campus of the University of California at Santa Cruz (UCSC). He shot them both to death in the car before driving off campus and later cut off their heads in the trunk of his car while it was parked in the street in front of his mother's apartment.

He told investigators the killings came on an impulse born out of anger with his mother.

"My mother and I had had a real tiff. I was pissed. I told her I was going to a movie and I jumped up and went straight to the campus because it was still early.

"I said, the first girl that's halfway decent that I pick up, I'm gonna blow her brains out," he revealed.

Kemper's final killings were those of his mother, Mrs. Clarnell Strandberg, 52, and her best friend, Mrs. Sara Hallett, 59, in his mother's apartment on Easter weekend. Then he began a cross-country flight, in a rented car loaded with guns and ammunition, that ended in a decision to surrender, "so I wouldn't kill again."

On April 24, 1973, he was arrested in a public telephone booth in Pueblo, Colo., after he had called policemen he knew in Santa Cruz to say he was the coed killer and told them where to find the bodies of his mother and Mrs. Hallett.

The afternoon I went to see Kemper in the Santa Cruz County jail where he was being kept pending sentencing the next morning, I expected to talk to him for an hour or so, in the presence of a jailer. Instead, I spent over five hours alone with him, locked up in a tiny glass-walled room within sight but not sound of the jailer's desk. Though he wore manacles on his ankles, his hands were free.

Disarming as he is at times, more than once during the long afternoon I was reminded that I was sitting face to face with a six-foot, nine-inch 255-pound giant who had murdered and mutilated six coeds, beaten his sleeping mother to death with a hammer and strangled his mother's best friend in a matter of seconds. The frequent traffic of jailers and inmates past the glass wall was reassuring comfort.

My visit with Kemper was an unforgettable experience, inducing a collage of feelings. As he talked on and on, he was many things.

- A lonely young man, grateful for companionship on the eve of what was certainly to be his last day outside prison.

- An angry and bitter sibling recalling what he felt was rejection and a lack of love from a divorced father who "cared more for his second family than he did us."

• A son who alternately hated and "loved" a mother he described as a "manhater" who had three husbands and "took her violent hatred of my father out on me."

• A sometimes wry and boastful raconteur, chronicling the events of his life and a person quick to see the humorous side of things and laugh, even if the joke is on him.

• An anguished and remorseful killer when speaking of the coeds whose bodies he had sexually assaulted after death and of the "pain" he had caused their families. "The day those fathers [of the Pesce and Luchessa girls] testified in court was very hard for me … I felt terrible. I wanted to talk to them about their daughters, comfort them … But what could I say?"

Kemper also was a person who momentarily precipitated in me a flush of terror and then allayed my misgivings by faultlessly assuming the role of the gracious host. He talked about the jury's verdict that morning. He had pleaded not guilty and not guilty by reason of insanity to each of the killings.

Court-appointed psychiatrists, called to testify by the prosecution, described Kemper as suffering from a "personality disorder," but said he was not criminally insane by California's legal standards. One doctor called Kemper a "sadistic sex maniac."

The jury found Kemper was guilty and sane.

He didn't disagree with the jury's verdict.

"I really wasn't surprised when it came out that way," he said. "There was just no way they could find me insane … Society just isn't ready for that yet. Ten or 20 years from now they would have, but they're not going to take a chance."

But he expressed regret that the "sane" verdict would mean he would go to prison, instead of possibly returning to Atascadero state hospital.

Kemper spent five years at Atascadero after he murdered his grandparents in 1964 at the age of 15. He recalled with pride the job he'd held there as head of the psychological testing lab at the age of 19 and working directly under the hospital's chief psychologist. He said:

"I felt I definitely could have done a lot of good there, helping people return to the streets ... I could have fit in there quicker than anybody else...

"After all," he explained, "I grew up there. That used to be like my home.

"Basically, I was born there, you know. I have a lot of fond memories of the place ... And I don't know anybody else who has," he added with a rueful laugh.

It was there that he became a member of the Junior Chamber of Commerce. During his trial, he wore his membership pin in his lapel, apparently with pride.

Because of his intelligence and ability, he apparently was a valuable aide in psychological testing and research. "I helped to develop some new tests and some new scales on MMPI... You've probably heard of it ... the Minnesota Multiphasic Personality Inventory," he said with a chuckle. "I helped to develop a new scale on that, the 'Overt Hostility Scale'... How's that for a..." He groped for a word.

"Ironic?" I suggested.

"Ironic note," he agreed. "There we go, it was an ironic note that I helped to develop that scale and then look what happened to me when I got back out on the streets."

Though Kemper couldn't give me a positive answer to why he did what he did, he partly blamed society, the courts and his parents as well, saying:

"I didn't have the supervision I should have had once I got out... I was supposed to see my parole officer every other week and a social worker the other week.

"I never did. I think if I had, I would have made it.

"Two weeks after I was on the streets, I got scared because I hadn't seen anyone.

"Finally, I called the district parole office and asked if I was doing something wrong... was I supposed to go to my parole officer, or would he come to see me, I asked."

Kemper said the man on the phone asked him, "What's the matter, you got a problem?" When Kemper told him, "no," the man replied, "Well, we're awfully busy with people who have; we'll get to you."

Kemper blamed the court for counteracting the plan of Atascadero doctors to release him in stages geared to get him accustomed to the world outside again. He said they planned to send him to a "halfway house" environment where he would still have counseling, have a chance to get acquainted with girls at social functions and become aware of persons in his own age group.

"When I got out on the street it was like being on a strange planet. People my age were not talking the same language. I had been living with people older than I was for so long that I was an old fogey."

Instead, Kemper was sent to a California Youth Authority institution by court order, only to be released abruptly five months later, paroled to the custody of a mother who was "an alcoholic and constantly bitched and screamed at me."

Kemper looked down at his hands and said, "She loved me in her way and despite all the violent screaming and yelling arguments we had, I loved her, too." "But," he continued, "she had to manage your life... and interfere in your personal affairs."

He said his mother was a "big, ugly, awkward woman who was six feet tall and she was always trying to get me to go out with girls who were just like her... friends of hers from the campus." (His mother was an administrative assistant at UCSC.)

"I may not be so much to look at myself," Kemper said with a laugh, "but I have always gone after pretty girls."

All of his hitchhiking coed victims were pretty and, with the exception of one girl, were small and delicate in stature.

Of his father, he said, "he didn't want me around, because I upset his second wife. Before I went to Atascadero, my presence gave her migraine headaches; when I came out she was going to have a heart attack if I came around."

It was because of that, Kemper said, that he was "shipped off" to his paternal grandparents to live in "complete isolation" on a California mountain top with "my senile grandfather" and "my grandmother who thought she had more balls than any man and was constantly emasculating me and my grandfather to prove it.

"I couldn't please her... It was like being in jail... I became a walking time bomb and I finally blew ... It was like that the second time, with my mother."

Kemper laughed as he recalled an incident with his grandmother when she left him home alone one day but took his grandfather's .45 automatic with her in her purse, because she was afraid he might "play" around with it in her absence. His grandparents were going to Fresno on a monthly shopping trip. He recalled:

"I saw her big black pocketbook bulging as she went out the door and I said to myself, 'Why that old bitch, she's taking the gun with her, because she doesn't trust me, even though I promised I wouldn't touch it.'"

He said he looked in his grandfather's bureau drawer and "sure enough the gun was gone from its usual place...

"I toyed with the idea of calling the chief of police in Fresno and telling him 'there's a little old lady walking around town with a forty-five in her purse and she's planning a holdup' and then give him my grandmother's description."

He laughed appreciatively at the idea and asked me: "How do you suppose she would have talked herself out of that?" There were moments, prior to her death, when he felt like punishing his mother, too. Kemper told investigators he had killed his mother to spare her the suffering and shame that knowledge of his crimes would bring. But, he said, as he sat in the little room with me:

"There were times when she was bitching and yelling at me that I felt like retaliating and walking over to the telephone in her presence and calling the police, to say, 'Hello, I'm the coed killer,' just to lay it on her."

Kemper's testimony in court revealed his desire to punish his mother did not end with the fatal hammer blow. He cut off his mother's head, "put it on a shelf and screamed at it for an hour ... threw darts at it," and ultimately, "smashed her face in," he recalled for the horrified court.

Once during the long afternoon, a deputy brought us in some coffee. Another one came to inquire if Kemper needed any medication. (Under doctor's orders he was allowed to have tranquillizers as required and sleeping pills at night.)

The jail nurse also came in while I was there and changed the bandage on his wrist where he had slashed an artery in one of his four suicide attempts after his arrest.

"Would you like to see my wound," he said, holding his arm out to me.

(The cutting instrument he had used to make the suicidal incision had been fashioned from the metal casing of a ball point pen I had given him. Jailers at the neighboring San Mateo county jail, where he was kept for security reasons after two suicide attempts in Santa Cruz, had failed to remove the pen from his folder of papers when Kemper returned from court.)

He had previously assured me, "It's not your fault." He tried to explain his suicide attempts, saying that he did not have a suicidal feeling when he was first "locked up." Then the "kindness and respect with which I was treated by the people [jail personnel] after a while started to get to me ...

"I started feeling like I didn't deserve all that nice treatment after what I had done ... and I guess that's why I started cutting myself up."

Kemper also talked about his previous statements that, if he were sent to prison he would kill someone so he could die in the gas chamber, and indicated he had had a change of heart.

"I guess you heard me say that I wanted to kill 'Herbie' Mullin, my fellow mass murderer," he said. (The Mullin story, *Chalk Up Another for Mr. Kill-Crazy*, appeared in the June, 1973, issue of INSIDE DETECTIVE.)

"Well, there was a time when I thought it would be a good solution for everyone.

"It would be good for society and save everyone a bundle of money. Instead of spending thousands and thousands of dollars to lock the two of us up for life to protect us from people and people from us...."

Kemper had told investigators and psychiatrists he thought he would kill again if he ever were released. He also admitted under cross examination by District Attorney Peter Chang that he had fantasized killing "thousands of people," including Chang himself. He said:

"I figured that if I killed him [Mullin] and then they sent me to the gas chamber, it would be a good solution to the problem.

"I know I'd never get a chance to though and I don't have any intention of killing him or anyone else...."

(Mullin was convicted of two counts of first-degree murder and eight counts of second-degree murder in the shooting deaths of ten persons he killed during a 21-day rampage early in 1973 in Santa Cruz County. Five of the victims were complete strangers to him. He said he killed three others in 1972.)

Kemper and Mullin were next-door neighbors in their security prisoner cellblock at the San Mateo County jail before Mullin was tried and convicted. Kemper made no secret of his disdain for Mullin from the first moment of their meeting in San Mateo.

"You're a no-class killer," he taunted him.

During Kemper's trial, under questioning from Chang, Kemper admitted he had thrown water through the cell bars onto Mullin to "shut him up when he was disturbing everybody by singing off- key in his high-pitched, squeaky voice."

Kemper added, though, "When he was a good boy, I gave him peanuts. He liked peanuts."

Kemper said of the alternate water treatment and the peanuts, "It was behavioral modification treatment... The jailers were very pleased with me."

"You know, though," Kemper told me, as he looked out of the window in the little room, "It really sticks in my craw that Mullin only got two 'firsts' and I got eight.

"He was just a cold-blooded killer, running over a three-week period killing everybody he saw for no good reason."

He paused for a moment, then broke into laughter, saying, "I guess that's kind of hilarious, my sitting here so self-righteously talking, like that, after what I've done."

When Kemper assured me that he had given up thoughts of trying to take his own life again, I asked him what he planned to do with the rest of his years in prison. He told me he knew he would be locked up in tight security for the first few years and that he thought he would try to do a lot of reading and studying. "I've always loved science and math," he said, "and I'd also like to study French and German.

"After that, I hope, I can find a way to help other people... Maybe they can study me and find out what makes people like me do the things they do."

(The next morning. Judge Harry F. Brauer sentenced Kemper to life in prison and told him he was going to recommend "in the strongest terms possible" that Kemper not be released for "the rest of your natural life.")

One relationship that obviously has touched Kemper is that with Bruce Colomy, Santa Cruz County sheriff's deputy. Colomy has been with Kemper more than any other officer, transporting him to and from San Mateo County Jail to Santa Cruz for court appearances and remaining with him at all times when he was out of his cell.

Kemper said of Colomy, only a few years older than himself, "He's more like a father to me than anyone I have ever known ... He's like the father I wish I had had."

(Deputy Colomy told me later that one of the last things Kemper did before he left the Santa Cruz courthouse for state prison was to remove his cherished Junior Chamber of Commerce membership pin from his coat lapel "and give it to me." The deputy said, "Ed looked at it for a long time and tears came to his eyes. Then he handed it to me and said, 'Here, I want you to have it.'")

For all of his seeming ability to relate to people in an animated and warm exchange, Kemper also has the ability to withdraw without warning into a kind of frightening reverie, reliving his acts of violence. I watched it happen.

He had paused in his outpouring of talk about himself and looked at me curiously. "You haven't asked the questions I expected a reporter to ask," he said.

"What do you mean," I replied. "Give me some examples."

He drawled, "Oh, what is it like to have sex with a dead body? ... What does it feel like to sit on your living room couch and look over and see two decapitated girls' heads on the arm of the couch?" (He interjected an unsolicited answer: "The first time, it makes you sick to your stomach.")

He continued, "What do you think, now, when you see a pretty girl walking down the street?"

Again, an unsolicited answer: "One side of me says, 'Wow, what an attractive chick. I'd like to talk to her, date her. The other side of me says, 'I wonder how her head would look on a stick?'"

The public defender appointed as Kemper's attorney told jurors in his closing argument: "There are two people locked up in the body of this young giant, one good and one evil... One is fighting to be here with us and the other is slipping off to his own little world of fantasy where he is happy."

"Oh, for God's sake, Ed," I said, just a trifle piqued by the feeling he was putting me on and hoping that was it, "the jury found you legally sane and I agree with that. But, at the same time, I can't help but believe that, as you yourself said, you must have been sick when you did the things you did.

Kemper, himself, earlier had told me he thought his actions were that of a "demented person."

"In my estimation," I continued, "it doesn't make any more sense to ask a delirious patient what he's thinking than it would to ask you what you were thinking when these things were going on."

Despite that, for the first time, he began to detail to me how he killed one of his victims. The illustration he chose made me even more uncomfortable. It was the killing of Mrs. Hallett, not a coed but a mature woman, like me.

Kemper straightened up in his chair and began a graphic description. "I came up behind her and crooked my arm around her neck, like this," he said, bending his powerful arm in front of himself at chin level.

"I squeezed and just lifted her off the floor. She just hung there and, for a moment, I didn't realize she was dead ... I had broken her neck and her head was just wobbling around with the bones of her neck disconnected in the skin sack of her neck."

He began to wobble his head around, never changing the position of his arms and gazing fixedly at me. His jail-pale face had become slightly flushed, his eyes glazed, his breath coming a little quickly and he stuttered almost imperceptibly as, he spoke.

"Holy Christ," I said to myself, "what am I doing here?"

I reached for a cigarette in my pocket and said the first thing that came into my mind to try and change the subject without showing I was upset. "Have you always been so strong, Ed," I asked in a nonchalant tone.

"No," he replied. "As a matter of fact..." he relaxed and then we were off and talking about other more comfortable topics.

The sky outside the windows of the little room had grown dark and I made efforts to leave, saying I had been "virtually incommunicado all day as far as my family was concerned and they would wonder why I had not arrived for dinner."

Kemper was reluctant for me to go. "Well, you can always tell them later, you have been over talking with Ed Kemper all afternoon," he laughed.

As it turned out, though, I stayed for dinner with Ed. The trusty had brought his dinner and it was getting cold. When I insisted that we should stop talking and that Kemper should eat, the jailer invited me to stay for dinner.

"Big Ed" urged me to accept and I did. He carried the trays into the little room himself and arranged them on the desk chairs. We chatted as we ate and he was the host. He ate hungrily and I noticed he had finished his rice with meat sauce. I had more than I could eat, so I offered to share. What seemed like a large portion to me must have been but a morsel to a large man like him.

He gratefully accepted the added food, but cautioned me as I scraped it from my tray on to his, "Save some for yourself."

I gave him my milk as well, saying, "I really hate milk, you can have it."

"Do you?" he said. "I love it."

When dinner was over, I said I must go and, when he got up and proceeded toward the door, I said, "Do you think you could knock on the window and get the jailer to spring me, Ed?"

He laughed and replied, "I'll try."

He stood in the doorway, his hair brushing the top of the door jamb, watching me leave, as if he were graciously bidding a guest goodbye from his home.

He said to a deputy, "Could I have some matches?" (I had been lighting his cigarettes all afternoon with my lighter.)

The sergeant on duty at the desk said to the deputy, "He can't have any matches, but light his cigarette for him." Kemper looked at me and grinned like a teenager. "Yesterday," he said, "I had matches, but isn't it funny when you're convicted, you immediately become combustible."

"Well, Ed," I retorted, "if you'd learn to stay out of trouble, you wouldn't find yourself in these predicaments."

"Right on," he said, with a final salute of his hand and a smile.

VACAVILLE — The petition quietly filed last month in Solano County Superior Court by California prison inmate No. B-52453 was a strange and unusual pleading.

It asked that the convict be allowed to undergo psychosurgery – an operation in which a portion of his brain would, quite literally, be killed.

"I have led a very violent life and wish to stop the violence while I can," the neatly handwritten petition explained. "I have been through, between 1964 and 1970, every accepted form of therapy with the result of eight more deaths at my hand."

Inmate B-52453 is 27-year-old Edmund Emil Kemper III of Santa Cruz County, murderer of 10 persons (among them his mother, two grandparents and six young women hitchhikers), all of them killed in hideous ways, most of them butchered after death.

Superior Court Judge Thomas Healy has denied Kemper's petition but left the door open to further proceedings if Kemper can prove his contention he has a "right" to psychosurgery. He ordered that Kemper receive legal counsel to explore the matter.

In his early teens, the juvenile court ordered Kemper confide to a state hospital for the criminally insane after it was discovered he had murdered his grandparents. Six years later, in 1970, he was released as rehabilitated.

In the spring of 1972, Kemper began killing again. Over the next year, six girls became his victims, then his mother and another woman, before he voluntarily surrendered to police on April 24, 1973, and confessed the eight killings.

Here at the California Medical Facility, where he has been confined under maximum security conditions since November 1973. Kemper is considered a "model" prisoner. He follows the rules, works hard at his job as a kitchen helper, and gets along well with both fellow inmates and prison staff.

That sort of convict report card would count a lot for an average inmate going before the Adult Authority in quest of a parole date.

In Kemper's case, he knows it doesn't mean anything.

"Ed's no different from any of us," said an inmate source housed in the same unit. "He dreams that one day they'll let him out — but he knows they won't unless he some way proves he's been "cured."

According to several Vacaville sources, Kemper believes psychosurgery will rid of him of his violent tendencies and allow him to live a normal life as a free man again . . . somewhere down the line. But the hope to be free of violence outweighs the dream of parole, those who know Kemper say.

But the California Department of Corrections does not share Kemper's faith in psychosurgery. In fact, the CDC, by policy rather than law, has virtually outlawed the controversial method as a treatment for severely mentally-ill inmates.

The main reason is because it has yet to be proven that psychosurgery really can cure someone of, say, the urge to kill.

"There is just no way psychosurgery can be realistically evaluated at this time," said Dr. Eugene Prout, chief medical officer at the Vacaville facility. "Much more study is needed and I agree with those who say that the prison system his no place to be studying it."

Dr. Prout emphasized that Kemper has never "formally requested" of the CDC that the operation be performed. Instead, he went straight to the courts "And I want to stress this," he added, "I can assure you that no member of this staff has suggested or recommended to Kemper that it be done."

Kemper has enlisted the support of one medical man, Dr. M. Hunter Brown, in his efforts to have such an operation.

His petition states he has engaged in "extended written contact" with the Santa Monica neurosurgeon.

Dr. Brown, Kemper said in his petition, "has convinced me that he can, with a proven form of psychosurgery, relieve me of the violence of my life."

Dr. Brown, who has reportedly performed nearly 300 psychosurgery operations, could not be reached for comment on Kemper's case.

What's involved in psychosurgery, according to Dr. Prout, is an operational procedure known as stereotactic neurosurgery, so-called "because the position of the probe that is inserted into the brain is determined by X rays from two different angles. Sort of like determining your position on the nautical chart."

There are three different methods that may be employed too, as Dr. Prout put it, "obliterate very small portions of the brain." Each method begins the same way, with the drilling of a hole in the patient's skull."

When the area of the brain to be "obliterated" is reached, the tissue can be killed by the application of either extreme cold (a procedure known as cryosurgery) or certain chemicals, such as absolute alcohol (chemosurgery).

A third—and in recent years the most widely employed—method involves the insertion of a probe with a steel wire loop that, "like a cantaloupe scoop," cuts the desired portion of the brain away from its life source—its supply of blood. The cutaway area, about the size of a marble, is not removed. It merely dies, becoming scar tissue.

Critics of psychosurgery contend that while today's methods are more sophisticated than those involved in the era of frontal lobotomy, the results still are unproven. The usual procedure then was to insert an instrument similar to an ice pick through the eye socket to blindly stab away at the brain tissue.

"The height of enthusiasm for the ice pick method was in the 1940s," said Dr. Prout. It "waned" in the 1950s, he said, and "there probably hasn't been such an operation in the last 15 years—it was a pretty crude approach. It was never employed in the CDC, but it was expanded within state mental hospitals."

In 1968, three convicts underwent operations in which portions of their brain tissue were killed. "These were inmates suffering from temporal lobe epilepsy," explained Dr. Prout. "The operations were medical—they were not performed for the purpose of personality control or change, though afterwards we obviously looked for that, too."

The result: "They weren't particularly successful. The inmates still suffered seizures and exhibited sociopathic traits," said Dr. Prout. That was the last such surgery in California prisons.

Vacaville officials will not discuss Kemper's case specifically, anticipating that they may one day have to appear in court on the matter. As things stand at the moment, Kemper's petition has been "denied without prejudice." Judge Healy ruled that "it does not appear that the legislature thus far has provided for the initiation of (such) proceedings by an individual prisoner ..."

The Solano County public defender's office, Kemper's new legal counsel, will only say that "we're looking into it."

Kemper himself has declined interviews.

ED KEMPER FAILED Tuesday in his half-hearted first attempt to win parole, admitting to a three-member panel of the board he doesn't "see my release as feasible – as morally or legally feasible."

Without emotion, panel chairman Ruth Rushen Tuesday detailed the eights murders, Kemper's decapitation of his victims and his disposal of their bodies in various counties, but Kemper demanded the official record be changed to reflect the accurate "facts" and proceeded to recount each of the slayings again.

At the time he made statements to authorities in 1973, he said he was "suicidal" and "in my unwise immature judgment, I thought I was trying to build a psychiatric case against me. I needed help. I wanted help. And I made statements unsubstantiated by fact that are now being introduced as fact."

"I was suicidal in my feelings at the time. I was trying to seal my fate."

Officials, he went on Tuesday, were so anxious to convict him of the slayings "they left loopholes that I could use for an appeal, but I do not intend to take advantage of them."

His actions "distressed me greatly" at the time, but "things still happen out there on the streets," he added.

Kemper, who received an award two weeks ago for contributing 2 900 hours during the past two years tape recording books for the blind has sought court permission three times for psycho-surgery. He denied Tuesday the request was an attempt to gain his release or that he still felt an urge to kill.

"I felt I had one foot in a coffin and one on a banana peel" and his circumstances in the medical facility might result in violence, he suggested, "I didn't like being controlled by my dislikes."

Kemper, who also told the panel he has become a Christian while at Vacaville and has "learned to live with myself and God," admitted the State of California has "more than enough reason to keep me locked up for the rest of my life. I have to say eight people are dead and I murdered them."

After a half-hour deliberation, Rushen reconvened the hearing and said, "Mr. Kemper, you are not suitable for parole."

She cited the "extreme violence and depravity" of his crimes and called Kemper "an unreasonable risk to society at this time." His crimes, she went on, were premeditated and planned in meticulous detail, including bizarre conduct in "abusing, defiling and mutilating the victims' bodies, which shows a total disregard for the worth of another human being."

During a break in Edmund Kemper's parole hearing at Vacaville Tuesday, Richard F. Verbrugge, inspector with the Santa Cruz County District Attorney's Office, said Kemper was questioned by Sonoma County authorities as a suspect in the murder of several hitchhiking girls here that began in 1972.

Verbrugge said he worked closely with sheriff's homicide Detective Sgt. Butch Carlsted on the Sonoma County cases, but that Kemper was ruled out as a suspect.

"He was like a little boy, telling us everything and taking us everywhere," the inspector said. Kemper was also given truth serum by officials during his initial examination. However, Verbrugge said Kemper did admit he picked up young girl hitchhikers in Sonoma County during his cruise through Bay Area counties seeking young girls that met "his criteria" for victims, but none of them apparently had the characteristics he sought.

EDITOR'S NOTE – Due to a decision by the state Parole Board, only one reporter from this area was allowed to be present at Edmund Kemper's parole hearing Tuesday. That reporter was Mark Von B of the *Watsonville Register-Pajaronian*, who filed this report.

COED KILLER ED KEMPER, IMPRISONED IN 1973 ON EIGHT first-degree murder counts, will not be freed next year, a state prison parole board decided Tuesday.

Kemper, 30, was found to be "unsuitable for release at this time," but the board's decision did not seem to dismay him.

He told the three-member board at the conclusion of a three-hour hearing at the Vacaville State Medical Facility, "I'd have refused to be considered for parole but I didn't want to be provocative."

Earlier, he had stated to the board that he felt his release on parole was not "feasible, legal or moral," saying he had been sentenced to prison by Santa Cruz County Superior Court Judge Harry F. Brauer "for the rest of your natural life."

EDMUND EMIL KEMPER
Called 'unreasonable risk'

In addition, Kemper said, "I don't want to set a precedent of being a person two-times released after multiple murders. I don't want to ever hurt anybody again."

Kemper killed his grandmother and grandfather when he was 15, and was sent to Atascadero State Mental Hospital and then to the California Youth Authority where he was paroled in 1970.

But during the hearing, in which he was represented by a lawyer, Steve Bedient of Sacramento, Kemper seemed bent on personally straightening out the state's recorded versions of his crimes.

Part of the hearing procedure was the reading of a summary of his criminal history into the record by the chairman, Ruth Rushen.

It was a recitation of brutality, sexual depravity and violence, detailing the killing of six young women, Kemper's mother and one of her best friends.

According to a confession made to police after his surrender, Kemper said he had sexually assaulted the coeds after killing them, and then had dismembered their bodies disposing of them in sites in Santa Cruz and other adjacent counties.

As Mrs. Rushen read on, in a strange contrast, birds chirped in a tree outside the windows of the second story prison conference room.

Then Santa Cruz District Attorney Art Danner was asked to add his comments for the record, and he noted that the material related by

Mrs. Rushen did not reflect the fact that "parts" of one of the bodies of Kemper's victims had been "cannibalized by the defendant."

Nor, Danner said, did it reflect that Kemper had "mutilated" parts of his mother's body "by putting it into the garbage disposal."

Kemper refuted the confession, saying that in telling the police the lurid details, "In my unwise and immature judgment, I thought I was building a case supporting my psychiatric plea (of not guilty by reason of insanity)."

"I disclaim any sexual misconduct during any of my crimes," he said emphatically. "I made those statements when it was understood that I was to be the only witness at my trial."

And he added, "I am not a cannibal. That's unsubstantiated and only claimed by me."

"As every hunter knows, I could get physically ill or die from eating an animal or person in that state," Kemper argued.

In his account of the murders, Kemper said he had been trying to "go to Atascadero instead of state prison. I was trying to get myself locked up for good."

"I was trying to seal my fate, and the state in presenting its case botched it. I have ample opportunity now to save myself in the courts," Kemper said.

But then he continued, "I'm not going to avail myself of them."

Kemper also denied that he recently sought court permission to have psychosurgery to help him get out of prison later. Kemper said, "I asked for multi-target neurosurgery in the hope of gaining relief from any kind of homicidal tendencies whatsoever."

The court denied his request.

Asked if he was "still having urges to kill people," Kemper said, "No."

But he explained, "I felt as if I had one foot in the coffin and one on a banana peel."

He said he was afraid that "if some time I had a bad day and a prison officer or technician had a bad day and was provocative or insulting, I might smack his head up against the wall, and I would die in CDC (California Department of Corrections)."

Kemper referred to a state law which demands the death penalty for the murder of a prison guard or official.

But then he said mildly, "I am not known for a very short temper. I am a passive aggressive."

And in a sort of aside to himself, Kemper, who works as a clerk in a prison psychotherapy ward, said, "I've had nine diagnoses in my time. I wonder how many of them are valid?"

Kemper also appeared offended at a statement in a psychiatric report that he had shown no remorse for all the killings.

"I feel very strongly about what I've done," he said. "I do feel remorse in what I've done."

But when pressed for a reason behind his killings. Kemper always seemed to return to his relationship with his mother.

"I hate her fucking guts," he said in a rare explosive moment during the hearing.

He said he had turned to killing the six women because he was "feeling persecuted and destroyed by my mother."

And it was his childhood hatred of his mother that led him to kill his grandparents, too, he revealed.

But he explained, "I'm not blaming my mother. I'm saying I hate my mother."

After the coed murders, Kemper said he was "sick of killing," but murdered his mother knowing that would "blow the whistle."

He said, "If she died they (the police) were going to get me, and if they got me for her, they would get me for the others."

Kemper denied he killed his mother's friend to make persons think the two women were always together for a weekend and give him time to flee before an investigation of their disappearance.

Incongruously he said, "I killed her because she had hurt my mother very grievously."

The board members also talked with Kemper about his adjustment to prison life.

According to prison reports he is "doing an outstanding job" as a therapy clerk, has no disciplinary problems and "gets along with the staff and his peers."

He was asked by board member Craig Brown why he got along well in Vacaville and other institutions "and in the community you become violent?"

"Because when I am in a structured situation. I can get help when I need it," Kemper replied. "But on the streets I felt rather forgotten and sometimes I felt abandoned."

The loquacious Kemper later expounded on his life in prison saying, "I was convinced when I came here, I would soon be dead."

"But the last six months have been the best of my life. I've learned to live with myself and with God. I believe I have an obligation to myself and the people around me."

He also spoke with pride of his work in recording books on tape for the blind and the handicapped which recently won him a public service award.

However, Danner warned the board not to be complacent about Kemper.

"It's the kind of complacency he wants," Danner said, "the kind that was seen at Atascadero where he was released to kill again."

The district attorney said, "Mr. Kemper poses such an unreasonable risk and danger to society, he is now unsuitable for release and probably will remain so for the rest of his life."

After a 30-minute deliberation in private, the board called Kemper, the lawyers and the press back into the room and announced its decision.

Chairman Rushen outlined the reasons for denying the parole.

First, she said Kemper's crimes "contained elements of such extraordinary violence that it was incomprehensible to think that he should be released at this time."

Also:

> – He had a previous record of violence and although his juvenile record was sealed, "he stated several times during the hearing that he had killed his grandparents.

> – "His violent and bizarre conduct after the crimes which included mutilation and defiling of the corpses of the victims, showed a total disregard for the dignity and worth of a fellow human ... and this included the victims and their families."

> – The psychology reports do not support the suitability for release.

Mrs. Rushen noted that the latest report on Kemper, dated in March of this year, diagnosed him as a paranoid schizophrenic in a state of "good remission." But she added the report said that there was no way to predict the possibility of his violence in the future if he is released.

Kemper greeted the decision with a smile and thanked the board.

Referring to an initial outburst and his demand that the press and one reporter in particular be barred from the hearing. Kemper said, "I would like to apologize for my untoward and abusive behavior, although it's probably better than some you've had in here," he added with a chuckle.

Then with a wave of his hand, the six-foot, nine-inch inmate, known as "Big Ed" ambled down the long hall and was admitted into the locked area of the prison building.

"NO PAROLE FOR HOMICIDAL GIANT" - THE PRESS DEMOCRAT (MAY 1ST, 1980) - JAMES E. REID

No parole for homicidal giant

By JAMES E. REID

VACAVILLE — Commenting that he was "trying to keep a light air here, rather than being extremely serious," Edmund E. Kemper III Wednesday told the Community Release Board, "I don't see a place for me in society ever again."

At the second of his parole hearings, John Brooks, chairman of the three-man panel, told the six-foot nine-inch murderer he is "unsuitable for parole."

Kemper was convicted of killing his mother and her friend, as well as six young women he picked up as they were hitchhiking in the Bay Area. He was sent to the California Medical Facility at Vacaville Nov. 9, 1973.

Kemper also killed his maternal grandparents in Madera County when he was 15 and was placed with the California Youth Authority, which in turn sent him to Atascadero State Hospital. He was released Feb. 1, 1971, when he turned 21, and he went on to murder eight women.

The release board hearings are conducted on the second floor of the medical facility, in a room with dark paneling and broad tables. The proceedings are tape recorded and a court reporter also takes notes of the discussions.

Wednesday, someone had tied a small noose in the end of a venitian blind cord across the room from where Kemper calmly sat in his blue denim prison uniform.

Kemper criticized the news media for interpreting his remarks at his first, half-hearted parole hearing last year as meaning he does not want to be released from state prison.

"I have tried the door, gentlemen, and I assure you all is secure," he told the release board last year, adding that the State of California has "more than enough reason to keep me locked up for the rest of my life. I have to say eight people are dead and I murdered them."

At Wednesday's hearing, Kemper seemed to show more interest in seeking his own release from prison, but he appeared like a small boy in a candy store, not only afraid to reach out and touch the candy, but also unwilling to admit to himself or others that he wanted some.

"I literally sink my own boat and I do it quite frequently," he said. But he said the issue is not a matter of his not wanting to be released, it is the fact that he believes he can find no place for himself in society. He said he is a "maniac" in the eyes of society, and he believes he has 230 million enemies in the United States and 5 billion beyond its borders.

"I might as well be on Mars," he went on. "I don't see a parole in my future, so I've made no formal plans" for his life following release from prison, which is a routine question asked by the board.

In addition to objecting to the presence of four reporters at his hearing, Kemper also said the presence of a deputy district attorney and investigator from Santa Cruz County turned what he interpreted as an "information exchange" hearing into an adversary proceeding.

Prison psychologist R J. Brooks advised the panel Kemper has "narcissistic and schizo-typical personality disorders" and said he is constantly suspicious of other people's motives, as well as his own.

However, the psychologist said Kemper is learning to accept criticism and made a difficult emotional decision in the past year which led to his quitting the prison project making tapes of books for the blind, at which he spent 3,600 volunteer hours during his incarceration.

Santa Cruz Deputy DA John Hopkins argued, however, that Kemper lacked a basic understanding of the enormous atrocity of his crimes and seemed to "gloss" over the events. Kemper's victims were dismembered after they were brutally slain.

Hopkins said Kemper's crimes were "especially heinous and atrocious" and they were comitted in a

---

COMMENTING that he was "trying to keep a light air here, rather than being extremely serious," Edmund E. Kemper III Wednesday told the Community Release Board, "I don't see a place for me in society ever again."

At the second of his parole hearings, John Brooks, chairman of the three-man panel, told the six-foot nine-inch murderer he is "unsuitable for parole."

Kemper was convicted of killing his mother and her friend, as well as six young women he picked up as they were hitchhiking in the Bay

Area. He was sent to the California Medical Facility at Vacaville, Nov. 9, 1973.

Kemper also killed his maternal grandparents in Madera County when he was 15 and was placed with the California Youth Authority which in turn sent him to Atacadero State Hospital. He was released Feb. 1, 1971, when he turned 21, and he went on to murder eight women.

The release board hearings are conducted on the second floor of the California Medical Facility, in a room with dark paneling and broad tables. The proceedings are tape recorded and a court reporter also takes notes of the discussions.

Wednesday, someone had tied a small noose in the end of a venetian blind cord across the room from where Kemper calmly sat in his blue denim prison uniform.

Kemper criticized the news media for interpreting his remarks at his first half-hearted parole hearing last year as meaning he does not want to be released from state prison.

"I have tried the door, gentlemen, and I assure you all is secure," he told the release board last year, adding that the State of California has "more than enough reason to keep me locked up for the rest of my life. I have to say eight people are dead and I murdered them."

At Wednesday's hearing, Kemper seemed to show more interest in seeking his own release from prison, but he appeared like a small boy in a candy store, not only afraid to reach out and touch the candy, but also unwilling to admit to himself or others that he wanted some.

"I literally sink my own boat and I do it quite frequently," he said. But he said the issue is not a matter of his not wanting to be released, it is the fact that he believes he can find no place for himself in society. He said he is a "maniac" in the eyes of society, and he believes he has 230 million enemies in the United States and 5 billion beyond its borders.

"I might as well be on Mars," he went on. "I don't see a parole in my future, so I've made no formal plans" for his life following release from prison, which is a routine question asked by the board.

In addition to objecting to the presence of four reporters at his hearing, Kemper also said the presence of a deputy district attorney and investigator from Santa Cruz County turned what he interpreted as an "information exchange" hearing into an adversary proceeding.

Prison psychologist R.J. Brooks advised the panel Kemper has "narcissistic and schizo-typical personality disorders" and said he is constantly suspicious of other people's motives, as well as his own.

However, the psychologist said Kemper is learning to accept criticism and made a difficult emotional decision in the past year which led to his quitting the prison project making tapes of books for the blind, at which he spent 3,600 volunteer hours during his incarceration.

Santa Cruz Deputy DA John Hopkins argued, however, that Kemper lacked a basic understanding of the enormous atrocity of his crimes and seemed to "gloss" over the events. Kemper's victims were dismembered after they were brutally slain.

Hopkins said Kemper's crimes were "especially heinous and atrocious" and they were committed in a "dispassionate and calculated manner, with no real explicable motive."

"He seems to gloss over things, despite his attention to minute detail, and seems unable to really contemplate what underlies this" hearing, Hopkins said. He is making every "effort to distract attention from what's really been done."

Kemper, on the other hand, said he has wasted 25 years of his life and feels "an obligation to do something positive, not just sit here and cry for society."

After approximately 45 minutes of deliberation by the board, Brooks told Kemper he is still "unsuitable for parole." Adding that his murders were extremely violent, including dismemberment and decapitation of his victims, which showed "a total disregard for human dignity."

Brooks said the board would follow his psychiatrist's recommendation that he be held for "a long period of observation."

"A DAY WITH KEMPER" (MAY 1980) - A REMEMBRANCE BY JOEY TRANCHINA

OVER THE COURSE of 10 hours, on an otherwise sunny Northern California day, I shot 10 rolls of Tri-X & 5 rolls of Kodachrome focused on the prison life of convicted serial killer, Ed Kemper.

Even though I had worked very happily with Leonard Wolf, both as grad student and professional collaborator, I was not enthusiastic about this project and I had made my objections known to Leonard.

The gruesome character of Kemper's ten murders certify him as deeply disturbed, by any human standard, yet Kemp's intense mental acuity, masked evidence of psychosis, if he didn't come pre-packaged with a scrap-book of victims, I don't know that I would have sorted him out as a potential killer. That was the most frightening element of the day spent shadowing his life. When I was with him, he looked nothing like a killer on the hunt, I wouldn't have seen it, had I not already known the man he was, by knowing what he had done.

The nature of this assignment required that I'd do more than show up without doing homework. Weeks before our day trip to Vacaville, I spent hours in the library at San Francisco State, pulling together the information that, now, you could find in 2 minutes on the internet.

For homework, I read all of the jaw-droopingly shocking quotes, of a thoughtful, reflective, and articulate man who became a monster.

Having seen more than enough horror in my life, none of what I learned attracted me to the project. When I drive by an auto accident, I look only long enough to make sure that there's someone at the scene taking care of the victims. Once I see that there is, I turn away. I have no fascination with the gruesome or grotesque. Add to that the fact that I grew up in the Santa Cruz mountains, where Kemper stalked and killed his victims, I was turned off to the idea of being in the same space with this person.

Several times I thought that Leonard Wolf doubted that I had the proper open mind-set, to accomplish his mission, until finally, we had a conversation where he spoke about the psychological perversity of Kemper's childhood, and about his life in virtual isolation — never as a way to attempt to excuse Kemper's inexcusable acts rather as a way to attempt to understand them. This was bridging a chasm.

That conversation, more than anything else, brought me around to the challenge to tell a dark and complex story in images. I set out to construct a bridge between the monster and the man. Thus began my constant quasi-desperate search to unearth Ed Kemper's humanity, without becoming an apologist for acts of inhumanity.

I would attempt to see Edmund Kemper, the human being and not try to characterize him as one of the most notorious, violent, terrifying serial killers of my lifetime.

What I came to appreciate about working with Kemp and dealing with our time together afterwards, was the fact that he did not seem to gloat over his actions or take perverse pride in what he had done; rather he had, of necessity I'd guess, developed a respect for his inner turmoil — the rage that drove him to commit those anti-human acts. What Garcia Lorca wrote about as *"el duende"* — the inner demon &

well-spring of creative expression — is also the combination to a lock on darker capacities.

The first question I asked Edmund Kemper was: "How does it make you feel when people come from all over the world to interview you?" To which Kemp answered: "How would you feel if people came from around the world to talk to you and all they EVER wanted to talk about was the 13 worst things you EVER did?" I realized that even though my hit-singles were not in the same league with cutting my mother's head off and shoving her voice box down a garbage disposal, on a human level, what he asked me to think about made me feel bad. This man who had, unquestionably, done terrible things; was now facing the rest of — what could be and has turned out to be — a long life in prison to contemplate the evil forces that drove him to commit unpardonable acts.

It is sad that Ed Kemper will never be released from prison, but it is not unjust. Kemper's demonstrable capacity to commit otherwise unimaginable horrors is undeniable. The risk of Kemp's liberty would be too great, yet, in the same breath, it must be acknowledged that Ed Kemper has used his life sentence in the service of his prison community while he did work that benefited the community at large.

Imperfect criminal justice systems execute the innocent along with the guilty — Kemper's case does not fit that rubric. However, Kemper's execution would have done nothing to change the unpardonable acts of his past, while it would have precluded every decent, useful and beautiful that he has done in prison. Considering the lives of his victims, Kemper's execution could not fairly have been called an injustice, but considering the life he has lead in prison, it would have been a mistake. However, it is Kemper's remarkable art work that, ultimately, confirmed my faith in the futility of the death penalty.

Because of powerful forces beyond his control Edmund Kemper is too high-risk to be on the street, but in 41 years of incarceration, he has been a model prison-citizen, an effective functionary and a very interesting artist, whose ceramic designs have amazed me and astonished my friends for almost 35 years. The cup Kemp mailed to me, almost 35 years ago, continues to delight me every day.

May 1980

After several weeks of intermittently serious discussion, Leonard Wolf realized that my not unreasonable angst toward Ed Kemper had evolved to the point that I was prepared to be in the same space with him, which was the basic requirement for the job. The standard that I demanded of myself was higher. Before I would take on the assignment, I had to believe that I could approach a man, who I knew to be a vicious serial murderer, as a human being. After long discussions with Leonard Wolf I believed that I could do that — not without some discomfort.

Since there was paperwork involved in obtaining permission for me to enter a state prison — I know the sign reads "Correctional Facility" but it's a prison — it was a couple of weeks before Leonard and I set off on a lovely fall morning for the 62 mile drive from San Francisco State University to California State Correctional Facility Vacaville. I've been trying to remember what we talked about on the drive but, as clearly as I can recall, there was nothing more said to prep me for meeting Kemper. What I remember most clearly is that I was anxious to get on with it.

If you've never been to a prison, imagine driving up to a medieval fort built of concrete, steel and razor wire instead of stone... hold the moat. After a little over an hour in the car, we parked in a surprisingly large parking lot, unloaded camera equipment and walked up to the gate. If you've ever heard the thunk of pneumatic locks that unlock and roll-back huge steel gates then slam-shut behind you, you know the feeling of being in prison. Knowing that you have only to ask, in order to be able to leave, improves your long term outlook but does nothing to alleviate the sinking feeling you get in the pit of your guts when those doors slam shut....

Walking into the reception center where all inmates and professional visitors must pass, I am more than ready to pass this bureaucratic barrier to meet Edmund Kemper. I expect the next hurdle to be the awkward formality of an introduction to a person who has murdered ten people six of whom went to school with people I knew.

I was looking forward to breezing through that official barrier, by letting Dr. Wolf manage the bureaucrats, so that I could get on to explore a relationship with a challenging new subject through my camera. "Foiled again..." as they say in 19th century crime novels. There was a delay. A sort of serial-killer paparazzi traffic jam, as a German film-crew was already in with Kemper, so we would have to wait our turn with the great man...

This is when I learned that Kemper lived in an interesting neighborhood... his across-the-hall-neighbor, was Charles Manson... on a street with assorted other illuminati. Lieutenant Strong, who was to be out chaperone, for the afternoon, asked why we weren't interested in Manson,"He's the fascinating one."

After about an hour, the German TV crew emerged, Leonard, who began life as a Yiddish poet, spoke German with the producer. Having no German language skills, I tried my Dutch on the cameraman. Fortunately, for both of us, he spoke English, but it didn't take much talking to sense that the entire crew was visibly shaken. All I remember him saying was that Ed Kemper was not at all what they expected. They'd been traveling around America, shooting prison interviews with serial killers, but this experience was somehow more disturbing. The last thing he said was: "Talk with him, after you talk with him you will understand." Finally, I was going to get a chance to do that...

As I'd hoped, Leonard took care of everything with the administration, so that all I had to do was show my drivers license and walk in. Carrying a silver Halliburton case with two Nikon Fs and a Leica M4, strobe lights and a Gitzo tripod down the corridors, was a very unusual way to enter prison. It seemed like rows of convicts thought so too. until we turned into the short and relatively quiet corridor where Edmund Emil Kemper III lived, across the hall from a cell which was occupied by Charlie Manson's guitar — at least that's all I ever saw of him.

Finally, finally, finally… we turned left and there was Ed Kemper. What do they say in Ireland: "He's a fine door-full of a man," well at 6'9" and about 300 pounds, he was all that. Lieutenant Strong, quite discretely I thought, pulled back into the corridor and allowed us some privacy — or at least the illusion of privacy — for our interview. Leonard introduced us" Joey, Ed" — "Ed, Joey." Hello Joey; Hi Ed. What does one say, not knowing serial killer etiquette? Then he said: "Call me Kemp." Yes, sir.. "Good to meet you Kemp, I've waited for a long time." He said; I've heard.

There we were. Then next thing he was showing us around his "house." Books, bed, desk. short tour except that he had a ceramics project in progress on his desk — More on this later…

I'm in; I'm here in the room with this reputed monster, who seems like a polite and gentle giant. My antennae got no danger signals. i'd been around the world a couple of times and around the block more than once. I expected to sense the danger in this person. It was not there, which disturbed more than sensing something to put me on guard. How could I not tell that the person with whom I was sharing a very tight space, was not just a killer but a cannibal?

I was very disturbed. I should have been speechless and let Leonard guide the conversation — after all, he had spent hundreds of hours with Kemper. At this point Leonard knew Kemper, probably, better than anyone ever had, including the psychiatrist who told the parole board that Kemper represented "no threat to society" and could be safely released, after he had killed only two of his 10 eventual victims.   Anyway, rather than going about this the methodical, probably mature, way, I did two things simultaneously, I reached down, opened my camera case and took out my Nikon F with the big Sports Finder, and began to mount it on the tripod, while I asked a question: "Kemp, we waited for an hour while you were with that German film crew. How does it make you feel that people come from all over to interview you?

Kemper's answer so rocked me that I will leave you to think about it, until next installment. All I'll say her is that Kemp's answer blew my mind... and I'd not yet exposed a single frame of film...

FROM THE KILLING OF AMERICA
- INTERVIEW (1981)

FROM THE KILLING OF AMERICA, *a documentary about the decline of America directed by Sheldon Renan. It features footage (most exclusive to this film) from race riots to serial killers.*

"I'M AN AMERICAN AND I WENT OFF THE DEEP END."

When someone abandons himself to being a victim, he's gonna' have to be one.

I've been saying I'd wanted to kill my mother since I was eight years old and I'm not proud of it. It started with surrogates at a non-human level. Physical objects, my possessions, other people's destruction of things that are cared about and then its destruction of things that are living on a lower level. Small animals. Insects, animals, and then finally people.

It started coming to a head again, so went back down. I ran away back down there and then a month later I'm up living with my grandparents in the mountains and ten months later, I murdered them.

It made it worse to be on top of a mountain. I was literally on top of a mountain when it happened. I could sense everybody in the world just stopping and what they were doing, turning around and saw what I did and were coming to get me. I knew I was paranoid at that moment. I knew anybody that came up there and gave me a funny look or a fishy eye or quizzical look, I woulda' blown their brains out thinking they were coming to get me. If it'd been in a city, I'd have been a mass murderer at age 15. I would have killed until they gunned me down. I wouldn't have been able to reason my way out of it. I was scared to death and I was violent. I felt my back hit that wall. I was the rabbit that always ran, that always backed away, always burned his bridges. Suddenly, there weren't any more and my back hit that wall and I came out screaming and kicking and shooting.

I got paroled to my mother. Atascadero decided that I didn't ever need to talk to her again at all. Don't give her a Christmas present! Leave her alone. She got her pound of flesh out of you. I wasn't sniveling about my mother to them. I didn't like to hear what they had to say about her. She went through three husbands like a hot knife through butter.

When four months after I was out, I was back into the fantasy bag. My first date was an absolute disaster. It wasn't her fault, you know, and I didn't blame her even then. I'm sayin' it was a terrible tragedy, but boy she didn't ever talk to me again. It was awful. It wasn't sexual, or grabbin' at her at all. I was just such a dork, taking her to a John Wayne movie and ... Denny's. It was terrible. I'd never been on a date. At sixteen, it was cool! You know, I'd never been on a date, you know. I was locked up since I was 15. But I can't tell her that. 'Oh gee,' you know, 'don't mind me,' you know. She kinda got hung up on my looks or whatever, you know. She was a gorgeous young lady. Pure class, and she saw something there that I guess wasn't there, and boy she found out quick.

THOSE GLASSES

Yep. These are the ones. [*he puts on a pair of dorky eye glasses*] Now would you get in a car with this man? Huh? Hmm? The State has made me much more credible as a human being.

FALLING APART

But I was losing a grasp on something that was too violent to keep inside forever. As I'm sitting there with a severed head in my hand, talking to it, or looking at it, and I'm about to go crazy, literally. I'm about to go completely fly-wheel loose, and just fall apart. I say 'wow! This is insane,' and then I told myself 'no it isn't. You're saying that, and that makes it not insane.' I said 'I'm sane, and I'm looking at a severe.' And I said 'well, wait a minute, wait a minute,' I'd see old paintings and drawings of Viking heroes talking to severed heads and takin' them to parties; old enemies in leather bags. Part of our heritage. This is me back then in 1972 and '73. I'm able to live with the fact that I just stabbed to death and cut the throat of an innocent young woman––innocent in the sense that she did not plan on that to be happening––she didn't do anything specifically for that to happen to her.

Yet, she was a very active participant in her own death, and in my memory of that. She was 19-years-old, and her roommate in the trunk who died right after that was eighteen. I didn't go hog-wild and totally limp. What I'm saying is I found myself doing things in an attempt to make things fit together inside. I was doing sexual probings and things I mean, in a sense of striking out, or reaching out and grabbing and pulling to me. I'd be appalled at the sense that it wasn't working. That isn't the way it's supposed to be. That isn't the way I want it. You see what I'm saying? And yet I get during that time I become engaged to someone who is young and is beautiful, and very much the same advantages, and very much the same upbringing, and Disneyland values, and she's very much the reason I surrendered.

I picked up two girls who were so much like the first two it was unbelievable, almost identical circumstances, and I let them go. Everything went towards killing them, and I didn't. But I'm sayin' 'wow, it's uncanny.' It was almost like it was meant to be that way, and I said 'wow! This has got to stop,' and I let them out. They never even knew what was going on. I let them out. I would've gotten away with those two being murdered. I said 'no, it's gotta' stop,' and a week later I murdered my mother. Went back to Santa Cruz and killed her.

I am an American and I killed Americans. I am a human being and I killed human beings. I did it in my society.

Mass Murderer Kemper Denied Parole Again

By MARK BERGSTROM
Sentinel Staff Writer

VACAVILLE — The state Board of Prison Terms denied parole Thursday to Edmund Kemper, telling the convicted murderer of eight he still is a threat to society.

It was the fourth denial in as many years for the 33-year-old Kemper, who was convicted of the murders in 1973 and became eligible for parole in 1979.

The three-member panel also agreed with requests by Assistant District Attorney Jon Hopkins and by Kemper, himself, that the next parole hearing be put off three years as provided for in a new state law.

Kemper was almost unrecognizable as he walked into the hearing room Thursday at the Correctional Medical Facility here, where he has been incarcerated since his conviction in Santa Cruz Superior Court.

He told the parole board he has been exercising and jogging the past year and has shed 80 pounds from his 6-foot-9 frame. When he was convicted, Kemper weighed some 280 pounds. He is now sporting slightly longer and neatly combed hair.

Kemper said he did not wish to testify at the hour-long hearing, but answered a number of questions from the panelists, describing his job as therapy clerk, volunteer work reading books onto tape for the blind and the

Kemper buried two of his victims' heads in the backyard of his mother's Aptos home, pointing the heads toward his bedroom.

Kemper also was convicted of killing his mother, Clarnell Strandberg, and her best friend, Sara Hallett, both employees at UCSC.

After killing and mutilating his mother, Kemper put her head on the mantle and threw darts at it, according to testimony from his 1973 trial in Santa Cruz.

During that trial, Kemper said the eight killings were his way of acting out homicidal and sexual fantasies from early childhood.

Kemper testified he killed his mother, who he said he hated and frequently argued with, to keep her from finding out about the other killings.

After murdering his mother and her friend, Kemper fled the Santa Cruz area, but stopped in Pueblo, Colo., and called Santa Cruz Police to confess to the murders.

Following a three-week trial, the jury deliberated only five hours before finding Kemper guilty. Judge Harry Brauer sentenced Kemper to life in prison, but according to law at the time, he became eligible for parole consideration after serving just over six years.

The parole board also told Kemper it considered his previous conviction for murdering his grandparents.

Kemper, 15 at the time, was committed to Atascadero State Hospital and then to the California Youth Authority for those slayings.

His CYA parole ended in 1973, at which time a five-member panel of psychiatrists concluded Kemper no longer represented a threat to the public. Kemper reportedly drove to that hearing, to determine if his juvenile record should be sealed, with the body one of his eight new victims in the trunk of his car.

Bedient, Kemper's appointed attorney, conceded Thursday that Kemper's multiple murder conviction plus his former conviction stand strongly against him.

But, he urged the panel to consider the other factors required by law — Kemper's behavior while institutionalized and the psychiatric report, which he said stand strongly in Kemper's favor.

Bedient also said Kemper has shown remorse and added, "If 2½ million feet of tape (which Kemper said he has read for the blind) is not paying back society, I don't know what is."

Hopkins said little at the hearing, telling the panel he had little to add to the strong objections to release he'd made at two previous hearings.

But, he did say, "Clearly, the feeling of the people of Santa Cruz County remains the same."

Vacaville – The state Board of Prison Terms denied parole Thursday to Edmund Kemper, telling the convicted murderer of eight he still is a threat to society.

It was the fourth denial in as many years for the 33-year-old Kemper, who was convicted of the murders in 1973 and became eligible for parole in 1979.

The three-member panel also agreed with requests by Assistant District Attorney John Hopkins and by Kemper, himself, that the next parole hearing be put off three years as provided for in a new state law.

Kemper was almost unrecognizable as he walked into the hearing room Thursday at the California Medical Facility here, where he has been incarcerated since his conviction in Santa Cruz Superior Court.

He told the parole board he has been exercising and jogging the past year and has shed 80 pounds from his 6-foot-9 frame. When he was convicted, Kemper weighed some 280 pounds. He is now sporting slightly longer and neatly-combed hair.

Kemper said he did not wish to testify at the hour-long hearing, but answered a number of questions from the panelists, describing his job as therapy clerk, volunteer work reading books on tape for the blind and the progress he said he has made in sessions with his psychiatrist.

But Kemper said in response to a question from Robert Roos, he doesn't feel he's ready to be returned to the street.

Ted Rich, chairman of the panel, later told Kemper that that admission played a part in the board's denial of parole.

In announcing the decision after a short deliberation, Rich commended Kemper for his behavior inside the institution and for the progress reflected in the psychiatric report.

Kemper replied, "Thank you, I appreciate that."

The report by Dr. R. Brooks said, in part, that Kemper "has made considerable progress in re-establishing his working relationship with his family, in many ways to a level which surpasses his highest functioning in the family in the past."

Kemper told the panel he corresponds with his two sisters, but no longer with his father. "I blew it," he said of the break-off of communication.

One of Kemper's eight victims was his mother and he previously was convicted of killing his grandparents.

Brooks also wrote: "As he releases some of his intellectual defenses and experiences and expresses his emotional responses, he has become more 'real,' stepping out of his 'monster' role."

Rich complimented Kemper for not being "contentious" as he had been at the previous parole hearings.

But, he reminded Kemper the murders were committed in an "especially heinous and atrocious manner" and that Kemper had "(sexually) abused and mutilated" his victims.

Kemper was accused of murdering and beheading six co-eds. He scattered their body parts in this and surrounding counties.

Kemper buried two of his victims' heads in the backyard of his mother's Aptos home, pointing the heads toward his bedroom.

Kemper also was convicted of killing his mother, Clarnell Strandberg, and her best friend, Sara Hallett, both employees at UCSC.

After killing and mutilating his mother, Kemper put her head on the mantle and threw darts at it, according to testimony from his 1973 trial in Santa Cruz.

During that trial, Kemper said the eight killings were his way of acting out homicidal and sexual fantasies from early childhood.

Kemper testified he killed his mother, who he said he hated and frequently argued with, to keep her from finding out about the other killings.

After murdering his mother and her friend, Kemper fled the Santa Cruz area but stopped in Pueblo, Colo. and called Santa Cruz Police to confess to the murders.

Following a three-week trial, the jury deliberated only five hours before finding Kemper guilty. Judge Harry Brauer sentenced Kemper to life in prison but according to law at the time, he became eligible for parole consideration after serving just over six years.

The parole board also told Kemper it considered his previous conviction for murdering his grandparents. Kemper, 15 at the time, was committed to Atascadero State Hospital and then to the California Youth Authority for those slayings.

His CYA parole ended in 1973 at which time a five-member panel of psychiatrists concluded Kemper no longer represented a threat to the public. Kemper reportedly drove to that hearing to determine if his juvenile record should be sealed, with the body of one of his eight new victims in the trunk of his car.

Bedient, Kemper's appointed attorney, conceded Thursday that Kemper's multiple murder conviction plus his former conviction stand strongly against him.

But, he urged the panel to consider the other factors required by law: Kemper's behavior while institutionalized and the psychiatric report, which he said stand strongly in Kemper's favor.

Bedient also said Kemper has shown remorse and added, "If 2 ½ million feet of tape (which Kemper said he has read for the blind) is not paying back society, I don't know what is."

Hopkins said little at the hearing, telling the panel he had little to add to the strong objections to release he'd made at two previous hearings.

But, he did say, "Clearly the feeling of the people of Santa Cruz County remains the same."

MURDER: No Apparent Motive (1984) *is a documentary about serial killers and FBI Behavioral Sciences Profilers. It features interviews with serial killers Ed Kemper and Ted Bundy and various crime victims and law enforcement officials. The documentary also includes some dramatic recreations.*

ON BEING A KILLER

Well, I'm not an expert. I'm not an authority. I'm someone that has been a murderer for almost twenty years.

Can you say how many people might be doing crimes like you were doing?

It would be a guess, but it's far more than thirty-five. It isn't that impossible in this society. It happens.

Were there more people?

They didn't give up. He/she didn't give up. *I* did. I came in out of the cold, and what I'm saying is that there are some people who prefer it in the cold.

What do people see?

A nice guy.

You were able to appear like an ordinary person, non-threatening to ...

I lived as an ordinary person. I was leading a parallel, and an increasingly sick life. One victim let me back in the car. I locked myself out. She opened the door for me. My gun was under the seat. What the hell am I doing telling you that? Am I a masochist? Am I looking to be tormented further? I'm trying to show you just how awful this got ... how commanding these rages got.

I was raging inside. There were these incredible energies, positive *and* negative, depending on a mood that would trigger one or the other, and outside I looked troubled at times. Other times, I looked moody. Other times, perfectly serene. Not very sane. Again, people weren't even aware what was happening.

ON HIS MOTHER

You were involved in the campus because your mother worked there.

Yes. I was also involved in killing coeds, because my mother was associated with college work. College coeds. Women, and had had a very strong and violently outspoken position on men for much of my upbringing.

My mother was a sick, angry, hungry and very sad woman. Hated her! But, I wanted to love my mother. I watched her alcohol increase. I watched her social life drop off. I watched her get bizarre. She had terrible pain from her life. Her early life ... her upbringing. A failed marriage with my father. I'm a constant reminder of that failure.

I hate to distill it down into a one-word realities like that. There's a lot that leads into that happening, but that is what happened. It represented not what may mother was, but what she liked. What she coveted. What was important to her. I was destroying it.

ON HIS MOTIVE TO KILL

Why did you actually kill the girls?

My frustration. My inability to communicate socially, sexually ... I wasn't impotent. But emotionally I was impotent. I was scared to death of failing in male and female relationships. I knew nothing about that whole area, even if [I was] just sitting down and talking with the young lady. I need to be able to communicate, and ironically enough, that's why I began picking people up ... and I'm picking up young women and I'm going a little bit farther each time. It's a *daring* kind of a thing.

At first, there wasn't a gun. I'm driving along. We go to a vulnerable place where there *aren't* people watching. I could act out, and I say, 'no, I can't.' And then a gun is in the car, hidden, and this craving—this awful raging eating feeling inside—I could feel it consuming my insides, this *fantastic* passion. It was overwhelming me. It was like drugs! It was like alcohol. A little isn't enough. At first it is, and as you adjust to that, psychological and physically, you take more and more and more. It's the same process.

So, it finally came down to the thing of 'do I dare bring this gun out?' Already realizing that if the gun comes out, something has to happen. It was going to happen. I didn't see it then, but it was going to happen. I was playing a dangerous game with a loaded gun that got us all.

THE FIRST KILLINGS

In that first killing in May of '72, when that gun was pulled out, I launched it out for I had it under my leg, out of sight, parallel to my leg and the seat. It was something that had been thought out in fantasy. Acted out, *felt* out hundreds of times before it ever happened.

Kemper drove them at gunpoint to a secluded area near a park.[1] He took one of them[2] into the woods, leaving the second girl[3] tied in the car.

I had just gone from a horrible experience with her roommate, stabbing her, and I was in shock because of that. I couldn't believe that it was that way. And I'm walking back there bewildered: 'I gotta' kill her. I can't let her go. She's gonna' tell on me. Everybody's gonna' get me.' She sees the blood on my hands.

"What are you doing?"

She pulled back and she gasped, and I'm thinking, *Woah, I don't want her to know what happened.*

I said, "Your friend got smart with me. She'd been really getting smart with me a lot, but I never hit her. I killed her, but I never hit her," I said. "Your friend got smart with me and I think I broke her nose and you'd better come help. She's about to die." Why did she have to know that? I couldn't deal with telling her that, and when I attacked her, she didn't at first realize what was happening. It [the knife] didn't go through. She had very heavy coveralls on. It knocked her right up in the lid of the car, but it didn't pierce the clothing. It wasn't that swell a knife, anyway. I went out and bought a pawn shop huge knife. I kept on mindlessly attacking. She falls back into the trunk. I just killed a young woman. I slammed down the lid of the trunk. She isn't dead, she's dying, and I panicked, and I thought, 'I just locked the car keys, I can't find them in my pocket. Oh my god, I locked them in the trunk.' I'm kicking on the trunk lid and yanking on it. 'Oh no, I don't believe this!' I started to run and I tripped over the gun that I had in my pants that I had totally forgotten that was there. I stopped and says, stop and think! I collected my wits. 'Check all your pockets.' I picked the gun up. I stuck it back in my pants, now remembering I had one. I checked all my pockets and there's the keys in the back pocket. I never put them in my back pocket.

I thought I was pretty slick, and I tripped all over myself [during those] first two murders. During the first 24 hours, there were three clear times I should have been busted, and I wasn't because three different individuals, three different groups of people, got scared and minded their own business and looked the other way.

THE "A" STICKER

My mother worked at the campus, and I had an "A" sticker on my car and obvious access, day or night, to the campus. I was picking up some very lovely young women.

You know what we were talking about as we're driving around? Almost as often as not? This guy that's going around doing this stuff, and the second they started talking that, they didn't realize it, but they were getting a free ride. I couldn't touch that with a ten-foot pole, I swear. But they'd be telling me all about this guy and they're comparing notes, speculating on what he looks like, how he carries himself, why he's doing this stuff, telling me about it.

So how come they'd get in a car with somebody at that time?

She judged me not to be that guy. I "didn't look like him."

THE EASE OF MURDER

It was getting easier to do. I was getting better at it. I was getting less detectable. I started flaunting that invisibility, severing a human head ... two of them, at night, in front of my mother's residence with her at home, my neighbors at home upstairs, their picture window open, the curtains open, 11:00 at night. The lights are on, all they have to do is walk by, look out and I've had it.

ON KEEPING THE HEADS

Something out of my childhood. I could put it on an incident. I mean my father chopping the heads off of our two pet chickens and my mother insisting that I eat 'em for dinner. You know? We could say it was something that simple. I don't think it was. When my dad heads out back with that hatchet, I just got on my bike to try to stop it. I remember that. I got on a back and rode around the block. I was crying. I haven't talked about that for a lot of years. I'm sure that may have implemented something. That may have gotten something rolling along fantasy lines, but it took a lot of years of development along those lines to really get off.

How are you able to, in one minute, have someone's head in your hand, and very shortly thereafter ...

Through a fantasy, however way that would relate to that severed head, and then five minutes later, I'd put it away ... and there'd be a knock on the door, and I put it away and answer the door. The landlady would be there and we'd discuss reality. *Her* reality, not mine. Some people go crazy at that point. I felt it. It was one hell of a tweak, to just flip out and not know where I was, to be walking up the stairs with a camera bag that belonged to a young woman that had her severed head in it, walking up to my apartment. I passed a happy young couple coming down the stairs who nodded and smiled at me as they went by.

"Good evening."

They're going out on a date where I'd love to be going, and I'm aware of both of those realities, and the distance between those two is so dramatic, so amazing, so violent, that I could really feel the wheels squeaking inside that was really pulling on it and I imagine at that point, some people break, but I didn't literally go insane. I didn't get lost.

THE JURY ROOM

They'd buy me a beer. I'd buy them a beer. A casual relationship, but that I was poking around a little bit trying to find some things out. I knew they wouldn't be privy to hot information, but there were some things that were bothering me, like were there any speculations on how they were dying?

Did the cops like you?

Like I said, a "friendly nuisance." I got in the way, and it was deliberate. Again, friendly nuisances are dismissed.

How did you get the knowledge to outsmart the police?

Watching television. Believe it or not. Joseph Wambaugh. *Police Story* got some tremendous insights, and not just the gimmicks, the actual things, the tidbits that you pick up from their procedures, but the mechanics behind that, the logic behind it. I would not allow myself to walk into even a potential trap of behavior, and one of those was talking about those crimes too much to people, initiating conversations about that.

There was a memorial service for two of the victims.

Yes.

Were you tempted to go?

Yes, but I'd seen one too many episodes of one too many crime shows where that is one of the available resources for clues, tracking down the attenders, one man taking pictures of the people there to eliminate as potential suspects.

LOOKING FOR A GUN

Some police department actually came to your house to pick up a handgun.

The sheriff's representatives, one of the detectives was upset because he heard I had a .44 magnum pistol and was a convicted mental patient and killed. He came to take the gun away. They were staking out the wrong houses across the street and I'm playing around with a car, standing next to the gun in the trunk. They come over and asked, "Excuse me, sir. Do you know who lives in this houser across the street?" Well, that house was 609 Harriet. He crossed back over to this side, 609 Ord, and they were looking for me and didn't even know that was me. Bad news. Well, at any rate, we walk in the house and have them ask my mother about this other house, and I'm saying, "Hey, which 609 are you looking for?" They said, "Are you Ed Kemper?" "Yes," and it goes on and I needed to find out what they were looking for, the murder weapon, the .22 automatic or the .44 magnum, and I don't want to advertise that I've got a whole bunch of guns. So, I made a comment just to divine between the two and I suggest, "quite a little gun, isn't it?"

He reported, ".44 magnum, I hope so." Okay, because that loaded .22 was under the front seat and guarantee me an arrest right on the spot and the .44 was in the trunk. I forgot that. I took them in the house we went into my bedroom and the closet doors open and I have a high-powered rifle with a scope on it with some other stuff in the house.

You had some other stuff in the house, yes?

Yeah, I had the personal effects and the last two coeds that had been murdered about two months before, right next to the guns in the closet in a box.

Could he have seen it?

No, But when he arrested me for having all those guns and went through the closet looking to see if there were any pistols or anything else, he wouldn't have ... couldn't have helped notice a purse, a book bag and coed ID inside of those belonging to their two latest murder victims. I back up and I say, "Oh, excuse me. I just remembered something," and instantly he responds to what I'm saying. My hand moves, back we go outside, and he's still thinking, 'Boy, this is a really nice and helpful guy here.'

END GAME

It was springtime. It was April. For two months I hadn't killed. I said, 'It's not going to happen to any more girls.' It's got to stay between me and my mother and it's gotta' ... I cannot get away from her. We're still fighting. She's still belittling. I'm like a puppet on a string, and I entertain her. She knows all my buttons and I dance like a puppet with that pain. It had even gotten physical, to where I had physically grabbed her and thrown her on her bed, trying to emphasize a point that she's threatening to kill her, so here I pick up these two young ladies at Berkeley on Ashby Avenue.[4] One has flowers in her hand. Petite little dolls. They're in granny dresses and they're hitchhiking, A couple of real experts. I want to see how together I am, if I can resist this temptation.

They get in my car. They want to go one way. I know they need to go the other. If they go the way they're insisting on, we're headed right back out to where the first two coeds were murdered. But I'm saying to myself, *oh my God, all I got to do is relax and they'll take me to their death.* I've got the gun in the car, the same one I've been doing it with, I insisted, as gently as I could, I took them where they needed to go to their college.

That was one week before I murdered my mother. I said, "She's got to die, and I've got to die or girls like that are gonna' die, and that's when I decided, I'm going to murder my mother. I knew a week before she died, I was 'gonna kill her. She went out to a party. She got soused. She came home, went to sleep. I was woken up by that. I came out. I walked up to her bed. She's laying there reading a paperback as many thousands of nights before, and she said, "Oh, I suppose you're going to want to sit up all night and talk now." Shit [*his voice starts to break*] I looked at her and I said, "No, have a good night," and I knew I was gonna' kill her, you know? And I'm so cold. It's so hard, and that's the first time in ten years I've looked at it that way. I mean, that intensely and that honestly. It hurts, because I'm not a lizard. I'm not from under a rock. I came out of her vagina. I came out of my mother, and in a rage I went right back in. For seven years ,she said "I haven't had sex with a man because of you, my murderous son." It was one of our arguments. I cut off her head and I humiliated her corpse. It's a dare, you know?" Six young women dead because of the way she raises her son, and the way her son is raised, he grows up, and her closing words, "I suppose you want to sit up all night and talk." God, I wish I had.

Your grandmother and your mother were two women very important in your life, and you killed them both. Could you say what they were like that led them to the same fate?

The same thing that kept them from ever being friends. They're both aggressive matriarchal women. They've been the daughters of strong matriarchal women, I still loved my mother. It's hard for somebody to comprehend that you murder your mother through love. It isn't a rational process. It's a very painful process. It isn't rational, and I've got to still live with that.

Why did you wind up giving yourself up?

It had to stop. It had to stop. Once my mother was dead, there's almost a cathartic process at that point. I got physically ill right then when she died. When I murdered her and once she was dead, there was no way I could back out. I backed down from giving up a thousand times, you know. I just used to get drunk and go sit out in front of the sheriff's department in a parking lot across the street on one of those little concrete parking berms, I just sit there and say, "Woah, I still can't, the clanging doors. I could still hear them. No, 'cuz it'll never open again."

I rationalized that to give up would be insane. To give up would be crazy. I'd be giving away my freedom and I don't need to. But I look back on that and wish I had earlier when I was saying those things to myself. The people who were later dead wouldn't be the regret that came later, would have not had to be. Those *people*, not things, those people would still be with their families, with their loved ones, they would have their own families. If I had had the courage to make that decision instead of painting myself into the corner.

Where might you be if you'd never given in to the impulse to murder?

Where might I be? If my parole had been successful, I believe I'd be married, have children. I'd be heading toward my first grandchildren.

There's somebody out there that is watching this and hasn't done that —hasn't killed people, and wants to, and rages inside and struggles with that feeling, or is so sure they have it under control. They need to talk to somebody about it. Trust somebody enough to sit down and talk about something that isn't a crime; thinking that way isn't a crime. Doing it isn't just a crime; it's a horrible thing. It doesn't know when to quit, and it can't be stopped easily once it starts.

---

1. near Alameda, California
2. Mary Ann Pesce
3. Anita Luchessa
4. Ashby Avenue was an on-ramp to Interstate 80, and a popular spot for hitchhikers seeking a free ride to San Francisco, a fact al too aware to Kemper who took advantage of it (by his own admission) on more than one occasion.

Killer of eight women waives parole

VACAVILLE (UPI) — Edmund Kemper III, the 6-9 former construction worker serving eight life terms for killing eight women including his mother, decided to skip his fifth parole hearing after the news media showed up.

"He felt he could not adequately state his case in front of the press," prison spokesman Lt. Joe McGrath said Monday after Kemper announced his last-minute decision to waive the hearing.

Kemper, 36, who has been rejected for parole four times, was to have appeared before the state Board of Prison terms.

But the 290-pound inmate told prison officials he was not suitable for release and would wait three years before requesting another parole hearing, McGrath said.

Kemper had been turned down for parole at hearings in 1979, 1980, 1981 and 1982 in which he variously argued for parole and stated he was not suitable for parole, McGrath said. He said Kemper had a "spotless" prison record.

The parole board accepted Kemper's waiver request.

Kemper was convicted in 1973 of murdering his mother, her best friend and six coed hitchhikers in a year-long murder spree in the Santa Cruz area, saying he was driven by sexual fantasies.

Serial killer Edmund Kemper testifies at parole hearing.

The Associated Press

VACAVILLE – A parole date was denied on June 15, 1988 for serial killer Edmund Kemper, even though a prison psychiatric evaluation termed Kemper suitable for release.

Kemper, 40, is serving a life sentence at the California Medical Facility for murdering eight women, including his mother, in 1972-

73. The law at the time provided for the possibility of parole on life sentences.

A three-member panel from the Board of Prison Terms rejected the psychiatric evaluation by Dr. Jack Fleming. Board member David Brown said Kemper poses an unreasonable risk to society.

Brown told Kemper his crimes "shock the public conscience."

During an almost three-hour hearing, Kemper told the panel he did not practice cannibalism or perform sex acts on his victims when they were dead or dying. He said he made those confessions to police when he was tired and confused.

He did acknowledge that he beheaded seven of his victims, including his mother, Clarnell Strandberg, because of a childhood fascination with decapitation. And, he put his mother's head on a mantle and threw darts at it.

Kemper buried the head of one of his young victims in the backyard of the house he shared with his mother in Seacliff. He pointed the face toward his bedroom, according to testimony at his trial in 1973.

He appeared surprised during the hearing by a letter written by a cousin, Patricia Kemper, urging the panel to deny Kemper a parole date. Kemper said he had not known of such a letter.

In the letter, the woman said that as a child, Kemper mutilated the family cat. And, she said she watched him one day wait for hours with a rifle over a squirrel's hole to blow its head off when it peeked out. He went on to kill his grandparents and then the seven women and his mother, she wrote.

She said Kemper was and still is a deeply disturbed person who will kill again if he's ever released.

District Attorney Art Danner said he was shocked, but not surprised by the latest psychiatric evaluation of Kemper. Danner said

Fleming's report "flies in the face of everything known about Kemper."

Danner told the parole board Kemper's greatest danger is that he may some day con his way back out on the street.

He pointed out that Kemper had led psychiatrists and psychologists to believe he was no threat after a five-year commitment for killing his grandparents.

Even Kemper testified that he was shocked in the 1970s when two doctors would rule him sane and no danger to society, even after he had begun killing again.

He explained that he was sent to be interviewed by two doctors in Merced County in 1972 when he was seeking to have his conviction for killing his grandparents sealed from public view.

After meeting with the first psychiatrist, Kemper said, he went out and got drunk. "He thought I was Mr. Wonderful or something," Kemper said. He knew after the first interview that he would be judged sane.

He said he went to the second interview, later in the day, "blasted off my tail on beer," but the doctor didn't notice.

The two psychiatrists wrote that Kemper posed no danger to himself or others.

Kemper hadn't told them he had already begun killing again, just two days before and had driven to his interviews with a woman's head in the trunk of the car.

He told the parole board he picked up more than 1,000 hitchhikers during his year-long murder spree. He did not say why he selected the victims he did, other than say the selection was random.

He said he only murdered the women hitchhikers because the women in his life, especially his mother, had caused his only grief.

Kemper talked at length about his mother and drunken fights he said they had after his release from custody after killing his grandparents.

Kemper said he returned from the California Youth Authority at age 20 with great hope for the future. He said his mother fought him every step of the way. "She was 6 feet tall and 220 pounds at the time of her death," Kemper said, adding, "she was not intimidated by anybody."

Kemper said he can't simply explain why he murdered his mother to spare her from finding out that he was responsible for all the co-ed killings in Santa Cruz.

"There was love and there was hate," Kemper said of his relationship with his mother.

"I didn't want to put her through what I created," he said. And even though he said she helped create what he was, "she was a victim and not a perpetrator."

Kemper fled Santa Cruz County after killing his mother. He said he drove for four days, listening to the radio for news that police had a break in the case.

He said he had three guns and a knife in the car. "When I heard on the news there was a break in the case it would mean in a few hours I'd be dead," Kemper explained.

He said he planned to stop the car as soon as he heard the bulletin. "I was going to get my weapons and go to high ground and attack authorities when they came for me," Kemper said.

He said he believed at the time that he would have to be killed or he would keep on killing.

As it turns out, a showdown never happened. The bodies of his mother and her friend had not been found, and a panicked Kemper finally telephoned Santa Cruz police from Pueblo, Colorado, and confessed. Police there arrested him at a telephone booth.

Kemper's last appearance before the parole board was in 1982. At the time, he had lost weight and looked noticeably different that at the time of his trial.

Now, he appeared to look more like the 6-foot-9, 280-pound giant of a man Santa Cruz residents remember.

In 1985, Kemper waived his right for a hearing, saying he was unsuitable for release. He did not say that this time, but did concede he does not expect to be released from prison anytime soon.

His next parole consideration will be in 1991.

VACAVILLE

I altered how I approached these young ladies from the point of capture from the first time. What I had wanted to do was to secure them and to suffocate them with plastic bags over their heads. I had some completely unrealistic perspective that that was quick, [and] that they would lose consciousness rapidly. But the first young lady that was in the backseat, it was Marianne Peche, I finally secured her. She argued a lot. She was dialoguing and trying to change up control of the situation. She had already decided I was in control. I was trying to gain control. I was convinced she was in control of it. So, for about twenty minutes, we were arguing back and forth over what was going to happen, and I was trying to keep it away from what was intended, which was murder. I decided at that time I wasn't going to tell anyone I was going to rape them. I didn't say that at the time. But I left it wide open as the avenue, that it was going to be a sexual release and that got me very distressed, and it was obvious to me that if I was going to pursue what I was doing, that distress had to stop. So I went into an unfortunately more effective behavior of letting them help me. I let more of my personality come out and I was suicidal.

Very disturbed. Grasping out of someone ... I had abducted them and I wasn't going to let them out of the car because I was tired of people walking away from me, so someone that was very true, but I manipulated that to allow them to help me to the point of resolving their behavior until we got to a place where they could be killed. And that has the biggest problem with that, on my guilt basis because, obviously, that entitled unusual trust between captor of the perpetrator and the victim of the crime.

At one point, in fact, on the fourth victim of the crime, Miss Shaw, she actually got back into the trunk under her own power. I had a cast on my left arm that was broken. I walked her back to the trunk of the car where I told her I was going to keep her under covers so that I could get her to my home, or we could talk, but I didn't want neighbors seeing her coming to the house or leaving the house. I made that sound realistic to her. So she didn't want to get into the trunk, but was willing to ... when she got into the trunk I shot her.

I'm trying to remember this from a long time ago but another round had entered and exited that padding area ... so there were three holes in that padding area that was head level with her. It was off to her right to my left. She was moving then out in the back quadrant there trying to avoid the shots. That wouldn't have happened. I realized if I'd never done it, it wouldn't have happened, but my original intention was to make it very quick and either one of them to be aware what was happening, and it was not to keep them from stopping the crime. It was to keep them from suffering. I had a real bad problem depriving people of their lives. It wasn't the aspect of killing them, but it was the aspect of possessing their bodies afterwards. So it was almost an after-effect of evicting someone from their human body. I'm sorry it sounds so cold, but that's about what it analogizes to.

At the time, I wanted my case to look like random killings. Unrelated. As you know, there was no real understanding of serial killing at the time and when I told the police, they asked me how many people I thought I could have killed in the fashion that I did, of the approximately 1,000 individuals that got in my car over a three-year period that I was out there. This being a hobby ... a side hobby of mine was driving around. I loved to drive and picking up anybody who wanted to ride, and then later on focusing on more difficult cases people I was convinced wouldn't want to get in because a single male. A young adult ... car ... excuse me, two-door car, they're not going to want to get in and ride with me. I made that a challenge, almost like a chess game, and the more clever they got about checking me out ahead of time, the more clever I got about appearing innocuous and in a hurry and a businessman. The best one for assuaging that last check of me was just a glance at my watch, look slightly irritated. "No? Well, I guess I can stop and give this person a ride." It seemed to have a very positive effect, even with the most sophisticated hitchers, which included the Peche and Luchessa girls, the first two victims.

So really, You are a psychologist in your own right, from the standpoint of how to size up people, how they'll respond to you ...

How about a sociologist at a very lay level? A psychiatrist is looking for pathology, I was looking for ways to influence people.

FROM FORGIVEN (CIRCA- 1990)

How long have you been in prison?

17 years.

Did you believe in God when you first came to prison?

When I first came to prison, I had been a baptized Christian ... a fundamentalist Protestant Christian on the streets some years before. I got caught up in a lot of trinkets, a lot of flashy things. Involvements that weren't Christian, that were not wholesome and I completely fell away from my faith and from my devotion to Christ.

When I came to prison, there was a lot of distraction in here, too. But also, there was a lot of time to contemplate ... a lot of time to think about all the damage that happened to me and people around me, because of my attitude, because of life out there ... distractions out there and not facing up to some real problems I needed to deal with.

As you know, much has been written about you. When you first came to prison, you were described as a "monster," a "maniac." How different is the Ed Kemper before our camera today?

It's possible for people to be more relaxed with me than with some other people. It might well be thought to be an uptight situation. I'm a very large person. Six-foot-nine. I weigh about 350 pounds and you would think someone that large is going to be prone toward violence, aggression and an overbearing personality and I'm working toward quite the opposite and so I would say the difference between 16, 17 years ago where I was considered friendly—an easygoing person— that was a facade. Now it's real.

Are you concerned about what people on the street think of you?

People on the streets, that could be of great benefit to lead [*hesitates as a loud female voice is heard from a loudspeaker*] ...repeat it at least once, c'mon ...

Let me rephrase that. From your your early childhood, and from a mother who at the very least mentally abused you, to the victims' families who in some instances have hated you. How do you deal with all this negativity?

That's one thing that those emotions being spent on a person brings to the fore is whether you have an ability to deal with it or not and if you don't, you learn one or you fall because it's a real trap. Hatred, revenge, vengeance, retribution ... it's interesting how often people say that that's the "Greek" way. They put some class to it and say, "That's a classic Greek statement that at least with a revenge there's a kind of solace and I don't really believe that. I think that's a cop-out. It's easy for me to say that being a violent criminal in my past, but I haven't had to deal with feelings directly related to murder, to retribution, to forgiveness in all of my life until I became this, until I *lived* this for 17 solid years. In fact, 22 out of the last 25 years and I'm in for life. I'm doing life. I'm not satisfied with that. I accept it. It's something that took a long time to accept and I'm not serving a sentence, but I'm not trying to beat anyone out the retribution. I'm living a life. I won't waste a life again.

You came to Christ at the point you accepted responsibility for all the murders, yet I understand it happened in an unlikely place. Where was that?

In the hole during time in the lock-up. I could just squander my life away, who wasted away into nothing quietly. Die in a little corner, or start living my life and it was over a period of months. It was very ugly. It's the worst place I've ever lived in my life, and it's the best place I've ever lived because during that three years there, I came to grips with myself, with my feelings with who I was. I became a human being for the first time in my life instead of a caricature.

What would your life be like without Jesus Christ?

If Christ were not in my life, now, if peace were not in my life, if love were not in my life, I'd probably be dead. If I weren't,. I'd bet wishing I were dead.

Although you will probably never be released, you once told me that if you got out, you'd go far away. Where?

There's a lot of missionary work out there and a lot of people in the world that don't know Christ and won't know Christ unless people lay down their comforts and the fun things ... the fast cars and a few watches and the cute girlfriends and the telephones and go somewhere where the mosquitoes are as big as hummingbirds, and the alligators bite and share the work and share the peace and ask them to exchange ritual and tradition and history for something that works with other people.

I understand that part of what helped you to dedicate your life to Christ was the faithfulness of a Christian volunteer who visited you through a prison ministry called M-2. Tell us about that.

The people close to me, family members and close friends drift their way over the years. They had other things to do than to drag into prison continually, so for a period of time I had very few or no visits at all from the outside and the way I learned about Match 2 was by word of mouth. I know a few people involved with it here, and had seen a few in the visiting room in earlier years. So, I got an application and filled it out and talked to one of the representatives from the outside who came in to see me and one thing that was remarkable about that and it's remained that way since. A remarkable thing is that that man came to my housing unit, to my wing, to my cel to talk to me and the notice I got of that meeting said "Please be on your wing at your house see people familiar with the nomenclature in here we don't like to call it a cell. It isn't a cell. It's our house. It's where we live. It's not where we do time, it's where we live our lives and that's rather insensitive to reality. I'd like to think that that's dealing with reality or either serving time or we're living our lives, and you either do it wastefully or you do it usefully. The man wanted to come see me in my house and for a civilian to come inside and to come right in where we live, it was meaningful to me. It meant quite a bit that it touched me as very sincere. I've known the man some years now and that's never wavered.

It sounds like the faithfulness of this Christian man had a great impact on you.

My match to this sponsor is a very short man, he's not even average in height. He's very slender. He's a businessman and not at all imposing and we get along quite well, very well in fact. He is a very dear friend of mine after just a few months. The man is sincere. He's honest. He cares and he's here to learn too. It started out a bit shaky because he scared. This is prison. It was his first prison. I was his first match up and I'm a notorious criminal. People talk about "monster this and maniac that"...

What is the most difficult aspect of your incarceration?

It's hard to answer what it is that I've lost the most. I'd say I lost touch where I would have been or might have been had I still been in society those 17 years.

Have there been times of deep sadness, even desperation?

It had been a rat race, yes, which I guess is an overused term, but that's what it felt like to me. Like a big race and all of a sudden it comes to a screeching halt. I was just standing there and I didn't have any reason to live. I was wavering between suicide and trying not to be violent again, and it was a very violent atmosphere. I was aimed on him in the hole and the violence down there is like 65% higher than it is on the mainline of a prison, so it's hard to avoid that and it's so easy to fall into the suicidal trip that it's scary.

How do you survive?

Two ways: with Christ and without. When I first came to prison, I had a lot of notoriety attached to myself and my case and the first three years in prison where in what we call 'the hole" in the adjustment center in the prison. I spent probably the first year of that in what I saw as the blackest pit of my life. The state had put me in a little concrete room. I had a garment to keep from freezing. Some food to keep from starving. A place to deposit it when I was done with it and that was it. I was told that's what I needed to live. I guess the most shocking thing was all my life being especially a California person, I'd been listening to media conversation: "But you need this" and "You have to have that" and "you just can't live without this product or this item or this support system." I've heard that all my life and now I've sat in a little concrete room and I was told by people in authority that that's all I needed to stay alive. What I found myself doing was facing myself for the first time in my life, and at that time I was 24-years-old.

Do you have many opportunities to share your faith in Christ with the other inmates?

Yes, I'm able to share Christ in here in prison with other people, both other Christians and people who feel pain when the issue of Christ comes up. When the issue of love and mercy comes up because it's like a scalding, these people have pain, they have scars, they have bitterness. They don't have ways of resolving that and to see someone come by with a smile on his face and with peace in his heart and that radiates ... that's painful. Those people tend to be violent or aggressive toward that kind of involvement, so if you're going to be a Christian and a genuine one, it's a burden. It's a cross and it's the cross Christ asked us to bear. It's the ridicule or the tempting of other people to sway away from what we've been doing. Rather than try to justify my involvement with Christ and Christianity, I'd like to see this contest and I think ... I've learned in the past that we're the patients of Christ, the patients of that love. The other guy does comes around, it's not a matter of a game or a contest in that sense, but it's a patience just are showing that every day is real. Every day the smiles there. Every day sharing is there, and then the man says, "Wow, Ed, I'm getting out in six months. I'm going home. You're not ever going home and you know it. You've said it, yet every day you get in a. Better mood. Every day you get a little bit mellower and every day I get a little more bitter and a little more burned out." What's the answer? There it is.

Thank-you.

*FROM SERIAL KILLERS (1991) –
STEPHANE BOURGOIN*

THE AVAILABLE FOOTAGE *of* Stephane Bourgoin's meeting with *Ed Kemper is not available as one complete beginning-to-end interview, but has been split into fragments and made available through various documentary sources. We have split up each of these sources using ornamental breaks and did not attempt to reconstruct the interview to match its original order.*

[KEMPER ENTERING THE ROOM FOR HIS INTERVIEW AT VACAVILLE *Prison. The tape begins with Kemper in mid-sentence.*]

I guess I didn't even ask him that—just offered the information that he wouldn't hesitate a second to pull the lever on any serial killer, right? And I'm thinking, gee, he just killed me, you know? If you stop and think about it, if I were to have been executed in a timely fashion they would have had absolutely no input and they'd be scratching their heads about what makes a serial murder tick, other than the experts all jumping up to give their opinions, which you've been doing for a lot of years, and unfortunately they don't hit too well—

they don't have too good of a track record. Obviously very few of them could if there's only 35 serial killers [*the then-current estimate of acting serial killers in the United States*].

No no, they're talking about close to 100 [serial killers in the United States] right now.

I was saying that ten years ago. You also have to include his cohorts—they were saying as a unit, the BSU was saying. And having come from that generation—having been locked up and through the drakes, and knowing some of those characters and watching how easy it was for me to stumble into what I did, I didn't go into it pre-planned or anything, but I couldn't believe that was a unique act; no one else could find it out. That's just one avenue into it. While a lot of people can stereotype the type of criminal that a serial killer would be, society has to loosen up his belt a bit and admit that jailers, like at the Tucker Farm down in Arkansas who get tired of recalcitrant troublemaker inmates take them out back and kill them and bury them, are serial killers; different motive, but it's a wide range of activities that get included in something like that. They've had that 100 years ago in the Old West, where someone would set up a boarding house and people who came by never left. Whole families, individual travelers would go on for years before they get discovered —it's things I've read about.

You had H.H. Holmes[1] also in the 1890s.

Poisoners, people like that. Are we starting our interview?

[*Kemper continues from some other point in the tape that has been cut.*]

I would say, oh yes, I'm doing my time and I'm miserable, and they say "good." That's not what it's about. Uh oh, we're getting serious, now. I can tell.

The tape is going. Could you tell us how long you've been imprisoned?

This month is eighteen years that I've actually been in prison.

What were you convicted of?

Eight counts of first degree murder.

What was your sentence?

Seven years to life, CC—that's called concurrent, which means all the sentences run at the same time.

That means they run consecutively?

No, that's the opposite of consecutive. Consecutive would be one at a time and, of course, you can't serve multiple life sentences. There was some question before on my case, the legality of that, so when my case went through, the judge sentenced me to one term of seven-to-life, which at that time was the maximum non-death penalty, and all to run concurrent at the same time.

In considering your crimes and crimes done by other serial killers, what do you think society should do in general with serial killers?

It's a difficult question to answer from my point of view because I'm obviously an involved subject so, any answer I would give, that would be *other* than the death penalty_would sound very self-serving. I look at people who on the surface don't have any redeeming qualities whatsoever—they don't do anything or say anything or behave in any way that would make your average person want to save their life—to keep them alive—and feed them and house them and clothe them for decades. When I first came to prison, I had much the same attitude, it was a very defensive attitude, very self-preservative attitude, because those immediately about me were very much set on destructive attitudes toward me, so I put up screens, so to speak, to screen out those feelings and those reactions to me.

The only interview I ever did back at the time of my case—this is just a little anecdote—I went through the whole investigation, the whole trial with no interviews with the media, and then this one woman who had treated me pretty fairly in the media, she tried to do a more in-depth piece around it and so I did an interview with her the day before I was sentenced.

I was at the jury room to the courthouse and my lawyer hadn't shown up yet. She was up there talking to the police officer that was with me, and I said, "My lawyer does not want me talking to the media at all." So, I see him coming down the hall, and I said, "Let's set up a little scenario and act like I'm giving this really incriminating interview that screws everything up." She kind of laughed because it was breaking the tension in the room. So we set up this little scenario and she's busily acting like she's writing and I'm about all of this hair brain stuff that relates to the case and feelings, and he just starts turning bright red as he gets within hearing range—he's like a big clown with this huge forehead and huge hair standing out all over— and he's bright red, and he stomps into the room and slams his briefcase onto the desk and we all start laughing. He gets really mad and says to us, "What are you laughing about?" And I said, "This is just a setup just for you—I'm not doing any interviews." But later on I gave her an interview because she treated me so fairly up to that point.

She also gave me a pen that day, it was a cast aluminum ballpoint pen, and I took it back to my high-security jail cell up in Redwood City. I was really slammed down tight: a two-man cell by myself. They have a camera on me 24-hours a day. The lights are on—two sets of these four-footers—it's bright as day 24-hours a day, and I was there for five months, and I get strip shook leaving the cell and strip shook coming back in. I brought this pen in with my legal papers, and a few months later in the middle of the trial, I smashed the pen on the floor with my boot, sharpened it—got a sharp edge on the metal—and slashed my wrist. I was bleeding all over the place. It was very messy and very exciting, and everybody was dragging me off to the hospital and I got sewed up. I got shot up with industrial strength mace. They had about a quart of it and they just gassed me with that whole thing and dragged me off to the hospital. I made a quippy comment—I don't think the police translated it properly for the media because they missed it, you know how they love to get in to puns on broadcast television— "the pen is mightier than the sword"—I turned the pen into the sword. Both times I attempted suicide I did it with a pen or parts of a pen, and I thought that was kind of interesting, but the media never picked up on that. They were too busy being serious.

At one point I could see every aspect of my life, my crimes, who I was, how I really felt about things without any defensive or protective accoutrements. It was fascinating to me: I was semi-conscious— actually, I was conscious, I just couldn't get up and move around a lot, and at the end of the two hours, I didn't want to stop. I wanted to keep on with this. I hadn't gotten to the crimes themselves, I was kind of oriented around other things related to my life. I asked to continue on, and the doctor didn't want to, so I insisted. They were using an IV and shot me up with another two-hour batch of this stuff, and as soon as he was done with what he wanted to do, he got up and left.

He had an appointment and it had gone longer than he planned on it so he had to leave and my lawyer had to go. So I'm stuck with these two deputies and a registered nurse watching me until I come down off of this stuff. Well, when the doctor left, he decided to give me a shot of medicine to snap me out of this, and I asked him what it was, and he said it was Methedrine[2]—hospital-grade speed. I've asked doctors since then, both medical doctors and psychiatrists, if that was an appropriate action, and they said absolutely not. They should have let me sleep it off. It is suggested that the doctor knew full well it would put me through hell. It amplified everything I was feeling, it got me really down, and for two days after that they were trying to scrape me off the ceiling—they couldn't even talk to me. I was raving and ranting. They had to put me in a strip cell because I refused to go back to my regular cell. There was television available there. I had canteen. I had some food items, but I wouldn't accept it.

I went to a strip cell two cells down where all I had was a mattress over a hole in the floor. I was just on and on 24-hours a day. The convicts and the criminals in the back that were locked up with me—they were in the tank—were talking with me very casually about different things, and I put them all on what we call "front street."[3] I exposed all of them to all of the negative sides of our relationships. I called them cowards and punks and this and that because they were even talking to me. That was when I made the statement that I should be hung upside down on the bars and beaten daily for what I did.

Under the influence of those drugs, I was seeing what I did through other people's eyes, not through mine; as someone else would view it —pure horror—how someone with nothing to do with violence in their life would see it. It was an awful experience. Within hours of coming down off that stuff two days later, I wasn't making comments like that, [my] defenses were back in place—they were a bit ruffled. It had been an eye-opening experience because it gave me some perspectives on my case that I would never forget—some anxieties on my case that I would never forget—and all I can give you to gauge it by is that when I went into that hospital, the nurse came out—she was the typical battle-axe,[4] professional nurse, been on the job for twenty years ... great woman ... with the wheelchair, severe stern face, and she's looking at me with razor blades.

I'm in the chair and she wheels me inside. Five hours later when I come out of there, she's wheeling me out and as I'm getting into the car, I've got this tortured look on my face. I've been crying and tearing at myself. She looks at me with this very compassionate look, and she says, "Good luck." She got a good look at what was really inside. She was already aware of the evil I was capable of and the horror that had happened in the case, and then she saw a lot of my real feelings. With her knowledge of chemicals and medicine and treatments, she knew I wasn't faking. So, from her I got good luck and she was serious. I've never seen her since, but ironically, the deputies that were stuck with me that day, they figured 'he's so outraged right now, let's just keep him here until he calms down a bit, then we'll take him back to jail.'

But I didn't calm down.

I just kept going on and on, and at one point I asked the deputies to handcuff me to the rails of the bed because I was afraid I would rip my eyes out. I was really acting up, and he had known me for a few months and he didn't want to do that. He said, "Oh, come on Ed, that's not really necessary." I said, "Man, you better put them on, or I'm going to tear that goddamn gun belt off and blast you, and I might beat you to death with it." So, he comes over with the cuffs. He was a little offended by that ... so he came over with the cuffs and started putting them on my wrists and I just went through some incredible convulsion and I just yanked him clear across the bed. He had the other hand cuffed already. Zing! Off he goes, he's hanging onto this handcuff and at that point he cuffed me up real quick and finished and I already had my leg irons at the foot of the bed and I was just yanking those rails up and down with my wrists. That was very painful with handcuffs on. We went like that for a few hours and finally they said, "We got to get him back to jail, he's not going to change in the near future."

In general, people see serial killers as one category, but they're actually several different types of serial killers. Would you care to explain to us what types of serial killers ...

To be honest with you, I couldn't really tell you, because the categorization process as you know is back east—or the Behavioral Sciences Unit. When I was locked up originally, they called it mass murderer: anybody who killed more than two or three people was a mass murderer, whether it was all at one place or over an extended period of time. In the early 80s they came up with this differentiation called serial killing, which was living two lives, basically. If one orients to the negative side of that living, he would say this person is living in a cover life that was wrapped around doing those crimes, which couldn't be very realistic, someone doesn't live their life to murder people; their life was not set for that from birth. From my point of view, what I saw was there was a great hole in my life. There was a lot missing from my life. And it didn't necessarily mean feelings, it meant that I had holed off this emptiness in my life. I had an upbringing that some have called dysfunctional: parents divorced when I was young, my mother started drinking heavily, she was working to raise three kids, we were not being cooperative about it, she drank more, she punished us harder—probably out of desperation, so character sets were being developed at that point, rather than me going to Boys Scouts getting achievement badges. I was finding devious ways to get around the rules of the home. I watched the whole home life deteriorate from what typical kids on the block were doing to coming home from school, which I didn't like anyway—ironically I have a high IQ, which I didn't know that when I was locked up the first time for murder. I always thought I was missing up here in my head, a little short, because I was always called stupid or called slow—that was the problem, I wasn't thinking when I did things. I just did by rote, I did by memory, I did by example. I had absolutely no faith in myself, I had no interaction going on in my own mind. I was not a thinker. I was not an individual. I had a teacher in the ninth grade who changed all of that; he made me think. He would not tolerate my not thinking. He was an art teacher. It was a devastating experience for me because there were gears in my head that were just rusty and they were barely moving or not at all, and that's when I found out that's what the state of my mind's functioning was: I didn't think—to the point of he points at a stapler on his desk and says what does that say and I looked at is and said, "Silverline," and he says, "Look again" and he's raving at me, and I look again and it said, "Swingline." All I had to do was look at it and read it, but I glanced at it and threw it back at him out of panic. He made me think, and he gave me puzzles to work out in school in my class where I had to resolve these to continue on with the class. I had to think. I had to use abstracts. After that started, that became fascinating to me, so I got more and more involved in thinking—and about my surroundings and things like that, but by then, I was locked up.

What was your relationship like with your sister?

Which one? I have two.

The one you were playing strange games of death with her.

My younger sister. My older sister was five years older than me, so she was off with her friends and in a distant relationship with me. My younger sister is two years younger. I developed some morbid games. My life had started going that way at about eight. We lived in a house where there was a basement—some people think there was a trap door on that basement, but that was a different house—it was a walk-in basement but it was in Montana, it was a full basement with granite walls, hewn wood floorboards, and it looked like some old dungeon or out of a castle or something. I was eight years old and I was very susceptible, my imagination was very limited. There was an old furnace in the basement that had been converted from burning coal and wood to burning gas, that was a central heating system with your typical radiators, and if you've ever lived in a home like that you know the binging, the clang, the pop, the rattles, the weird sounds in the night that can be spooky to a kid. At a certain time of the evening the family left the center room, the living room of the house. My mother and my sisters or my sisters themselves would go to bed upstairs where I used to go to bed, upstairs. I had to go down to the basement. An eight-year-old child had a tough time differentiating the reasoning of that: "Why am I going to the basement? I'm going to hell, they're going to heaven." Earth is the living room. I'm going down to deal with demons and monsters and ghosts and all the things that scare me, while they don't have to. There's a house with three women and one male, me, and I got a little defensive. I was saying gee, this is kind of ganging up. My older sister had a basement bedroom and it was a storage room that was about 18-feet wide and 35-feet long, and it was a concrete room with no windows. It had a light bulb over a big industrial iron laundry sink and had a pull string on the light. The bed was in the opposite corner of the room. There was a dresser, a couple carpets thrown on the floor, and there was a lot of storage stuff along the wall. I was in that room for about six months and I developed some very, very particular and articulate rituals that I felt I had to go through to protect myself. Again, it was embarrassing. I was a youngster, and if you can imagine me going down a staircase of rough hewn wood, there's no guard rail, so one step wrong and you're off into this black pit, I turn on the light, it's a little circular light switch, and a single naked bulb goes on down at the bottom of these stairs, so I turned that light on, I opened the door then I closed the door because my mother complained of the cold coming in from the basement, I go down the stairs, get to the bottom and do a 180 degree turn and I walk the full length of the house on this floor with these pipes rattling and wheezing and banging over my head. It's pitch black ahead of me and the only light is behind me hanging down from the ceiling. I'm now cut off from the house—cut off from them. I walk this full length into the darkness from this gradience of light into complete darkness. Groping around in the dark, I do a 45-degree angle when I get to the end and I pull the string and the lights up this end. Then I'm supposed to walk all the way back to the other end and turn that light off and walk toward the light from the dark and I've got this horrible terror going on inside me; this is every night—this is every day because it's pitch black down there with no windows. She didn't intend all of this and I sniffled about it when I complained and I cried about it and got smacked in the head—what's the matter with you? Quit being such a wimp. She was trying to solve a problem: she had not enough room upstairs to where I didn't have to share a bedroom with a sister, I'm eight years old, I need to go to the basement.

What were those morbid games that you played with your sister?

Well, the one I remember, someone talking about in a book, we were playing gas chamber or electric chair or something, and we had this big old overstuffed chair up in my room. It was not just my sister and I, it was my sister and I and a close friend, and we got into all these games. We got into one game where we'd roll up in a rug and a person would try to get out of it. It was like a large throw rug. I guess what fascinated us individually about it is that it was completely .... It broke up the monotony I guess to what we were doing. We didn't have a lot of toys to play with and we got bored of those pretty quickly, so we looked for things to do. You roll up in the rug and you try to get out and the other two would leave the room and we would see who could get out fastest, you know, you try to work your way out sideways or scoot out the end of it or whatever. It went from that to being tied in this overstuffed chair with a cord or something or pieces of sheet or sash or something. It went through this process. This was back in 1960 when Caryl Chessman was executed down in California. We're up in Montana, so there was a lot of media coverage on that because he was an author, he'd written books, they were trying to save his life, he'd not killed anybody so why are they executing him? So that's where I think the fascination with that came in—that gas chamber effect, but I think it overly fascinated some people. I'm preparing my mindset for doing deathly kinds of things.

I don't know if this story is true, that you beheaded one of your sister's dolls and cut off the hands of the doll.

It's interesting you bring that up . . . I had a cap gun, it was made by Mattel. A Fanner-50 was a very fancy cap gun. I got it in New York City, I went there for one summer with a cousin and when I came back my little sister kemwas kind of jealous. For years I never really put any value on what happened. I tried to figure out beyond the obvious what happened in this scenario. I've since found it plausible to believe that when she was angry or jealous about something, she would fuel her attitude towards resolving something. She hated that cap gun because it came between us as brother and sister. It was something I had that she didn't have. That trip represented something she really wanted and didn't get and I did. Very soon after getting back from that trip, she got in an argument with me over something really petty. She got really outraged and picked up that cap pistol, and I said, "Don't throw that!" And she threw it right at me—wham! Hard. It hit the floor and my toe and it hurt bad, and it broke the gun. The inner mechanism wouldn't work after that. It wouldn't cock and pull the trigger anymore, and that really outraged me, so I said, "So you want to play like that, huh?"

So I go running into her room and she says, "What are you doing?" She's shrieking and chasing me. I grab her Barbie doll—it was the one fancy doll she had—she had a pair of sewing scissors sitting there in a sewing kit, so I grabbed the scissors, but the head popped off, so I said well that's going to go right back on, that's no damage, so I took the scissors and I cut the hands off the doll and I said, "Here—now you've got a toy that doesn't work too. Good! And I got a toy that doesn't work too. Good!" That was my attitude. It wasn't just quite me going and dismembering her doll. I think that's a little bit too quick an assignation—it's not me to judge these professionals, but when they look at me here on Monday morning after the football game and they say, "Gee, here's all these little parts of the puzzle: oh, this indicates what he was going to do. And if that's the case, I want to know about the pre-teen kids and the pre- and post-puberty kids, they're going through these raging moods and attitudes that go out and kill neighborhood cats—they hang them up from a telephone pole or hang them up from a tree shoot them full of arrows and set fire to them."

I was reading about that in "Dear Abby." Where are those children today? Are they serial killers? Or are they police chiefs and mayors and aldermen and assemblymen? I'm saying there are periods when kids go through very violent development—I mean, potentially violent—they break things, they steal things, they lie, they go through these changes; yet I've had these people—one or two doctors in particular who I won't go into—who very casually just slapped all these assignations on there and said of course if you run into a kid that's doing this kind of thing you've got a developing serial killer, you better put him in treatment real quick and save his life. To a point, I agree with them, that someone who is acting out and has a dysfunctional childhood or has just gone through a dysfunctional childhood and hasn't gotten violent yet or is heading toward that direction—passive aggressive—violence was the last thing I exhibited and then it was murderous violence. So sure, there's a lot of value in getting youngsters like that help to where they can find themselves and they can find value in themselves and they can find value in interacting with others and they go in a different direction than what I did. But to just sit there and casually lay these . . . I guess it just bothers my ego.

Year after year the psychiatrists and psychologists I deal with are in a prison setting. They're there eight hours a day. They have to deal with me every day. If I am their patient and I screw up, they can kiss their job goodbye. I mean there's going to be a lot of hell on them for not seeing this in advance and saying, "Oh, we should lock him up, he might be violent." Any professional out there is going to tell you that if they are going into my mind and into my past, into my feelings, there's a potential there for acting out or getting uncontrolled or being violent because they're stripping away the veneer of my civilization and the protections of myself, and there's a lot of things that can come jumping out of there. Then to walk out of that therapy session into this kind of a setting, prison, where it's very violent and aggressive, it's a distilled medium that you might encounter on a street corner somewhere—the street corner thug or punk—or the alleyway where someone is going to take terrible advantage of you or put you in a terrible situation that you may have to be violent to get out of—that's this main line. That's where all these guys go. And I'm going to walk out of a therapy session where this man has been peeling my mind so to speak and getting into my psyche and soul, and finding out what makes me tick or trying to help put me back together or help try to put me together for the first time, and then I'm going to walk out of that into this medium. That's not very conducive to good health. I'm aware of that going into this situation, so I'm twice as leery as the doctor is, but unfortunately he's got all of these mindsets and these theories and these books he's read and that he's trained under, and I guess what has happened in my life kind of jumps out of the book a few chapters ahead, and the way I've experienced it, the psyches don't want to go that far. They don't want to go out there and work the pages back into the book so that I fit in there or my kind of criminal fits in there, too. They kind of just stand on the edge of the book and they put on their feathers and they put on their paint and they get their rattles and they hop around and they go into the witch doctor routine and that I resent and, unfortunately, so do they. When they have to put on their rattles and put their crosses up and say, Ah! He's evil! Get him away from us! He'll take advantage of us and he'll rape, pillage and burn!" That's where I'm on the cutting edge of humanity. I find out now, and it doesn't matter that I find this out because I've already been cast out by society, so any things I find out or discover—even beautiful little things I discover about the ability of the human spirit to heal itself just to an extent enough where he can make friendships, he can form bonds, he can cry when someone dies of AIDS, or he can feel bad when a friend gets injured or killed by someone else, or grows old and dies, unable to go back out to the streets because they won't let him out early and he's dying. The feeling that can develop, it can develop hard, wicked feelings, it can develop some very tender and some very sad feelings, and then you're trying to deal with the widow of that man through the mail—the very restrictive mail procedures we have here, we're not supposed to co-correspond across these lattices of relationship—it's tough to deal with. That's my world now. That's what allows me to be sane—"sane" that's what allows me to function as a human being, not doing time with these considerable constraints that I've caused to be on me, it's living my life with the limitations that I've caused to happen, living with my life is different than doing time.

Because then there's the ability to work into that picture positive things giving back, like working in the blind project—the volunteers of Vacaville where we read books on the tape for the blind all over the United States, and sometimes in foreign countries. I participated in that program for the last 14 years. I started out in very, very little involvement reading books, working on baseballs for blind sports, doing some clerk work, working on their newsletter—different jobs in there—become the reader supervisor teaching guys how to read the books on the tape, all the way up to the point where I became the inmate coordinator, which is the lead man there. It's the guy that's in charge of making sure everything works right all the time. When I first went into that activity, they were saying there were things I could never do. To ask you a question about *your* interview, did you see a trophy case when you came in?

Uh, yes.

Out in the foyer there's a trophy case, take a look at it. There's several trophies in there and a couple of them have my name on them. There's a big 40-inch trophy in there, triple-tier trophy, very impressive looking. That's the volunteer of the year award. It has a little speech on the front of it, on the brass plaque that says: this award is given to the person who most epitomizes what they stand for, the help for the service of the handicap visually-impaired. This is a very time honored award. They've been in existence now for 31 years. I've been in that group for 14 of those years. When the first couple of years I was there, the trophy case used to be in the blind project and I used to walk up and I'd look at the trophy, and I'd never had a trophy in my life. I'd never had a ribbon, never had a plaque, none of that stuff. I'd never tried for it.

Well, you had the Junior Chamber of Commerce.

Okay, yeah. I forgot, they don't call it that, though, they had to get rid of that name because the Chamber of Commerce took offense to that. United States Jaycees—at one point I was the youngest Jaycee in America because I was 19 when I was put in as an associate member who couldn't vote, and by the time I was 20, I was on the Board of Directors.

Okay, no trophies, no plaques. I got some certificates, but again, that was in the institution, that's where I'm learning to achieve. I developed a better image of self and those around me, and I really love cooking. I started doing things, real positive. I felt good about it, and that continued on to the streets. I went to the Jaycees on the streets, but as my relationship I was paroled to my mother. What these experts don't notice in the picture, I haven't seen it in writing anywhere, it could be somewhere, was that when I was 14 years old, I ran away from my mother, they mentioned that. But if you look at the overall picture—why did I run away? I wanted to be with my father. That's a very topical approach to it. I wanted to get away from my mother because I was dreaming, thinking, fantasizing murder all day long. I couldn't get it out of my head. I couldn't battle with her because I was very intimidated by her; she's six-feet-tall. She weighs 225 pounds. She's not a fat woman, she's just this great big woman who I was terrified of. She had verbal capabilities you wouldn't believe. I used to watch her field strip grown men in little emotional contests, and when they get to a point where they wanted to smack her, then she started attacking them on beating women—slap the woman around—and then she'd toy with him on that. I'd watch these guys dance around the room having fits, knocking out windows, punch a hole in the door and stomp off. She could control people like that. I'm sitting there watching that in awe from one point of view, and in terror from the other. I grew up with this stuff. She did that to my dad when they were always battling before the divorce, I'm not trying to put on her what happened to the girls or to her, but what I'm saying is there was a lot of psychological involvement there.

Did you feel early on [tape cut]

[*after tape cut*] I got in the legs one time I turned around shrieking and she [*his mother*] hit me in the mouth and the little keeper—the little silver buckle thing on the clasp flew off. So she smacked me and this thing breaks off on my mouth. She hits me across the face with his belt and says, "Shut up! The neighbors are going to think I'm beating you." I'm looking at her.

"What?"

I'm not supposed to cry out, which is a natural reaction to these great red welts that are going on me. Sure, I was a little shit. I got rude downstairs so she took me upstairs and beat the hell out of me. I would like to think it was a better part of my character that was resisting this kind of pressure to fit into some mold that she had an image of as being the "good little kid." I'll be damned if I'm going to be that good little kid. I'm getting the hell beat out of me for not being that little kid. I got resistant to it. But again, it's not in manly ways or in prideful ways, it was sneaky little devious ways—I'd get around that. One of the ways was she won't give me allowance, so I'll take money out of her purse. I never robbed her—take all of it—I'd take a dime here, a quarter there, 15 cents there, 50 cents here. She comes in drunk at night, she's not going to know how much change she has. So to rebound on that, she started counting her money at all kinds of odd times to keep on top of me. It was like a game we played for years. At the age of 13, she finally let me go visit my father down in L.A., where I was born. I'm in Montana where she was born. I don't like Montana, it's cold in the winter, hot in the summer, it's miserable and the people up there are nice people, but hey, they're not *my* people. That's what I'm saying. Now I wasn't viewing or voicing those things then, I was feeling them, but I didn't know how to put them into words.

So, I finally get to come down and see my dad again down in L.A. One month. I never touched her purse again. That scared her. That really bothered her because she beat me halfway senseless with that belt, and terror tactics: "Okay, we're going to eat dinner and I'm gonna' beat your ass afterwards," so that I can think about it for a half hour. Or, after some little thing she's doing, she tried psychological tactics. She tried, "I'm going to put you in an orphanage, I'm going to disavow you!" None of that shit worked. So, I go see my Dad for 30 days, and my step-brother and I go out and mow lawns. We say, "Gee Dad, you're going out to dinner tonight, can we go someplace and eat?" And he'd say, "Sure" and he'd give us a few dollars. We'd go down to some little diner down the street. He treated us like little men, like *he* wanted to be treated. He came from a matriarchal household, too. I guess if you know how that stuff runs in families: matriarchal household, the son goes out and finds a mother image and marries her. I didn't know all this stuff back then. It would have made a lot more sense. But I got this domineering grandmother on my father's side. I got this domineering grandmother on my mother's side who died before I was born, but now she's reincarnated in my mother and her sister, my aunt. They're two very domineering, very aggressive, very successful women. So these two women are in terrible conflict with each other. Competition. They didn't get along at all. So, I'm in the middle of that trying to find my way, and I go stay with my Dad and I can only say he reflected back on his childhood, said, "Gee, I wish I had been treated this way," so that's how he treated me and my step-brother. We responded to that. If we needed spending money we'd go out and we'd do tasks around the neighborhood: clean yards, rake this, mow that, water the flowers, and make a few dollars and we'd have some fun.

Sometimes he'd ask us to do something and we'd do it because he was always fair with us and kind and he was generous with us, so 30 days of doing this opened up new feelings in me that I'd never had before, and I wish I'd had more experience with my father growing up so I could orient more to being tall around not tall peers. I call it an artificial paranoia that developed while I walk into a room.

Everybody stops and looks at me because I'm the tallest guy they've seen or the tallest guy in the room. They stop and they look, and ironically, the average or short guy is sitting over there looking at me with a great resentment because he wants that attention. I've got it, and he thinks it's really neat because he's looking at it from a vicarious position. He doesn't realize that there's thorny sides to that attention. I don't want that attention. I just want to blend into the room. I just want to kind of sidle in. So I see two kinds of tall men or tall men or tall female personalities: those who are very passive because of all of this thrust on them, or those who are very aggressive and they use that and they apply it towards ends, like the little guy who goes on to become the bank president, needs the champion this and did that and never saw the fourth grade. He's real aggressive because he's denied all those little attention. He's got to grab them and he has to go out and put himself in the limelight. I get it naturally, so there's resentment, and little guys tormented me all the time I'm growing up.

Did you feel like an outsider early on?

Always. I always felt like an outsider and it's again, because I didn't ever fit in. I moved around a lot for one thing, I went to different schools when I was in Los Angeles from age five until seven when I'm going to kindergarten, first grade, second grade. I got in trouble in public school and I look fondly back on those times because that's when I was acting out, and I was normal. I'm not saying I went around and kidnapping people in classrooms or broke windows out—we didn't get into stuff like that—but I was tardy and I was messing around and I was recalcitrant. I was getting bad marks for it, and my parents were getting called by the PTA, but that's a hell of a lot better than a few years later when I'm real spooky. I'm real quiet and nobody ever hears from me, and I'm in school and I go home and very few people knew me because I'm in that basement, and now I'm pulling into myself and now things are getting very morbid in their orientation. I start becoming fascinated with things evolving around death and destruction and evil and all of that. I'm not saying I became a satan worshiper because I was afraid of evil things, afraid of those powers that we all don't understand, and as a little kid, I had a very, very strange orientation to those. I mean, it wasn't rational.

What were your morbid fantasies at that time?

At what about age? Eight? Or nine?

Or later on when you said you were thinking all the time about death.

What I was fantasizing about was building up big loads of frustration inside, big loads of hatred, because I had no outlet for it. I should have developed outlets, but I didn't know how at that time. So the outlets that developed themselves, or I developed without knowing it, were fantasies about me being the last—I got that out of a school book, this thing of being the last person alive in the world, and the thing that was posed to me in this textbook was social studies and it was meant to play upon the loneliness youngsters can feel, and it's a very uncomfortable feeling and you can't have love and you can't have adventure and you can't have excitement without being able to share it with other people because that's where a lot of the dimension comes from, so they post this thing. I mean, what if you were the last person in the world and you had all these cars and airplanes and boats and ships and things to do, but nobody to share it with? Wouldn't that be awful? And I thought, hey, that's a thought, I never thought of that before, so it became a seed, like a little core to fantasies for me. Some mysterious thing has happened and everybody else is gone and I got all these things I can do and no inhibitions. No restrictions. I can do what I want. I don't get yelled at anymore. That soon became very hollow, and so I built upon that and added to it while people were still around, but they were inanimate. They couldn't affect me. It couldn't hurt me. Then it went further and further and further until finally, by the time I'm approaching puberty, and I'm starting to sense myself and I've already been accosted by a girlfriend—not sexually or physically—but emotionally. She was a little ahead of me. We were the same age, but she was pretty aggressive and a beautiful young girl, but I wasn't ready for that kind of a relationship and I was scared by it, and she kind of cowed me into backing away from the relationship altogether because she wanted to get physical. She wanted to kiss and to neck and to smooch and imitate what she saw in older kids and that kind of terrified me because I didn't understand the feelings inside.

At one point your sister teased you also about a woman's school teacher, and you said, "If I wanted to kiss her, I would have to kill her, first."

You can imagine how that goes, the deep dark secrets that one sibling shares with another. It's troubling inside of me. That was from that period that a more advanced period where people were still there, they just weren't animate, they could not react or respond to what I was feeling or what I was sharing because what I was sharing was very embarrassing. Very humiliating. It's hard to talk about now because it obviously affects how a person feels about himself. It's not too hard to get around that because then I look at the wreckage I have behind me; the dead people caused by my self-indulgence in fantasy life and my self-indulgence and not doing something about it, like getting help or taking action against myself. A lot of people have committed suicide at an early age and they don't understand why. A lot of times, again, by troubled parents, and school counselors will water it down into "Well, he couldn't adjust and he was having a difficult time, so he took his life." I would not want to say too casually that they're probably pretty lucky he did. Not in every case and not even in most cases, but in some of those cases you might have had some very inwardly violent young people that they had on the one hand the prospect of what they're about to act out on and the other in a very violent way or a very unsocial and socially abhorrent way. On the other hand, they keep holding it in, you know? Then sometimes they kill themselves.

I played with death. One of my favorite tricks back then was to go out and lay in front of the cars in the traffic. I'm walking down the sidewalk with a friend, you know, it's a roustabout friend and we're clowning around about something. I'll say, "Hey! Check this out," and I'll go lay in the street like a stiff. I'll lay in the street like I got run over and a car comes driving by and of course I'm expecting this guy isn't drunk. I'm expecting this guy isn't slightly demented and say, "Hey! There's a kid laying in front of me! Yeah, it's his fault." Bump, bump, just shift gears going over me. They always stop and they jump out of the car and get all upset when I get up and walk off or run away. It was a little game we played. He didn't go lay in front of the car, so I was doing that. You know, I laugh now because it's embarrassing, but it indicated, I think, how little I thought of myself. I think it indicated that a part of me would rather I got run over right then, then I pursued what I was continuing to pursue in my life because looking at myself and how I was developing inside, nothing good could come of that.

You also had a great admiration for John Wayne at the time.

He looked a lot like my Dad and he acted a lot like my Dad. My Dad was kind of a big loud guy. Actually, John Wayne was six-foot-four, had very little tiny feet. My Dad was six-foot-seven. He had little tiny feet. And you notice how comedians when they imitate how John Wayne walked, uh, there's this rambling thing [*imitates a swaggering walk*] with the hips waving and they always do this trick. You ever wonder why? He didn't just pick that way to walk. I found quite by accident that very big men with very little feet, who have abnormally small feet, have a tough time balancing, and it's a little balancing act they're going through.

I went to Grauman's Chinese Theater[5] after it was renamed and I went and checked all those different footprints out, and here I'd grown up as a kid, not as a very tall kid looking at other people being like this [*holds the flat of his hand at a smaller height than his*], much shorter than me. In my mind's eye, it was all balanced. When I saw pictures of other kids and me, or other people and me, and there's this great difference, it's always shocking to me too, because I never saw it that way. But here I went, I watch all these movies and TV programs and I see these people as being bigger than me because I'm a youth. Then I go to this physical exhibit where it shows their foot size and I step on John Wayne's boot print with this cowboy boot and my shoe completely covers it over. It's gone. When I was 14-years-old, I had bigger feet than he did. You know? When I was 14-years-old, I had bigger feet than my father. I was 6-foot-three-and-a-half, he's six-seven. He works on a construction site as an electrician. I'm going to junior high school. We go to Kenny's, we get the same kind of Oxford shoes. Black Oxfords. I wear a 14-and-a-half ... excuse me [*thinking*] ...I wear a 12-and-a-half, he wears a 12. Alright? In the mix up of getting up and going to work and going to school in the morning, he comes running around the house looking for his shoes. He grabs mine. I can't find mine, so I go running around the house and I grab his, and all day long I'm walking around with his pinched feet. I got blisters developing. He's flopping around at work, half a sizer too big in his shoe and he says, "Goddamn it, I got my kid's shoes again." And they're all saying, "Gee Big Ed," you know, "your kid, you got his shoes on and you're flopping around in them?" And he thought that was great. Well that was a big laugh, right? Hey, I was kind of proud of that, too, because following father's footsteps.

When I was 14-years-old, I put his old Army jacket on, his Class-A uniform. I put his jacket on and if I had pulled my shoulders forward I would have ripped it right up the back because I had broader shoulders than he had. My head's larger than his is. I have a very large head. I wear an 8-3/4 helmet for a motorcycle. 8-3/4 is very big. It's hard to find a helmet like that.

Actually, what's strange is that another serial killer from Santa Cruz, Herb Mullin,[6] grew up hating John Wayne, actually.

I wouldn't blame him, I was in a jail cell right next to him for months and I was in prison up in the hole here, in the lock-up unit, for going on three years with him. About two-and-a-half years, and at one point I got him a job in the kitchen. I was already on the kitchen crew and the sergeant pulled me aside and asked me to talk to the guys about him coming on the crew, because he'd alienated a lot of the guys and they were afraid there'd be violence. So, I talked to them and there was no problem, so they brought him out to the crew. He worked a few months and he goes to the main line. I'm still sitting in the hole saying, "Geez, what happened here?"

You know, I knew Herbie. I don't call him "Herbert Mullin." And of course, I don't call myself Edmund Emil Kemper III either ... I never heard that in my life until I was locked up for murder, right? But little Herbie was, when I met him in Redwood City Jail, okay? Our first meeting was I bumped him out of the priority cell, where they could look from the office and see through the steel door, the glass in the door and see him, physically. Or they could watch the monitor and watch him. He got bumped next door. There was a shower in the priority cell. You never had to leave the cell. For him to shower from the other cell, he had to go out in the main area, they had to lock everybody in one of the ... uh, I guess you call them "tanks." They moved 15 guys... 30 guys, out of the tank into the activity area. They'd walk him around into their tank. He'd shower. He'd come back out and all the way over there and all the way back there. They're cat-calling him. They're calling him names. They're yelling, because he caused them great interruption in their day. Right? He resented that. He got bumped out of the priority cell into a non-shower cell. I got the shower cell. Right?

So, he wasn't too friendly at first. I'd say, "Excuse me, Mr. Mullin." I say, "Do you have a bar of soap? There's no soap over here." He took it all with him. He had no need for it, but he took it with him. He'd say, "yes," and I'd say, "Well, can I use a bar of it?" He said, "No." I'd say, "Oh, I got one of these little shits here ... " and what it is, that he's a little wimpy guy that hates big guys because he always feels intimidated by them. Right? And that's how we started out. So, I started thinking about that and I went back to my old relationships in therapy and group therapy in Atascadero and Youth Authority and stuff and I'm saying, "Okay, well we can deal with this." So I started. I said, "Well, I have to be kind to him." So I found out something he liked. He loved Planter's Peanuts. Little bags of peanuts. Shelled peanuts. So I bought 20-30 bags of them. I didn't care for them myself. I offered him some one day. They were both on camera 24-hours-a-day. So I said, "Herbie, would you like some peanuts?" And he'd say, "Yeah!" And I said, "Oh, I got to him, right down to the inner core there?" "Yeah!" This little childhood thing comes out and it says, "Oh, here!" And he was fascinated by this thought of "Gee! He's just giving me some peanuts and I didn't do anything for them. I don't know him. I'm not being nice to him. Wh would he be giving me some peanuts?" So he comes over to the bars. We can't even see each other, and I reach out with these peanuts around the side, and I see this little hand come out and I thought of it almost as a little monkey paw. It's what it seemed like. So innocent. This little hand comes out, starts to reach for the peanuts, and then he hesitated. He pulls back and I thought, 'Oh, geez, he's defensive. He's thinking I'm gonna' grab his hand and rip his arm off or something. I'm this great big guy, right? So, without saying anything, I just reached around and I laid them on the bars and the pulled my hand away. He took them and he enjoyed them and all of that and I'd say later, I'd say, "Gee, uh, Herbie, did you eat all those peanuts?"

He'd say, "Oh, no, I still got some left."

I said, "Well, I got plenty more, go ahead and enjoy them."

So what I did, I started giving him bags of peanuts, and he had this horrible habit. There's guys back in the tank, and he and I are in these cells facing them through three bars. Three sets of bars. I can't see him and he can't see me. I don't know where on the set of bars he is.

The set of bars [*stretches out his arms wide*] is nine feet wide and eight or nine feet high. When he would get to acting up, he'd sit there for hours writing and writing at this little desk and the other guys were ignoring him, so that night they're watching *Saturday Night Special*, you know, with all of this rock music playing and stuff and they're enjoying it. He'd get up and make this real loud speech about how bad television is for you and why you shouldn't watch it. All the things it'll do to you. And they're having fits. They're trying to throw things at him and they can't get at him. They're raging. They're mad, because he's destroying the one thing they really enjoy and he's just having a ball doing this. They'll sit for hours all day writing this two-hour speech, exactly as long as it takes to watch that show. So, he'd also sit over there and sing these horrible songs. He couldn't sing a lick at all. He's singing these horrible songs and one time I was in the car coming back to Redwood City and the cop got so upset at this singing he's doing at the back of the station wagon, he turns around with his can of mace and says, "I had it, get out of the way Kemper. I'm saying, "Hey, wait a minute! You're going to get me with that stuff." They're just trying to mace the guy in the back of the car because he won't shut up! He's trying to get him to shut up, and the guy just ignored him. He had this way of really getting on people's nerves. So he'd pull these little stunts, these horrible songs and the speeches and things and I say, "Herbie, why do you do stuff like that?" He says, "I have a right to do what I want to do, too." And then "Yeah, okay, right." So, I started this, they call just real basic behavior modification therapy, okay? I had a little bit of psychology study. I worked in the psych testing area in Atascadero. I knew some of these things. So I set up a very basic and very essential—just bare minimum—behavior mod experiment. Behavior modification, right? You reward them when they're good. You punish them when they're bad, and if you're absolutely accurate in when you do these things, quick punishment when they do bad and quick reward when they do good, supposedly this is supposed to attack you at a subliminal level. A subconscious level, and you don't have a lot of control over your reactions. That would improve your behavior, essentially and then have these great elaborate experiments, like in Youth Authority when I went through where they try these things. So, what I did was when he was bad, I'd get a cup full of water in a styrofoam cup and I'd reach around and throw it on him. It's embarrassing and it also gets his papers wet, and, you know . . . so we got this cat and mouse game. When he was good. I'd give him peanuts and I tried gas him when he was bad. It's called "gassing." You throw this water on him, and he'd duck all over the house. I couldn't figure out where he was at so I kept missing him.

So, what I did is I waited one day till I knew he was asleep or I suspected he was. I called one of the guys over to the bars from the place in the back. The tank and I went like this [*Kemper pretends he is sleeping with his folded hands beneath his face for a pillow*]. I says [*he holds his hands out in a mime-gesture to ask 'what is he doing?'*] He reads it and says [*nods yes*]. I say, "Sshh." I called him over to the bars and I said, "Hey, I want to work something out where I can get Herbie with these cups of water and he can't figure out how I'm doing it." I said, "I just thought of a way." He says, "What's that?" And I said, "I want you to set up a grid on the bars where you're at, put a little piece of string, or a little piece of plastic, or a little something he won't notice. Count over how many bars there are on his cell, on his cell front, and from the wall go over that far on your set and set up boundaries. Then, when I give you a signal, that will be a hand signal, very casually walk over, don't look at me, just casually walk over and drape yourself on the bars where he's at so I'll know. If he's back away from the bars, go back that far and position yourself so it's a grid. It's a targeting grid. So he would do this, and Herbie would hear me turn the water on or maybe I'd have some already set up, and I would reach through the bars and I blasted him. I got him every time. He couldn't figure out how all of a sudden I got so accurate. It was without fail. I'd get him with that water. Wham! You know, it's embarrassing and everybody's laughing back there and "Good shot,

Ed!" And all that stuff, and then I'd ask him if he'd do something, or "Hey, can we do this" or whatever, you know, and he'd participate in something with me. I'd give him peanuts. When he's bad, he gets blasted with water. This went on for two or three weeks.

He actually got away from the bad behavior when he said, "Hey! I want to sing!"

I says, "Well, hey guys in the back, do you mind if he sings?"

"Oh, we don't want to hear that shit, man!"

I said, "Hey, you want to hear it now or do you want to hear it tonight when you're watching the show?"

"Yeah, okay."

"So, go ahead, Herbie, sing."

He'd sing for 30-40 seconds, and then get bored and say, "Gee, I don't want to do this anymore." You know? Because the fun was gone out of it. But the point is, I got a handle on his behavior, and the cops are watching this. The deputies are on camera watching me. I mean, they're on the monitors watching every move I'm making. Right? And they're fascinated. They're watching this thing go back and forth with me and Herbie. They're not involving themselves. They're just watching it, and after a while, one of them come in and said, "Herbie is completely cooperative now. He's not messing around." Because, I've been ... as we're talking, these little frictions out between he and I, I'm showing him some insights into why people don't like him, and showing some insights into what his behavior is causing in them and he has realized by that point that it was just he's reacting to how people are reacting to him. It's just a self-perpetuating thing, and it was the only way he could get out his negative feelings. I said, "Well, why don't you focus on the positive. Focus on the positive instead and the negative will go away." I don't think anybody ever did that with him before, because he responded real well to it, and later when we were up here in the hole together, and we weren't even supposed to be together, they didn't want us together. But we were up in the hole together. I was the only guy he could talk to.

He had a lot of pain inside. He had a lot of anguish inside. He had a lot of hate inside and it was addressed to people he didn't even know because he didn't dare do anything to the people he knew because he was aware of all of the structure around that, and that would be the end of his life. So I started ... the way I found out about these things is I would pose little comments or questions aimed at him as we're sitting up there on the tier, on the concrete floor, sitting against the wall talking to one another.

I would say, "How did you feel, you know, when you bought that little Saturday Night Special. 22? Did you ever go out shooting with that? You know, just target shooting?"

He says, "Well, not much."

I say, "Well, try this on. You loaded it up, you went out. You set up bottles, You set up cans. You set them around in little areas right around close and practice shooting them real fast." And he looks at me all shocked, he says, "How do you know that?" I said, "Because that's what I used to do. Those were people, those weren't cans and bottles and you never told anybody." So he got all fascinated about how I was able to read his mind and stuff. I wasn't. I saw a kindred spirit there, somebody who was doing something very similar to what I was doing as a child. He went to mental institutions and he went through these processes where these doctors told him what was wrong with him, and these doctors treated things that they decided were wrong with him and he just sat back very passively and went through these treatments and they had almost no effect on him because he didn't dare say what was really going on in his head. They would cast him off somewhere. He'd be totally separated from the human race and there were certain things he and certain things I enjoyed in being in the human race and being part of the human race we weren't willing to let go of. So that was that little desperate hanging on. So here comes these professionals saying, "Oh *this* is what's wrong with you little lad and *this* is what's wrong with you and we're gonna' fix this up," and "Okay, okay I'm well and yeah." He goes out and buys a gun and starts killing people, and I talk about what happened when he killed those people.

"Oh, they fell dead."

"No, they did this, they did that, they gurgled and that some of them kept moving like you hadn't even shot them and you shot them again."

He says, "How did you know this? You weren't there!"

I says, "I know."

"I never told anybody that!"

"I know. I was there on my own trip. I know what happened. Herbie don't give me that bullshit about earthquakes[7] and don't give me that crap about God was telling you." I said, "You couldn't even be talking to me now if God was talking to you because of the pressure I'm putting on you right now; these little shocking insights into what you did. God would start talking to you right now if you were really that kind of ill because I grew up with people like that. Where? In a maximum security hospital for the criminally-insane. Adults. I was 15-years-old when I went there.

To go back before that time, when you ran away from your mother and went to your grandmother...

No. I went to my father.

Yes, but afterwards, when you went to your grandmother, you were 14, I think? Why did you feel you had to kill her?

That was an outburst. It wasn't a head. I felt I had to ... I went up there hoping ... I didn't go there, for one thing. I got left there. We went there for Christmas, from my father's in L.A. We went up to the mountains to stay for Christmas and I got left behind. I was having friction with my step-brother and my step-mother. There was problems there. We were vying for his interests and vying for his love. They were desperate because they're the new family. I'm desperate because I've never had the man of my life. I wanted my father's love. I wanted his approval. I wanted his recognitions and we all got very greedy and desperate at that time so we fought each other a lot, and it was a lot of friction and he couldn't handle that. So, he got rid of me. I was old family. I was already a failure. So, you know, I got parked up in the mountains. There's a lot of dressing on it, and window dressing and things, but I was up there with them for ten months. At first it was okay, because it was the calm of being away from Montana. There wasn't the hellious stuff. I was going to a good school. As the months went on, the veneer went away. My grandmother had made agreements with me from the gate that she wouldn't get into little humiliating mind-games with me like my mother and step-father had done. Right? I agreed I wouldn't do certain things. Then this mind game stuff started up. She decided she was going to raise me like she raised her three sons. She was going to get rid of all of this negative crap that my mother put on me. She's recognizing it as something my mother put on me and I didn't know that it wasn't . . . some of it was. But a lot of it was my inability to deal with complex critical psychological situations. I could not deal with them, so I resisted it. I ran away. That was my answer, to run.

I ran from the people in Montana. I ran from my mother in Montana. I let my father park me up there to get away from the strife in L.A. Now I'm stuck. All the bridges are burned because my grandparents are there 24-hours-a-day. I can't run from them. She never let me get out of her sight for more than an hour without yelling my name out to see where I was. She was convinced I wanted to go down the mountain into town, little North Fork, to hang around with kids. Rowdies and stuff and be a juvenile delinquent. So she would never let me go down there on my own. She never let me leave the property, and ... I just ... it started simmering, I guess. It started building, the passions and the tensions. I started developing the fantasies toward her, from my mother, killing her. And then the decapitation fantasies were even there. They were in place by then, already.

And what was those fantasies?

What were they?

Yes.

Possessing the severed heads of women. Men didn't turn me on. That wasn't very... I couldn't appreciate the appearances of a guy. I see movies as a youth and I'm, you know, I'm seeing ... this was a ... not common.... But it was a frequent feature in some movies where they use a shock effect. They'll have someone get their head cut off or there's a head sitting there when they come around the corner or open the drawer or something and it went from ... that got caught up in my morbid fascination. I made a comment and someone wrote about it, that when I was young—I was about 8 or 9 years old—I went to this little "Come On," it was like at a record store or something and they had this crowd of kids there and there was a magic show, and this guy, you've probably seen it, the fake guillotine, hand-pressed, and they put the potato there and someone puts their neck in the brace, and they slam this thing down and the potato down below chops in two, but the person's head doesn't fall off. Right? And everybody gets very fascinated by that ... "Oh my God!" And then when he puts the blade in place, and he pushes it down, it goes through that neck hole, but it never chops anybody's head off. Okay, so ... he wanted a volunteer out of the ... I'm not standing in this crowd watching this show. He wanted a volunteer out of the audience. Some quite beautiful little 16-year-old girl gets up there and this big laugh and you're all giddy and stuff. I started getting caught up in this and I said, "Wow!" Right at that moment, I departed reality because logically I should have been able to ascertain that that could not happen. You're not going to get away with chopping somebody's head off in the middle of Helena, Montana, the capital city. But the concept of it was so raw and it was titillating, I said, "Wow! Gee, I gotta' watch this." And he had her girlfriend come over and put her hands there to catch her head so it wouldn't fall in the basket, you know, and he was making jokes about this. I got caught up in this interplay between normal concerns. You don't want her to get a bump on her head, but hey, if you're chopping her head off it doesn't matter! Right? And this is catching in my mind somehow, and I'm saying, "Wow!"

Naturally, everybody let out a shriek, and they're all excited and wow, and as he chops in the potato fall and her head doesn't go anyplace. He unlocks the brace and she gets up laughing and he gives some little prize for coming up and participating in the experiment. That's the first time I'd ever seen a show like that. You know, you see things like that on TV, it's one thing, but to be there and watch things like that you get more caught up in it.

I went from there and it became another piece. That's the only way I can really ... the only event in my life that I can align that fascination with ... was the fact that she was a very alluring young lady. I'm coming close to approaching puberty. I think I hit it a little early, because between the ages of 10 and 13, I was going through some incredible emotional shifts. They say that going into puberty for a young man and girls, I guess, is a very upheaving time in our lives. Without a lot of positive input from parental or adult figures, it can go in some really wild directions. In my case, it was embedded in this negative orientation thing. I would go back to my basement bedroom and I would fantasize to protect myself. I'd go off into fantasy worlds that got vengeance on my enemies. It got even with the bullies who picked on the kids and me at school. It got even with someone who slighted me.

There's even adults, I mean, they talk in various relationships how we have our darker side and there's things that you have thought as an example, that you never want to share with anybody because they're so cruel or they're so unspeakably out of sync with what's going on, that you would be too ashamed to share it with someone. Like, "You, boy, I'd like to knock his head off, " or "I'd like to *kill* this guy!" Or, "She's such a bitch" you know ...we all do that. I didn't know that. So, I'm adding to this problem, the impetus of this negative orientation. I must be a really evil little kid because I'm thinking all these horrible things. I was thinking of them in increasing amounts and increasing frequency so it's a kind of conditioning, and negative conditioning that I wasn't aware of other than effect. I noticed that if I worked on a certain scenario, or a certain kind of patterning in my fantasies, right after a while it became numb. It became insignificant. It became not enough, so I had to add embellishments to it. A new level, and it is just very subtle, but over many many years it just kept going more and more. Ive known young people that Ive been able to talk to honestly and they've ... knowing them well enough and friendly enough over enough years, share with me because it a cure, it was real importance to me to know where I dove off the deep end. They would admit that sometimes they ... and they went off into happier orientations. They had a period where they went off into some real morbid or negative fascinations, but they "grew out of it."

It stopped providing a service they needed. It stopped filling a hole or a gap or, let's say an adult came along and started sharing something with them or showed them a new avenue of acting out that completely obliterated that need or vacated it, and they let it go. I didn't. The adult wasn't there. My mother was there. She was there to beat me. She was there to humiliate me,. She was there to use me as an example of how inferior men are. That was a great little lady there. She kind of preceded this female movement we have now of getting rights. Of getting equal rights, of getting equal standing, of getting equal presence in various theaters. I was finding out the hard way what women's rights and women's antagonisms. Women are driven about things like that. They get upset about the belittlements they get and the lack of equal quality that they should ... that they have that they experience. Unfortunately, my mother developed and I'm not ... it's not fair to talk about a dead person that way, they can't defend themselves, they can't give you another perspective on what really happened. I can only surmise to try to be fair.

Looking back on it, I'm seeing that she was making an effort to balance her pain with what she was experiencing. If you look at her dad, he's a wimp. He never did anything. Mom did everything, so she orientated toward her, so she comes out doing that stuff, I find out in sociological studies and psychological studies that that's normal. Not necessarily healthy, but that happens. And my Dad being the wimp out of his family goes and finds my Mom who's the dynamo out of her family and they get married, and it'll either work or it won't. In his case it didn't work because she kept hammering on him. She wanted him to change *this*. She wanted him to change *that*. He couldn't handle that. After 13 years he'd had enough. What I resented was that I had a mother, I had a father. Father worked, he brought in a big paycheck. We had a nice house. We had friends. We went to school. We had birthdays. We had Christmas. We had vacations. Huh? He had Saturday night with the poker buddies out in the guest house by the garage. We were living pretty good and she absolutely hated that, this stereotypical response of this deadhead, this muttonhead she's married to, of wanting to go out and play cards in a smoke-filled room, drinking beer and with these old war buddies. She had another problem. My father was in the first Special Service Force in World War II. They did a book and a movie called *The Devil's Brigade*[8]. He was a combat sergeant in that group and he volunteered for that as a single man. They would not take married men. Thats how my parents met. She was working as a secretary in Helena, Montana, the capital city. He's a few miles out of town at an old retired closed down cavalry fort for the U.S. Army that was reopened as a secret base for these guys to train out of at Fort William Henry Harrison just outside of town. They got to know each other. They quite .. it wasn't secretly, but it was very quietly, got married. They didn't know he got married. He'd have been kicked out of the group. This is what was described as a suicide brigade. 5,000 men trained in just in all his devastation ways., he goes off to war and he does some horrible things. He can't talk about those things [...]

[*tape cuts off*]

Two years before you committed crimes, I think you traveled quite a lot on the freeways at night or picking ups hitchhikers ...

During the day.

During the day?

Yeah, I traveled a lot because I'd been locked up for five-and-a-half-years. I never had a license... well, I just gotten a license when I got locked up the first time, the Montana license, and so I was free. The driving around was a way to exhibit that freedom, to demonstrate it, to get the cobwebs out of me. When I first got out, I loved to drive. I always did love as a kid to drive. I stayed driving when I was 10 or 12-years-old, but I got a license when I was 15 up in Montana, and then I got locked up and then here in California, and I got out and got a license and I just started driving, and that was my main hobby, I'd say. I saw a lot of people out hitchhiking and I didn't select girls to pick up. I picked up anybody who wanted a ride. Over that whole three-year period, it was the same way. If someone needed a ride, I picked them up, unless specifically I was looking for someone to do in.

The crimes, it goes from May to September [1972] ... May 7th - Sunday to Thursday - September 14th, then it hops over to January [1973], right? And then to February. It's speeding up. It's coming to a head. It's getting to where it wasn't a cyclical thing, but it was coming to where it was coming more often, and something I didn't tell a whole lot of people—I guess I did tell in one interview—shortly before it all ended, I drove up to the Bay Area and I was ... well, I was living there ... I was up in Alameda living with my mother in Santa Cruz and commuting because I had to work up there and I stayed with a friend. I went out to Berkeley and I drove Ashby Avenue, one of the places I used to drive looking for coeds. I drove from HWY-80 up Ashby Avenue to HWY-13. The first two coeds I killed were on Ashby Avenue.

They were 5'-2", slight of figure, you know, we call "petite," and the one is black hair, one's blonde hair, okay? Now I'm driving the opposite direction of Ashby Avenue. It's a year later. I'm seeing if I can maintain. I'm not hunting. I'm out seeing if I can maintain. I have a weapon in the car. I have everything else fitting the situation. I'm seeing if I can maintain. If I can just let go of it and maintain and marry this young lady and go on. I go driving up there and here's two young ladies, 5'-2". One's got blonde hair. One's got black hair. They're in granny dresses and I'm having shit-fits because it's like *déjà vu* and I ... oh my God, I just acted in a way that they wouldn't be paranoid, because I'm a young man, by myself in this car. I defused the situation as I drove up. I'd gotten practice at that. All that driving around? It wasn't rehearsing. I made a game out of driving around picking people up and later on I discerned that some people wouldn't get in my car because of the situation. I'm a young man by myself. It's unsafe. So, I thought, 'Well, gee, that kind of put me off. I'm not doing anything to anybody, so I want to see if I can change that situation where they'll want to get in and I can take them where they're going because I know I'm not going to do anything, and I got to where I could defuse that situation. Is [it] how you're looking if you're looking at ... [like] "Oh, boy! How are you?" You start cranking the car over there. They're not going to get in your car, because they can see you from half a block away drooling. But if you look at your watch and say, "Jeez, I don't know if I have enough time" and you're kind of looking in the mirror, looking around, you pull over and it's guys .... It's the "businessman going somewhere" and get in this car and we'll go where we're going, and it's little games I played. So they get in the car and then we chatted. I talked about things. I found out where their orientations were and their little ... what they used to judge, and who could get in and who they could get in with, and who they couldn't, right? In that sense it's been interpreted as ... what do you call it? "Rehearsing." Not true. It's like playing chess and then turning it into something ugly. I played chess casually, I played chess more and more thoroughly till I got very good at it, which was picking up people to where I could make you a bet. I could pick up those two ladies, and they'd say, "Oh man, you're crazy! Those are two very crafty young ladies who won't get in a car with a young man by himself, etc. etc. I'd win the bet because I knew how to defuse the situation, even if they asked, "Where're you headed?" Right? And they had a sign saying where they're going, but they'd asked ... or, even if they didn't, they'd say, "Where are you headed?" I had ways of developing it to where they wouldn't get suspicious. But it didn't mean I was going to kill them. It meant I was playing a game and then later when I started killing people, I used that against them. But initially, it was just a hobby. It was a habit. It was trying to fill in the blanks of five-and-a-half years of not being in society. I missed that flower child generation. I missed the entry into Vietnam. All that stuff, and all these kids are like aliens to me. Yeah, I say "kids." I missed 16-17-18-19-20-21. I'm supposed to be associating with people in their adult years, but I missed a big chunk, so I'm out there trying to fill in the gaps, to find out why these kids are the way they are now because they were totally different from the kids that I was when I was that age. Totally different. I'm trying to fill the gaps in, and then later I changed that to something ugly. Why? My mother works at the university. My mother won't introduce me to any young ladies at the university because I'm like my father and I don't deserve to know any of those young ladies, so here she is holding these little girls up there as "too good" for me. Very special. If anything, I was destroying icons. I was hurting her without her even knowing it.

Again, it's that picking, you know... petty and ineffectual "I'm getting back at you but I don't have the heart top tell you what doing." See? Why would I admit those things on a camera? That's embarrassing. It's humiliating.

How would you select your victims?

I didn't select them. It was random, and it was also the development of the passion. If I was drove, they died. Like the last two victims. I was so pissed, I'd have killed anybody that got in the car. But there was times I drove a woman and her son, clear up into Oregon, crossed over to the Coast highway and drove back down, and like 8:30-9:00 at night, falling misty highway, and I'm driving along, there's not a car near me, it's a totally alien county. This is way up around Eureka or something ... and there's these two, I say, probably high school girls. They looked to be 17 or 18-years-old. They're hitching the first ride into town because they snuck off the farm, they'd gone the half a mile or so off the road. They're gonna' hit on into town, have a good time and sneak back. It was obvious, because they were grabbing the first ride they could get.

And here I've been, fighting my inner impulses to not go off on this woman and her 12-year-old son whose hitchhiking clear back to Seattle. Right? I'm struggling with these feelings. I don't want to do it, man. You don't know how to do it anyway. You're weak. You're a punk. I don't want to do it. All day long I'm doing this. By the time I'm coming back down that highway, I'm exhausted. I'm driving along just to get home. Here's a perfect situation. I cannot get busted. It exceeds the criterion of picking someone up and not getting caught. No one knows me in the county. No one seen me going through it, right? It's a fog-shrouded night. Nobody could even see me if their home was in view, and I don't know that. I picked them up. We drove into town about two miles, three miles. I dropped them off. I got some gas and kept right on going. I was not in a proper state of mind to do something like that. It blew me away, I couldn't believe it. It was like it was handed to me on a platter. Scared the hell out of me. I couldn't do it. I had everything I needed.

Again, so about the selection and the preparation, if I was selecting and preparing and everything was all set, that's it. I got 'em. But I didn't. They're not dead. As I said, that is an example of [how] many times that kind of thing happened. All of a sudden, somebody shows up out of nowhere. I pick them up to take them where they're going, but I didn't do that to them because the mindset was all wrong. The only time people got killed was when she and I was fighting like cats and dogs and I couldn't deal with it. I couldn't vent it any other way. I look back on it, and I'm not saying Im right or wrong, but I'm looking back on it saying I think they were surrogates. I was killing her, not them. I was attacking her station. I was attacking her stance in that university setting. Also, I hated the university for what it was doing to her. She worked her butt off; they took every bit of it: "Oh, yeah, we love that ... okay, here's some more, you want some more authority? You want some more responsibility? Here ..." It was eating her up. She went into that job sober. She came out of that job damn near canned because she went to work drunk one day. She couldn't cope with it and it was destroying her a little at a time. She needed help, but if you told her she needed a mental hospital ... if *I* told her she needed a mental hospital, if my little sister told her she needed a mental hospital, or a "dry out" program, she would have peeled our skin for us. We did not mess with that woman. My sister... my little sister was cheating on her husband when my mother was murdered. If she had known my littler sister was doing that, she probably would've been out of the family. That was totally outrageous to her Victorian mores, as she grew up in this twisted Victorian bullshit ideals that her mother laid on her as a kid and twisted her life with ... then she tried to run that shit on my Dad.

You said you had a lot of sympathy and empathy toward Mary Anne Pesce when you talked to her, but isn't that strange to say that after you had killed her in such a brutal fashion?

There was a draw... there was a draw to the young lady that was haunting. I'm not saying I had compassion toward her when I talked to her. I tried to remember what we talked about. In fact, I think what I said about her was that she epitomized what really drove me. She was a haughty young lady. She's kind of stuck-up. Distant. I look back on it and I see a girl that was not beautiful. She was not plain. She was somewhere in between and she was caught up in that beauty thing, like kids in the Valley are, okay? Valley girls[9] trying to make something of themselves and exploit little attributes they have, and to downplay other ones, and she was playing Little Miss Distant with me, and her friend was very open and very ... her roommate was very open and very ... a country girl talking and stuff and it's sad because Peche was the ... Mary Anne was the expert at hitchhiking. She had half her life in Europe. She'd hitchhiked around Europe. She'd done it in the United States. She was good at it. She didn't want to get in the car, but she had talked her ... she had two roommates, okay? And one went on the trip with her to Berkeley and to Stanford and back to Fresno State. Only one would go with her, and apparently—I'm thinking back—the other one was so close to going that later when she found out what happened to her two roommates, she dropped out of college. She came to testify at my trial and she was devastated by the whole thing, so I'm thinking she almost went and she realized she might have died, too. Who knows? But I don't even know that Id have picked them up if there's three of them. I don't know. I don't know if they'd have been where they were. All the circumstances could have changed, but I'm thinking that it ... because it had such a violent effect on her college education, she was that close to going.

The other girl, Anita Luchessa, wasn't a hitchhiker. She had been raised by her family [who told her] "don't do things like that. That's totally out of line," and her friend talked her into it. Once she got into it and she saw how much fun it was and they meet the different people and then talk with people that by the time they're leaving Berkeley, right? It's all about who gets the front seat and who gets the back seat. So she opened the door and asked where I was headed, and it said "STANFORD" right on the sign they were holding up, and I said, "I'm going to Palo Alto, I could drop you off." "Oh, great!" And she jumps in, grabs her stuff and jumps in, opens the back seat up for her friend who's standing there looking at me and serious about whether or not, because I could tell at the time. She knows better than to get in. Single adult. It's a coupe instead of a four-door car, so she cannot get out other than through the front seat. So, that's all the warning signs of not getting in with a single kind of a situation. All of the things were wrong about it, but when I drove up I pulled that little stunt of looking at my watch. You know ... [miming that he is glancing at a wrist watch], "Do I have time to pick them up?" You wouldn't believe how much effect that kind of thing has and when she kept staring at me and looking ... looking for something wrong in my eyes. I gave this look back like, "I don't understand, why are you looking at me like this?"I gave her that back and she said, "Aw, this guy's a dork. He's innocent as hell." She gets in. Okay.

We're driving along and I'm looking at this lady in the rear-view mirror, and I look back at it years later and I'm saying, 'she kept looking at me back too.' Right in the eyeballs. I'm wearing dark glasses, but they're not totally dark, and I'm realizing now that she could see me looking at her and she was looking right back at me and instead of saying something to me, like "What are you looking at?" Or, "Hey, maybe you got to drop us off" or something like that ... she just kept looking back at me and I'm looking at her, and she keeps looking at me. I think she's playing this little game. It's not really teasing, so to speak, it's just this little psychological game back and forth that men and women do sometimes. The young girl in the front, Anita, was at one point in the driving—and I'm sure they were doing little looks at each other and little comments that I didn't pick up on because I'm driving, and looking for places to go—that somewhere in that communication she gave me this sexy little look, you know, like 'Oh boy, you're a pretty good-looking guy, you know, da-da-da.' I smiled back at her, but not this hungry"I'd like to get down with you" kind of thing. It was just I smiled back at her and I saw it for what it was; it's an 18-year-old girl that's feeling her oats. She's not doing anything wrong. It's sad. It's real pathetic, but some of this stuff, I was getting real caught up with this girl in the backseat. You know, I was … she was, you know, to me at that point, she was really beautiful. She had the most incredible blue eye, right? She had this really shiny black hair that was turning me on. I was getting drove, because I just kept playing this game of picking people up, and I had plugged in those fantasies of killing people and, you know, the titillating little fantasies. I keep walking away from that and I put myself down as being weak for not being able to do something about that. Right?

So, I kept driving. I drive around myself saying, 'I got to do something. I got to do something about this.'

How were you feeling while you were killing?

Well, especially the first two which were very messy. It was a shock that first time. That horrified me. I did everything stupid. I did everything wrong if I were trying to get away with it. It was just really really dumb. The knife I fell back on, that was a fall back position. I was trying to smother her. That didn't work, and she was struggling against that and arguing with me about it and I got frustrated and I reached in my pocket and I had that folding knife and I pulled it out. For a lot of years—and I made a point of saying back then to the investigators—when I pulled the knife out and locked it into place, it clicked and she said, "What's that?" That's a quote, "What's that?" And she was kind of like a nagging kind of thing: "What's that?" I couldn't figure out why she said that. Like, it's not that big an impact. A little clicking sound behind her, you know, amongst what's going on and it hadn't been murderous up to that point. It had been an aggravation and I had her tied up. Handcuffed. It took me years for it to dawn on me, trying to look at it from different points of view to understand these things, why she said that.

You know she said that? Because I had brandished this gun, and I had cocked it once and it clicked. So, in her mind, very possibly, I had pulled the gun out and was going to shoot her. So, she said, "What's that?" And thinking I pulled the gun out now and I'm cocking it, not realizing I'd pulled a knife out. I still had the gun in my pants. I stabbed her. She didn't fall dead. You're supposed to fall dead. You're supposed to go "ohhh" and fall dead. I've seen it in all the movies, right? It doesn't work that way. When you stab someone, they leak to death. They lose blood pressure and you stab them more and more and more. You complicate it many times by where you're hitting; the pain you're causing; and, the aggravation of the person involved. Plus, whether or not they leak a little faster. It wasn't working worth a damn. I stabbed her all over her back and she even turned around, I stabbed her in the side and int he stomach once. Why? As she turned around I could have stabbed her through the heart. But her breasts were there, and had actually deflected me. I couldn't see stabbing a young woman in her breast. That's embarrassing. I didn't say that to them back then. I don't think ... I may have, but that's humiliating to admit that I was that affected by her presence. I stabbed her in the belly. That had to hurt worse. I didn't do it to make it hurt. I was trying to shut her up. She ended up getting her throat cut. I learned the term "ear-to-ear," what that meant because that's the way it went. She went out of it completely right then. She lost consciousness and died probably just moments after that. But I just backed up out of the car. My hands are covered in blood, and I'm saying, "Oh God, I did it! I did it! I don't believe it! I did it! Shit! I've done it now. I got to kill the other one."

Toward the end when I picked those two girls, I said they were just like the first two, like Mary Anne Pesce and Anita Luchessa, who taunted me all this time, and now two more just like them get in my car. We drive up HWY-13 and we get to this figure 8 cloverleaf interchange where it hits HWY-580, and they want to go under the freeway back up on and head out this way, and out that way I happen to know just a couple of miles down the road is Palomares Road where I took Anita Luchessa and Mary Ann Pesce and killed them.

Mills College is back this way [Kemper points to his right], toward downtown, They don't think so, they want to go [pointing to his left] this way. I'm saying, "Gee, you don't want to go that way," and I can't tell them why.

"You do not want to go that way. Mills College is *this* way."

"Well, no, we go there and we know, we live there and we want to go."

And as we're approaching this interchange, I'm saying "No, we need to go in the right lane, get up on the freeway and go downtown. You want to get theft lane, go under, cross up and that's going to be another step closer to you dying." Because even if I don't go all the way out to Palomares Road, up 580, if I stop where it starts to go out in the country, and get back on the freeway, that's where I used to work on the highways. That's one of the places where it's a cul-de-sac, you drive down there. It's a very quiet street. It comes down up onto the freeway very sharply and they're dead. If these urges take over, and if I go that way, it's not encouraging me to stop. It's testing beyond where I want to test. We've already gone beyond that with them getting in the car, because, geez, it's just like those first two.

I was actually scared to death I was going to kill them. By that point, I had killed all of the coeds. Those two months after the last two, and I'm seeing if I can pull out of it, like drinking or something, or smoking, and at the point where we're bickering, if they'd started shrieking or banging on the windows, I'm busted! They're going to pull me over. Someone's going to call a cop or something. They're gonna' get me and probably bust me on these other cases on a fluke. I'm trying to save their lives. I don't want them going that way because I know Mills College is this other way. They get scared shitless.

"Oh, my God, we shouldn't have gotten in this guy's car!" And they're getting all puckered up. I said, "Just bear with me, be patient. If I'm wrong, I'll get on the turn-off and we'll go right back around to take you out your way, but I know it's the next turn-off, the one past it this way. Downtown. Trust me, please." And they're sitting like this [mocks the girls sitting stiffly and afraid] and they couldn't talk and they're looking straight ahead and I'm saying, 'Shit! Gun is under the seat. It's all just, you know, woah!" I get up on the freeway two turn offs. The next one said, "Mills College - Next Exit." But they;'re not relaxing or nothing. I had refused to take them the way they wanted to go and pushed it the other way. That's what scared them. But, they didn't know that the irony of it was if I had gone along their way, I'd have probably said, "Yeah, yeah, well I just follow through and oops! We'll do it one more time." How do you "oops" human lives? I don't know those two young ladies. I don't know where they are today, and I don't know that they remember that little incident. But when I drove them to Mills College, inside of Mills College to their college entrance, right to the building to the dormitory and they got out of that car and flew up those stairs, never even looked back. I'll bet they quit hitchhiking quite so casually after that, but you know what? I don't think they know to this day how close that came, and the irony of it is just to shut them up and not have them freak out, I could have gone the other way. But by that time, then we're going back up that groove of what I had done already, and what I was familiar with. See what I'm saying? And that day I knew that I could not stop doing it. I knew I had no control over it. I had just minimal controls, but mainly I could not stop it. It was going to happen again and between that weekend day, it was a Saturday or a Sunday, I think it was a Sunday, between that Sunday and the next Saturday, all that week I was working, I built an image in my head my mother's going to die. I'm going to kill her and I'm going to go to it with the police and we're going to hold court in the street, and they're going to pound me in the ground and they can fill in the blanks because I don't want to be around to explain it.

All that week, I just ... it was a conviction that just got deeper and deeper in me. I got more and more morose. I got less and less talkative at work. I got more somber about what I was doing, because almost every minute of every day I knew that's what that next weekend held. That was Easter weekend, right? Worked half-a-day, Friday. Went back to Santa Cruz Friday afternoon. Was drinking Friday night. I fell asleep before my mother came home. Woke up after she came home and the last words we had were an argument, right? I walked into her bedroom to chat with her. I was back home. I'm not going to try and blame her dying, I'm just saying in the back of my mind I was hoping she could say something, or I'd say something that could stop all of this shit. A little childish hope in the back of my mind and she'd say something. I'd just play it off.

But you still went with a hammer?

Wait a minute. You're wiping out the moment here. I went in there hoping I could stop this stuff in the back of my head. I'm not planning on it. I'm just a little hope and the first thing out of her mouth was .. she's reading this book and she just flaps it down on herself and says, "Oh my God. I suppose now you want to stay up all night and talk." That was one of her favorite peeves when I come in late at night and want to talk and once in a long while, like that night, I'd spun on my heel and said, "Nope! Goodnight." I walked back out, and she knew she'd hurt my feelings and the next day we'd sit down and talk. Except I knew that we weren't going to talk. I went back into my room and I laid down. I did not go to sleep. I laid there for three to four hours, till 4:00-5:00 in the morning. A little after five in the morning, and walked in there with a hammer. I came to the side of her head and cut her throat.

[tape cut]

At first I did, yeah, but that stopped because at first I was hoping I could get off.. I could get a vicarious thrill out of seeing those pictures and say, "Well, this will be satisfying enough." One, two people died, it doesn't have to go past that, and I'll see why I don't want to do it again. Those pictures lasted about two weeks. I come back from work two days after I did it. I mean, Tuesday, right? Sunday it happened. Monday, I took off. Took CTO ... compensatory time off ... and I go back to work Tuesday. I come home from work Tuesday, a hard day at work. I'm feeling like I used to feel. I've done some work that day. I've accomplished something, and I'm saying, "I can't believe I did this stuff! I must have dreamed it. This must be some kind of weird dream." I come back to the house. I pick up the corner of the carpet. I pull out these pictures and an envelope and I said, "Jeez, I don't believe this." Now I've got to believe it. That really happened. See? That was distance from what I had done just one day later that I couldn't believe, or two physical days later, that I couldn't believe that I'd actually done that. After two weeks, I couldn't handle the reality of those pictures. I've seen ... I've read where guys have hung criminals, like in the Old West, and tanned the guy's hide and made a pair of shoes on it ... the doctor did. I think it was a city doctor, and took his skull and made an inkwell out of it with gold hinges on it for the pens. This was some kind of notorious criminal, right? I said, "Gee, that's kind of grisly." [...]

[*tape cut*]

The two girls were killed around 6:00 p.m. By eleven the next morning, they are both completely gone out of my life. Physically. All right? That's not even 24 hours. The third murder,[10] which was the second incident, okay? I'm in the middle of trying to get my record sealed. Right? Thursday night, I killed her. I took off Friday. I didn't go to work. I called in sick, took CTO, all right? Dismembered her body, got rid of her body but kept her head and her hands because they're identifiable. They're highly identifiable. I kept those at the apartment, okay? That Friday night ... uh, Thursday night. Friday morning, she was dismembered. Friday night, she was disposed of, right? Saturday morning, I left. Right? And I wasn't satisfied that I took the head along with the hands. But I couldn't put them someplace that I couldn't be sure they would be dug up by an animal, or just be somewhere. It's scary, going out there, trying to bury somebody, or dispose of body parts in a community or out even in the boonies [11] where you don't know where you're at and who can come up at any moment. I had some real close calls there. Or, people that come out of nowhere, and if a body's found and they remember this beige-looking car sitting there that night. That's evidence! So, it was very hard to get rid of this stuff. Anyway, it's Saturday morning. I went to see the psychiatrist in Fresno. Saturday afternoon, I saw the other one. Saturday evening, I'm with my fiancé and her family over in Turlock. Sunday night, I come back to my apartment. [...]

[tape cut]

It was like a trophy thing. It was ... it's disgusting, but it was kind of a power trip. I always felt intimidated by women. I always felt overpowered by them as a kid. When I stopped making it as an adult .... when I was doing great socially on the job base, making friends locally, having buddies and stuff, you know, have a pizza and a beer and stuff, no problem. I got friends for that. But making women friends was real tough. Battling my mom on the one hand and trying to make friend with women is a little bit of a problem because there was a lot of crossover there and she was opening a lot of old wounds, pushing a lot of buttons and she liked to watch me twitch. That's the only thing I can say. There was a little bit of sadism in her too, and I hated her for that because she was the one person in the world to push every button I had because she knew where they all were. As I got better and smarter and better at what I did and more involved in the public and a better all-around adult, it's as if she were offended by that and you ask, "Why?" Okay? Just look at the vanity of being a mother. She raised me at a horrible time from Day One as an individual parent raised. I fight every day, right? The state comes in, she's a proud woman. She's a vain woman, she was real proud and she's raised that way, the state of California takes her son away from her and says, "We are taking your son away because you must be an unfit mother. He is a murderer. He killed people." I've tried to look any it from her point of view.

"If you could raise your son right, you wouldn't kill people, lady. We're taking him."

And in the mere 5-and-a-half years of bureaucracy, and she had nothing. No respect for California bureaucracy. She used to make jokes about that all the time, about if you want to waste the rest of your life doing nothing, apply for something through a bureaucratic process in California. Those bureaucrats took me away from her and in 5-and-a-half years of filter farming around, they hand me back and now I'm an over-achiever? Huh? Good-looking strapping young man, wants to go work, wants to make a living for himself, wants to be sociable, he isn't paranoid and pulling away from people anymore ... that shocked the hell out of her. It had to have... she didn't share that with me, but I'm saying that must have really tore her and made her feel all the more a bad mother. I have a feeling that she couldn't be a part of that healing process, so she attacked it because I became a cancer in his life. I reminded her every day what a rotten mother she must be, and I'm saying she was ... she must be a rotten mother, look what the state did for me, and she couldn't. They couldn't have insulted her any worse if they'd have tried, and they didn't try. They were trying to solve a problem by paroling me to her, so I'll stay out of trouble and go be a good adult. Pay taxes, and guess what? That's the one furnace they should not have put me back in because, hey, she had no help on the other end to sort through her feelings because she was too proud to get help. So we fought and we fought, and that's the only excuse I can make in my head. She's not here to discuss it, that's the only balance I can put in there, is that I must have been a terrible accuser to her, a terrible accusal of what a rotten mother she was, or she could have done better. Even the state raised me with apparent ease. They locked me away in an adult institution where I should have been raped and I should have been mutilated and I should have been screwed over and been like Charlie Manson when he was raped as a kid in prison and Youth Authority, now, and then he starts raping other people, and he's a leader of that stuff, and he's manipulating people. [...]

[*tape cuts*]

---

1. H.H. Holmes - Herman Webster Mudgett (May 16, 1861 – May 7, 1896), better known as Dr. Henry Howard Holmes or H. H. Holmes, was an American serial killer.
2. Methedrine is a synthesis of Methyl and Benzedrine. Methedrine is a term used for methamphetamine hydrochloride, which was marketed under the trade name Methedrine. Although Methedrine was prescribed for clinical purposes, methamphetamines have few medical uses now and have been shown to cause many adverse physical and psychological effects when abused.
3. Front street - in prison slang, it is to share private information in a public setting; to hold someone accountable for their actions.
4. Battle-axe - a term, generally considered pejorative, for an aggressive, domineering and forceful woman.
5. Grauman's Chinese Theater is a movie palace on the historic Hollywood Walk of Fame at 6925 Hollywood Blvd. in Hollywood, Los Angeles. It was renamed Mann's Chinese Theatre in 1973
6. Herbert Mullin (born April 18, 1947) is an American serial killer who killed thirteen people in California in the early 1970s in the same geographic locale as Kemper during the same time period. Mullin confessed to the killings. In 1973, after a trial to determine whether he was insane or culpable, he was convicted of two murders in the first degree and nine in the second, and sentenced to life imprisonment. He has been denied parole 10 times and is unlikely to ever be released.
7. Herbert Mullin, a diagnosed schizophrenic, claimed that he had to kill thirteen people to prevent an earthquake. Mullin stated, "We human beings, through the history of the world, have protected our continents from cataclysmic earthquakes by murder. In other words, a minor natural disaster avoids a major natural disaster."
8. *The Devil's Brigade* was written by Robert H. Adleman and adapted into a film of the same title and released in 1968.
9. Kemper is referring to a then-present fashionable young female populace of San Fernando Valley who tended got come from affluent families.
10. Aiko Koo, murdered on the evening of September 14, 1972.
11. "Boonies" is vernacular for a rural location.

EXCERPT FROM "IN AT THE
KILL" GQ (BRITAIN) (FEBRUARY
1991) JOHN A. JENKINS

*F*ROM *C*HARLES *M*ANSON *to the Yorkshire Ripper, Son of Sam to the Monster of Florence, John Douglas tests his wits against the best criminal minds of his generation.*

*E*DMUND *K*EMPER IS, BY HIS OWN RIGHTS, A MAN OF SUPERIOR intellect and no small achievements. He boasts of once having been America's youngest fully-fledged civic booster, a twenty-year-old Christian living what he calls a "Jesus-first" life.

But that distinction is just an ironic footnote in Kemper's *vitae*. He is a legend for far more weighty reasons, and he implores his visitor to please, just please, get the story right.

"I did not butcher people," Ed Kemper, now 41-years old, insists with the petty certitude of a grammarian arguing over nuance. "Decapitation is not butchering. The papers and the magazines had me butchering my victims. But I only dismembered two bodies. They were all decapitated; all but my mother's friend. Why? Why didn't I just pop some teeth out, or crunch some bones up? I was starting to branch out in my thoughts about how to do things and get away with it. The psychological trip was, the person is the head. For some reason, someone looks entirely different with no head. I noticed that."

In an interview room at Vacaville prison in California, John Douglas, an energetic man not particularly suited to the sedentary, just sits there for a change and listens. There is little choice. Kemper talks fast, like someone trying to finish a long story before he runs out of the door. But Kemper is going nowhere.

Kemper is a giant of a man, 6'9" and 302 pounds, and as the words spew out, his voice betrays macabre enthusiasm while an intermittent giggle gives away his self-consciousness. These are awful stories. Over a span of maybe half-a-dozen years, Kemper killed ten people: his grandparents, his mother, her best friend, and six hitchhiking students. He chopped their heads and hands off, are parts of them, and, in his nagging mother's case, propped up her severed head on the kitchen table, ranted and raved at it, ripped out her larynx and ground it up in the waste disposal. "Mom didn't give a fuck. She was using us for her own little comforts." Nice guy.

Maybe it's a stretch of the imagination to see Kemper as the pride of the Junior Chamber of Commerce chapter at the Atascadero State Hospital for the criminally insane, California. But then he was much younger and the shrinks thought there was still hope; at that time he'd only hacked up his grandparents.

As Douglas listens to this serial killer offhandedly describe the young women he stalked and murdered after his release from Atascadero, the word that comes to Douglas's mind is nothing to be proud of, but at least he is being honest with himself. Douglas spells it out: "p-u-s-s-y." A coward. The word refers to Edmund Kemper, not to those who are dead, although Douglas has called murdered girls by that cruel name, too, when he thought doing so would please a murderer enough to make him relive the thrill of the kill.

Which is what Douglas wants.

The dead cannot speak, but their killers can, andDouglas has probably talked to more of them than any other man alive.

THIS IS *an excerpt from a letter to an unknown recipient that came up for sale on a web site specializing in serial killer ephemera. In it, Kemper details some early partying history and lashes out at FBI profilers.*

YOU ASKED ME WHAT KIND OF PICTURES I LIKE AND I MAY HAVE told you the ones you sent are plenty interesting to me. I like to remember the house parties I attended & held with buddies & chics from related interests ... although somewhat "dated" from those you have today. Most liked beer, some pot, some little pills that made them hallucinate ... but addicts have been bad news and too complicated to be friends for the same reasons back then ... often times because they were "hot" and sometimes even wired for sound ... like much more often today as the technology becomes cheaper. I did much of my partying in the City (SF) or suburbs or Oakland or even Alameda, where I lived for maybe a year. Sometimes I went up to Saratoga & Clear Lake, know spots among the Northern California hip. Having read some of the crap the media has printed about me, especially those opportunists Ressler & Douglas who couldn't wait to "retire" from the FBI so they could cash-in on their so-called expertise in "profiling." Quiet as it's kept, there was profiling in existence before I fell & one of the best was brought in to try & solve my crimes. He came up with absolutely nothing … so naturally there is a great amount of Monday morning quarterbacking coming down the pike ever since. The winners write the history. Where're the "35 serial killers" Ressler & Douglas estimated were out there … they've had 20 years to trap them, right? In most cases, it was the good old police science that busted the ones they have. How much have those two made in "guest speaker" fees, "lecture" fees, book signing appearance fees … etc. Those guys can't even get the facts of my case right, what if you multiply that times ALL the criminals they pontificate about? Boo. You'll never see the three of us in a live debate because neither of them can stand the light of day … as long as they're in possession of the media horn (& I kid you not about "possession" - - the so-called legitimate media has plenty of skeletons in my case alone.) If I had any interest beyond scorn to redress the whitewash/disinformation that's been laid on my house, I'd have said it before now. It ain't my job to straighten out the record … this is a free America & I will stand in amazement as it is. As screwed up as the record of my life is, it's a wonderfully honest portrayal of the influences involved in the telling.

Mass murderer denied parole for third time

By ROBERT GAMMON
Sentinel staff writer

VACAVILLE — No one thinks Edmund Kemper, an Aptos serial killer who haunted Santa Cruz in the early 1970s, should be paroled — including Kemper.

Kemper, 49, refused to attend his parole hearing Thursday but he directed his appointed attorney to read a short statement. "The severity of my commitment offenses, I believe, preclude my release at this time," read Marcia Hurst.

A three-member panel from the state Board of Prison Terms agreed with Kemper, saying he remains a threat to society.

"Mr. Kemper terrorized Northern California," said Commissioner Carol Bentley at the California Medical Facility in Vacaville. "He poses an unreasonable risk to the public."

During an 11-month killing spree

Edmund Kemper killed eight people during 1972-73.

Kemper viciously murdered eight women, including his mother. He decapitated most of his victims, had sex with the corpses and ate parts of one woman. Six of the murder victims were young hitchhikers.

Since 1988 this is the third consecutive time Kemper, who has diabetes, has declined to appear before a parole board and he has repeatedly stated that he does not believe he should be freed. In fact in the late 1970s, he twice tried unsuccessfully to get state doctors to perform psychosurgery on him — similar to a lobotomy — claiming surgery may be the only way to squelch his urge to kill.

Assistant District Attorney Bob Lee represented Santa Cruz County at the hearing and recalled Kemper's "absolutely shocking, violent, depraved acts."

"I was a 12-year-old boy at the time and I remember instead of having a monster in our dreams we had him in real life," Lee told the parole board.

The serial murders began 25 years ago, but Kemper actually started killing eight years before that, when at the age of 15 he fatally shot his grandmother in the back of the head in her home in North Fork. He also killed his grandfather and was sentenced to the California Youth Authority for their murders. He was released from Atascadero State Hospital when he turned 20.

A few years later, Kemper drove to Fresno to be examined by psychiatrists in an effort to have his juvenile murder record expunged. The 6-foot, 9-inch man, whose friends nicknamed "Forklift" because of his strength, convinced the experts that he was no longer a danger. But they didn't know that he had begun killing again and the head of one of his victims was in the trunk of his car.

Kemper was eventually caught because he was convinced that police were hot on his trail after sheriff's deputies confiscated his gun because he had been convicted of murdering his grandparents. The detectives had no evidence against him at the time, but Kemper believed they did, recalled Watsonville police Capt. Mickey Aluffi.

"The most memorable part for me ... I think it was about 5 a.m. when I got a phone call," Aluffi said Thursday. "I felt like all the blood just rushed out of my body."

On the phone that day in late April, 1973, was the Sheriff's Office saying Kemper had called from Pueblo, Colo., and confessed to the murders including the killing of his mother, Clarnell Strandberg, a UCSC employee.

Kemper, who attempted suicide four times before and during his trial, testified that he killed his mother because he didn't want her to think he was the serial killer being reported in all the news accounts.

Santa Cruz County was dubbed the "murder capital of the world" at the time because the county had two mass murderers on killing sprees: Kemper and Herbert Mullin, who killed 10 people.

And just two years before that, John Lindley Frazier also murdered five people in the county. Both Mullin and Frazier also are serving life sentences. All three serial killers were tried when the death penalty was illegal.

Jim Jackson, who defended the three murderers and is now a Santa Cruz County assistant district attorney, said that while the county has not seen a rash of killers like Kemper, Mullin and Frazier in the last two decades, he does not believe there are fewer mass murderers today.

"Who knows how many people are out there now, lurking," Jackson said.

According to the parole board, Kemper has been a model prisoner at Vacaville. He works in the library and has had no disciplinary action taken against him in the last 23 years. However, no one wrote a letter to the parole board or came forward Thursday to say he should be released. His next parole hearing is in 2002.

No one thinks Edmund Kemper, an Aptos serial killer who haunted Santa Cruz in the early 1970s, should be paroled – including Kemper.

Kemper, 49, refused to attend his parole hearing Thursday but he directed his appointed attorney to read a short statement. "The severity of my commitment offenses, I believe, preclude my release at this time," read Marcia Hurst.

A three-member panel from the state Board of Prison Terms agreed with Kemper, saying he remains a threat to society.

"Mr. Kemper terrorized Northern California," said Commissioner Carol Bentley at the California Medical Facility in Vacaville. "He poses an unreasonable risk to the public."

During an 11-month killing spree, Kemper viciously murdered eight women, including his mother. He decapitated most of his victims, had sex with the corpses and ate parts of one woman. Six of the murder victims were young hitchhikers.

Since 1988, this is the third consecutive time Kemper, who has diabetes, has declined to appear before a parole board and he has repeatedly stated that he does not believe he should be freed. In fact in the late 1970s, he twice tried unsuccessfully to get state doctors to perform psychosurgery on him – similar to a lobotomy – claiming surgery may be the only way to squelch his urge to kill.

Assistant District Attorney Bob Lee represented Santa Cruz County at the hearing and recalled Kemper's "absolutely shocking, violent, depraved acts."

"I was a 12-year-old boy at the time and I remember instead of having a monster in our dreams we had him in real life," Lee told the parole board.

The serial murders began 25 years ago, but Kemper actually started killing eight years before that, when at the age of 15 he fatally shot his grandmother in the back of the head in her home in North Fork. He also killed his grandfather and was sentenced to the California Youth Authority for their murders. He was released from Atascadero State Hospital when he turned 20.

A few years later, Kemper drove to Fresno to be examined by psychiatrists in an effort to have his juvenile murder record expunged. The 6-foot, 9-inch man, whose friends nicknamed "Forklift" because of his strength, convinced the experts that he was no longer a danger. But they didn't know that he had begun killing again and the head of one of his victims was in the trunk of his car.

Kemper was eventually caught because he was convinced that police were hot on his trail after sheriff's deputies confiscated his gun because he had been convicted of murdering his grandparents. The detectives had no evidence against him at the time, but Kemper believed they did, recalled Watsonville police Capt. Mickey Aluffi.

"The most memorable part for me ... I think it was about 5 a.m. when I got a phone call," Aluffi said Thursday. "I felt like all the blood just rushed out of my body."

On the phone that day in Laye April 1973 was the Sheriff's Office saying Kemper had called Pueblo, Colo. and confessed to the murders including the killing of his mother, Clarnell Strandberg, a UCSC employee.

Kemper, who attempted suicide four times before and during his trial, testified that he killed his mother because he didn't want her to think he was the serial killer being reported in all the news accounts.

Santa Cruz was dubbed the "murder capital of the world" at the time because the county had two mass murderers on killing sprees: Kemper and Herbert Mullin, who killed 10 people.

And just two years before that, John Lindley Frazier also murdered five people in the county. Both Mullin and Frazier also are serving life sentences. All three serial killers were tried when the death penalty was illegal.

Jim Jackson, who defended the three murderers and is now a Santa Cruz County district attorney, said that while the county has not seen a rash of killers like Kemper, Mullin and Frazier in the last two decades, he does not believe there are fewer mass murderers today.

"Who knows how many people are out there now, lurking," Jackson said.

According to the parole board, Kemper has been a model prisoner at Vacaville. He works in the library and has had no disciplinary action taken against him in the last 23 years. However, no one wrote a letter to the parole board or came forward Thursday to say he should be released. His next parole hearing is in 2002.

"KEMPER WAIVES PAROLE HEARING", SANTA CRUZ SENTINEL (JUNE 28, 2002) – JASON SCHULTZ

Kemper waives parole hearing

By JASON SCHULTZ
SENTINEL STAFF WRITER

Santa Cruz County's deadliest serial killer will be in prison for at least another five years.

VACAVILLE Edmund Emil Kemper, 54, has been in prison since 1973, when he was convicted of savagely killing, decapitating and dismembering six UC Santa Cruz students, his mother and his mother's friend in 1972 and 1973.

Kemper was set to face the state parole board Wednesday. But earlier this week, he waived his right to the hearing, and agreed not to seek parole again until at least 2007, according to Denise Schmidt, spokeswoman for the state Board of Prison Terms.

Kemper's agreement came as a surprise to county prosecutor Ariadne Symons. She said Kemper had indicated he would attend the parole hearing at the California Medical Facility in Vacaville, and Symons was prepared to go — and to argue that he must remain behind bars.

She wrote in a letter to the parole board that she does not think Kemper is at all reformed, and that he remains a threat to society.

"Apparently Kemper does not like to be referred to as a 'monster,' " Symons wrote. "However, the term is apt, even though it is woefully inadequate. Mere words cannot convey the horror of what he did."

Though it's been 30 years since Kemper's crimes, the brutality of the murders has never been forgotten by those involved in the case.

After Kemper killed his mother and her friend in April of 1973, he fled across country, expecting to die in an armed conflict with police. Instead he called Santa Cruz police from Colorado to confess to the murders.

Local detectives flew to Colorado and drove Kemper back to Santa Cruz in his own rental car. During the drive, he confessed in great detail.

He told the officers he would prowl the UCSC campus for young female hitchhikers. He would pick them up, murder them, in some instances sexually assaulting their corpses. He then decapitated and dismembered the bodies, dumping body parts in the ocean, nearby mountains and even in his own yard.

Mickey Aluffi was one of the detectives who drove Kemper back. He said he still thinks about the case, and that a recent television story on the case broadcast on Court TV brought up a lot of emotions he had suppressed for nearly three decades.

Aluffi now works for the UCSC Police Department. He said he thinks about the case often as he patrols the same campus roads Kemper prowled.

Kemper will be 59 when he becomes eligible for parole again.

Both Aluffi and Symons say that no matter when Kemper comes up for parole, he should not be be released.

In her letter to the parole board, Symons wrote:

"In an interview at the time of his arrest, Kemper stated 'I certainly wouldn't trust me in society again.' Let us give weight to those words."

Contact Jason Schultz at jschultz@santa-cruz.com

SANTA CRUZ's deadliest serial killer will be in prison for at least another five years.

Edmund Emil Kemper, 54, has been in prison since 1973, when he was convicted of savagely killing, decapitating and dismembering six UC Santa Cruz students, his mother and his mother's friend in 1972 and 1973.

Kemper was set to face the state parole board Wednesday. But earlier this week, he waived his right to the hearing, and agreed not to seek parole again until at least 2007, according to Denise Schmidt, spokeswoman for the state Board of Prison Terms.

Kemper's agreement came as a surprise to county prosecutor Ariadne Symons. She said Kemper had indicated he would attend the parole hearing at the California Medical Facility in Vacaville, and Symons was prepared to go – and to argue that he must remain behind bars.

She wrote in a letter to the parole board that she does not think Kemper is at all reformed, and that he remains a threat to society.

"Apparently Kemper does not like to be referred to as a 'monster,'" Symons wrote. "However, the term is apt, even though it is woefully inadequate. Mere words cannot convey the horror of what he did."

Kemper will be 59 when he becomes eligible for parole again.

Symons says that no matter when Kemper comes up for parole, he should not be released.

In her letter to the parole board, Symons wrote:

"In an interview at the time of his arrest, Kemper stated 'I certainly wouldn't trust me in society again.' Let us give weight to those words."

ERROL MORRIS (EM): When Werner and I first met each other, we took a trip to visit this serial killer in prison in Northern California.

Werner Herzog (WH): Vacaville, yeah.

EM: There were three of us. And Kemper's lawyer. To circumvent a lot of red tape, the lawyer identified us as psychiatrists. Werner's producer, Walter Saxer, came along with us. So there was Dr. Saxer, Dr. Morris, and Dr. Herzog allowed in because—

WH: We were scared shitless because Kemper was a very huge man, fairly young, I think still twenty-six by then. But something like six-foot-five or six-foot-four.

EM: I think bigger.

WH: Maybe bigger, yes.

EM: Very large.

WH: Capital punishment was suspended at the time he was condemned. And he chose seven or eight consecutive life terms, but he wanted to die in the gas chamber. And the only way to get to the gas chamber when it was reinstated at that time was to kill someone inside the prison. So the attorney was really scared. And he was in a way relieved that he had some solid men as his guards or his company. And reading all the transcripts of Kemper, I had the feeling that what was interesting was that the man, in my opinion—and I'm speaking of Edmund Emil Kemper—he made a lot of sense. In a way he makes a lot of sense, why he killed and how it all originated.

And at the end, after having killed seven or eight or so coeds, hitchhikers, he killed his mother and put the severed head on the mantel and threw darts at it. And then there happened to be some leftover turkey in the fridge from Thanksgiving and he called the lady next door, the neighbor, and asked—am I correct? Yeah, asked her if she would like to pick up the turkey leftovers, and she walks in and then he killed her as well, and put her in a closet. And then he fled in his mother's car and crisscrossed the West until he ran out of money and ran out of gas. And in Pueblo, Colorado, he kept calling the police. [*To Morris*] You know better what happened there. I think they thought he was kind of gaga and didn't believe him.

EM: He desperately tried to turn himself in to the police by making repeated phone calls from this phone booth. Now he would have had a cell phone. So I guess it's easier now for serial killers to turn themselves in. And the police kept hanging up on him. They just—

WH: And he was down to his last quarter to make his last call, and then two detectives actually picked him up at this phone booth. I remember their names because they sound very German: Schmidt and Grubb. And Schmidt and Grubb took him to the police station, and what was smart of them was, they just randomly turned on a tape recorder and Kemper spoke for six hours, pretty much nonstop.

And this transcript is really wonderful—

EM: Quite amazing, yes.

WH: Very, very amazing. And Kemper was, in a way, a very sensitive person. When you looked at his hands, like the hands of a violin player, in a way. I remember he looked like an elephant with a Mozart soul.

EM: Yeah. That's the way Werner described him at the time. An elephant with the soul of Mozart. I'm not sure that most of the prison authorities would have described him in the same way, but at the time I found Werner's description very interesting. I thought for a long time about it. It made it *situational,* as if God in his infinite perversity had somehow mismatched Kemper's various attributes in order to produce some kind of nightmare, some kind of tragedy. I remember thinking, Yeah, if Othello had been in Hamlet's place, and vice versa, there would be no tragedy.

It's so mixed up in my mind—Werner in these early years, graduate school, and what I myself was thinking. I was a very disaffected graduate student at the University of California, Berkeley. That's where I first met Werner. It was just shortly after he finished *Aguirre* and his films were being shown in the United States for the first time. It was an amazing experience to see Werner's work. There was really nothing quite like it in America at that time, and probably not since that time.

And I became really fascinated by Werner's films. I'm thinking about it even now, now that we're talking about it, our attempts to understand what people are thinking. What is going on in another person's mind? How do they see the world? Kemper was a perfect example. I would drive every day from Berkeley to Santa Cruz and I would attend the Kemper trial. I became a regular fixture. And I would say the trial transformed my thinking about many, many, many things.

In those days, murder trials were chopped into two pieces. There would be a guilt and innocence phase and a penalty phase.

And there was this wacko psychiatrist, Dr. Joel Fort, who took the stand and said that Kemper was not even neurotic. Kemper had killed a dozen people. He had killed his grandparents. He had been put away in a juvenile facility, released under California law when he reached eighteen, and then went on to kill eight more people. And Kemper had described how these murders occurred. He would pick up women hitchhiking. He would be killing a woman with a knife and talking to her, saying, "I hope this isn't really unpleasant. I hope you're not uncomfortable. I hope this is not too frightening."

So, the psychiatrist—I'll make this as short as possible—the psychiatrist took the stand and said, "You know, this man is not even neurotic. Not only is he not psychotic, he's not even neurotic, because he can't empathize with the victim. He has a sociopathy or a psychopathy. He can be completely dispassionate while he is killing another person." And I started to wonder—I still wonder about this stuff—I started to wonder how in god's name does the psychiatrist know what Ed is thinking? Maybe Ed has this fantasy of being in control. Maybe in this writing after the fact he imagined himself as being dispassionate. Perhaps he was completely out of control, deeply psychotic. This kind of discrepancy between the accounts that we provide about ourselves and the world.

And I think it's very much—in a different way—but it's very much in your films as well, and something that deeply inspired me.

BOARD OF PAROLE HEARINGS

In the matter of the Life Term Parole Consideration Hearing of:

EDMUND EMIL KEMPER
(CDC Number: B-52453)
CALIFORNIA MEDICAL FACILITY VACAVILLE,
CALIFORNIA
JULY 25, 2017
9:00 A.M.

CYNTHIA FRITZ, Presiding Commissioner

DANIEL BLAKE, Deputy Commissioner

OTHERS PRESENT:

EDMUND KEMPER, Inmate

JEFFREY HALL, Attorney for Inmate

CELIA WEST, Assistant Deputy District Attorney

PAT KEMPER, Victims Family Member

ANGEL PAYAN, Correctional Case Records Manager SYLVIA NIETO, Victim Advocate

TWO CORRECTIONAL OFFICERS, Unidentified

KATHILYNN LIADIS, Transcriber, DE

PROCEEDINGS

DEPUTY COMMISSIONER BLAKE: Okay, we're on the record.

PRESIDING COMMISSIONER FRITZ: We're on record. The time's 9:00 a.m. This is for the Subsequent Parole Consideration Hearing of Edmund Kemper, K-E-M-P-E-R, CDC number B52453. Today date's, July 25th, 2017. We're located at the California Medical Facility. Mr. Kemper was received into the Department of Corrections and Rehabilitation on November 9th, 1973. He was taken to the Department of Corrections and Rehabilitation for the offense of murder first, Penal Code Section 187, eight counts, and the county of commitment is Santa Cruz. This hearing's being tape recorded. We're gonna go around room, put our names on the record. Please give your names: spell your last name, when I get to you. Mr. Kemper, give your CDC number, also. Start with myself, Cynthia Fritz, F-R-I-T-Z, Commissioner.

DEPUTY COMMISSIONER BLAKE: I'm Dan Blake, B-L-A- K-E, Deputy Commissioner.

ASSISTANT DISTRICT ATTORNEY ROWLAND: Celia Rowland ... Celia Rowland with the Santa Cruz District Attorney's Office.

PRESIDING COMMISSIONER FRITZ: You're supposed to be looking forward, sir. Go ahead, yeah.

MS. PAYAN: Angel Payan, P-A-Y-A-N, Correctional Case Records Manager.

MS. KEMPER: Pat Kemper, K-E-M-P-E-R. Did you want me to say my relationship?

PRESIDING COMMISSIONER FRITZ: Yes.

PAT KEMPER: Uh, the victims were my grandparents.

PRESIDING COMMISSIONER FRITZ: Thank you.

MS. NIETO: Sylvia Nieto, N-I-E-T-O, Victim Advocate.

PRESIDING COMMISSIONER FRITZ: Thank you.

ATTORNEY HALL: Jeffrey Hall, H-A-L-L, attorney for Mr. Edmund Kemper.

INMATE KEMPER: Edmund Kemper, uh, the third, uh, Bravo 52453.

PRESIDING COMMISSIONER FRITZ: Spell your last name.

INMATE KEMPER: K-E-M-P-E-R.

PRESIDING COMMISSIONER FRITZ: Thank you. All right, we also have two correctional officers present for security purposes only.

DEPUTY COMMISSIONER BLAKE: Commissioner, would you move the mic? There you go. Perfect.

PRESIDING COMMISSIONER FRITZ: Did you get all that? Or ...

DEPUTY COMMISSIONER BLAKE: I got it, but it was, uh, (*inaudible*)

PRESIDING COMMISSIONER FRITZ: Okay.

DEPUTY COMMISSIONER BLAKE: Thank you.

PRESIDING COMMISSIONER FRITZ: All right, Mr. Kemper, raise your right hand so I can swear you in. Do you swear or affirm to tell the truth, the whole truth, and nothing but the truth?

INMATE KEMPER: Yes.

PRESIDING COMMISSIONER FRITZ: Okay. You can put your hand down. Let's see if you need any accommodations under the Americans with Disabilities Act. I'm gonna ask you some questions. I'll note that you came in, in a wheelchair. You ... it's intermittent wheelchair use, correct? Do you know what that means?

INMATE KEMPER: Yes.

PRESIDING COMMISSIONER FRITZ: Okay so you can ... you can walk, but you use it on occasion?

INMATE KEMPER: Mostly.

PRESIDING COMMISSIONER FRITZ: Mostly. And do you, um, I ... I have that you had a mobility vest, too. Do you have that?

INMATE KEMPER: Yeah.

PRESIDING COMMISSIONER FRITZ: Do you wear the vest?

INMATE KEMPER: I don't wear it.

PRESIDING COMMISSIONER FRITZ: Oh, you don't wear it? Okay. All right, you're wearing your glasses. So are your glasses working okay?

INMATE KEMPER: Yes.

PRESIDING COMMISSIONER FRITZ: Can you hear me okay?

INMATE KEMPER: Yes, ma'am.

PRESIDING COMMISSIONER FRITZ: All right. Are you CCCMS[1] or EOP[2]?

INMATE KEMPER: No.

PRESIDING COMMISSIONER FRITZ: No. Have you ever been in ... in the mental health?

INMATE KEMPER: Yes.

PRESIDING COMMISSIONER FRITZ: When's the last time you were in the mental health?

INMATE KEMPER: Back when I first got here.

PRESIDING COMMISSIONER FRITZ: Okay. Are you taking any psychotropic medication?

INMATE KEMPER: No.

PRESIDING COMMISSIONER FRITZ: Any medication for any medical reason?

INMATE KEMPER: A number of them.

PRESIDING COMMISSIONER FRITZ: Okay, so let us know. You're on elderly parole, okay? So this is an elderly parole hearing so medical issues are, um, ... we give special consideration to your age, the amount of time you've been in prison, and any medical issues. So, if you can remember any of the medications or medical issues that you have, can you put that on the record?

INMATE KEMPER: My primary medication is, uh, diabetic and it's, uh, metformin[3] 850 mg three times a day.

PRESIDING COMMISSIONER FRITZ: All right, anything else?

INMATE KEMPER: And I take that K.O.P., which means "keep on person." I carry my own medication. Uh, there's two or three different kinds of, uh, blood pressure meds; lisinopril and, uh, oh ...

oh, I can't remember the others. I had a stroke a couple of years ago so that's one of the problems I have.

PRESIDING COMMISSIONER FRITZ: Any memory problems if … if you're aware of it?

INMATE KEMPER: No.

PRESIDING COMMISSIONER FRITZ: No, okay. All right, any other issues because of the stroke?

INMATE KEMPER: Yes, uh … uh, PBA, pseudo-bulbar affect, which means I'll burst into laughter or crying inappropriately. It just happens …

PRESIDING COMMISSIONER FRITZ: And that's the affective …

INMATE KEMPER: … nothing to … nothing to do with emotion.

PRESIDING COMMISSIONER FRITZ: That's an affect of the stroke?

INMATE KEMPER: Yes, damage to the brain.

PRESIDING COMMISSIONER FRITZ: Got it. Anything else?

INMATE KEMPER: Not that I can think of.

PRESIDING COMMISSIONER FRITZ: Okay, all right. Besides wheelchair, glasses, I have your TABE[4] score as 12.9, that's the highest you can receive. Um, any other … and then you're not wearing the mobility vest, but you said you just don't wear it, right?

INMATE KEMPER: It's hot, yeah.

PRESIDING COMMISSIONER FRITZ: Okay. Um, any other accommodations that you need to go forward with the hearing today?

INMATE KEMPER: Not that I can think of.

PRESIDING COMMISSIONER FRITZ: Any other accommodations your client needs to go forward?

ATTORNEY HALL: I … I think that's complete.

PRESIDING COMMISSIONER FRITZ: Okay.

ATTORNEY HALL: Thank you.

PRESIDING COMMISSIONER FRITZ: Wheelchair, glasses, he's not using the mobility vest. If you need any breaks at any time let us know. Um, let's go through your Notice of Hearing Rights. Do you recall receiving your board forms from your correctional counselor, reviewing and signing your forms?

INMATE KEMPER: Yes.

PRESIDING COMMISSIONER FRITZ: All right, I have that you signed them November 11th … I'm sorry, strike that, May 11th, 2017. Does that sound right?

INMATE KEMPER: Mm-hmm.

PRESIDING COMMISSIONER FRITZ: Is that a yes or a no? I need something audible for the hearing.

INMATE KEMPER: Yes, I'm sorry.

PRESIDING COMMISSIONER FRITZ: Okay, that's fine. Okay, so let's go through portion of the forms with you. The purpose of your parole consideration hearing is to determine if you're suitable for parole. When you're prior to your minimum eligible parole date, a parole consideration hearing will be held. You have a right to attend the hearing, ask and answer questions, and speak on your own behalf. You're entitled to be represented by an attorney. You may not call any witnesses at your hearing. The district attorney from the county where the offenses were committed will be invited to the hearing to represent the interest of the People. Notice of the hearing will also be given to the judge, um, … the sentencing judge, law enforcement agency, attorney who represented you at sentencing, victims or next of kin, other designated representatives may also attend and address the hearing panel. You have a right to review the non-confidential documents in your prison central file. We already went through your Americans with Disability Act accommodations. Do you want to go forward with the hearing today?

INMATE KEMPER: Do I want to go forward?

PRESIDING COMMISSIONER FRITZ: Yes.

INMATE KEMPER: Yes.

PRESIDING COMMISSIONER FRITZ: All right. You're entitled to a hearing by an impartial hearing panel. You're entitled to a copy of the record of the hearing. You're entitled to a copy of the decision. We'll give you the decision today. Any questions regarding your hearing rights?

INMATE KEMPER: No.

PRESIDING COMMISSIONER FRITZ: All right. Have your client's rights been met thus far?

ATTORNEY HALL: They have, Commissioner, thank you.

PRESIDING COMMISSIONER FRITZ: Any preliminary objections?

ATTORNEY HALL: No objections.

PRESIDING COMMISSIONER FRITZ: All right. So let's go through procedures. I think it's been a while since you've been to an actual full hearing, right?

INMATE KEMPER: It has.

PRESIDING COMMISSIONER FRITZ: Okay. So let me explain how it's gonna' work today. We break it down into three parts. The first part is pre-conviction or everything that happened before you came to prison, background information, prior criminality, and then we'll into the crimes and why you came to prison. From there we'll move into the second part of the hearing, it is how you [have] been doing in prison, and so we'll go through any upgrades that you've had in education, vocation, work history, and self-help programming. We'll go through your wr ... recent risk assessment. We'll also go through ... the third part of the hearing is parole plans so if you were given a grant release where would you live, what would you do, how would you support yourself. Those are the three parts of the hearing. Once we've completed our questioning, the two panel members and the District Attorney will have the opportunity to ask clarifying questions. Your attorney can also ask clarifying questions. Once all the questioning is done, we'll take closing statements. First, from the district attorney's office, second from your attorney and then you can also make a closing statement if you want to, okay? Once that's done I'll hand it back over to the district attorney's office and if, uh, a victim's family member would like to make a statement, you're welcome to do so at that time, okay? Once all that is completed, then we're gonna take a break and the two panel members will discuss your case. We'll go into what's called "deliberations" and then we'll come and we'll give you a decision today. Do you have any questions on how it's gonna work?

INMATE KEMPER: No.

PRESIDING COMMISSIONER FRITZ: Okay, the hearing's being tape recorded so that you know that we have a clear record. We don't want you to guess to anything. If you don't know ... if you don't know an answer, you don't know an answer. If you don't understand a question, we're asking you to let us know so we can try and ask it a different way. We do need audible answers. We need yes/no instead of shakes of the head and ah-huhs, okay? Because the transcriber can't pick that up. We'll try not to talk over each other so that the transcription is clear. So, if you see us correcting you, those are usually the areas that we're correcting you on so that we have a clear record. Are ... are we clear on that?

INMATE KEMPER: Mm-hmm.

PRESIDING COMMISSIONER FRITZ: Yes, I need a yes.

INMATE KEMPER: Uh, yes, ma'am.

PRESIDING COMMISSIONER FRITZ: Okay, are you sure you're clear on that? All right, um, okay, so any questions so far? And again, if you need a break at any time or that goes for anybody in the hearings cause they do get long sometimes, let us know so we can take a break. So with that, any questions on the procedures?

INMATE KEMPER: No.

PRESIDING COMMISSIONER FRITZ: Okay. Did you receive, uh, Mr. Hall, 10-day/65-day packets?

ATTORNEY HALL: I did, Commissioner.

PRESIDING COMMISSIONER FRITZ: All right. Di you receive all the packets 10-day/65-day?

ASSISTANT DISTRICT ATTORNEY WEST: Yes, I did as well.

PRESIDING COMMISSIONER FRITZ: Thank you. Are there other documents you want to submit on behalf of your client?

ATTORNEY HALL: No additional documents.

PRESIDING COMMISSIONER FRITZ: Okay. All right, Mr. Kemper, are there any questions you have before we get started?

INMATE KEMPER: No.

PRESIDING COMMISSIONER FRITZ: Okay. So let's get started. The first part of the hearing is everything ... it's, uh, what happened before you came to prison. So, um, ... so we're gonna start off with just a little, uh ... uh, a brief summary of your background. So it's a brief summary, um, just to kind of figure out what was going on in your life before you came to prison. If you think there are things you'd like to add, correct, or clarify about what we're saying about you, let us know, all right?

INMATE KEMPER: Yes, ma'am.

PRESIDING COMMISSIONER FRITZ: Okay. So I have that, um, it looks like you came from a family where your parents divorced when you were about eight or nine. It looks like your mother had some type of mental health problems. She was an abusive alcoholic toward you. Um, and you also routinely would see parents with their ... with multiple stepfathers engage in domestic violence. Um, you stated that it was instigated by your mother who "started shit with almost everyone ... everybody." That is what you told the psychologist recently. Um, you were scared and depressed when you watched your mother beat your father. Um, but then it looks like your father, um, also was involved in some violence. Um, at a young age it looks like you were killing your cats, buried one alive, playing games with your sister like, um, playing execution chair, gas chamber, is that right? Are those the types of games you played with your sister?

INMATE KEMPER: Among others.

PRESIDING COMMISSIONER FRITZ: Right, you'd rip up her dolls, decapitate them, um ...

INMATE KEMPER: Actually, that's something she did.

PRESIDING COMMISSIONER FRITZ: Is that right?

INMATE KEMPER: I made a trip when I was 10 years old, which she got a bit jealous about. When I came back I had a Mattel Fanner 50[5], I don't know if you're familiar with the ... the, uh, toy, but it's basically a cap gun, and, uh, I got that in New York, and one day she came in my room, picked it up, and seemed to be mad at me. She has since admitted that this happened and for the reasons that it happened, that she's into theatrics.

PRESIDING COMMISSIONER FRITZ: All right, so your sister's jealous and theatrical, your mother's abusive.

INMATE KEMPER: So she took the ... the pistol from where it was sitting and flung it at me, and it hit my toe ... my big toe and the floor at the same time, and it broke. Not apart, but it broke inside and it couldn't be, uh, fired normally by pulling the trigger. It could only be fanned. When I picked it up I was calling out for her not to throw it, and I said, please don't throw that, and she threw it at me. And, uh, it broke and I picked it up and determined that it was broken, and I chased her out of my bedroom over to her bedroom, when in looking for something of equal value to break, and all I saw in the room basically was her Barbie doll which was seated on its cabinet ... clothing cabinet. And, uh, I snatched it up and I grabbed the head of it and yanked it off and said here, how's this. And I thought it pops ... it pops off.

PRESIDING COMMISSIONER FRITZ: Okay, well I mean ...

INMATE KEMPER: Well, that isn't broken. That's just, uh, disabled for a few moments.

PRESIDING COMMISSIONER FRITZ: Okay, well, all this is just sibling ...

INMATE KEMPER: So I picked up a pair of ...

PRESIDING COMMISSIONER FRITZ: ... rive ... but all this stuff is just sibling rivalry stuff ...

INMATE KEMPER: I know.

PRESIDING COMMISSIONER FRITZ: ... that happens in every family.

INMATE KEMPER: That's all ... that's all that was back done.

PRESIDING COMMISSIONER FRITZ: So, I mean, but the killing of the cats, the burying of a cat alive, the smothering of a dog is not stuff that people normally do.

INMATE KEMPER: Well it got better. The thing with the doll. I picked up a pair of shears that she had in there and I cut the hands off. Those couldn't ...

PRESIDING COMMISSIONER FRITZ: Are we still at the ... we're talk ... talking about the dolls?

INMATE KEMPER: The doll, yeah.

PRESIDING COMMISSIONER FRITZ: Oh, okay, we're ... we're going back to that?

INMATE KEMPER: That ... that couldn't be stuck back on, but I figured it ... it broke her toy in equal fashion to mine, and I threw it down. She got all hysterical about it, and, uh, we went on arguing.

PRESIDING COMMISSIONER FRITZ: Okay, well let's move on, all right?

INMATE KEMPER: Yes.

PRESIDING COMMISSIONER FRITZ: All right. Um ... um, okay, so why were you killing animals?

INMATE KEMPER: Instead of people.

PRESIDING COMMISSIONER FRITZ: Okay, but why were you killing animals?

INMATE KEMPER: Instead of people.

PRESIDING COMMISSIONER FRITZ: So, what? You wanted to kill people but you killed animals instead? Is that what you're saying?

INMATE KEMPER: Yes.

PRESIDING COMMISSIONER FRITZ: At ... at what age? 8, 9, 10, 11? How old were you?

INMATE KEMPER: Probably, uh, 11 or 12.

PRESIDING COMMISSIONER FRITZ: Okay. No other explanation?

INMATE KEMPER: Uh, well, the cats were treated ... it was a cat, one cat at a time. The cat was treated as a family member. It was, uh, loved and cared for by all, and, uh, one day ...

PRESIDING COMMISSIONER FRITZ: Well, wait, we ... we don't need to get into details.

INMATE KEMPER: Yeah.

PRESIDING COMMISSIONER FRITZ: I want to know why? I mean besides the fact that you said you wanted to kill people and so you killed the animals. Do you have any other explanations? It sounds like to me if they were family members and they were treated nicely, you're probably jealous of them, right?

INMATE KEMPER: No.

PRESIDING COMMISSIONER FRITZ: Thought about that?

INMATE KEMPER: No.

PRESIDING COMMISSIONER FRITZ: Okay. Any other explanations that you can give?

INMATE KEMPER: Not really.

PRESIDING COMMISSIONER FRITZ: Okay. Then your parents were divorced. I guess you moved to Montana. You're trying to get back with your father who you had a better relationship with; sounds like there were some issues there. Um, but, at some point you go ... you move in with your grandparents. They seem to have treated you well.

INMATE KEMPER: I was moved in with my grandparents. Uh, what happened was it was Christmas time and all the family members went up there to their house, and, uh, for the holiday. My stepbrother didn't go this year and it turns out he ... he understood why he didn't want to go is cause I was gonna be left up there. This was his mother telling him not to let me know. They were German ... ethnic German, and, uh, she told him in German, uh, don't be telling him ...

PRESIDING COMMISSIONER FRITZ: Okay.

INMATE KEMPER: ... what's happening.

PRESIDING COMMISSIONER FRITZ: So you start living with your grandparents, but you were left there. You didn't know that you were gonna' be living with them. But they ... did they treat you well?

INMATE KEMPER: Generally.

PRESIDING COMMISSIONER FRITZ: Okay, and then you killed them both when you were 15?

INMATE KEMPER: Yes.

PRESIDING COMMISSIONER FRITZ: So, why'd you kill your grandparents?

INMATE KEMPER: That's a complex question for an immediate answer.

PRESIDING COMMISSIONER FRITZ: Well, would you like to answer it? You ... it's up to you.

INMATE KEMPER: Uh, basically I had gone to the window where my grandmother was typing and the dog was laying in the shade, my pet dog, Anka. And, uh, I went there to get the dog, I was gonna' go hunting, and I stood there and I started having basically an emotional, uh ... uh, I had a moment that I was, uh, going through my history with my mother, my, uh, grandmother. They were a lot alike, my grandmother and my mother, very assertive, very aggressive, and, uh, self-confident. And, uh, while I was standing there not pointing the gun basically at my grandmother, but it happened to be in my ... in my possession under my arm, and was held in her general direction. She didn't see it because she was facing away from me. But I started thinking about all the times and the years I had been dealing with my mother and my grandmother.

PRESIDING COMMISSIONER FRITZ: But your grandmother didn't do anything bad to you. I mean your mother was a ... we know your mother was abusive towards you, but I didn't get that impression at all that your grand ... maybe she had the same types of character as your mother as far as being assertive and aggressive, but she didn't do anything bad to you.

INMATE KEMPER: Not really.

PRESIDING COMMISSIONER FRITZ: Okay, and then you shoot her?

INMATE KEMPER: Huh?

PRESIDING COMMISSIONER FRITZ: Then you shot her?

INMATE KEMPER: At the end of that, uh, period of, uh, thinking about ...

PRESIDING COMMISSIONER FRITZ: Because you keep saying because you kept going back to how your mother and your grandmother treated you.

INMATE KEMPER: Well I was going ...

PRESIDING COMMISSIONER FRITZ: Your grandmother didn't treat your bad. I'm just trying to figure out what ...

INMATE KEMPER: Not, not generally ...

PRESIDING COMMISSIONER FRITZ: Yeah.

INMATE KEMPER: ... but there were ... there were moments.

PRESIDING COMMISSIONER FRITZ: Just because ... well okay, so like everybody, right?

INMATE KEMPER: Yeah.

PRESIDING COMMISSIONER FRITZ: I mean no one's perfect and so you just didn't like that she was an assertive, self-confident, aggressive woman. Is that what you're saying?

INMATE KEMPER: Kind of flew in my face.

PRESIDING COMMISSIONER FRITZ: Well, uh ... well, so what I'm trying to get at here and ... and we're gonna get to it because all of your victims are women. You clearly have an issue with your mother. To me I see ... I think it's hatred, but we'll get there.

INMATE KEMPER: Yeah.

PRESIDING COMMISSIONER FRITZ: Um, seems to be like you must have had some issues with your grandmother for no reason, so, um, you just don't ... don't like assertive, aggressive women?

INMATE KEMPER: Well she had placed herself in the position of being, in essence, my warden. And she said if you ever want to get to go live with your father again, you had better do what I say.

PRESIDING COMMISSIONER FRITZ: You're a 15-year-old kid, okay?

INMATE KEMPER: Yeah.

PRESIDING COMMISSIONER FRITZ: So that's pretty normal when someone's under the care of someone else.

INMATE KEMPER: But that wasn't a good idea when you're talking, uh, in my ... in my ...

PRESIDING COMMISSIONER FRITZ: Who to ... to you?

INMATE KEMPER: ... in my case I was talking from a position of disturbance, uh, I was trying to ... to share my sense of disturbance, uh, with her cause it bothered me ...

PRESIDING COMMISSIONER FRITZ: Okay.

INMATE KEMPER: ... and it bothered her too and she wasn't familiar with it and she told me not to bring that up again.

PRESIDING COMMISSIONER FRITZ: Sense, uh ... what do mean? What are ... what are we talking about here? Sense of disturbance.

INMATE KEMPER: Uh, inner problems I was having - -

PRESIDING COMMISSIONER FRITZ: Ahh, okay.

INMATE KEMPER: ... in coping with other people.

PRESIDING COMMISSIONER FRITZ: Got it, all right.

INMATE KEMPER: And, uh ...

PRESIDING COMMISSIONER FRITZ: ... you killed your grandmother. Any other reason because of you thought she was assertive, aggressive, self-confident woman, and she treated you good generally but there are a couple of times that apparently that she didn't, but, okay, and that she was trying to, um, sounds to me like act like a responsible adult in trying to give you some guidelines.

INMATE KEMPER: Well we had a walk-up freezer in my bedroom. It was a six foot long lift top, uh, freezer. There were four half-gallons of my favorite ice-cream in the whole world in there and they stayed in there the whole time I was there.

PRESIDING COMMISSIONER FRITZ: Okay.

INMATE KEMPER: Now why did she buy those? She'd heard the story about my mother had brought home a half- gallon of ice-cream, put it in the freezer, and I had turned it around, opened it up surreptitiously, and scraped off little bits of ice-cream.

PRESIDING COMMISSIONER FRITZ: Why didn't you just ask why there were there then?

INMATE KEMPER: Well I wasn't getting any. A week later, it was hollowed out to where there was just about a half inch or three quarters of an inch of ice-cream at the top end. And that was the ... the end facing people looking in there.

PRESIDING COMMISSIONER FRITZ: So wait, are you telling me your grandmother was messing with you or something; is that what you're saying?

INMATE KEMPER: Well my mother I'm saying ...

PRESIDING COMMISSIONER FRITZ: Oh, your mother.

INMATE KEMPER: ... pulled the half-gallon out, set it on the table, opened the top, took this big spoon to serve with ...

PRESIDING COMMISSIONER FRITZ: Okay, all right, but we're talking about your grandmother.

INMATE KEMPER: ... and it fell ... right ... it fell apart, it caved in and she went off.

PRESIDING COMMISSIONER FRITZ: Okay, we're talking about your grandmother. I'm still trying figure out ...

INMATE KEMPER: And she realized the deception.

PRESIDING COMMISSIONER FRITZ: All right, um, so you kill your grandmother and then why'd you kill your grandfather.

INMATE KEMPER: Fear.

PRESIDING COMMISSIONER FRITZ: Fear of your grandfather?

INMATE KEMPER: Yeah.

PRESIDING COMMISSIONER FRITZ: Why'd you fear your grandfather?

INMATE KEMPER: Well when he ... I'd heard stories about when he was younger. He was a pretty fierce guy. He was an original cowboy. He carried a 45 on his hip. He was, uh, a tough guy wrangler, and my father had told me that he back-handed him clear across the kitchen one night when he got, I guess, smart with him.

PRESIDING COMMISSIONER FRITZ: Did there ... your grandfather ever hit you?

INMATE KEMPER: No.

PRESIDING COMMISSIONER FRITZ: No, okay I don't know if I'm ... I'm ... I'm following this. You killed your ...

INMATE KEMPER: Well ...

PRESIDING COMMISSIONER FRITZ: Hold on.

INMATE KEMPER: Yes.

PRESIDING COMMISSIONER FRITZ: I know you're trying to get out what you want to get out, but I have questions that I would like answered, okay?

INMATE KEMPER: Mm-hmm.

PRESIDING COMMISSIONER FRITZ: So you kill your grandmother first because you just happen to have the shotgun to hunting with your dog ...

INMATE KEMPER: Twenty-two.

PRESIDING COMMISSIONER FRITZ: ... 22, okay. And then do you immediately kill your grandfather afterward or what?

INMATE KEMPER: He wasn't there. He was down shopping in town.

PRESIDING COMMISSIONER FRITZ: So when he got back did you kill him?

INMATE KEMPER: Yeah.

PRESIDING COMMISSIONER FRITZ: Immediately?

INMATE KEMPER: Uh, within a few minutes, yes.

PRESIDING COMMISSIONER FRITZ: Did he even know

his wife ... that you killed his wife?

INMATE KEMPER: No.

PRESIDING COMMISSIONER FRITZ: Okay so but where would there be any ...

INMATE KEMPER: I started trying to tell him.

PRESIDING COMMISSIONER FRITZ: There would be no fear at this point. You didn't even ... I mean if that's what you're trying to ...

INMATE KEMPER: That built up. I was trying to tell him and I couldn't even talk. I was, uh, garbled.

PRESIDING COMMISSIONER FRITZ: All right.

INMATE KEMPER: The words kept coming out in batches of different starts, and, uh, he wasn't paying any attention to it, uh, he was getting a little senile, not totally, you know, responsive to moments.

PRESIDING COMMISSIONER FRITZ: No problems with your grandfather?

INMATE KEMPER: No.

PRESIDING COMMISSIONER FRITZ: Okay, so ...

INMATE KEMPER: But he was walking around to the other side of his truck and he was gonna open the passenger side where there was a bag of groceries for me to take in, and I was arguing with myself trying to figure out what to do, and it became very apparent in just a matter of minutes that there's no way I was gonna tell him what had happened to his wife of 50 years.

PRESIDING COMMISSIONER FRITZ: So it would seem then that you killed them because you wanted to get away with it or something, I mean, cause you weren't gonna tell him about the death. So then, he needed to be killed? I ... I don't get the whole fear thing cause I don't see that here. Um, so what else can you tell me?

INMATE KEMPER: I was walking along behind him.

I had the 22 in my hand. I tried to raise the barrel up and I couldn't.

PRESIDING COMMISSIONER FRITZ: How old was he at the time?

INMATE KEMPER: Was he?

PRESIDING COMMISSIONER FRITZ: How old was he?

INMATE KEMPER: Seventy-two.

PRESIDING COMMISSIONER FRITZ: So he's 72, you're 15; you're what, 6'5" at this point with a ...

INMATE KEMPER: Some ... something like that.

PRESIDING COMMISSIONER FRITZ: ... you're 6'5", you have a gun, you have a 22, he's bring ... trying to bring groceries in the house.

INMATE KEMPER: Just gonna open the door so I can get them.

PRESIDING COMMISSIONER FRITZ: Right, so ... so that's why I'm not ... I don't get this fear thing at all because he had no weapon, he had nothing.

INMATE KEMPER: It was something ... it was ... it was something that was building up.

PRESIDING COMMISSIONER FRITZ: Okay. You feel bad about what you did to your grandparents?

INMATE KEMPER: Yes.

PRESIDING COMMISSIONER FRITZ: Do you?

INMATE KEMPER: Yes, I do.

PRESIDING COMMISSIONER FRITZ: Okay so, um, what would you say to them right now? What would you like to say to them?

INMATE KEMPER: Well neither one of them knew what happened to them. They were shot in the head so they went down immediately.

PRESIDING COMMISSIONER FRITZ: So does that make ... okay, please ... does that make it better? Is that what you're saying, they didn't know they were getting killed? I want to know, you shot your grandparents.

INMATE KEMPER: Yes.

PRESIDING COMMISSIONER FRITZ: Sir, you shot your grandparents who were taking care of you.

INMATE KEMPER: Yes.

PRESIDING COMMISSIONER FRITZ: They didn't do anything to you. For no apparent reason and basically I asked you what would you say to them? You murdered both of them and you basically said they didn't know what was coming. So what? That makes it better? That's ... that's very disturbing.

INMATE KEMPER: No, I ... I'm saying in the reference to your statement that ...

PRESIDING COMMISSIONER FRITZ: What would you say?

INMATE KEMPER: ... what would I ... you asked what would I say to them.

PRESIDING COMMISSIONER FRITZ: And you'd say ...

INMATE KEMPER: First off ...

PRESIDING COMMISSIONER FRITZ: ... I shot you in the head so you didn't know what was coming.

INMATE KEMPER: If they were here suddenly just out of the past, there would be a lot of confusion. For one thing, they wouldn't realize why time had gone by.

PRESIDING COMMISSIONER FRITZ: Okay.

INMATE KEMPER: They didn't even know what happened to them.

PRESIDING COMMISSIONER FRITZ: Okay. All right, then you go to Ash, right?

INMATE KEMPER: No. I went to Youth Authority.

PRESIDING COMMISSIONER FRITZ: You went to Youth Authority but then ... then you went to Ash. I mean you got ... you were committed to Ash.

INMATE KEMPER: The Youth Authority and I was processed through Perkins, California.

PRESIDING COMMISSIONER FRITZ: Okay.

INMATE KEMPER: It's a northern reception center.

PRESIDING COMMISSIONER FRITZ: No, I ... I ... we ... I get it. I'm trying to move forward. You ended up in Ash.

INMATE KEMPER: Over where ... I know, but we're moving past something that was salient.

PRESIDING COMMISSIONER FRITZ: Oh, okay. Well tell me what it is.

INMATE KEMPER: I had a youth ... I had a youth authority number, I went through normal processing like everybody else. When I went to the board, the board members said you ... don't even sit down, he says, we can't even talk to you. And I looked at him with confusion and he said don't take a seat. And basically he told me I wasn't even suppose to be there because mental issues had been brought up at my trial by a psychiatrist hired by the judge, not by me.

PRESIDING COMMISSIONER FRITZ: Okay, I didn't ... I don't know how ...

INMATE KEMPER: He said I was mentally ill and I needed treatment, not punishment.

PRESIDING COMMISSIONER FRITZ: Well right, that's why you ended up at Ash.

INMATE KEMPER: No, the judge mocked at that and sent me YA anyway ...

PRESIDING COMMISSIONER FRITZ: Okay.

INMATE KEMPER: ... which he ... I wasn't aware of it at the time, but shortly thereafter that, that was illegal; he wasn't even allowed to do that. But he did it anyway because Madera County, as it turns out, is a hang 'em high county, they do what they want to do.

PRESIDING COMMISSIONER FRITZ: We don't need to go into all this, sir. What's salient about this whole thing? Tell ... just let me get to the bottom line here cause I'm trying to move forward into ...

INMATE KEMPER: I was sent back to Madera County for further processing and rejected by the Youth Authority. They left my case open, but they sent me back to Madera. And, uh, the judge kind of had a fit ...

PRESIDING COMMISSIONER FRITZ: But we don't need to get in to all this; okay, I'm just saying, if there's something salient, which I haven't found yet, what is it besides you complaining about the treatment that you had way back in the '70s and it's 2017. Bottom line is you eventually ended up at Ash, correct?

INMATE KEMPER: Yes.

PRESIDING COMMISSIONER FRITZ: Okay for mental health, correct or not? Were you there for mental health issues? Do you know?

INMATE KEMPER: Theoretically.

PRESIDING COMMISSIONER FRITZ: Do you think that you had a mental health problem?

INMATE KEMPER: Uh, yes.

PRESIDING COMMISSIONER FRITZ: Okay is there anything imp ... that you thinks was important about what you were just describing that would add to the story?

INMATE KEMPER: Well, there always is, but, uh, I think you'd be saying I'm holding things up again, so. PRESIDING COMMISSIONER FRITZ: Okay. So you're at Ash and then actually from what I read, and ... and maybe I have this wrong, the ... the psychologist actually their opinion was you should have stayed there, but somehow they ... you ended up getting released. Do you think you should have been released from Ash?

INMATE KEMPER: I wasn't released from Ash. I left there in chains.

PRESIDING COMMISSIONER FRITZ: Okay.

INMATE KEMPER: Four years and six months after I got there.

PRESIDING COMMISSIONER FRITZ: Right.

INMATE KEMPER: Because the county judge said I had a hold on me and I could not be released by Atascadero so the ... the psychiatrist asked me, what did I want to do at this point? Do I...would I want to stay for treatment or go back and face the music?

PRESIDING COMMISSIONER FRITZ: The psychologist asked you that? They gave you the choice?

INMATE KEMPER: Psychiatrist.

PRESIDING COMMISSIONER FRITZ: Psychiatrist, okay.

INMATE KEMPER: He was ... he was ... he was the head man of the unit, and, uh, I said well, you've given me therapy and you're saying that I'm ready for a minimum security hospital in a program there so I think I'll go back and face up to whatever they got. But he - - he was under the misapprehension that I was going back for trial as an adult.

PRESIDING COMMISSIONER FRITZ: Okay, so ...

INMATE KEMPER: I knew that I had been tried as a 15-year-old as a juvenile in juvenile court. It was a one day trial.

PRESIDING COMMISSIONER FRITZ: Do you think you should have been released from Ash? That's my questions that I want you to answer now.

INMATE KEMPER: No, I was being transferred.

PRESIDING COMMISSIONER FRITZ: But, no ... I know what happened but do you personally think you should have been released?

INMATE KEMPER: That wasn't the issue at the time. That wasn't what I came up for.

PRESIDING COMMISSIONER FRITZ: I ... I understand that, sir. Do you think you should have been released from Ash? Do you think CDCR made a mistake in releasing you?

INMATE KEMPER: I went back to Youth Authority.

PRESIDING COMMISSIONER FRITZ: Okay so your ... you just don't want to answer the question. Okay.

INMATE KEMPER: No. I went back to the Youth Authority.

PRESIDING COMMISSIONER FRITZ: But you're not ask ... answering the question ...

INMATE KEMPER: I wasn't up for ...

PRESIDING COMMISSIONER FRITZ: ... but that's okay ...

INMATE KEMPER: I wasn't up for release ...

PRESIDING COMMISSIONER FRITZ: ... you don't need to answer it.

INMATE KEMPER: I wasn't up for release.

PRESIDING COMMISSIONER FRITZ: Okay, uh, let's ...

INMATE KEMPER: The issue is ...

PRESIDING COMMISSIONER FRITZ: ... let's move on. It's okay, you don't need to answer questions, it's up to you. Um, all right, so you ... you're out ... out for a few years I guess and ... and then went on a crime scree ... spree where you ended up killing what, eight people, six were strangers, correct?

INMATE KEMPER: Yeah.

PRESIDING COMMISSIONER FRITZ: Uh, mostly college students, I think one high school student, all women hitchhikers. Um, I guess you lured them in, um, ended up killing them, dismembering them. According to this, you had sex with them after they were dismembered or died. And I'm just wondering why you did that?

INMATE KEMPER: At the time it was frustration.

PRESIDING COMMISSIONER FRITZ: Over what?

INMATE KEMPER: That I couldn't do anything with them when they were alive.

PRESIDING COMMISSIONER FRITZ: What do you mean you couldn't do anything with them when you ... they were alive.

INMATE KEMPER: Well the first two ...

PRESIDING COMMISSIONER FRITZ: Do you know ...

INMATE KEMPER: ... we got into quite an argument ...

PRESIDING COMMISSIONER FRITZ: Do you know their names?

INMATE KEMPER: Yes.

PRESIDING COMMISSIONER FRITZ: What are their names?

INMATE KEMPER: Mary Ann Pesce and Anita Luchessa.

PRESIDING COMMISSIONER FRITZ: Okay.

INMATE KEMPER: They were hitchhiking together. They were roommates at Fresno State. They were in Berkley hitchhiking going to Stanford on their way back to Fresno. And when I pulled my gun out, when I had them in a quiet place, uh, and they asked me what I was going to do, and I said, what do you think I'm going to do, I was referring to sex. They were thinking ... they didn't want to be thinking death so I wasn't encouraging that at all. And, uh, when they refused to be involved with me sexually, I stated that it could get worse, it, uh, you know, you could die today. You can end up getting dumped in the ditch, is that what you want? And, uh, they basically were, uh ... they were arguing against rape. And, uh, naturally that didn't happen. Also I didn't shoot them. I had a 9 mm automatic and I didn't use it other than for gesturing.

PRESIDING COMMISSIONER FRITZ: So instead you did what?

INMATE KEMPER: Reached in my pocket and pulled a knife out.

PRESIDING COMMISSIONER FRITZ: Okay so it made it better ... what that you didn't rape them and you didn't shoot? Instead you took a knife and ...

INMATE KEMPER: I wish I hadn't because, you know, I didn't have any experience with such things, and the ... well the only experience I had was theatrical stuff on television. When somebody gets stuck with a knife they fall over dead for theatrical purposes. That doesn't happen in real life.

PRESIDING COMMISSIONER FRITZ: So you took the more personal approach of using a knife. Why ... why'd you do that?

INMATE KEMPER: Well I thought it was going to be quick.

PRESIDING COMMISSIONER FRITZ: Well I ... the whole story doesn't make a whole lot of sense to me cause what, at this point you're 6'9", right?

INMATE KEMPER: Yeah.

PRESIDING COMMISSIONER FRITZ: You're this huge guy, you have a gun. You could've easily forced rape.

INMATE KEMPER: Neither one of them were impressed with the gun.

PRESIDING COMMISSIONER FRITZ: So, I mean, then you take a knife out and you're saying you ... you thought they would just die. Okay and then why ... did you dismember them?

INMATE KEMPER: Not immediately, no. It was later on.

PRESIDING COMMISSIONER FRITZ: But you did it, and so why'd you do that?

INMATE KEMPER: I didn't dismember them. I cut their heads off.

PRESIDING COMMISSIONER FRITZ: Okay. All right, so you beheaded them ...

INMATE KEMPER: Yes.

PRESIDING COMMISSIONER FRITZ: Or dismembered them; it just depends on how you want to say it, but you did it and I want to know why?

INMATE KEMPER: They're both beautiful, but after I got done with the knife, they weren't. They were bloody and, I mean, they were covered in blood.

PRESIDING COMMISSIONER FRITZ: Okay.

INMATE KEMPER: It was messy and I didn't ... once I got into it, it just got ... I got sucked in deeper and deeper, it just ... it didn't go away. So something had to be dealt with.

PRESIDING COMMISSIONER FRITZ: So ... so, I ... I - - I need to ... I'm ... I'm gonna redirect you again cause I ... I'm still waiting for the answer on why you beheaded them.

INMATE KEMPER: And I took their heads up to my apartment. I cleaned them up. I cleaned their hair out and posed them as they would have ... as they were two hours earlier.

PRESIDING COMMISSIONER FRITZ: For what reason?

INMATE KEMPER: To look at.

PRESIDING COMMISSIONER FRITZ: Why?

INMATE KEMPER: I was a nut. I wasn't able to do anything more than that.

PRESIDING COMMISSIONER FRITZ: Well okay. I ... I think that's kind of a poor choice of words, but okay. Um, so they were you trophies. That's the way you treated them, like objects?

INMATE KEMPER: Yeah.

PRESIDING COMMISSIONER FRITZ: Why is that? Cause that's, uh, what your whole history is, is treating women like objects. So I'm kind of ...

INMATE KEMPER: Yes.

PRESIDING COMMISSIONER FRITZ: ... wondering why.

INMATE KEMPER: Huh?

PRESIDING COMMISSIONER FRITZ: Why? Where'd that come from?

INMATE KEMPER: Uh, my limited exposure to women at ... at that time.

PRESIDING COMMISSIONER FRITZ: Well ...

INMATE KEMPER: I had never been on a date and I'm suddenly paroled by the Youth Authority.

PRESIDING COMMISSIONER FRITZ: But there's plenty of people that are not experienced with dating and things like that, and they don't go on a crime spree, and you know, killing ...

INMATE KEMPER: Atascadero intended that I go on dates, and you know, work my way out into society ...

PRESIDING COMMISSIONER FRITZ: But you're not hearing me. Sir, you're not hearing me. There's plenty of people that are ... were similar as far as abusive families or abusive mothers, and you know, not involved ...

INMATE KEMPER: Highly erotic you ...

PRESIDING COMMISSIONER FRITZ: ... well ... wait ... wait ... wait don't interrupt me, and, um, you know not experienced with women and stuff, and they don't go out and kill six women and then dismember them and what? You had sex with the corpses? That's what I read. Is that right?

INMATE KEMPER: Occasionally.

PRESIDING COMMISSIONER FRITZ: All about ..

INMATE KEMPER: Frustration.

PRESIDING COMMISSIONER FRITZ: ... your reasoning for six murders?

INMATE KEMPER: Well, it grew. It didn't start out that way.

PRESIDING COMMISSIONER FRITZ: Um, but that's your ... that's your reasoning that you were frustrated.

INMATE KEMPER: And not being able to treat them more normally.

PRESIDING COMMISSIONER FRITZ: So, instead of treating them more normally, you killed them, dismembered them, and had sex with them when they were dead?

INMATE KEMPER: I dismembered two of them because I had a broken arm. I had a motorcycle and I shattered my left arm. It was in a cast all the way to my shoulder. So I couldn't carry them normally, so I had to be very careful how I treated them.

PRESIDING COMMISSIONER FRITZ: The first two you cut off their heads and then you displayed them in your house. All right, okay, so you don't like that being called dismembered. We'll call it beheaded, um ...

INMATE KEMPER: Partial dismemberment.

PRESIDING COMMISSIONER FRITZ: ... partially, all right, you know, I guess semantics are important to you.

INMATE KEMPER: But there were some very thorough dismemberment, too.

PRESIDING COMMISSIONER FRITZ: Oh, I know. Um, all right, and then you're saying because you had a broken arm you couldn't carry them correctly so you had to dismember them? Is that really what you're telling me?

INMATE KEMPER: I couldn't safely carry them from my car to my house or my house to the car.

PRESIDING COMMISSIONER FRITZ: Did you enjoy dismembering them?

INMATE KEMPER: No.

PRESIDING COMMISSIONER FRITZ: But you did it with almost every single one at some ... either partially or beheading or however you want to describe it, right?

INMATE KEMPER: Yes.

PRESIDING COMMISSIONER FRITZ: So, sometimes you had the broken arm, sometimes you didn't 'cause this was over a period of a year-and-a-half or more. So then there is no reasoning for any of the others unless you just enjoyed doing it or unless you have another explanation for me.

INMATE KEMPER: Well you are over simplifying, I think.

PRESIDING COMMISSIONER FRITZ: Well, I've been trying to get the answers from you but I'm only getting frustration. So if you want to get into more ... in more ... a ... a different explanation, I ... I'd like to hear it.

INMATE KEMPER: Uh, well there's embarrassment now too in this whole thing. It is a very embarrassing memory. It's not a pleasant memory. It hasn't been for years. I've had years and years of therapy; twelve years of therapy here in prison, and, uh, it's a very involved explanation. Nothing explains a way, right?

PRESIDING COMMISSIONER FRITZ: Well let's hear it.

INMATE KEMPER: Nothing like explains a way. But, it's not a simple answer on the head of pin, you know, bing, here's your answer.

PRESIDING COMMISSIONER FRITZ: Well just tell me besides just telling me that it's not simple. Tell me then what it is.

INMATE KEMPER: Very complex problem.

PRESIDING COMMISSIONER FRITZ: Okay, you keep saying that, but I ... now I just want to hear it. Like, you know, okay we get it. It's complex, I think we get it, so let's hear it.

INMATE KEMPER: Well some of the issues are not available to me right now because I've gotten frustrated, and, uh ...

PRESIDING COMMISSIONER FRITZ: You've gotten frustrated right now?

INMATE KEMPER: Yeah.

PRESIDING COMMISSIONER FRITZ: Okay.

INMATE KEMPER: One thing I've not ever had a problem with is people throwing how did you do it or what did you do and run it down to me in one sentence, you know?

PRESIDING COMMISSIONER FRITZ: Well I'm not asking for a one sentence answer.

INMATE KEMPER: No, I'm saying ...

PRESIDING COMMISSIONER FRITZ: I'm just asking for something besides a one word answer, frustration, and ...

INMATE KEMPER: No ...

PRESIDING COMMISSIONER FRITZ: ... and some issues are not available to me right now cause I'm getting frustrated. But, I'm just thinking to myself, this is what I'm thinking; you've been here for how many years?

INMATE KEMPER: Over 40.

PRESIDING COMMISSIONER FRITZ: Okay, so you've had a long time to think about why you've killed all these people. You've been to tons of therapy. Um, if you actually wanted to think about it and not be embarrassed by it, and ... and having no pleasure in it. I'm sure the victims would think otherwise, but you've been here for almost 40 years, you've been through tons of therapy, and I'm not ... this is what I'm getting? That some of the issues aren't available right now cause I'm frustrated and it was because of frustration and embar ... I'm embarrassed.

INMATE KEMPER: No, I said it's an embarrassing issue.

PRESIDING COMMISSIONER FRITZ: Okay, I would ...

INMATE KEMPER: It's an embarrassing memory.

PRESIDING COMMISSIONER FRITZ: I think again, a different choice of words is perhaps something that, uh, should be used, but any way.

INMATE KEMPER: There's no simple explanation.

PRESIDING COMMISSIONER FRITZ: We know, and you keep saying that, so I'm gonna ask you one more time and then we're just gonna move on because you keep saying there's no simple explanation so I'm waiting to hear this complex explanation. Um, I know you're capable of it. I mean ... I mean, you don't have any ... as far as you don't have any intellectual issues that would hinder you from being able to get through this process to explain why you did this, but ... so, what ... just one more time and then I'm not gonna keep pressing you on it, cause like I said you don't have to answer questions if you don't want to, but you keep saying it's more than ... it's ... it's not simple, but ... then what is it?

INMATE KEMPER: I explained it, uh, in years past a lot.

PRESIDING COMMISSIONER FRITZ: Okay, but it's a new hearing.

INMATE KEMPER: It's still embarrassing. It's still dimin ... diminishing of my manhood. I'm not much of a man for having done things like that to people who are innocent and just looking for a ride.

PRESIDING COMMISSIONER FRITZ: Okay. And then you, what, kill your mother and her friend?

INMATE KEMPER: Yes.

PRESIDING COMMISSIONER FRITZ: And so what was that all about?

INMATE KEMPER: My mother ... I went to Mary Ann Pesce's grave and I made an oath to her that my mother and I were going to pay for what happened to her.

PRESIDING COMMISSIONER FRITZ: So you blame your mother for your murder?

INMATE KEMPER: I blamed her for a role in it.

PRESIDING COMMISSIONER FRITZ: Why? What's your mother have to do with your actions?

INMATE KEMPER: She played a role in the decisions I made earlier in life. For her is expediency or frustration or humor or whatever motivated her at the time. Sometimes it was alcoholic and sometimes it was sober as hell. But, I knew that as long as she lived, I wasn't going to stop doing that to other people ... to strangers, cause that I could get away with.

PRESIDING COMMISSIONER FRITZ: I'm sorry; you could get away with killing strangers?

INMATE KEMPER: Yeah, that was not linking back to me.

PRESIDING COMMISSIONER FRITZ: Got it, okay. All right, so you ...

INMATE KEMPER: And every time I got mad at her I went out and got in my car, went driving around, found someone to pick up, took them off somewhere quiet, and blew them away with a .22.

PRESIDING COMMISSIONER FRITZ: Or stabbed them, right?

INMATE KEMPER: No.

PRESIDING COMMISSIONER FRITZ: No?

INMATE KEMPER: I stopped that very early on. I did that to the first two.

PRESIDING COMMISSIONER FRITZ: Okay.

INMATE KEMPER: To the third girl, Aiko Koo, I smothered her.

PRESIDING COMMISSIONER FRITZ: And you call her girl, what, she was a college student, right? No, she was a high school student.

INMATE KEMPER: High school.

PRESIDING COMMISSIONER FRITZ: Okay.

INMATE KEMPER: She was pretending to be at University at Berkeley. She was hitchhiking in front of Berkley and pretending to be 18 - 19 years of age, and I mistook her for that. I wouldn't of killed a high school girl.

PRESIDING COMMISSIONER FRITZ: All right, so all of these were precipitated on having a … some type of argument with your mother. So the … the point, it … I think what you're trying to tell me is you … you needed to kill your mother so you would stop killing other people, is that what you're saying?

INMATE KEMPER: Or kill myself and for some reason the frustration that I had lived earlier in life didn't allow me to simplify by killing myself.

PRESIDING COMMISSIONER FRITZ: Well when you …

INMATE KEMPER: I made the effort.

PRESIDING COMMISSIONER FRITZ: … when you have a narcissistic personality, sir, narcissists don't usually kill themselves. Do you know what that means?

INMATE KEMPER: Generally.

PRESIDING COMMISSIONER FRITZ: You think you're a narcissist?

INMATE KEMPER: No.

PRESIDING COMMISSIONER FRITZ: No? You don't think so?

INMATE KEMPER: No, one of my therapists since then, here, someone I had for five years one on one, said it was a toss up between that and another type of disease that, uh, I can't recall. It was a complicated name. And then finally he said it wasn't the narcissist one, it was the other. It was, uh ...

PRESIDING COMMISSIONER FRITZ: Okay, but other ...

INMATE KEMPER: ... some kind ... some kind of psychosis.

PRESIDING COMMISSIONER FRITZ: But other psychologists, many have said that you have a narcissistic personality trait. So I guess there's one that ...

INMATE KEMPER: Eh, when you see someone one time, I mean, you know they can get images.

PRESIDING COMMISSIONER FRITZ: But all the psychologists?

INMATE KEMPER: Hmm?

PRESIDING COMMISSIONER FRITZ: All the different psychologists that have come to the same conclusion; they're all wrong?

INMATE KEMPER: Mm, they cited other people before them.

PRESIDING COMMISSIONER FRITZ: Okay, um, all right, so that ... I guess that's the explanation for killing your mother. Why'd you kill her friend?

INMATE KEMPER: Her friend, her lover, uh, it sounds really dumb saying it this way, but my mother had her only vacation and it was a big one, and she went to Europe; two weeks in England and two weeks in France. And she was suppose to do it with this woman, Sally Hallett. They planned on it all summer long or spring long, and, uh, made serious plans, and her friend, Sally, in fact got mad at her when she ... when she over it ... iterated that, uh, you know, be sure and let me know if you're gonna change your mind or if you're not gonna' be involved, and she said, of course I am, quit asking me that. Then at the last minute, this is a non- refundable down-payment of sixty ... six hundred dollars that has to be paid by each party, and Sunday night was the deadline for that six hundred dollar deposit, and my mother was frantically calling Sally all weekend trying to get a hold of her. She couldn't reach her even though she was local. So finally she went ahead and made the decision to make ... mail the deposit ...

PRESIDING COMMISSIONER FRITZ: Okay, I ...

INMATE KEMPER: ... on Sunday night ...

PRESIDING COMMISSIONER FRITZ: ... you really like

gone way ...

INMATE KEMPER: ... on Monday morning ...

PRESIDING COMMISSIONER FRITZ: Hold on, wait a second. What does this have to do with killing her friend? Let's get to ... let's focus. You kind of ...

INMATE KEMPER: Revenge.

PRESIDING COMMISSIONER FRITZ: Revenge. Okay, got it. So wh ... revenge for what?

INMATE KEMPER: Ruining my mother's holiday.

PRESIDING COMMISSIONER FRITZ: Oh, okay.

INMATE KEMPER: Her vacation. She came, eh ... Monday she found out that Sally had changed her mind and then made herself unavailable. So she had to go by herself and she went over to Europe. She spent this vacation time by herself going to places and seeing things by herself when she had intended to go with this other woman. And when she got back, she tried sharing those vacation moments with Sally, and Sally got very loud with her and rude, and told her I don't want to hear about that. I didn't even go on that vacation, why are you brining this up? So she ... that cut off that release. So here I am at the house having heard this from my mother and she's frustrated and I said I'd like to know, I'd like you to share with me. So she went and got all of her travel logs and the ...

PRESIDING COMMISSIONER FRITZ: okay, I got. Um ...

INMATE KEMPER: And the ... and the papers and stuff from the places that she went and she started systematically sharing this stuff with me, and then all of a sudden she stops and she looks at me in this strange way, and she said, I'm not gonna let you pity me. And she just walked away from the whole thing. And I said, hey, I wanted to hear this stuff.

PRESIDING COMMISSIONER FRITZ: Okay. So, I mean ... I ...

INMATE KEMPER: So what I did, I said to myself ... self ...

PRESIDING COMMISSIONER FRITZ: Now, wait! You're interrupting me again, okay? You said it was revenge for your mother's vacation, I get that. But, I get the impression you hated your mother, I mean that's why you killed all these people.

INMATE KEMPER: Off and on.

PRESIDING COMMISSIONER FRITZ: And, um, so that ...

INMATE KEMPER: I loved my mother, but I also had a lot of hatred for her too.

PRESIDING COMMISSIONER FRITZ: So then why would you revenge your mother's vacation by killing the friend if you had ...

INMATE KEMPER: I had told myself that if my mother ever dies over this stuff that I did, she's going with her. That's one trip she's not gonna miss. She's not gonna back off on that one.

PRESIDING COMMISSIONER FRITZ: Okay, um …

INMATE KEMPER: I swore an oath to it. I was angry at the time.

PRESIDING COMMISSIONER FRITZ: All right.

INMATE KEMPER: I haven't sworn many oaths in my life and everyone that I have sworn I followed through with.

PRESIDING COMMISSIONER FRITZ: Do you, um … did you have sex with any of the victims before they were killed?

INMATE KEMPER: No, uh, well …

PRESIDING COMMISSIONER FRITZ: You did, well that's what it says.

INMATE KEMPER: No.

PRESIDING COMMISSIONER FRITZ: No?

INMATE KEMPER: Not the victims, no … no.

PRESIDING COMMISSIONER FRITZ: Okay, and I don't know if I ever got the answer as to why you had sex with some of the victims after they were killed.

INMATE KEMPER: They were beautiful women.

PRESIDING COMMISSIONER FRITZ: But, they were dead.

INMATE KEMPER: That's true.

PRESIDING COMMISSIONER FRITZ: Did you have sex with your mom after you bludgeoned her with the hammer?

INMATE KEMPER: No.

PRESIDING COMMISSIONER FRITZ: No? I thought I read that somewhere, too.

INMATE KEMPER: I said something to that affect at my trial, but that was a choice of moments and words.

PRESIDING COMMISSIONER FRITZ: Why'd you use a hammer because you said you used the knives in the beginning, it was too messy for you, started using the gun, then you used a hammer.

INMATE KEMPER: And that made it very quick.

PRESIDING COMMISSIONER FRITZ: I'm sorry?

INMATE KEMPER: Using the gun, the .22 pistol, became very quick.

PRESIDING COMMISSIONER FRITZ: Okay so then why did you use a hammer to kill your mother?

INMATE KEMPER: That was a childhood fantasy.

PRESIDING COMMISSIONER FRITZ: To kill your mother with a hammer?

INMATE KEMPER: To bludgeon her with a hammer, uh, one time to hit her with a hammer and incapacitate her and then cut her throat.

PRESIDING COMMISSIONER FRITZ: Okay.

INMATE KEMPER: That was a fantasy from when I was eight years old, and locked in the basement and I used to sneak up in the middle of the night when everybody was asleep and I went through the ritual, but I didn't follow through with the act.

PRESIDING COMMISSIONER FRITZ: I guess she thought you were gonna harm your sister so that was why she put you in the basement? That's what I read.

INMATE KEMPER: No.

PRESIDING COMMISSIONER FRITZ: No?

INMATE KEMPER: That was a solution for my older sister sneaking out. She was five years my senior; she was 13 at the time and she was caught at a, uh, teenage hangout along with another woman's son. And the wo ... other woman told her, oh by the way your sis ... your daughter, Sue, was there too. And, uh, she called Sue up and had this little conversation with her doing homework and stuff like that and let her get herself deep and then said, I know that you were at the Dutch Maid.

PRESIDING COMMISSIONER FRITZ: Well you still have a lot of frustration towards your fam ... your mother, your sisters, cause it ... it comes out in your testimony which is surprising after all this time, but you still feel like you got short-shifted or something because it comes out. You have a lot of issues related to that. I'm ... you ... you ...

INMATE KEMPER: I got put in the basement when I was scared to death of the dark. That was my fear.

PRESIDING COMMISSIONER FRITZ: Okay, any questions?

DEPUTY COMMISSIONER BLAKE: I have developed some questions, thank you. Um ... um, Mr. Kemper, do you think you've ever had a, well one could call a normal relationship with a woman?

INMATE KEMPER: I've had several.

DEPUTY COMMISSIONER BLAKE: Okay, where?

INMATE KEMPER: But not necessarily sexual.

DEPUTY COMMISSIONER BLAKE: Okay, I mean friendships or professional ...

INMATE KEMPER: But I have ... I have had sexual relationships with women also.

DEPUTY COMMISSIONER BLAKE: Have you?

INMATE KEMPER: On the streets.

DEPUTY COMMISSIONER BLAKE: Okay.

INMATE KEMPER: And ironically ...

DEPUTY COMMISSIONER BLAKE: What do ...

INMATE KEMPER: ... some of them were at assistance in the provost up at UCSC. You ... something that escaped our conversation earlier was that a lot of my mother's friends, uh, got hot pants for me. They wanted to do it. And that was obvious after our first meeting, and you know, they raise the ... the ... the hem of the skirt, and, uh, of a ... a lovely woman that's so old enough to be my grandmother, I mean, you know, uh, 50 some years old. But, I said to myself, self, she wants to get in your pants, and it turned out to be very true and at a later meeting we did it, and my mother, of course, found out about it because they would talk about when I'm like in bed. And she got so mad and she come at me with, uh, I can't even bring my friends by the house anymore cause here, uh, and I said why not? And she says cause your scrotum.

DEPUTY COMMISSIONER BLAKE: Did you think the ... those were normal relationships?

INMATE KEMPER: No ... no ... no, I'm saying that was, uh, something in the wr ... in the ... my case ...

DEPUTY COMMISSIONER BLAKE: I understand.

INMATE KEMPER: Like one woman I could have done the same thing to her as I did to Sally Hallett, but I didn't because she was a lover. She was someone I had a normal relationship with and we both had enjoyed it, and I had no intentions of doing anything harmful to her.

DEPUTY COMMISSIONER BLAKE: Okay.

INMATE KEMPER: So while I had that opportunity, I didn't take advantage it.

DEPUTY COMMISSIONER BLAKE: Yeah, you mean the opportunity to ... to kill her? Is that what you mean?

INMATE KEMPER: Yeah.

DEPUTY COMMISSIONER BLAKE: Why would that even occur to you that you would have an opportunity to ... to kill this person?

INMATE KEMPER: Thoughts after my mother passed - -

DEPUTY COMMISSIONER BLAKE: Okay, sir ...

INMATE KEMPER: ... I'm trying to think is there anything else I want to do along that line and different names came up, and for various reasons I said no.

DEPUTY COMMISSIONER BLAKE: Did you ... so ... let's ... the ... the question was whether you've ever had, uh, a normal relationship with a woman. Can you think of something where you can describe a friendship you had with a female peer or a working relationship, or, um, I mean, um ...

INMATE KEMPER: Here.

DEPUTY COMMISSIONER BLAKE: Here, okay ...

INMATE KEMPER: Yeah, in prison.

DEPUTY COMMISSIONER BLAKE: Okay.

INMATE KEMPER: Yeah.

DEPUTY COMMISSIONER BLAKE: Who's that?

INMATE KEMPER: Right now there's a young woman in her 30s in France who's very heavily involved in a relationship with me on paper because that's all we can do right now is write. But, uh, and she sends money, sends pictures, and, uh, now she sought me out through the media.

DEPUTY COMMISSIONER BLAKE: Um ...

INMATE KEMPER: It's not someone I sought out, it's someone who sought me out.

DEPUTY COMMISSIONER BLAKE: When you ... when you say you had, um, sexual relationship ... relationships on the streets, did you ever have, uh, a girlfriend or anyone close to your age?

INMATE KEMPER: Not at the time. There were times when I had relationships with young women, and, uh, in one case it was jailbait, it was someone that was underage, but she was in a bar faking age, and I took her home that night, and we did it, and she brought her girlfriend by the gas station I worked at to introduce me to her as, you know, I'm ... I'm her young lover, right. What she didn't know is that she had given me a really nasty case of gonorrhea, and I had been getting it treated. Wasn't too happy about it, so when she brought this young lady by and introduced her I ... I was pretty sarcastic about, uh ... and we didn't see each other anymore.

DEPUTY COMMISSIONER BLAKE: I ... I got the sense that you were sexually inexperienced when you began murdering your victims.

INMATE KEMPER: Essentially, I was.

DEPUTY COMMISSIONER BLAKE: Did you believe that you probably wouldn't be able to have sex with the victims unless they were dead? I mean it sounds like you just gave up on the idea.

INMATE KEMPER: My sister had said to, uh, one of the psyches investigating my case

DEPUTY COMMISSIONER BLAKE: Mm-hmm.

INMATE KEMPER: ... that I had said something to that affect about a teacher, uh, a grade school teacher that I really ... really liked how she looked, and I'd say I couldn't kiss her cause I'd have to kill her.

DEPUTY COMMISSIONER BLAKE: Mm-hmm.

INMATE KEMPER: So she said that and I'm thinking, oh boy that takes some explaining. But, in essence it was my ... my ... my, uh, youth and my fear of dealing with advanced issues like, uh, sexuality or groping or things like that. That all comes later in life when you're in your late teens-20s, I was not even a teenager at that time. But, that wasn't the case with, uh ... I just ... I felt like it was a real waste, and again this is embarrassing. It's shocking and it's embarrassing to me, too.

DEPUTY COMMISSIONER BLAKE: It was a waste? How?

INMATE KEMPER: I've murdered someone, and I'd say, what a waste cause I used to say that at movies when I'd see somebody get offed and I'd say, what a waste as she gets rolled into a ditch and they all go on and ... and nothing ... as if nothing happened. And I say, what a ... what a freakin' waste. That's still a human being.

DEPUTY COMMISSIONER BLAKE: That you could have sex with? Is that what ... is that what you ...

INMATE KEMPER: Theoretically. I'd ... I, uh, made myself believe that, yes.

DEPUTY COMMISSIONER BLAKE: Um, can you think of anything that really, uh, would've made anything different in your life that, uh, where would you would have had a relatively normal life or at least you wouldn't have, uh, engaged in these violent acts? Is there any things or anything that you can think of?

INMATE KEMPER: I can think of a whole lot of accidents I almost had that would have ended it as even a consideration. But then I start wondering about why those things didn't happen, you know. And, uh ...

DEPUTY COMMISSIONER BLAKE: How ... how ... for example ... what do you ... I mean ...

INMATE KEMPER: Like I'm on a bridge.

DEPUTY COMMISSIONER BLAKE: Okay.

INMATE KEMPER: The Golden Gate Bridge, and I'm, uh, I had a fleeting thought about jumping over the side.

DEPUTY COMMISSIONER BLAKE: Right.

INMATE KEMPER: And I said to myself, well why I didn't I? Later on, I'm saying well why in the hell didn't I, before I did any of that stuff. When I worked in Caltrans before it was Caltrans it was Division of Highways, and I'm working with this highway crew in a very dangerous job with speeding cars going by both sides of me, and it's like standing on a chain saw on the side of the blade with the ... with the blades whizzing by at 60 miles an hour, and that can be very scary. I got very used to it and I got sometimes within just inches of being clipped by a car. And in that case, if I'd a been even clipped, I'd a been whacked out, completely whacked out.

DEPUTY COMMISSIONER BLAKE: I ...

INMATE KEMPER: Uh, why didn't that happen?

DEPUTY COMMISSIONER BLAKE: Well I didn't mean that Mr. Kemper, I'm sorry, I didn't mean things would have been different had you died ...

INMATE KEMPER: Yeah.

DEPUTY COMMISSIONER BLAKE: ... and not been alive to commit these crimes. I mean, is there anything you can think of where ... I mean there's never only one thing, but I mean, you know, obviously your siblings, your sisters, they probably didn't have these issues that you had.

INMATE KEMPER: That was all very comp ... all very complicated. A bunch of relationships and I wish I had done better in them.

DEPUTY COMMISSIONER BLAKE: Okay.

INMATE KEMPER: But it would have been a very different existence for me if it were gonna be benign.

DEPUTY COMMISSIONER BLAKE: Is there anything, uh, different about you now than when you first came to prison? Any sort of, um, time for, uh, reflection or any in ... insight that you gained back then?

INMATE KEMPER: Very much.

DEPUTY COMMISSIONER BLAKE: Okay.

INMATE KEMPER: What I did before has no chance of happening again in my life.

DEPUTY COMMISSIONER BLAKE: Why not?

INMATE KEMPER: For one thing, I'm not happy with the results. It's not like I, you know, I'm thinking, oh if I had this head, you know, it doesn't go like that. I'm shocked that I did things like that. The memory of that has me wincing and saying, I can't believe I did that. But, I did and I've become very responsible for what I did and very responsible for the skeletons in my closet, and I've been busy over the years opening that closet and kicking those stupid skeletons out and dealing with them issue by issue, and sometimes with non-professional people, just people I live with.

DEPUTY COMMISSIONER BLAKE: Okay. We'll ... we'll ... we'll talk more about that in the next segment of the hearing.

INMATE KEMPER: All right.

DEPUTY COMMISSIONER BLAKE: Thank you. Thank you.

PRESIDING COMMISSIONER FRITZ: Okay, all right, so we might have some more questions about that, but we're gonna move on. Um, do you remember how long you, um, had the interview with the psychologist ...

INMATE KEMPER: How long?

PRESIDING COMMISSIONER FRITZ: ... back in March 14th, 2017, how long was the interview?

INMATE KEMPER: Two or three hours.

PRESIDING COMMISSIONER FRITZ: Okay, all right. Well let's go through parts of the (*inaudible*) ...

INMATE KEMPER: And he made a comment about my ... I didn't mean to interrupt, but, uh ...

PRESIDING COMMISSIONER FRITZ: But you keep doing it.

INMATE KEMPER: Well, I ...

PRESIDING COMMISSIONER FRITZ: You can't help yourself right? It's just your personality, I guess.

INMATE KEMPER: Well, it's moving along quickly here and I thought of this at the moment and I'm sorry I spoke so quickly about it, but, uh, part of his report speaks at how I was at the end of the first session when I became non-responsive and quiet, and he put some other words in there like psychotic and some other stuff. Hey, I had had a stroke less than two years earlier and I've just spent two or three hours going through this very intensive stuff psychologically, and even though I've had therapy to that effect, it's having, uh, an impact on me. I was exhausted.

PRESIDING COMMISSIONER FRITZ: Okay, thank you. Um, so let me ask you question. How do you feel about killing all these people?

INMATE KEMPER: About who?

PRESIDING COMMISSIONER FRITZ: Killing all these people. You've killed what; 10 people in your life?

INMATE KEMPER: Oh, badly. I wish I could take all of them back. But that's almost an insult because it's obvious I can't.

PRESIDING COMMISSIONER FRITZ: Okay, all right. So it's 26 pages, you said it was about a couple hours long. We're not gonna go through all of it, um, but in the background information on page 426, there is something that I wanted an explanation about. Um, it says that you weren't close to anybody growing up, you did have some friends grow ... this is at the bottom of that page and I'm just paraphrasing ... you had friends several years ago but saw that the relationship was not going well because the man was "playing a role and supposedly going to find out my secrets and then reveal them to others. Other friends about six or seven years ago were more or less adolescent and beneath my station." What does that mean? You think people are beneath your station? What are you talking about? It's in quotes so you said it, and I was ...

INMATE KEMPER: That's not familiar.

PRESIDING COMMISSIONER FRITZ: It's not familiar to you?

INMATE KEMPER: No.

PRESIDING COMMISSIONER FRITZ: Do you think you're better than other people?

INMATE KEMPER: Well, some people, I am. I don't know how ...

PRESIDING COMMISSIONER FRITZ: You do think you're better than other people?

INMATE KEMPER: No, there are some people that ... I have a high IQ, they don't.

PRESIDING COMMISSIONER FRITZ: So?

INMATE KEMPER: Uh, well, I'm saying.

PRESIDING COMMISSIONER FRITZ: I mean, so what. Lots ... tons of people in this room have high IQs. That doesn't make us better than anybody else, right?

INMATE KEMPER: Not in ...

PRESIDING COMMISSIONER FRITZ: Does it make you feel good about yourself to say, "Oh, I have a high IQ, so I'm better than other people?"

INMATE KEMPER: No.

PRESIDING COMMISSIONER FRITZ: Okay, so then what do you mean by "you are better than other people" besides having a high IQ?

INMATE KEMPER: Some people, some of my acquaintances, uh, speak in, uh, a fashion that, uh, tells me they're happy with much simpler accomplishments moment to moment, day to day, and I might put a lot more energy into that; a lot more effort into that than to so speak up to something. In that sense.

PRESIDING COMMISSIONER FRITZ: Okay, all right. can't empathize or be happy with the accomplishments they have 'cause you think they're simple accomplishments versus your accomplishments?

INMATE KEMPER: Well, some accomplishments ... as an example, at Atascadero, I was in the ... working in the, uh, scullery of a kitchen, and a young man that was a couple of years ... well I guess he was about my age, and, uh, he was rolling up a towel and snapping it at people. He thought that was funny. Well he ran by this one guy that was a massive guy, he was over 300 pounds, and, uh, he was not, uh ... advertising how he felt, but he was getting more and more frustrated at how this kid was acting, and when he snapped him and ran by, this big guy got up, headed toward him, grabbed the towel away from him, wrapped it around his neck and squeezed it, and forced him to the floor, and we all sat there going, you know, just the mouth hanging open, like what the hell is that.

PRESIDING COMMISSIONER FRITZ: Okay, well I'm trying to figure out what this has to do with accomplishments.

INMATE KEMPER: And I said ... I jumped up out of me seat, ran around the steel table looking for a weapon and I found a big steel hot teapot and I was heading for it and yelled as loudly and as lowly as I could with a low voice, hey, you know, and it caught his attention, and he backed up off of this kid and started almost babbling, he was talking very quickly. He had snapped and he was killing the kid. He was strangling him. The kid wasn't making a peep of a noise. There was no staff around to stop it.

PRESIDING COMMISSIONER FRITZ: Okay, what does this story have to do with anything?

INMATE KEMPER: I saved the kid's life.

PRESIDING COMMISSIONER FRITZ: Okay.

INMATE KEMPER: That's an accomplishment. I didn't think a lot about it. But, there were times that I reminded myself that there were some good things that I had done.

PRESIDING COMMISSIONER FRITZ: Okay, I thought we were talking about other people's good accomplishments, not yours, but okay. Let's move on. Um, on page 5 you go into this whole thing about this relationship with the woman from France, you think that ... you also ... there's a man in Australia expressed interest in you, um, the man looks a lot better as a woman, could have been interested in her before, so you're getting into these more recent relationships. You say you absolutely have a sexual interest toward the woman in France. That's the one that's giving ... bring ... giving you money, right; sending you money or something?

INMATE KEMPER: Occasionally.

PRESIDING COMMISSIONER FRITZ: And you got emotionally caught up with a woman in Maryland, um, but she was married at the time, and to a federal parole agent; this could be fatal depending on what kind of man he was. That's a little disturbing.

INMATE KEMPER: He ended up in prison.

PRESIDING COMMISSIONER FRITZ: Um, that … so my thing with this is, all right, well you know, you can talk to whoever you want to, but, to me a lot of your issues before this stem from having problems with relationships.

INMATE KEMPER: Yep.

PRESIDING COMMISSIONER FRITZ: I don't know if you recognize that or not.

INMATE KEMPER: I certainly do.

PRESIDING COMMISSIONER FRITZ: Um, so you're involved in these relationships now, but what have you done as far as trying how to figure out how would you deal with them in a pro-social way?

INMATE KEMPER: Pro-social way?

PRESIDING COMMISSIONER FRITZ: Well … well, uh, let me just scratch that. Let's just say "non-violent" way.

INMATE KEMPER: In a strictly social … social setting?

PRESIDING COMMISSIONER FRITZ: Any setting, sir. I mean.

INMATE KEMPER: Uh, that would have to be a, uh, non-alcoholic, non, uh, drug related relationship.

PRESIDING COMMISSIONER FRITZ: Okay, all right, thank you. Um, all right. In part of this, um, discussion with the psychologist, you went into things about when you were younger how you were a voting member of the Board of Directors, and the youngest Jaycee in America, but this was all at point where you were actually at Atascadero ...

INMATE KEMPER: Yeah.

PRESIDING COMMISSIONER FRITZ: ... so it couldn't have happened. So what was that all about?

INMATE KEMPER: It couldn't have happened?

PRESIDING COMMISSIONER FRITZ: Well it couldn't have happened during that time period that you described.

INMATE KEMPER: Why not?

PRESIDING COMMISSIONER FRITZ: Cause you were ...

INMATE KEMPER: They have a Jaycee local there.

PRESIDING COMMISSIONER FRITZ: I'm sorry?

INMATE KEMPER: We had a Jaycee local there.

PRESIDING COMMISSIONER FRITZ: Oh, okay. So that's what you're saying.

INMATE KEMPER: And I was, uh, at one point I was allowed to be an associate member, non-voting member ...

PRESIDING COMMISSIONER FRITZ: Okay.

INMATE KEMPER: ... when I first got involved with them. By a year later, I not only had a vote, I was external director.

PRESIDING COMMISSIONER FRITZ: Got it, okay. Um, so it goes into, um, the discussion, very lengthy about all of the crimes. I'm, um, a lot of it's you know, um, in quotes and things like that about what you stated recently about what happened, uh, so I'm not gonna read through it again cause we've been talking about it for a lengthy period of time. I ... I do have to say, um, I was a bit surprised at your verbiage that you use when describing the victims. Um, especially many of the female victims which I thought was very derogatory and demeaning toward women, and I just thought it was surprising that at this point in your life, in 2017, that you still would describe, um, the murders and the way things happened in such a derogatory and demeaning way towards your victims. Do you have an explanation for that?

INMATE KEMPER: From memory.

PRESIDING COMMISSIONER FRITZ: From memory?

INMATE KEMPER: Okay.

PRESIDING COMMISSIONER FRITZ: Right, I get that. But ... so everybody has a memory of what they did in the past, right?

INMATE KEMPER: Yeah.

PRESIDING COMMISSIONER FRITZ: And they may have described it at the time in a certain way, but presumably after so much therapy and things like that ...

INMATE KEMPER: I'm gonna change the value of what I thought?

PRESIDING COMMISSIONER FRITZ: Well, you're not gonna describe the victims in such a demeaning and derogatory way. You're gonna describe it ...

INMATE KEMPER: Can you make some examples?

PRESIDING COMMISSIONER FRITZ: Yeah, talking about, uh, their tits, how you wanted to fuck them, I mean, those ... those are the words that you used ...

INMATE KEMPER: Yeah.

PRESIDING COMMISSIONER FRITZ: ... today in 2017. Um, and so I find that ... I ... I just wanted an explanation for it.

INMATE KEMPER: That was being blunt.

PRESIDING COMMISSIONER FRITZ: Okay.

INMATE KEMPER: I didn't appreciate talking about it, let alone thinking along those lines.

PRESIDING COMMISSIONER FRITZ: Okay so that ...

INMATE KEMPER: But that's the terms that I had used when I was a young man.

PRESIDING COMMISSIONER FRITZ: Those are the terms you use as an older man too cause you used them this year when you were describing the crimes. That's why I was so surprised.

INMATE KEMPER: Mm-hmm.

PRESIDING COMMISSIONER FRITZ: 'Cause like I said, people that have gone through therapy and programming, and all that ... everything you have gone through this process of rehabilitation especially when they have issues with women wouldn't describe them in that way if they had gone through the process.

INMATE KEMPER: More habilitation than rehabilitation because when have I ever been normal?

PRESIDING COMMISSIONER FRITZ: Okay, um, any ... any further thought on that before I move on?

INMATE KEMPER: Uh, not really.

PRESIDING COMMISSIONER FRITZ: Okay. All right, so your PCL-R[6] score when it goes through the, um ... well wait, let me go back a little bit. The mental status examination starts on page 11, the substance abuse information is on page 12, its alcohol use disorder in sustained remission. Where you ever under the influence when you committed crimes?

INMATE KEMPER: No.

PRESIDING COMMISSIONER FRITZ: Okay. Your diagnosis is antisocial, narcissistic, and schizotypal personality disorder that's on page 13. You continue to maintain a rather, um, egocentric stance, appears focused on touting, domination, or manipulation of others. Interpersonally explosive, lacks empathy, tendency to over-personalize situations, has odd beliefs and fantasies, and on thought ... has on thoughts in speech, ongoing suspiciousness, has an appropriate affect related to content, and lacks close friends. That's page 13. Historic factors; your PCLR is above the mean of North American male inmates, but below the cutoff for psychopathic personality; that's page 16. Gives it ... gets into the clinical that's quite lengthy so I'm not gonna put it on the record, but it is in ... in the record, um, that goes through, um, 20 ... page 21. Um, and then[7] there's other risk considerations, the medical and elderly parole starts on page 22, says your 68 years old, um, talks about your advancing age and medical problems, um, it says you are ... you do appear significantly, physically restricted, but you are able to move about temporarily without a wheelchair. Um, and in some parts crimes are without the need for physical agility or prowess; there is some. Um, there ... uh, a Static-99 was administered. Um, low moderate risk range, page 23. Uh, risk for future violence in the high risk for violence. Um, the psychologist said that you have spent many years in prison, participated in therapy years ago, um, continue to discuss women rather disrespectfully and with objectification with little evidence of understanding mature relationships, your guided by rather superficial grain ... grandiose delusions of women's interest in you. Misread cues, if the cues are even there. Uh, ascribe motivations and sentiments to women beyond the information presented. Describe the crimes rather matter-of-factly with little emotion. Um, and it goes into more lengthy discussions. Um, I'm ... I'm not gonna put them all on the record, but, uh, that's, wh ... he came to the conclusions for high risk; it's Charles Taylor (phonetic). Um, there was some information about how you turned yourself in and I wanted to ask you, why did you turn yourself in?

INMATE KEMPER: To stop what I was doing.

PRESIDING COMMISSIONER FRITZ: To stop what you were doing?

INMATE KEMPER: What I had done to that point ... yeah.

PRESIDING COMMISSIONER FRITZ: Okay.

INMATE KEMPER: I've since thought better about that whole process rather than just calling Santa Cruz from long distance, and, uh, insisting that they arrest me. I could have gone to an attorney's office, and, uh, surrendered myself to him or her.

PRESIDING COMMISSIONER FRITZ: Okay.

INMATE KEMPER: And had them call the authorities. It probably would've, uh, taken the drawn guns out of the picture. It certainly would have reduced the possibility that I was gonna get blasted during the process of surrendering.

PRESIDING COMMISSIONER FRITZ: Well, let me ask you a question, uh, so it seems to me like you were killing strangers and you weren't getting caught for it.

INMATE KEMPER: Yes.

PRESIDING COMMISSIONER FRITZ: And when I look at your profile, your character traits and stuff, I have to ask you the question of whether you wanted to get caught because you wanted to be known.

INMATE KEMPER: No.

PRESIDING COMMISSIONER FRITZ: Because it seems as if there's a ... bit of a ... that there's some pleasure in telling the story about what happened. That's the impression ...

INMATE KEMPER: [There was] no communication with the authorities while I was out there at all.

PRESIDING COMMISSIONER FRITZ: Do you like that you are, um, known?

INMATE KEMPER: No.

PRESIDING COMMISSIONER FRITZ: No? You ... you've never bragged about it or ... I mean, I feel like I've read that places that you have been ... you like to brag about it and you take, uh, pleasure in being kind of known as a ...

INMATE KEMPER: No.

PRESIDING COMMISSIONER FRITZ: No?

INMATE KEMPER: No.

PRESIDING COMMISSIONER FRITZ: Okay.

INMATE KEMPER: That sounds like some of that stuff from, uh, yellow journalism that always parallels the, uh, legitimate media.

PRESIDING COMMISSIONER FRITZ: Did you read all of that stuff?

INMATE KEMPER: No.

PRESIDING COMMISSIONER FRITZ: No? Mm. All right ...

INMATE KEMPER: Some of it.

PRESIDING COMMISSIONER FRITZ: You've read some it? Yeah, okay. Any questions?

DEPUTY COMMISSIONER BLAKE: Oh, well, uh, so you're really being cooperative today, but I ... I know you mentioned to Dr. Taylor that you probably wouldn't be interested in participating in the hearing, but it ... things are going fine, so, um, what ... did you change your mind or where you feeling at the time that you were talking to Dr. Taylor that this wasn't something you wanted to participate in? Or do you remember? You said you were gonna drop your drawers or something like that.

INMATE KEMPER: Uh, years ago I had a young attorney and I explained to him my feeling about ...

PRESIDING COMMISSIONER FRITZ: Whoa ... whoa ... wait ... wait ... you see you keep getting unfocused. We're talking about the psychologist, Taylor, the recent one from 2017.

INMATE KEMPER: Yes.

PRESIDING COMMISSIONER FRITZ: Right? So let's focus on the question. We want you to answer *our* questions.

INMATE KEMPER: Yes.

PRESIDING COMMISSIONER FRITZ: I know that you are interested in saying what you want to say, but you'll have the opportunity to do that in your closing statement, so please answer our questions.

INMATE KEMPER: Mm-hmm.

PRESIDING COMMISSIONER FRITZ: And if you don't want to answer it, you don't have, but then we gotta move on, okay?

INMATE KEMPER: Yes, ma'am.

PRESIDING COMMISSIONER FRITZ: All right.

DEPUTY COMMISSIONER BLAKE: But you ... you changed your mind obviously, things were ... I mean were you seriously didn't want to participate because you're here and we're ... we're doing the hearing, so, um, is there a reason why you told Dr. Taylor that you ... that you weren't interested really in participating.

INMATE KEMPER: I didn't believe there was any realistic chance for me to get out and years ago, um, there was some indication that the Board members, the ... the media was present ...

DEPUTY COMMISSIONER BLAKE: Okay.

INMATE KEMPER: ... at the hearings, and, uh, it's as if I were a form of entertainment, and that's not air ... ever, uh, ego inductive. That's pretty much what that's related to, what I said to Dr. Taylor.

DEPUTY COMMISSIONER BLAKE: I understand.

INMATE KEMPER: And as far as ... I was talking about twirling and dropping my drawers to say basically "kiss my ass" ...

DEPUTY COMMISSIONER BLAKE: Yeah.

INMATE KEMPER: ... in front of the media. It wasn't gonna' happen, but

DEPUTY COMMISSIONER BLAKE: I know.

INMATE KEMPER: ... the Board wouldn't want it to happen either, so, when there were times that ... that, uh, they could accept or not accept my attempt at passing on a hearing ...

DEPUTY COMMISSIONER BLAKE: I see. It's true.

INMATE KEMPER: ... they tend to do encourage them. Who wants to be the first guy to drop his drawers and say, "Hey, kiss my ass!" you know?

DEPUTY COMMISSIONER BLAKE: Okay.

INMATE KEMPER: That's not a good way to get out ...

DEPUTY COMMISSIONER BLAKE: No.

INMATE KEMPER: for anybody.

DEPUTY COMMISSIONER BLAKE: Okay, well thank you.

INMATE KEMPER: But I was making an effort back then at that time, not to get out, but to impress upon the Board members that I was working as hard as I could to be who ... realistic and to be righteous about this whole thing. And suddenly I got the ... the district attorney from the county, damn near flipping the table over, he's talking such trash. They took it out of the hearing minutes. The lady taking the notes, it suddenly ... his stuff stopped appearing and my attorney was still saying, you can't talk like that, you can't say that, right? He's allowed to say that, but the ... it's to nothing, you know.

PRESIDING COMMISSIONER FRITZ: Okay but, I ... you keep bringing this up cause you brought it up here, we - - we see it, but again we're not getting focused on the questions that ...

DEPUTY COMMISSIONER BLAKE: Okay I ... I ... I asked you sort of an open-end question and I ... I think you're ... you're doing the best. I ... I think I ... I'm satisfied with the answer that you gave. And it wasn't ... I was just curious about it because, uh, I was concerned maybe when I read that that things wouldn't ... weren't go that well, but that's obviously not in the case today, so.

INMATE KEMPER: No.

DEPUTY COMMISSIONER BLAKE: Thank you.

PRESIDING COMMISSIONER FRITZ: Okay, uh, we're gonna' move on to post-conviction. Does anybody need a break or anything? Okay, all right.

DEPUTY COMMISSIONER BLAKE: So, Mr. Kemper, it's the portion of the hearing where we discuss your life in prison and it's been ... it's been a long time, it's been most of your life.

INMATE KEMPER: Yeah.

DEPUTY COMMISSIONER BLAKE: Probably about two-thirds or so, right?

INMATE KEMPER: Yes.

DEPUTY COMMISSIONER BLAKE: You've, uh, you've never been in trouble. You only got, uh, ... you've only had one 115[8] issued and that was about a year ago ...

INMATE KEMPER: Mm-hmm.

DEPUTY COMMISSIONER BLAKE: ... uh, or, uh, it was deemed, uh, fitter ... for refusal to provide a urine sample for a test.

INMATE KEMPER: Which I found out at the time is the only way they write it up.

DEPUTY COMMISSIONER BLAKE: For ... well ...

INMATE KEMPER: I didn't refuse. I was attempting at trying for three solid hours and that's all you have is three hours to do it in and all I did was fill up with water and I just couldn't do it. I couldn't pee.

DEPUTY COMMISSIONER BLAKE: Okay, do you have ...

INMATE KEMPER: In private or in public.

DEPUTY COMMISSIONER BLAKE: Do you have medical issues that would effect that?

INMATE KEMPER: A few years ago I had a operation on the central part of my, uh, anatomy down there where you have a type of hernia.

DEPUTY COMMISSIONER BLAKE: Okay.

INMATE KEMPER: Not ... not a hernia over the leg, but a hernia over the groin and it gotten really bad. It was about 20 years old and it got to the point where I was forcing myself back in ...

DEPUTY COMMISSIONER BLAKE: Right.

INMATE KEMPER: ... so I can, uh, defecate.

DEPUTY COMMISSIONER BLAKE: So, uh, let me ask you this Do you ... is common for you to have, uh, some issues urinating?

INMATE KEMPER: For a while I was urinating all over myself at the turn of a hat. I mean, I was in a diaper for a long time. Uh ...

DEPUTY COMMISSIONER BLAKE: But since the surgery ... uh, this was in ...

INMATE KEMPER: Since the surgery.

DEPUTY COMMISSIONER BLAKE: ... 2016, is it something that's happening today? Because it's ...

INMATE KEMPER: It's declining. That kind of ... that kind of problem is going away slowly. My doctor doesn't want to put me on a, uh, a bag, you know on the leg where you, uh, catheter.

DEPUTY COMMISSIONER BLAKE: Well how's your ... how's your ability to urinate on command? Is it okay or is it, uh ... does it still cause problems?

INMATE KEMPER: It still causes problems, but I haven't been asked recently.

DEPUTY COMMISSIONER BLAKE: All right. For a urine sample?

INMATE KEMPER: To do it. In fact, it's not asked, it's told. Today you're going to do that ...

DEPUTY COMMISSIONER BLAKE: Right.

INMATE KEMPER: Between this time and that time.

DEPUTY COMMISSIONER BLAKE: So do you understand the suspicion behind the failure to provide a sample?

INMATE KEMPER: Please be aware that every result of a test that I've taken has been negative ...

DEPUTY COMMISSIONER BLAKE: Right.

INMATE KEMPER: ... every time. I've asked to take blood tests, I've asked to take catheterizations; they won't do it. They just want to do it their way and that's it. You do it their way or you're beefed.

DEPUTY COMMISSIONER BLAKE: Uh, for your hearing that you had of the ... for your 115, was there any information provided by health care that would sort of help solve this problem because you were found guilty of it, and, uh ...

INMATE KEMPER: And punished.

DEPUTY COMMISSIONER BLAKE: Right, so ...

INMATE KEMPER: It was the first time in 42-43 years.

DEPUTY COMMISSIONER BLAKE: Is there any way that you get this information, um, in writing in the file because apparently, I mean, you know, they conduct them ...

INMATE KEMPER: I've asked my doctor to ... if he would do a chrono, pointing out that I have problems in this area, but he refuses to that reluctantly because the doctors don't want to get involved in that custodial part of my treatment. And ... and why he doesn't want to put something on paper? I think is more of a personal issue with him rather than, uh, all of the doctors.

DEPUTY COMMISSIONER BLAKE: How do you mean?

INMATE KEMPER: And more of a personal, uh ... he understands I have a problem ...

DEPUTY COMMISSIONER BLAKE: Uh-huh.

INMATE KEMPER: ... urinating, and my body just does it when it wants to do it and if I've sitting in a wheelchair, I do it in the wheelchair, which are not waterproof by the way. Uh ...

DEPUTY COMMISSIONER BLAKE: So I ... you ...

INMATE KEMPER: It's embarrassing. It's ...

DEPUTY COMMISSIONER BLAKE: Don't you think this is gonna happen again if you're subjected to a random urine test that, uh, ... I mean, it's gonna keep happening, and ...

INMATE KEMPER: Hopefully they'll give me a little more time to work it out rather than the ... the hard and fast three hour limit.

DEPUTY COMMISSIONER BLAKE: Well if ... if you have a legitimate, uh, medical concern regarding your ability to urinate that should be in, uh, available to the ... to custodial staff in your file. Is there anything that you can do? Uh, I mean what ... what steps should you take to make sure this doesn't happen again of you? Have you filed, uh ... uh, a health care appeal or grievance?

INMATE KEMPER: No, I haven't. I ... I didn't appeal the conviction either.

DEPUTY COMMISSIONER BLAKE: Why not?

INMATE KEMPER: Just the way I am. It's, uh, it's something that happened, and, uh, it cost me six months of visits because they would put me behind the glass for an hour at a time instead of all day visiting, contact visiting.

DEPUTY COMMISSIONER BLAKE: Right.

INMATE KEMPER: My sister was coming up to see me pretty regular, my onl ... younger sister, and all of a sudden I gotta tell her don't come up for a while because ...

DEPUTY COMMISSIONER BLAKE: So then ...

INMATE KEMPER: ... you know.

DEPUTY COMMISSIONER BLAKE: It would seem that you ... you really want this to not happen again, right? It causes problems for you and ...

INMATE KEMPER: Right.

DEPUTY COMMISSIONER BLAKE: There's no evidence that you were using ... I am not aware of any evidence that you were using ...

INMATE KEMPER: No.

DEPUTY COMMISSIONER BLAKE: ... drugs or alcohol. Um, the question is ...

INMATE KEMPER: I have up Pruno[9] many years ago, over 30 years ago.

DEPUTY COMMISSIONER BLAKE: I know you were drinking heavily when you were ... prior to prison, right? I mean ...

INMATE KEMPER: And ironically, my lawyer at the trial said, were you intoxicated when you committed any of these crimes? And I thought about it and thought about it and I said, no I was sober every time. And he just looked at me like he could not believe it. He said, do you realize, he said you must be a pathological truth teller. He says, you ... you got a case where the DA has to show you weren't drunk, you know, when you did it. You just saw you were drunk and that's it, that's a fact.

DEPUTY COMMISSIONER BLAKE: Okay. I ... you know what, I have no reason to doubt that.

INMATE KEMPER: But I never was.

DEPUTY COMMISSIONER BLAKE: Okay, and I ... I ... what I'm trying to say here, Mr. Kemper, is that I don't ... I'm not aware of you, um, there's no evidence that you would be avoiding, uh, detection of drugs or alcohol other than the fact that you ... according to the 115 you refused to provide a sample. My question that is, you know, if it's causing a problem for you why ... why don't you just proceed to ...

INMATE KEMPER: You didn't say all through the write up. If you looked at the actual write up, I said all through that thing and they wrote it down that way.

DEPUTY COMMISSIONER BLAKE: I ... I know, you denied your ... that ...

INMATE KEMPER: I ... I say hey I'm trying, I'm trying, I just can't pee. And for that whole three hour period, I didn't.

DEPUTY COMMISSIONER BLAKE: All right. I ... I will admit ...

INMATE KEMPER: I was bloated and I was going for two hours after that, but by then I was already written up.

DEPUTY COMMISSIONER BLAKE: Okay, it was over a year ago, um ...

INMATE KEMPER: And it was a young cop just starting out and, uh, the cop ... the other cops on the wing have told me that's a fresh cop that did that ... wrote you up. The rest of us know you better ...

DEPUTY COMMISSIONER BLAKE: Okay.

INMATE KEMPER: ... we're gonna give you more time. If we have to give you until the next day, we're gonna do that because your ... your gonna come up with a sample ...

DEPUTY COMMISSIONER BLAKE: Okay.

INMATE KEMPER: ... eventually.

DEPUTY COMMISSIONER BLAKE: So it sounds like maybe you're not too worried about this situation occurring again. It's probably gonna be okay?

INMATE KEMPER: Well now that it's back to random instead of mandatory ...

DEPUTY COMMISSIONER BLAKE: Uh-huh.

INMATE KEMPER: ... for a year it was mandatory so I had to do mandatory and random at the same time, and they got frequent, but it ... it's such a nightmare when that happens.

DEPUTY COMMISSIONER BLAKE: Right.

INMATE KEMPER: Because for me it's ... it's, uh - - it's a nightmare, it just I ... I couldn't perform. I start drinking coffee which encourages urination.

DEPUTY COMMISSIONER BLAKE: Okay.

INMATE KEMPER: I drank water. Anything I could think of.

DEPUTY COMMISSIONER BLAKE: Here's the thing. I just ... it'd be helpful for the, um, for you to not get anymore of these 115s. Obviously we ... we spent some time talking about this, so, um, try to do what you can to not get written up for this again. And when I say that, I mean, if ... if you're gonna lose, uh, you know, things that are important to you like visitation time, then there are procedures that you can follow, and I ... I just want to make sure that there's no ... there isn't a reason why ... there's no reason why you haven't pursued that.

INMATE KEMPER: I was told that I couldn't do a catheterization, right, cause that's too complicated. But one time during this year period that I was penalized. I had to take a mandatory test while I was in the hospital, I'm physically in the hospital. Then it's no problem doing a urination and when the guy ... when the, uh, MTA ... the nurse ... the nurse couldn't get a sample for me, he broke out, uh, a catheterization kit and catheterized me.

PRESIDING COMMISSIONER FRITZ: I think we've heard enough.

DEPUTY COMMISSIONER BLAKE: Yeah, all right. Let ... that's fine. I just want to ... just make sure that you ... if there's ... if there's paperwork that you can do or ... or procedures you can follow so we don't have to go ... have this discussion again because obviously you don't want to be ... you don't want to be catheterized just for a urine sample.

INMATE KEMPER: It's painful.

DEPUTY COMMISSIONER BLAKE: Yeah. Okay. Uh,

INMATE KEMPER: It's the only time I was catheterized my whole life.

DEPUTY COMMISSIONER BLAKE: Yeah, it's ... I imagine it's ... it's not pleasant. Um, so what ... what else have you done here? You ... you stayed out of trouble, uh, and you've ... you've worked but it's a while, right? You used to be ... you've had ... held jobs as clerks, you've had clerk positions?

INMATE KEMPER: Forty-two years.

DEPUTY COMMISSIONER BLAKE: Okay, so generally you did, uh ...

INMATE KEMPER: I got retired.

DEPUTY COMMISSIONER BLAKE: Yeah, okay.

INMATE KEMPER: Isn't that something? I had a special committee, right? They usually brought me to a special time instead of annually and I said, why am I here, and they said thank you for your 42 or 40 years of clerking. And I said, where ... where's that going? And they said, well we're retiring you.

DEPUTY COMMISSIONER BLAKE: Well you ...

INMATE KEMPER: They made totally medically disabled.

DEPUTY COMMISSIONER BLAKE: Okay.

INMATE KEMPER: Because of my stroke.

DEPUTY COMMISSIONER BLAKE: Right, okay.

INMATE KEMPER: And I was working with computers and that scared them into thinking, you know, he's gonna force something to happen because he's ...

DEPUTY COMMISSIONER BLAKE: You did ... you were - - you generally were, um ... did a good job in your positions.

INMATE KEMPER: Yeah.

DEPUTY COMMISSIONER BLAKE: Supervisors were okay with your performance, right?

INMATE KEMPER: Absolutely.

DEPUTY COMMISSIONER BLAKE: Okay. When was the last time you, uh, actually had a clerk job?

INMATE KEMPER: Uh, the one I just talked about being retired.

DEPUTY COMMISSIONER BLAKE: Yeah.

INMATE KEMPER: It was probably ...

DEPUTY COMMISSIONER BLAKE: A while ago.

INMATE KEMPER: Late last year.

DEPUTY COMMISSIONER BLAKE: All right. So, um,

all right, 42 years. Did you learn any job skills, uh, that would be useful to you, um, if you were, uh, living outside of prison? Cause you worked in gas stations a couple times, and I mean you worked for Caltrans for the Department of Transportation, uh, any way that you can support yourself if that ... that were the case? I mean ...

INMATE KEMPER: At 68 years old ...

DEPUTY COMMISSIONER BLAKE: Right.

INMATE KEMPER: ... and probably going on 69 and 70, I don't think I'd have to.

DEPUTY COMMISSIONER BLAKE: okay.

INMATE KEMPER: I'd be stuck in a retirement home somewhere.

DEPUTY COMMISSIONER BLAKE: Okay.

INMATE KEMPER: But not because of my, uh ... what do you call it, um ... uh ... uh, can't even ... well that's one of my problems now with that stroke it scatters my thoughts around ...

DEPUTY COMMISSIONER BLAKE: Okay.

INMATE KEMPER: ... and it's hard to think of specific issues.

DEPUTY COMMISSIONER BLAKE: I was just ... I was just thinking of if you ... if you ... if you ...

INMATE KEMPER: Medicaid, Medicare, that kind of stuff.

DEPUTY COMMISSIONER BLAKE: All right.

INMATE KEMPER: What ... it doesn't even exist for me. I haven't had ... I haven't been employed long enough ...

DEPUTY COMMISSIONER BLAKE: I see.

INMATE KEMPER: ... to qualify ...

DEPUTY COMMISSIONER BLAKE: Okay.

INMATE KEMPER: ... for those things.

DEPUTY COMMISSIONER BLAKE: Um, so you ... you ... we can talk about parole plans later. I was just talking about things that you ... the kind of work you did here in prison. It sounds like you were a clerk which involves providing, uh, assistance to the staff when they run their programs, right?

INMATE KEMPER: Yeah, I was the, uh ... the clerk in therapy ...

DEPUTY COMMISSIONER BLAKE: Okay.

INMATE KEMPER: ... for seven years and I was a clerk in the library in, uh, reference area.

DEPUTY COMMISSIONER BLAKE: Okay.

INMATE KEMPER: And those guys were wishing to get me back when I got busted out of there cause I'd been there so long ...

DEPUTY COMMISSIONER BLAKE: Mm-hmm.

INMATE KEMPER: ... and they ... they made me swap out with another guy who was a captain's clerk in central services.

DEPUTY COMMISSIONER BLAKE: okay.

INMATE KEMPER: And, uh, they were wishing I can come back. They were putting up a petition. I'm serious.

DEPUTY COMMISSIONER BLAKE: Did you ... did you have other jobs? You got some hospice care training, right?

INMATE KEMPER: Yes.

DEPUTY COMMISSIONER BLAKE: Did you ever, uh ... um, have ...

INMATE KEMPER: That was voluntary.

DEPUTY COMMISSIONER BLAKE: Okay.

INMATE KEMPER: But I did that for 10 years.

DEPUTY COMMISSIONER BLAKE: You worked, uh ... was that here at CMF[10]?

INMATE KEMPER: Yeah.

DEPUTY COMMISSIONER BLAKE: And you ... you provide ... helped provide hospice care to the ... some of the dying inmates?

INMATE KEMPER: And unfortunately, uh, I was exposed to every kind of cancer you can get ...

DEPUTY COMMISSIONER BLAKE: Uh-huh.

INMATE KEMPER: ... and it was becoming a real nightmare to me.

DEPUTY COMMISSIONER BLAKE: Why?

INMATE KEMPER: I was dreaming about it. I mean I ... I could, uh, sit there and eat my dinner, a hot dinner in front of a guy ... a dying patient [in a] hospice with cancer.

DEPUTY COMMISSIONER BLAKE: Mm-hmm.

INMATE KEMPER: He appreciated the fact that I'd stay in the room and visit with him while I was eating. Other guys would throw up instead; they couldn't deal with it. It was horrible. You know ... do you know the smell of cancer?

DEPUTY COMMISSIONER BLAKE: I'm ... I'm not with the smell of cancer.

INMATE KEMPER: It ... it has a very diff ... a very definite odor, different kinds of cancer, very definite odor, and it's not pleasant.

DEPUTY COMMISSIONER BLAKE: Okay.

INMATE KEMPER: And the worse you are with it when you, you know getting terminal, uh, it's just a really eva, uh ...

DEPUTY COMMISSIONER BLAKE: Did you, uh, pick up some health care skills and medical skills while you were working in hospice? What kinds of things did you do?

INMATE KEMPER: Mostly weightlifting. Uh, I was, you know, I'd go to G1 hospital ...

DEPUTY COMMISSIONER BLAKE: Right.

INMATE KEMPER: ... and they'd say they need you down in hospice. I thought that's odd; [that they'd] talk to a volunteer that way so I turned right around and go down to hospice and it turns out there's, uh … a dope addict that was dying in bed literally tied down and he kept turning off his oxygen mask, and they couldn't deal with that [and] so they needed me.

DEPUTY COMMISSIONER BLAKE: Okay. Did you provide … did you do …

INMATE KEMPER: I held it an inch away from his face for four or five minutes and he totally relaxed. He's getting the oxygen finally and instead of thinking it's a poison, uh … uh, a poison thing, uh, he's getting oxygen and, uh, that's when he passed.

DEPUTY COMMISSIONER BLAKE: I see.

INMATE KEMPER: He totally relaxed and he just, shu, he went out. But things like that, I get called in, uh, to help others. A guy 400 and some pounds needs a bath but he can't take a regular shower so he has to get in a bed bath.

DEPUTY COMMISSIONER BLAKE: All right, would you help with that type of work?

INMATE KEMPER: I had to lift him into it, yeah, because I was big and strong, and, uh-huh …

DEPUTY COMMISSIONER BLAKE: Do you think you'd be able to continue with that type of, uh, work?

INMATE KEMPER: In a … on a … on a limited basis, yeah.

DEPUTY COMMISSIONER BLAKE: So, uh, I … I know you're kind of a heavy drinker, um, before you came to prison, um, I don't really see any issues with it while you're here, but I really don't see much evidence that you've … can you hear okay? We've got the machinery working down … outside.

INMATE KEMPER: Yeah, the backup … the backup horn.

DEPUTY COMMISSIONER BLAKE: Um, but I don't ... I don't see, uh, any evidence that you've, um, engaged in what we call self-help or rehabilitative programs, and ...

INMATE KEMPER: You don't see AA in there? That's the first thing I did when I got out of the hole is join AA.

DEPUTY COMMISSIONER BLAKE: No, okay, you ...

INMATE KEMPER: I got the oldest AA card back when it was Fred C. Marsh, uh, Memorial. They don't even call it that anymore.

DEPUTY COMMISSIONER BLAKE: Honestly, some of the things from the ... the 70s are little harder to find.

INMATE KEMPER: Mm-hmm.

DEPUTY COMMISSIONER BLAKE: The files that I have. But why don't you tell us about AA[11]? How did ... how did you ... what did you get out of it?

INMATE KEMPER: They got so tired of hearing me up there at that podium sharing my problems in the past. I think I drove some of those people back into drinking. Not to be too humorous about, but I'd finally just gave up on it because, uh, I think I had a six month pin and was working on three-quarters of the year.

DEPUTY COMMISSIONER BLAKE: Okay.

INMATE KEMPER: And, uh, I just said, I mean I was there about five years, and it just got really old to me so I ... I never did join NA[12] ...

DEPUTY COMMISSIONER BLAKE: Right.

INMATE KEMPER: ... 'cause I never was a narcotics abuser on the streets. But ...

DEPUTY COMMISSIONER BLAKE: Did you ...

INMATE KEMPER: ... I've known people in both groups, AA and NA.

DEPUTY COMMISSIONER BLAKE: So you did it for awhile. You did ... you attended AA for a while ...

INMATE KEMPER: Yes.

DEPUTY COMMISSIONER BLAKE: ... and it sounds as though you, uh, you freely participated ...

INMATE KEMPER: Mm-hmm.

DEPUTY COMMISSIONER BLAKE: ... and you weren't just sitting there. Um ... uh, do you think that it ... it helped you in any way? Did you get any ... learn anything about yourself or get any insight into anything about yourself?

INMATE KEMPER: Yeah.

DEPUTY COMMISSIONER BLAKE: Do you recall, um, what ... what do you recall from those days? What kind of insight do you think you gained? I mean I know it focuses on alcohol abuse and dependence, but I know there's more to it.

INMATE KEMPER: Why was I an alcohol abuser on the street?

DEPUTY COMMISSIONER BLAKE: Okay.

INMATE KEMPER: Everybody in the family was. Seriously. I mean my mom was, my dad was, and then he started cutting back on it. In fact, I told her later that, uh, he only drank not even socially. He had a bottle of brandy that was three-quarters full and a bottle of port wine that was untapped.

DEPUTY COMMISSIONER BLAKE: Right. Never went ...

INMATE KEMPER: And it sat in there the whole time I was there visiting ... or living with him.

DEPUTY COMMISSIONER BLAKE: Well then so you think you got a handle on your drinking now? I mean when was the last ... you said you had some Pruno many years ago?

INMATE KEMPER: Many years ago, yeah.

DEPUTY COMMISSIONER BLAKE: Okay.

INMATE KEMPER: I threw up just drinking it.

DEPUTY COMMISSIONER BLAKE: Okay.

INMATE KEMPER: It ... it ... I can't keep it down. It's un ... it's what do you call it, un ... "unfinished alcohol," uh, it's still cooking and it would cook inside of me ...

DEPUTY COMMISSIONER BLAKE: Right, it's ...

INMATE KEMPER: ... to the point where I'd throw up.

DEPUTY COMMISSIONER BLAKE: After all this time——and I know you haven't been drinking lately or there's no evidence that you have——you attended AA, uh, many years ago and then you ... you said you just ...

INMATE KEMPER: When I was a young man ...

DEPUTY COMMISSIONER BLAKE: ... in some way got tired of it. Um, what do you ... what connection can you make between your alcohol abuse and ... and all these crimes that you committed if you would ... if you hadn't been ...

INMATE KEMPER: I never hurt anybody when I had alcohol in me. That's one thing I did notice. So I started drinking more and more cause I didn't want to do it. I really didn't want him killing people so I drank like a fish.

DEPUTY COMMISSIONER BLAKE: So you're a ...

INMATE KEMPER: The cops even knew I was a heavy alcohol drinker. They were aware of that when I was going to trial. Almost all of the cops knew that I was a heavy drinker. Not just 'cause I drank at their bar, I was ... I got stopped two or three times. I never got busted ...

DEPUTY COMMISSIONER BLAKE: Mm-hmm.

INMATE KEMPER: ... but I got stopped two or three times and I was lit up.

DEPUTY COMMISSIONER BLAKE: Do you ever see, uh, I mean, you know, if you were to be released from prison, all ... you know, it's available everywhere. I mean, when you went to prison, I think there was some laws about being able to purchase alcohol near a campus or something like that. I mean you can buy alcohol ... alcohol is available every ... everywhere and there's a big, you know, a booming beer industry again in California and other places, so ...

INMATE KEMPER: Brew is something I love.

DEPUTY COMMISSIONER BLAKE: Okay well what do you ... do you think you might be ... have an issue would be ...

INMATE KEMPER: I think I would be tempted to drink near beer or something to that effect.

DEPUTY COMMISSIONER BLAKE: Why ... why do you say that?

INMATE KEMPER: It doesn't effect as much ...

DEPUTY COMMISSIONER BLAKE: Okay

INMATE KEMPER: ... as the hard stuff.

DEPUTY COMMISSIONER BLAKE: Okay. Do you ... you think, um, it would be a problem if you were to have alcohol?

INMATE KEMPER: I don't think so, but anything's possible.

DEPUTY COMMISSIONER BLAKE: Is there a reason why you haven't ...

INMATE KEMPER: That would tempt ... that would tempt me to go back to AA.

DEPUTY COMMISSIONER BLAKE: It would, okay. Well, we'll talk a little more too, um, we're getting more into parole plans now, but I'm trying to cover whatever rehabilitative programming you might have been engaged in here. And I know, you finished ... you finished high school or your GED when you were in Atascadero, right? Did you ever ...

INMATE KEMPER: I finished ... I took a GED ...

DEPUTY COMMISSIONER BLAKE: Okay.

INMATE KEMPER: ... when I jus ... just was able to when I just turned 18 ...

DEPUTY COMMISSIONER BLAKE: Right.

INMATE KEMPER: ... at Atascadero and passed it. And I got the second highest score of anybody that took it that week.

DEPUTY COMMISSIONER BLAKE: And I know you were taking college classes too back then. Have you ... have you taken them ...

INMATE KEMPER: Straight A's.

DEPUTY COMMISSIONER BLAKE: Pardon me, sir?

INMATE KEMPER: Straight A's.

DEPUTY COMMISSIONER BLAKE: What about, uh, your time in state prison as an adult, um, after 1973. Have you ...

INMATE KEMPER: I did go to ... to, uh, night school to college where they'd have professors come in from, um ... um, Solano

Community College.

DEPUTY COMMISSIONER BLAKE: Okay, that's here at CMF?

INMATE KEMPER: Yeah and they'd hold courses one semester at a time, and I wish I'd gone to more of those and gotten, uh, my certificate.

DEPUTY COMMISSIONER BLAKE: Uh ... uh, like an Associates Degree?

INMATE KEMPER: Yeah.

DEPUTY COMMISSIONER BLAKE: Why do you suppose you didn't do that? You had a lot of time to do that.

INMATE KEMPER: I figured it'd be ... it would there for longer than it was.

DEPUTY COMMISSIONER BLAKE: Okay. Are there other opportunities for, uh, someone in your situation to pursue education? Are you interested in doing them, I mean ...

INMATE KEMPER: At one point, um, I was interested enough. I don't know if you've heard of Leonard Wolf. He was a professor at San Francisco State.

DEPUTY COMMISSIONER BLAKE: All right, okay.

INMATE KEMPER: Full professor, and, uh, almost professor emeritus, and, uh, he was a visitor of mine back then. And at one point, I was gonna pursue education through San Francisco State with his backing - - his help in efforts of getting a PhD because I believed I could do and he did, too.

DEPUTY COMMISSIONER BLAKE: So, um, I ... when I'm asking about education and ... and upgrading your education ... that's how they call it here. We call it upgrading, um, you had some desire to further your education; doesn't seem like there's been a lot of followthrough, but am I missing something? Its ... it sounds like you had ... you got close in some instances, um, maybe getting a PhD would be, uh, more difficult now, but ...

INMATE KEMPER: Yeah, it would.

DEPUTY COMMISSIONER BLAKE: ... an AA, what about an Associates Degree? Have you ... a lot of inmates ...

INMATE KEMPER: If I get one more unit, I'd be a sophomore.

DEPUTY COMMISSIONER BLAKE: Okay, great.

INMATE KEMPER: So I'm the world's oldest freshman.

DEPUTY COMMISSIONER BLAKE: I see.

INMATE KEMPER: Now of course that's not true, but ...

DEPUTY COMMISSIONER BLAKE: Probably not.

INMATE KEMPER: ... um, I'm sure there's older people that me that are actually pursuing an education could make that claim, but if I got one more unit, I'd have half my credits necessary to get an AA.

DEPUTY COMMISSIONER BLAKE: Okay, have you, um, are you gonna' do that?

INMATE KEMPER: I could do that.

DEPUTY COMMISSIONER BLAKE: Okay.

INMATE KEMPER: 'Cause now they have, uh, courses here, but it's a different way than they did back then. Back then it was night school, uh, it was actual professors coming and teaching, and brining books in with them.

DEPUTY COMMISSIONER BLAKE: Okay.

INMATE KEMPER: Uh, now it's an ongoing regular course thing through education and I used to work in education as a clerk, too.

DEPUTY COMMISSIONER BLAKE: Okay.

INMATE KEMPER: And, uh ...

DEPUTY COMMISSIONER BLAKE: Are you gonna' do that then?

INMATE KEMPER: Huh?

DEPUTY COMMISSIONER BLAKE: Are you gonna' do that? Is that what your ... I know it ... more a correspondent ... it's a correspondence course.

INMATE KEMPER: No its, uh - it's, uh, actual course work.

DEPUTY COMMISSIONER BLAKE: Okay.

INMATE KEMPER: But ...

DEPUTY COMMISSIONER BLAKE: It's all right. That's fine.

INMATE KEMPER: It damaged my standing with my peer group a bit. I was a bit of a smart ass.

DEPUTY COMMISSIONER BLAKE: Okay.

INMATE KEMPER: I'm the guy that can ask question after question after question, and the teacher would really get involved in answering it because it was a sensible question and he had never had that one before. Another guy would do it just because I was doing it and then the teacher would shut him off.

DEPUTY COMMISSIONER BLAKE: Yeah.

INMATE KEMPER: 'Cause that's all it was, was wasting his time.

DEPUTY COMMISSIONER BLAKE: It gets annoying for the other people in the class probably at times. Um, but I ... okay, well it sounds like you have some interest in, uh, continuing with your education, and, um, obviously, uh, you ... you probably do some reading here, but, um, how would say you spend most of your time in prison? What do you ... what do you?

INMATE KEMPER: Watching television.

DEPUTY COMMISSIONER BLAKE: In your cell.

INMATE KEMPER: Catching up ... catching up on all the stuff I've missed out on for years and years.

DEPUTY COMMISSIONER BLAKE: Catching up on? What ... what do you ... what do you mean "you missed out"?

INMATE KEMPER: The TV shows, the movies.

DEPUTY COMMISSIONER BLAKE: How do you ... how do you catch up on ... did you ... did you ...

INMATE KEMPER: Well they're re-runs.

DEPUTY COMMISSIONER BLAKE: Oh, okay.

INMATE KEMPER: Shows and movies are re-runs, but they're ... I really enjoy them.

DEPUTY COMMISSIONER BLAKE: So you didn't watch TV for a while. You were ...

INMATE KEMPER: I was working and pulling in, uh ... uh, a good size pay number for a lot of years, and now I don't have any pay number. If I'm gonna get money some ... people have to send it in to me from the streets.

DEPUTY COMMISSIONER BLAKE: Okay. You ... you've also taken Anger Management. I think that was, uh ... uh, several years ago.

INMATE KEMPER: Yeah.

DEPUTY COMMISSIONER BLAKE: There's other programs available. You know, there's, uh, Lifer Programs, there's, uh, programs available for sort of victim awareness, things like that. And I know you've been engaged in therapy, right, so, uh, that's ... that's something that sounds like it's been helpful for you, but is there a reason why you haven't engaged in, you know, some of the ... the groups that are available to you or other ... other programs.

INMATE KEMPER: At one point, I wanted to be involved in the, uh, the victim's awareness, uh, aspect of it.

DEPUTY COMMISSIONER BLAKE: Okay.

INMATE KEMPER: But, a couple of the guys cautioned me against that because currently, and I don't even know if that's still valid, but, uh, currently they were, um, the ... the, uh, victims groups that were doing that stuff were doing it more for ammo to keep us in, arguing, you know, arguable stuff.

DEPUTY COMMISSIONER BLAKE: Yeah, I ... I ...

INMATE KEMPER: Reasons why they'd dislike us and reasons why they don't want us getting out.

DEPUTY COMMISSIONER BLAKE: I can tell you that anything like that probably ... I ... would not come out. That ... I mean it's ... I ... I ... yeah, I think you got some bad advice there. You got some bad advice.

INMATE KEMPER: Could be.

DEPUTY COMMISSIONER BLAKE: Um, did you ever talk to a counselor about signing up for any of these programs.

INMATE KEMPER: It's hard to see a counselor anymore

DEPUTY COMMISSIONER BLAKE: Um ...

INMATE KEMPER: I've had a number of counselors pass by. You know, had them for a period of time and then lost them, and ... and got somebody else without ever having asked them anything.

DEPUTY COMMISSIONER BLAKE: Have you ever, um, tried to write anything down. I mean, I ... you know, whether you wanted to write a ... uh, a remorse letter or not. It's ... it's kind of up to you, and I know your victim's dead, but have you ever thought about ...

INMATE KEMPER: Families ... families of the victims.

DEPUTY COMMISSIONER BLAKE: Yeah, have you thought about something like that.

INMATE KEMPER: Do you know that I was personally involved in locating my victim's remains?

DEPUTY COMMISSIONER BLAKE: I ... I know ... INMATE KEMPER: To ... to work on that.

DEPUTY COMMISSIONER BLAKE: Excuse me, sir. I

think we're gonna take a break and we can come back to this topic. So we're just gonna ... we're just gonna' take a five minute break.

PRESIDING COMMISSIONER FRITZ: There's some people that need, a ... a five minutes recess, so.

DEPUTY COMMISSIONER BLAKE: It's 11:00 o'clock.

PRESIDING COMMISSIONER FRITZ: We'll go off the record. It's 11:05 and we'll ... we'll get back to this topic.

DEPUTY COMMISSIONER BLAKE: Okay, all right.

RECESS

DEPUTY COMMISSIONER BLAKE: Okay, we're back on the record.

PRESIDING COMMISSIONER FRITZ: Okay, time's

11:18.

DEPUTY COMMISSIONER BLAKE: Mr. Kemper, we were,

uh, before we took a break we were discussing, um, your rehabilitative efforts, um, I ... I don't see that you've, uh ... we discussed victim impact I think as I said, I ...I think maybe you took, um, some bad advice from ... from some inmates regarding the purpose of that. Um, have you thought about printing down on paper, uh, putting your thoughts on paper regarding how you feel, uh, about what you've done, anything that you might want to say to the ... to the victims even though they're not around any longer or their ... their loved ones. Have you ... have you put anything on paper that, um, would be available to the ... to the Panel?

INMATE KEMPER: I'm concerned that, uh, the news media who still hasn't gotten their satisfaction from me, uh, as far as the whole story, the inside story, and, uh, they ... they still hound me for stuff like that. Or book writes, not necessarily news media, but book writers and people who do movies.

DEPUTY COMMISSIONER BLAKE: And would be, um, I know, you don't want to be the focus of that kind of spotlight, I ... I know, but you know the fact is that you ... you know, you were sentenced to life in prison, so what's ... why is that such a big ... I mean it seems like being in prison would be bad enough, but if people are writing about you, why is that an issue cause they're going to anyway? So wouldn't you want to have your ... your thoughts out there? And it might not even make it into the hands of media anyway, probably not.

INMATE KEMPER: There's a good possibility that my hand ... my writings would land in the hands of an editor ...

DEPUTY COMMISSIONER BLAKE: Okay.

INMATE KEMPER: ... and he'd edit out things he decided weren't interesting or not pertinent, and, uh, focus on different things that ... than I would.

DEPUTY COMMISSIONER BLAKE: I see.

INMATE KEMPER: Um, I've had a lot of decades to wish that I could do things differently with my own family. Uh, rather than, uh, so much a stranger because a stranger is ... feels attacked, they feel you know vi - - totally violated and out of, you know out of nowhere this stuff comes and they ... they just don't want to hear what the perpetrator has to say. Certainly not how sorry he is. But I did show, I demonstrated how sorry I was when as soon as I gave up the first thing I did was I told on the phone ... I told Santa Cruz contact Berkeley and let them know that Aiko Koo is not a runaway like they were posing, that's she's a victim. And ... and first thing I did, was after I got back in Santa Cruz and ... and Berkeley was to try and, uh, locate the remains as much as I could. I mean, I took them back to exact spots. But a lot of times, uh, animal activity undid, uh, the efforts I made later.

DEPUTY COMMISSIONER BLAKE: If you were to be found suitable for parole and you were released from prison ...

INMATE KEMPER: God, that sounds good.

DEPUTY COMMISSIONER BLAKE: It does?

INMATE KEMPER: Yeah, I mean it's so unlikely to even hear it cause you ...

DEPUTY COMMISSIONER BLAKE: Sounds good?

INMATE KEMPER: ... you guys didn't even want to say things like that decades ago because it might happen.

DEPUTY COMMISSIONER BLAKE: Well I'm not asking you now because, um ... um, the question is what would you do?

INMATE KEMPER: What would I do? What would I be telling people in the hallway? Hide. Head for the hills.

DEPUTY COMMISSIONER BLAKE: Why, what do you mean?

INMATE KEMPER: God, the media would hound me. They'd camp on my doorstep.

DEPUTY COMMISSIONER BLAKE: What would you do? I don't ... that's ... not what would the media do ...

INMATE KEMPER: Yeah.

DEPUTY COMMISSIONER BLAKE: ... but what ... but what are your parole plans and I'm sure you talked about this with your ... with the ... the clinician and Dr. Taylor, and probably with your lawyer. And I mean, this is one of the questions we ask so what ... what are your plans? Have you had ... put any thought into that?

INMATE KEMPER: I would try to be a tax payer instead of a tax burden ...

DEPUTY COMMISSIONER BLAKE: How would you do that?

INMATE KEMPER: ... for the first time in 40 years.

DEPUTY COMMISSIONER BLAKE: Okay. How ... how would you do that?

INMATE KEMPER: Work in any way I could.

DEPUTY COMMISSIONER BLAKE: Okay.

INMATE KEMPER: If it was selling papers by hand I'd be doing it. Nothings too good for me.

DEPUTY COMMISSIONER BLAKE: Do you have anything specific in mind that ... where you might work or what you might do?

INMATE KEMPER: Work at a gas station, but I understand that more ... most often those are self-serve now.

DEPUTY COMMISSIONER BLAKE: Okay, I mean realistically, Mr. Kemper, do you think that you'd be working? I mean, based on, you know, your health issues and ... and also your notoriety. I mean, I suppose it's possible, but I ... I ... what the question is, does the inmate, has the inmate developed realistic parole plans, and you know, I ... have you ... sounds like you're willing to work, but have you developed any plans whether ... you know, whether you're found suitable or not have you gone down that road at all?

INMATE KEMPER: Actually that's a form of torment ... self-imposed torment ...

DEPUTY COMMISSIONER BLAKE: I see.

INMATE KEMPER: ... if I toy with that too much because there hasn't been a real, uh ... uh, a realistic possibility for as long as I've been down.

DEPUTY COMMISSIONER BLAKE: Okay. But now you'd ... you'd like to be ...

INMATE KEMPER: I would love to be.

DEPUTY COMMISSIONER BLAKE: Well what ... what would you do? Where would you live? Who would you associate with?

INMATE KEMPER: I don't know if you believe it or not, but I've been invited to live in the house I lived in on the street in Aptos; 609-A Ord Street by a ... a group of youngsters; young men, uh, they're in their 30's ... 20's and 30's that, uh, have offered me an opportunity to live in that same address.

DEPUTY COMMISSIONER BLAKE: That's ... that's strange, isn't it?

INMATE KEMPER: Part of what I dreamt about last night. It's ... it's a bit scary, too. Uh, talk about bringing memories back.

DEPUTY COMMISSIONER BLAKE: Uh-huh.

INMATE KEMPER: And if you are at all a ... a believer in a ... in a the spiritual world ... the spiritual realm, I had a dream at Atascadero, and it was a … a focus. I was focusing on absolutely nothing. Everything went away, no sounds. And so I wasn't asleep, but I had a dream, a vision that I was at the neighbors property of my grandparents looking down on that house cause it was low … at a lower altitude than, uh, the neighbors were. Bill Bleyer and his wife used to live up there. When I got out on parole, I went back there, and it … and, uh, the Bleyer's 60-foot, uh, trailer was gone. It was on a cement base with the electric and everything and it was gone permanently. And I stood on that spot where I had been in that … in that, uh, vision. I was looking down on the old Kemper residence …

DEPUTY COMMISSIONER BLAKE: What, uh … what, um …

INMATE KEMPER: … and they had disconnected the bedroom that I had, had.

DEPUTY COMMISSIONER BLAKE: I see.

INMATE KEMPER: It was a breezeway bedroom. You know, they had 2x4's up and … and plastic, and … and sheeting and stuff covering the walls.

DEPUTY COMMISSIONER BLAKE Okay, I understand that, what does this have to do with, um, your possible parole plans, or standing at the house?

INMATE KEMPER: Wow. Uh …

DEPUTY COMMISSIONER BLAKE: I know that sounds like it was a very vivid memory for you, but, uh, okay, have you … have you considered transitional housing?

INMATE KEMPER: Yes.

DEPUTY COMMISSIONER BLAKE: Okay what do you think about that? Have you contacted anybody or?

INMATE KEMPER: I couldn't realistically, I mean at the present time.

DEPUTY COMMISSIONER BLAKE: Okay.

INMATE KEMPER: I have no status to do that, but, uh, I ... I have no address ... I guess I could find out some addresses.

DEPUTY COMMISSIONER BLAKE: Yeah ... yeah. You have ... have you talked to people about it about transitional housing, counselors or other needs, things like that?

INMATE KEMPER: I had done ... that's a painful memory. I did that the first time down.

DEPUTY COMMISSIONER BLAKE: Okay.

INMATE KEMPER: I tried doing that and you know what they told me? Do you want your parole or not? You know parole to your mother's house and that's it or you got no parole. I should have passed.

DEPUTY COMMISSIONER BLAKE: Yeah, well, uh, I would recommend that, you know ...

INMATE KEMPER: I didn't think we could have it that bad, her and I.

DEPUTY COMMISSIONER BLAKE: So, uh, coming up 'til now to present time, it's important for inmates to develop realistic parole plans, uh, means of support, um, and, uh, things like that. It sounds like you haven't had an opportunity to do that or you haven't followed through, but, um, what about people? What would you ...

INMATE KEMPER: Mm.

DEPUTY COMMISSIONER BLAKE: ... uh, would you ... are you interested in pursuing relationships with people? I know you mentioned the ... this person in France and another that was in Australia, but what about, um, relationships?

INMATE KEMPER: They'd take me in a minute.

DEPUTY COMMISSIONER BLAKE: Excuse me?

INMATE KEMPER: They'd take me in a minute, but I don't think Australia would be welcoming.

DEPUTY COMMISSIONER BLAKE: I ... I not asking you to live there, I mean, do you see yourself having relationships with people if you were to be living outside of prison?

INMATE KEMPER: Absolutely.

DEPUTY COMMISSIONER BLAKE: Okay, what ... which people? I mean, what ... what do you mean, neighbors or?

INMATE KEMPER: An expanded version of what I got now, uh, as far as, uh, penmanship friends.

DEPUTY COMMISSIONER BLAKE: Okay.

INMATE KEMPER: Um, answer more letters than I do. Part of the reason I stopped doing that was the lady in Maryland that was mentioned earlier. She came out here for a whole week visiting me every day for a solid week ...

DEPUTY COMMISSIONER BLAKE: Mm-hmm.

INMATE KEMPER: ... trying to convince me that I was the one ... I mean I should marry her.

DEPUTY COMMISSIONER BLAKE: Do you think that you would have relationships with women if you were released from prison, like have a romantic relationship? Is that something that's entered your mind?

INMATE KEMPER: That's a possibility, but I have to be careful with that because my feelings tend to run pretty loose. I don't just, you know, keep a real tight grip on, uh, letters. I follow the flow of, uh, emotions.

DEPUTY COMMISSIONER BLAKE: And why's that a problem?

INMATE KEMPER: The young lady in France. She loves me. I got love from her 200 times if I got it once and it started out when she started writing me, she said this isn't love, you know, this is this, this is that and other, but now she's talking really emotionally.

DEPUTY COMMISSIONER BLAKE: What about, uh ... where ... you know, it's been a while since you've been out of prison, but just think of a situation where you know you see a ... a young woman, you know around the age of your victims. Have you thought about that? What's, uh ...

INMATE KEMPER: It's a scary thought, isn't it?

DEPUTY COMMISSIONER BLAKE: I don't know. you're 68 years old now ...

INMATE KEMPER: Yeah.

DEPUTY COMMISSIONER BLAKE: What's, uh ... anything different? Or what? You said that's a thought, isn't it? Why ... why did you say that?

INMATE KEMPER: I haven't had an erection in two years.

DEPUTY COMMISSIONER BLAKE: Okay.

INMATE KEMPER: I don't think I can even do it anymore. Uh, platonic relationship it would have to be because I just haven't got it.

DEPUTY COMMISSIONER BLAKE: But assuming that you could ... that problem would be ameliorated, would you be interested in having a sexual relationship, would you find ...

INMATE KEMPER: Who wouldn't be?

DEPUTY COMMISSIONER BLAKE: Okay.

INMATE KEMPER: Who wouldn't be?

DEPUTY COMMISSIONER BLAKE: Well that's kind of ... you know, you haven't really done ...

INMATE KEMPER: I haven't put any effort in that area for quite some time now.

DEPUTY COMMISSIONER BLAKE: Well you've been in prison.

INMATE KEMPER: Yeah.

DEPUTY COMMISSIONER BLAKE: Okay. Is that ... is it ... should we be concerned about being attracted to women and ... and your thoughts, and desires, and feelings that might arouse in you?

INMATE KEMPER: Well every letter I've written as long as I've been in prison has been monitored, and by my exp ... but by my, uh, thoughts in that area has been recorded, not just monitored.

DEPUTY COMMISSIONER BLAKE: I see.

INMATE KEMPER: Or what they have copies of.

DEPUTY COMMISSIONER BLAKE: Okay. Are you concerned? Is that ... I mean I ...

INMATE KEMPER: If for nothing else, professional interests people would do stuff like that. I have been cautious about relationships.

DEPUTY COMMISSIONER BLAKE: Okay. I think we discussed your parole plans. Uh, it might be that some work that needs to be done there, but, um, you know you said you're willing to work and you considered transitional housing although you haven't really followed through. Uh, it's possible that you probably would spend some time living in a sort of a medical facility, um, you'll probably be required to register as a sex offender.

INMATE KEMPER: Believe it or not, no.

DEPUTY COMMISSIONER BLAKE: Interesting, really?

INMATE KEMPER: Uh, the ... the, uh, committees brought that up.

DEPUTY COMMISSIONER BLAKE: Okay it could be that you murdered, but not ...

INMATE KEMPER: Right. I ... I, uh, there's certain things that have to be met, uh, standards that have to met to ... after registering and they said specifically that I don't fit that.

DEPUTY COMMISSIONER BLAKE: Mm, okay.

INMATE KEMPER: And, uh, if I've committed one offense out of all the crimes I've had, it seems like I would have to register, but look at how many people have found ways to deceit that process.

DEPUTY COMMISSIONER BLAKE: Okay. But we're ... we're talking about you right now, um ...

INMATE KEMPER: Yeah.

DEPUTY COMMISSIONER BLAKE: ... any ... anything else that you'd like to tell us about parole plans. I know probably for along time you thought you would never have a chance, so.

INMATE KEMPER: Well, I was a ceramist at one point and I developed a line of ceramics that people have expressed interest in me following professionally.

DEPUTY COMMISSIONER BLAKE: Okay.

INMATE KEMPER: And, uh, like I would make a master cut with my patterns on it, and then issue it to a company that would copy that.

DEPUTY COMMISSIONER BLAKE: Okay.

INMATE KEMPER: And make dozens of copies for sale. I know that sounds ludicrous to the casual listener, but I've actually had people offer me, uh, serious money when I was, uh ... I put one cup out front for a hobby craft ... hobby, uh ... hobby show where everything was judged, and, uh, that cup wasn't even allowed to participate in that cause I wasn't technically in hobby, so ...

DEPUTY COMMISSIONER BLAKE: Well you ... you're going off on a tangent here ...

INMATE KEMPER: Well. I got the cup back.

DEPUTY COMMISSIONER BLAKE: Okay.

INMATE KEMPER: And I was angry about it and the people who did ... this was the first time in the California history ...

PRESIDING COMMISSIONER FRITZ: Mr. Kemper, we gotta' ... we gotta' move on. You're ... you're not answering the questions that we're asking you.

DEPUTY COMMISSIONER BLAKE: I'm just asking if you had anything ... any thought about what work you might do. It sounds like it's something you'd consider. But, uh, I appreciate it, um ...

INMATE KEMPER: Would you believe a hundred dollars a cup?

DEPUTY COMMISSIONER BLAKE: That's, uh ... it maybe ...

PRESIDING COMMISSIONER FRITZ: Okay so you're still not listening to me when I say we're moving on. So apparently you just are gonna do what you wanna do. Apparently you don't take direction very well.

INMATE KEMPER: I finished that thought ... I finished that thought.

PRESIDING COMMISSIONER FRITZ: Done? Any questions from the District Attorney's office?

ASSISTANT DISTRICT ATTORNEY WEST: Yes, thank you. Um, Commissioner Fritz, would you please ask the inmate if he killed the cat because the cat was actually like a member of the family.

PRESIDING COMMISSIONER FRITZ: Okay, first of all you need to look straight ahead and not at the district attorney like I've already admonished you once, okay? Now the question is, did you kill the cat because the cat was a family member?

INMATE KEMPER: No.

PRESIDING COMMISSIONER FRITZ: Okay.

INMATE KEMPER: I was trying to avoid pursuing any further thoughts of killing people.

PRESIDING COMMISSIONER FRITZ: Thank you.

ASSISTANT DISTRICT ATTORNEY WEST: Would you ask the Inmate if he believes that when he said he took responsibility for his crimes that that is consistent with blaming his mother?

PRESIDING COMMISSIONER FRITZ: Do you think that taking responsibility for your crimes is consistent with blaming your mother?

INMATE KEMPER: My mother played a big role of what I did.

PRESIDING COMMISSIONER FRITZ: Okay, all right.

ASSISTANT DISTRICT ATTORNEY WEST: When he took the podium for lengthy periods of time when he participated in AA did he share his experience ... experiences, strength, and hope or did he just talk about his experiences?

PRESIDING COMMISSIONER FRITZ: Did you talk about your experiences or did you talk about your experiences, strength, hope and what was it?

ASSISTANT DISTRICT ATTORNEY WEST: Just experiences ... experience, strength and hope which is the purpose of share.

PRESIDING COMMISSIONER FRITZ: Strength and hope, or just experiences?

INMATE KEMPER: Just ex ... back then it was just experiences.

PRESIDING COMMISSIONER FRITZ: Okay, thank you.

ASSISTANT DISTRICT ATTORNEY WEST: And if the inmate worked the steps, why didn't he write a letter to make amends to the victims in these cases, although because it would hurt them to receive it would be inappropriate to send it to them?

PRESIDING COMMISSIONER FRITZ: So ... so I think what she's getting at is [that] a lot of people send [an] amends letter to get through that step, but they just don't actually mail [it], but that's the part of getting through that.

INMATE KEMPER: It's against the law.

PRESIDING COMMISSIONER FRITZ: Okay, why didn't you write the amends letter and not mail it?

INMATE KEMPER: I guess I didn't get that far.

PRESIDING COMMISSIONER FRITZ: Okay.

ASSISTANT DISTRICT ATTORNEY WEST: The inmate has indicated that he would live in a household with men in their 30's and presumably they would have girlfriends who came to house. How would he handle his temptation to have sex with them?

PRESIDING COMMISSIONER FRITZ: How would you handle ... well one, do you think you'd have a temptation to have sex with your roommate's girlfriend's?

INMATE KEMPER: No.

PRESIDING COMMISSIONER FRITZ: Okay.

ASSISTANT DISTRICT ATTORNEY WEST: He indicated in his risk assessment that if he saw a lone woman he would look away essentially and try and think of something else. What would he do if in his living situation he came across women?

PRESIDING COMMISSIONER FRITZ: How about if in your living situation you came across a lone woman, what would you do?

INMATE KEMPER: Go in the opposite direction rather than play with temptation.

ASSISTANT DISTRICT ATTORNEY WEST: He indicated that the woman with whom he corresponds from France sought him out because of media attention. Did it occur to him that somebody who would seek him out because of his crimes was a disturbed individual?

PRESIDING COMMISSIONER FRITZ: Have you thought about that, that maybe she might have some issues for seeking you out for that reason?

INMATE KEMPER: I've given that some thought which has played a role in ... in, uh ... in my continued correspondence.

PRESIDING COMMISSIONER FRITZ: Okay, what does that mean?

INMATE KEMPER: My concern ... my concern has played a role.

PRESIDING COMMISSIONER FRITZ: Okay, all right.

ASSISTANT DISTRICT ATTORNEY WEST: He indicated that there was a time that his sister visited him including in 2016 but he was unable to have continued visits because of his 115. Did he ask her to write a letter in support of him for this hearing?

PRESIDING COMMISSIONER FRITZ: Did you ask her to write a support letter for you ... your sister?

INMATE KEMPER: No.

PRESIDING COMMISSIONER FRITZ: Okay.

ASSISTANT DISTRICT ATTORNEY WEST: With regard to the anger management programming he has participated in, does he think that he ... there's an issue about whether he benefited from that because he got so frustrated at one point when he was being questioned that he couldn't think of a way to respond to the Commissioner's question?

PRESIDING COMMISSIONER FRITZ: Do you think you've benefited from the anger management course that you've taken?

INMATE KEMPER: Absolutely.

PRESIDING COMMISSIONER FRITZ: Okay.

ASSISTANT DISTRICT ATTORNEY WEST: He indicated when he was responding to a question that at one of his hearings the DA almost flipped the table over, and I would just like to quote from the transcript of the hearing from April 30th, 1980, wherein on page 48 he said, "I would like to state I appreciate the district attorney's restraint in making these comments. It in fact laudable" and is that the district attorney he's talking who almost threw the table over?

PRESIDING COMMISSIONER FRITZ: Do you recall ... hold on ... do you recall was it in the 1980 hearing, was that the district attorney you were talking about?

INMATE KEMPER: The district attorney ... the district attorney later became a judge.

PRESIDING COMMISSIONER FRITZ: Okay, was that the district attorney you were taking about, yes or no?

INMATE KEMPER: No.

PRESIDING COMMISSIONER FRITZ: No, okay.

ASSISTANT DISTRICT ATTORNEY WEST: So in referring to the district attorney who later became a judge, that's Arthur Danner ...

INMATE KEMPER: Yes.

ASSISTANT DISTRICT ATTORNEY WEST: ... who was present on May 1st of 1979. Would you ask the inmate if there's some reason why he has hung on to experience since it was almost 30 year ... yeah ... 40 years ago?

PRESIDING COMMISSIONER FRITZ: Was [that the] district attorney you were talking about?

INMATE KEMPER: Yes.

PRESIDING COMMISSIONER FRITZ: And that's why I brought it up. This happened years ago. Why are you still holding on to this from 1979?

INMATE KEMPER: It was that shocking an event. He was looking for a rise. He was looking ...

PRESIDING COMMISSIONER FRITZ: Okay, we don't need to go into that. All right, any other questions? I mean it was a shocking event, that's what you're saying to you. Okay.

ASSISTANT DISTRICT ATTORNEY WEST: And you, uh, he indicated when he was speaking that on that occasion when the DA almost flipped the table over that, that things that the DA said and did were taken out of the minutes. Is ... is that something that he believes happens, that somehow minutes of hearings are doctored?

PRESIDING COMMISSIONER FRITZ: Is that what ... what you're saying? You felt that was taken ... I'm assuming not minutes, the transcript. Is that what you - that was what you're referring to?

INMATE KEMPER: I destroyed my copy of the minutes.

PRESIDING COMMISSIONER FRITZ: Okay, but listen to the question. Did you think that the ... that it was taken out of the transcript?

INMATE KEMPER: Yes.

PRESIDING COMMISSIONER FRITZ: Okay. He said yes.

ASSISTANT DISTRICT ATTORNEY WEST: Is there a reason why he has taken so few courses ... college level course if he's of the opinion that he could get a PhD?

PRESIDING COMMISSIONER FRITZ: Is there a reason why you haven't decided not to take any further college courses.

INMATE KEMPER: Leonard Wolf left.

PRESIDING COMMISSIONER FRITZ: Okay, that doesn't ...

INMATE KEMPER: He went to New York.

PRESIDING COMMISSIONER FRITZ: But what does that have to do with taking college courses or ...

INMATE KEMPER: He was my sponsor.

PRESIDING COMMISSIONER FRITZ: Got it. Okay.

ASSISTANT DISTRICT ATTORNEY WEST: Would you ask the inmate if he things that the community would be safe if he was released?

PRESIDING COMMISSIONER FRITZ: Do you think the community would be safe if you were released?

INMATE KEMPER: Absolutely. Would I be?

PRESIDING COMMISSIONER FRITZ: Okay, any other questions?

ASSISTANT DISTRICT ATTORNEY WEST: No. Thank you.

PRESIDING COMMISSIONER FRITZ: All right, any questions for your client?

ATTORNEY HALL: No questions, Commissioner.

PRESIDING COMMISSIONER FRITZ: All right, closing statement, District Attorney's office?

ASSISTANT DISTRICT ATTORNEY WEST: Thank you, I wrote a letter ...

PRESIDING COMMISSIONER FRITZ: Sir, I don't know have ... how many times I have to tell you ... you have to look over here.

INMATE KEMPER: I'm looking at my attorney's, uh ...

PRESIDING COMMISSIONER FRITZ: It didn't look like it, but, okay.

ASSISTANT DISTRICT ATTORNEY WEST: In his risk assessment conducted in the last several months he said to the doctor that denying him parole would be ultimately safe, which from the Peoples perspective means that he does have an understanding that he cannot control his temptation and would in fact hurt women whether that be in the form of rape, murder or both. When he was participating in that risk assessment, he was unable to identify even one trigger for why it is that he raped and murdered those women, which from, again from the Peoples perspective is incredibly dangerous is somebody isn't at all aware or self- conscious of something that might trigger that very violent behavior. Um, I would note that during this hearing I have never in my 29 year career hear somebody speak of such despicable actions in the dispassionate way that he has which has included avoiding answering questions and in startling detail talking about things that it appears he doesn't have any awareness of what it would be like to be a person hearing him talk about those things, which I find chilling. I won't go through the details of his crimes in as much as with describing the victim's experiences or the victim's family's experiences I ... as I indicated in my letter. One, I don't think there are words that can describe those experiences. I don't think our language permits a description of those experiences, but I would also say that for me to try and attempt to characterize those experiences would be arrogant and presumptuous in as much as I've never had any experience that in any way resembles the experiences of those women they knew he was gonna kill them and the families of those women some of whom thought their daughters, sisters, cousins, nieces we missing only to find that they weren't missing at all in the traditional somewhat hopeful sense. They were missing because they would never see them again and would never see their bodies intact. Again, I will ... I'll just iterate that as I was listening to him I was apoplectic because I never, ever in my life even in a movie heard somebody talk about what he did and they way he did and I frankly hope to never have that experience again because it was so disturbing. I don't think that there's any, not even reasonable possibility, but any possibility whatsoever that he would ever be suitable for release. He has unrealistic or nonexistent parole plans, he has a complete lack of insight and awareness into why he committed his crimes, and there isn't really any reason to believe he wouldn't continue to do it again. In all of the different parole hearings I have done, and I'm certainly not as experiences as the group of you three, I'm sure, but I've never had somebody who's been in prison for this length of time and was characterized as high risk and I think that, that is something that's very important to take in and honor, and I would ask, uh, the Board to permanently deny him any further hearings and I ... in that regard, uh, Patricia Kemper is going to speak about her experience, but I think it's very important to take into consideration the anxiety and fear that the possibility that he would ever be released creates in people. And those are my remarks. Thank you.

PRESIDING COMMISSIONER FRITZ: Thank you. Closing statement?

ATTORNEY HALL: Yes, Commissioner. Uh, you know, Mr. Kemper, I think has made a lot of very favorable strides, uh, over the last 10 years. I believe it's been 10 years since his last full taken to a ... a completion hearing. Uh, during that time he has, um, self-reflected, uh, about the, uh ... the murders which he testified to this morning, uh, that he showed remorse. We discovered that he had been taking many years of therapy, uh, which led to much discovery. Uh, he's, uh ... he's, uh, shared his remorse with the Board today and we also know that, uh, an elderly parole, uh, of 68-year-old man. He's been 42-43 years in, given his disabilities, the likelihood that he would, uh, behave the way he did when he was 22-23 is highly unlikely. However, I believe Mr. Kemper would agree with me that although he's very close, there is just a few things that I think the Board would want to see. Um, develop parole plans, uh, Mr. Kemper and I, uh, we talked about that, uh, and he shared with me that he ... he hadn't any parole plans, he hadn't made any, uh, communication with, uh, transitional housing given the number of years he's been down, that would be extremely helpful, uh, given his many disabilities, I don't believe that, uh, an issue of working is necessary. Uh, he's 68 so he would be eligible for SSI and Medi-Cal. Uh, he would not be eligible for Medicare nor Social Security cause he hasn't paid in 40 quarters, but never the less he ... he would have some benefits out there should he ever parole. So he needs to parole plans I believe with people, I think maybe a little more insight, um, would be helpful, and if Mr. Kemper can complete those two items given all the other things that he's shown very f ... very favorably here this morning that being the parole plans and some additional insight, I think he would then be a, um, a good candidate but right now he's just a ... a little short of that and perhaps no more than three years, uh, he can return to the Board with those two items completed. Thank you.

PRESIDING COMMISSIONER FRITZ: Thank you. Sir, closing statement? Do you have a closing statement that you'd like to make?

INMATE KEMPER: I don't think so.

PRESIDING COMMISSIONER FRITZ: Okay. Did ... then we'll hand it over to the district attorney's office. Did the victim's family member like to make statement?

ASSISTANT DISTRICT ATTORNEY WEST: I believe Patricia Kemper would like to make a statement in addition to the letter she submitted that was in the 10- day packet.

PRESIDING COMMISSIONER FRITZ: Sure, just come up to the microphone. Please put your name on the record again so that transcript can go ahead.

MS. KEMPER: My name's Pat ... sorry. My name's Pat Kemper, um, K-E-M-P-E-R. Um, it was my grandparents that he killed in addition to his own. We knew one another as children; we played together as children. He had a great sense of humor. Um, I want to say in honor of my grandparents that my grandmother was not aggressive. She was full of life and full of joy, and she loved him. She wanted to help him and that's why she took him in, and she told me that Christmas of 1963 that people told her she should take the gun away, but she wanted him to know that she loved and trusted him, and she was not going to take the gun away. She thought love conquered all. My grandfather was not senile. He was hard of hearing. He helped my sister with her algebra. That Christmas, often before that, he was ... they were both very intelligent, very loving people so I wanted to say that in their honor. I hope when I think of ... when I think of what my family has gone through because grandma and dada's deaths and the way they died and everyone blaming themselves, it's just changed everything. No one has lived a normal life that was in the family because of what Guy did. My father hardly ever leaves the house. That was his parents. I mean literally, hardly leaves the house and cannot bear any kind of conflict, any kind of news, any kind of talk about violence. He had to take a medical disability at 57 because he was a wreck and he couldn't cope anymore with ordinary life. I can't even imagine what it's like of the parents of those girls and their families. I know what it feels like to know grandma was ... was murdered and then dragged into another room and her body was disfigured, and for them to have a child or a sister who went through the fear they must have gone through before they died, and then to have their bodies dismembered and left for animals to get to. How can we take a risk of sending this man out again? What does it do to the families to come every five years and know that he can get out? And about ... I mean, I don't care how old he gets. He's safe here. People are safe from him here and I think he should stay and I don't think there should anymore parole hearings ever because it ... it's like sending the family members through a meat grinder. So thank you for listening.

PRESIDING COMMISSIONER FRITZ: Thank you.

DEPUTY COMMISSIONER BLAKE: Thank you.

PRESIDING COMMISSIONER FRITZ: Time is [*inaudible*]. We're gonna go into deliberations.

RECESS

CALIFORNIA BOARD OF PAROLE HEARINGS DECISION

DEPUTY COMMISSIONER BLAKE: We're on the record.

PRESIDING COMMISSIONER FRITZ: Okay, we're on record. Time's 12:21 p.m. All parties that were present prior to the recess are present now for the case of Kemper, K-E-M-P-E-R, CDC number B-52453. The Panel reviewed all information received from the public and all relevant information that was before us today in concluding that the prisoner is not suitable for parole and would pose an unreasonable risk of danger or a threat to public safety if released from from prison. Finding of unsuitability is based on weighing considerations provided in California Code of Regulations, Title 15. We also gave special consideration to Mr. Kemper's age, the amount of time that he's been in prison and any medical conditions that he has. This is a seven year denial. In determining unsuitability there were a number of factors that we thought linked Mr. Kemper to current dangerousness. One, being past and present mental state, past and present attitude about the crime. Two, lack of remorse. Three, um, lack of skills and tools to be successful out on parole. Four, institutional behavior. Um, and so let's go through some ... and five, parole plans. So let me go through these areas. Uh, so let's first go through past and present mental state, past and present attitude about the crime. I mean, uh, you know, we ... we still don't know to this day after so many years why you committed these crimes. Um, we spent a lot of time going back and forth over this. Um, it appears as if you just don't want to discuss it. I mean, that was the ... the ... what I got to because we would go on these tangents throughout this entire hearing about things that you wanted to discuss that had very relevance or, um, but you felt like you needed to get them on the record mostly because they were derogatory against your mother, sister, judge, DA, other things, um, that made other people look bad, so, uh, and you were able to go into great detail about prior memories about things, your prior history, social history, family, things like that. You were able to get in great detail about that, uh, but you certainly weren't able to do that when it came to the murders. Um, you know kept saying well it's very complicated and over and over again about how it's not a simple answer, but then you couldn't answer it, and basically what you said, I'm frustrated now and I can't answer it. So it brought up a lot of concerns because one, you aren't able to explain to us why you did what you did, um, and then to say that you got frustrated over it is even more concerning because frustration, anger is one of your issues that led you to prison, and you're still exhibiting that here at the hearing today. Um, so, you know, uh, in ... in order to get through this rehabilitation process you have to understand why you did what you did so you know what you can rehabilitate on so if you're still on step one and why this happened then there's a lot of work that needs to be done. You know your explanations of its painful and embarrassing, well that may be true, uh, I think it ... it gives really short shrift to what's going on here. The fact is I think you just don't want to, um ... you ... you don't want to go through the process, you don't want to accept it, you don't want to have to think about it because this is difficult to think about; the things that you did in the past. So you just choose to ignore it and not go through the process and that certainly what it ... how it showed today is someone who has not gone through the process, has not gone through rehabilitation, and certainly would not be safe ... could not be safely re ... released out on parole given your testimony today, and ... and ... and given some of the other things that happened at this hearing today. Um, as far as the remorse is concerned, um, all I can say is extremely chilling. Um, you know, a ... a void of all types of emotions, but you know, not only did you kill strangers you killed family members, and you know, there's just nothing there. You, uh, basically say you know you're sad about it. When I asked about your grandparents cause I thought perhaps because they were family members it would have elicited some other type of emotion versus strangers, you ... you took on this intellectual stance well wait a second they can't be here, and I ... it ... and they got killed fast so I guess they weren't in any pain. Uh, very scary, uh, very disturbing of that's how you would describe remorse and how you felt about things, um, and ... and have kind of this weird affect when you're discussing these types of things like you're actually enjoying telling the story and actually enjoying re ... reliving, um, the ... these murders and what happened to these people, which again is very disturbing and it's not something that other people could really see that aren't here at this hearing today. But, um, again, I did not see anything there that would suggest any type of remorse. We asked you a few times as far your grandparents, your mother, uh, the strangers that you in ... um, killed and basically it was, I feel badly and I wish I ... I wish I could take it back. Um, I haven't written letters, you know, because it's illegal, but then I've never written a letter cause I haven't gotten through that process before. Uh, and then you go into the fact that you ... well you turned yourself in and you tried to show them where the body parts were as a form of remorse. Uh, but I...I be...I felt ... I ... I believed that was a bit self-serving. Um, so again, until you can really show remorse for the victims and ... and really if you can ... if you can't really understand the pain and suffering that not only they went through at the time, but the ... they ... their families continue to go through, your own family continues to go through. But I ... I really saw it as a complete blank, um, that you really don't have that capacity or don't want to have that capacity to understand that then that is a very disturbing thing because upon release if you don't have any empathy for other people and to not understand the pain and suffering that they could go through or they have been through then there's no knowing what you would be capable of upon release, um, and so we do believe that - - that also is a connection to current dangerousness. Um, as far as your institutional behavior, you've had one rules violation. There's no pattern there. It's recent so it ... it's a concern, but it ... it would have been a ... it's a bigger concern if there were patterns of it and things like that. I didn't see that, but you better not have anymore rules violations or it will show a pattern. I think the bigger pattern here is the real lack of, uh, work that you've done on yourself. Um, you have taken therapy, um, hopefully it's helped; it did not come out in your testimony today. But I think, um, what was real telling today is it appears that some of your character defects ... defects are still present; that arrogance, that being self-absorbed. This hearing was a lot about you. We had to continue to go back to stories that you wanted to tell that had really had nothing to do with what we were asking because apparently you just wanted to tell it. You know, you interrupted, you tried to dominate this hearing, um, and I really want you think about that because that's exactly the type of person that you are. That's exactly some of the reasons why these murders occurred is your intimidation, dominance, you know, it's not necessarily about the sex, its about the control. We didn't hear anything about that, but here you are in this hearing in 2017 doing same or similar types of behaviors in a very structured environment where I continually ask you not to do ... in fact, you know, you would continue to do it. You ... you know, you decided hey, I'm gonna do it anyway. So it really shows just the fact that you are unwilling, um, to see or ... or you just don't want to because you just don't want a woman to tell you what to do. I mean that's basically what it comes down to. And I ... we saw it at this hearing and ... and that's your issue. I mean you have big, deep-seeded issues with woman probably stemming from your mother, I don't know, you need to tell us. Um, and, um, it ... it came out loud and clear today your frustration and anger not only with me but some of the other female participants at this hearing, and, um, I think you gotta take a look at that. That's why you're here. If you can't control that even in a structured environment with two correctional officers, what are you gonna do when you get out of prison? It's frightening. And we're talking about a guy who's 68 years old still acting like this. Um, as far as your no, uh, parole plans. I mean, you know they can get you transitional housing and things like that. We're ... I ... I'm not so much worried about actually where you're gonna go except for the fact that you think you're gonna stay with people that you don't know that apparently want to bring you in. You have, um, unrealistic relationships with other people and somehow you think that's gonna be part of your parole plans. I ... you ... your understanding of these relationships is mind boggling. For you to act like an immature kind of kid voice say because she loves or she loves is just disturbing. I mean you have to ... have to have ... if ... if you want to go out there and be released your issues are about relationships and that's how you're acting at your age about this relationship or support system that you have, which I think is good that you have support out there, but to act, um, like that in those terms again just shows how, uh ... how little you know about this process, how little you know about rehabilitation, how little you know about how you're gonna deal with things about the outside. You don't think that you're gonna have temptations. If you do, you say you're gonna walk away. Again, very simplistic immature way of dealing with things and that those are - - that's gonna be the answer to all your problems. You're here for eight murders. You're here because of relationship issues, issues with women, things that ... traumatic experiences that have happened to you. None of that was ... none of that came out of this hearing. We're basically telling you and so for you to act like that is a solution to these problems on the outside is extremely disturbing because you haven't thought about it. You don't want to think about it. You want to think about other things. You want to tell us about other things. You don't want to ta ... talk or think about your real issues. We know you're capable of it, you know, because ... you know, we believe that you're capable of doing it, you just don't want to do it or ... or you haven't thought about it which again after 40 years at your age is extremely disturbing that that's where you're at in this process because that just says that you have a long way to go. Um, the fact that you're still blaming your mother for the murders, I mean, it's mind boggling. She might have, uh ... she might have something to do with, um, how you were shaped in your childhood to the person that you are, but she certainly is not the blame for the ... the murders that you participated in, um, which I think shows that you really lack responsibility as far as your understanding and taking responsibility for your actions. Um, you have a lot of things that you need to work on. Um, have you made improvement in prison? Yes, of course. Um, you know, I mean, you haven't gotten in a lot of trouble. I think that should be commended. Um, some of the issues that you have outside of prison with the woman and relationships you don't have in prison so I ... I ... I would expect, but again, you could get in a lot more trouble than you have been so I think that that's something that you should be commended on. Um, is there anything that you want to ad?

DEPUTY COMMISSIONER BLAKE: No, thank you, Commissioner.

PRESIDING COMMISSIONER FRITZ: All right. Um, as far as the term calculations we put them in your paperwork. As far as Marsy's Law[13] is concerned, we first looked at 15 years by clear and convincing evidence based on your record as far as behavior is concerned. You don't require a more lengthy period of incarceration. Then the next threshold of 10 years, we even looked at 10 years for the reasons already sited. We also took into consideration you've taken some programming and therapy; you don't require a more lengthy period of incarceration. Then the next threshold is seven years. We looked at three, five, or seven, determined that seven years is the appropriate denial period and to get through these issues that we've discussed. If you feel like you're ready to come before then you can petition to advance and submit the paperwork to headquarters. They'll review and see if you can come back at an earlier date. I wish you the best of luck. Um, time is 12:35. We'll go off the record. Anything else you want to add?

DEPUTY COMMISSIONER BLAKE: No thank you.

PRESIDING COMMISSIONER FRITZ: Okay, all right.

ADJOURNMENT

---

1. Correctional Clinical Case Management System
2. Educational Opportunity Program
3. Metformin is an oral diabetes medicine that helps control blood sugar levels.
4. Tests of Adult Basic Education
5. The Mattel Fanner 50 was a realistic toy gun.
6. PCL-R - Psychopathy Checklist Revised
7. The Static-99 (Static 99) is an actuarial assessment instrument for use with adult male sexual offenders.
8. A 115 is a disciplinary action that could result in more time added to an inmate's sentence or some of their privileges being taken away, depending on the violation.
9. Pruno, or prison wine, is an alcoholic beverage variously made from apples, oranges, fruit cocktail, fruit juices, hard candy, sugar, high fructose syrup, and possibly other ingredients, including crumbled bread.
10. C.M.F. - California Medical Facility
11. AA - Alcoholics Anonymous
12. NA - Narcotics Anonymous
13. Under Marsy's Law, victims generally must assert their rights. For instance, they must ask to be notified of upcoming court dates, rather than be automatically notified.

Edmund Emil Kemper III, "Big Ed," or "Gus" has become the rare recipient of notorious fame without reaping any benefits from it. His stroke has left him unable to read and write and he no longer reads letters from "fans," nor will he write them back. He has stopped taking interviews. We can only assume, after years of imprisonment and basking in remorse, that he is merely waiting to die.

He has remained in the public eye long after his victims have disappeared into obscurity, save for their appearance in relation to this horrific final chapter in their lives.

Somewhere, out in the dark hinterlands of America, there are others like him lurking in the shadows, yet to stake their presence on a populace that has long since diminished its sanctity for life. After all the tests, interviews, special reports and documentaries on the "Co Ed Killer," it is doubtful that we have come any closer toward preventing the approach of another like him.

All we can do is wait and see.

ACKNOWLEDGMENTS

Thanks to *Santa Cruz Sentinel*; *Sacramento Bee*; *The San Francisco Examiner*; *John A. Jenkins*; and Joey & Geoff Tranchina. Thank you also to the Santa Cruz Sheriff's Department. There have been other interviews that I have been unable to track down for a reliable source, yet freshly transcribed from video sources. To them I also give a hearty thanks.